EGON R...

Jameson ...

Ireland

**Over 600 of the best Hotels, Restaurants & Pubs
in the Republic of Ireland and Northern Ireland**

Aer Lingus

Bord Fáilte
Irish Tourist Board

TIPPERARY
— Irish —
NATURAL
MINERAL WATER

JAMESON
IRISH WHISKEY

**Egon Ronay's Guides
35 Tadema Road
London SW10 0PZ**

Consultant **Egon Ronay**
Editorial Director **Bernard Branco**
Managing Editor **Andrew Eliel**
Publishing Director **Angela Nicholson**
Sales & Marketing Director **Stephen Prendergast**

Chairman **Roy Ackerman**
Leading Guides Ltd (part of the Richbell Group of Companies)

Cover Design © **Elizabeth Ayer**
Cover Concept © **Chris Ackerman-Eveleigh**
Cover Illustration © **Ian Drury**

The contents of this book are believed correct at
the time of printing. Nevertheless, the publisher
can accept no responsibility for errors or
omissions or changes in the details given.

**First published 1995 by Macmillan
Publishers Ltd, Cavaye Place,
London SW10 9PG**

9 8 7 6 5 4 3 2 1

ISBN 0333 62928 0

Typeset in Great Britain by Spottiswoode Ballantyne,
Colchester, Essex.
Printed and bound in Great Britain by BPC Hazell Books Ltd

*All restaurant, hotel and pub inspections are
anonymous and carried out by Egon Ronay's
Guides' team of professional inspectors.
Inspectors may reveal their identities at hotels
in order to check all the rooms and other facilities.
The Guide is independent in its editorial selection
and does not accept advertising, payment or
hospitality from listed establishments.*

Contents

A word of welcome from the distillers of Jameson Irish Whiskey.

Jameson, the world's most popular  Irish Whiskey is part of the renowned welcome and hospitality to be found in Ireland. So it is fitting that Jameson be associated with this Guide.

Whiskey is an intrinsic part of Irish life and whether you are enjoying the warmth of an Irish pub, relaxing in a hotel, or sitting back after a memorable meal, there is always an

occasion to savour a glass of Jameson Irish Whiskey.

We take great pride in the quality of Jameson. From the rich countryside of Ireland come nature's finest barley and crystal clear water. These natural ingredients are carefully distilled three times and then slowly matured for years in oak casks to produce an exceptionally smooth whiskey.

I hope you will enjoy using this Guide as you sample some of the best of Irish hospitality, food and – of course – Whiskey!

Richard Burrows
Chairman
Irish Distillers Group

JAMESON The Spirit of Ireland

FOREWORD
from the
Minister for Tourism and Trade,
Enda Kenny, TD

In their respective fields, Jameson Irish Whiskey and Egon Ronay's Guides are dedicated to quality. I am delighted therefore that they are partners in the production of this excellent Guide.

Food grown and produced in Ireland is of the highest quality. The priority and goodness of our food is matched by the care and attention given to its preparation and presentation in our hotels, restaurants and pubs. Standards have risen to top international levels in all sectors of the industry.

I am glad to see so many establishments receiving high recommendation in the Guide. In particular, I congratulate those who have been chosen to receive special awards.

In the highly competitive international leisure and tourism industry, there is a need to promote high standards in all sectors. A guarantee of quality is being sought not just be the large scale buyers of tourism products, but also by individual visitors who come to the island of Ireland on foot of promises made in the market place and justifiably expect to see those promises fulfilled.

I am sure that our international visitors will enjoy the hospitality, food and drink offered by the establishments listed in the Guide.

Introduction by **Georgina Campbell**,

author of *Good Food from Ireland* and *Meals for all Seasons*

Great changes have taken place in Ireland in the short time since our first guide appeared last year – the prospect of lasting peace in Northern Ireland opens up the possibility of a new era in hospitality for the area and, through co-operation and mutual development, for the whole country. As we go to press the peace process is still at an early stage and the opportunities it could lead to are almost too precious to dwell on – yet, put at its simplest, it means that thousands of people who have yet to visit Ireland may now feel the time is right to see for themselves the scenic attractions such as the Giant's Causeway – the 'eighth wonder of the world' – and the wonderful Mountains of Mourne, so evocatively captured in song, but until now immensely distant to many.

The Great Outdoors

Once in Ireland, it goes without saying that all will fall under the spell of this charming island and discover it all for themselves – and, heaven knows, there is plenty to discover. The outdoor life in general (and country pursuits in particular) is a major magnet for visitors from overcrowded European countries who, realising the truth of the saying 'if you don't like the weather in Ireland, wait five minutes', come well prepared and relish the space as well as good sporting opportunities available. Uncrowded country roads are as appealing for cycling or trundling along in a horse-drawn caravan as they are for driving those nifty little hire cars. Fishing and boating on the mighty Shannon (now linked to Lough Erne by the newly-opened Shannon-Erne Waterway) or the myriad of smaller lakes and rivers throughout the country are also major attractions; Co Cavan, until now the 'unknown Ireland' to all except dedicated fisherfolk, is now surely destined for new prosperity. Golf and equestrian activities of all kinds are also well represented and well-researched information on these plus many other special interests is available on request from tourist offices.

Business or Pleasure?

Although probably seen primarily as a holiday destination for a growing number of discerning visitors, the needs of the business traveller in Ireland – whether resident or visiting – are taken very seriously. There has been a noticeable improvement in the facilities provided for business guests in hotels throughout the country; nowadays one can often expect fax and computer points, generous desk space, one or two conveniently positioned direct-dial telephones and practical lighting, safes, trouser presses and mini-bars in business-oriented hotels; 'Executive rooms' are increasingly being furnished to down-play the bedroom function, with extra chairs and a proper table to sit around, making them suitable for private business meetings. Photocopying, secretarial and translation services in business centres, and well-equipped health and leisure facilities are also becoming more widely available. Our **Business Hotel of the Year**, *Castletroy Park Hotel* in Limerick, seeks constant feedback from guests and operates a wide range of incentives that includes membership of a Gold Card Club offering special privileges like an arrangement with Limerick County Golf and Country Club; happily, the restaurant is also recommended this year (which is certainly *not* the case in the majority of business-orientated hotels around the country).

Northern Lights

While there are as many reasons for wanting to visit Ireland as there are lakes in Connemara, what all visitors to the Emerald Isle have in common is the need for good food and accommodation – and here too we can confidently expect the steady improvements of the south to be matched by dramatic changes north of the border. That there is talent aplenty in the restaurants of Northern Ireland is undisputed – Paul and Jeanne Rankin's famous Belfast restaurant, *Roscoff*, must take a deal of credit for this as there are already lively competitors up and running alongside it whose staff have originally trained there. The Belfast-Bangor area now has a handful of very good, very up-to-date establishments such as *Deanes on the Square* at Helen's Bay, *Sullivans* of Holywood, *Back Street Café* in Bangor and now our Newcomer of the Year, *Shanks*. These busy, buzzy places all exude an air of excitement, confidence and promise. Our **Pub of the Year**, *The Hillside*, in Hillsborough is also poised to reap the benefits of the more relaxed atmosphere in the North.

Easy Access

Access to Ireland has never been easier, with Aer Lingus and other airlines offering frequent and increasingly competitive flights to Dublin and the regional airports. The east and south coasts are the most easily accessible by ferry: Sea Containers, Stena Sealink, Irish Ferries and Brittany Ferries operate various routes through Larne, Dublin, Dun Laoghaire, Cork and Rosslare. Our **Hotel of the Year**, *Kelly's Resort Hotel*, is a short hop from the ferry in Rosslare, while *Marlfield House*, run by Mary Bowe, our **Host of the Year**, is only a short distance up the road from Dublin in Gorey.

Cork and Dublin continue their traditional rivalry for supremacy in all areas: on the food side, Cork has the edge (and easy access to the country's most popular holiday area in the south-west), but Dublin has not only all the well-known attractions of the capital city, including our **International Hospitality Award** winner – *Jurys Hotel & Towers*, but has also acquired a reputation as one of Europe's hottest spots for nightlife. Temple Bar, known only half-jokingly as Dublin's Left Bank, has tremendous energy.

Pub Culture   .

The famous Irish pub culture is a perennial attraction for visitors and a new twist has recently been introduced in the trend towards continental-style café-bars; although most evident in Dublin, the first of this café-bar type, *Buzz's Bar*, has appeared in Carlow and wins our **Coffee Award for Excellence** this year. *Café en Seine*, on Dublin's Dawson Street, was the first to emulate the relaxed coffee-and-croissant style of the great Parisian cafés and there are now a growing number of very Irish hybrids. Our **Bar Food Award** this year goes to *The Roundwood Inn* in the scenic Wicklow Mountains. Wholesome home-baked bread plays such an important part in Irish food that we recognise this with our **Best Traditional Irish Bread** award, given to *Mary Ann's* in one of the country's prettiest villages, Castletownshend, West Cork.

Food trends generally are towards more sassy, informal bistro-style places, usually keenly-priced and often operated as second establishments alongside traditional, formal restaurants – *Michael's Bistro* and *Isaacs*, both in Cork, spring to mind, also *The Lime Tree* in Kenmare, which recently re-opened under new management, the *Inn Between* in Adare, *Destry Rides Again* in Clifden and *Morels* of Sandycove are all closely associated with well-established, serious restaurants. New informal restaurants are making an impact all over the country, often in the culinary "clusters" in holiday areas which have been growing over the last few years: notably Kinsale, Dingle, Adare, Ballyvaughan, Clifden and Carlingford. Newcomers to Cork in this style include the stylish *Harolds* in Cork and *Gregory's* of Carrigaline. Well-established Dublin success stories such as *Roly's Bistro* and our **Restaurant of the Year**, the dashing *La Stampa*, are being followed by more fashionable café-restaurants like *Fitzers Café* in Ballsbridge. Interestingly, however, restaurateurs are reporting a parallel revival of interest in formal dining: upmarket restaurants such as *Arbutus Lodge* in Cork, *The Rectory* in Glandore, *Restaurant Patrick Guilbaud*, *Le Coq Hardi*, *The Commons*, *Les Frères Jacques* and *Le Mistral* (all in Dublin) are retaining a busy, fashionable image at the more discreet end of the market. All of the culinary 'clusters' around the country offer a choice of styles that includes more formal dining, often in exceptionally good hotel restaurants, as for example *Aghadoe Heights Hotel*, Killarney (who receive this year's award for **Best Table Presentation**), *The Park Hotel* and *Sheen Falls Lodge*, both in Kenmare – and, of course, *Erriseask House* near Clifden, Co Galway, where our **Chef of the Year**, Stefan Matz, weaves his magic and wins a new star this year.

Exotic tastes

Oriental restaurants still play a relatively minor role at the cutting edge of Ireland's developing food story, but the range is growing and standards are improving. *Shiro Japanese Dinner House*, at Ahakista, Co Cork, is still out on its own from every point of view, but Dublin offers some fine ethnic choices, including our **Oriental Restaurant of the Year**, the Malaysian *Langkawi*, last year's winner *Zen*, the authentic *China-Sichuan* in Stillorgan (a perhaps unexpected winner of the *Irish Pork Award*) and northside Chinese restaurants *Wong's* and *Silks*; reliable Indian establishments include *Rajdoot* and *Eastern Tandoori* (who recently opened an outlet in Cork), and a promising new Thai restaurant in Malahide, *Siam*.

In tune with the trend towards a lighter, more colourful style evident across the board in restaurants, vegetarian dishes are becoming more imaginative and appealing on many menus. For example, *Drimcong House* and *Ballymaloe House* take the trouble to offer full vegetarian menus in addition to their other choices. Restaurants especially strong in this area include *Lettercollum House* in Timoleague and nearby *Dunworley Cottage Restaurant*; *Liss Ard Lake Lodge* near Skibbereen, *Truffles* in Sligo, *The Old Rectory* in Wicklow and *Harolds* in Cork city.

Whether it be the vegetables that are grown in one of Europe's 'greenest' environments, dairy produce from the green fields of the Emerald Isle, or the meats from sources that chefs are proud to name, Ireland's raw ingredients are tip-top. Michael Clifford at *Michael's Bistro* in Cork wins our **Irish Food Award** for his outstanding use of local ingredients (don't miss his supreme example of a classic Irish stew) and *Rathsallagh House* in Dunlavin wins our **Irish Beef & Lamb Award** for their careful use of only best-quality meat. Seafood is supreme throughout Ireland, but it is no coincidence that the recipients of our **Seafood Dish of the Year**, *King Sitric* in Howth, and **Seafood Restaurant of the Year**, *The Red Bank* in Skerries, are both situated in major fishing ports. Farmhouse cheeses are undoubtedly a major (if not *the* major) success story in the development of Irish food over the last fifteen years. Not surprisingly, perhaps, our second **Irish Cheeseboard of the Year** award goes to an establishment in the heart of lush County Cork countryside, *Assolas House* in Kanturk; a local cheese, Mary and Eugene Burns' richly-flavoured Ardrahan, always features on their board.

Room for improvement

However, while standards are undoubtedly improving overall, there are inevitably a few criticisms, too. Although some aspects of traditional cooking, notably home-baked breads, are thriving and some traditional produce such as black pudding and crubeens (pigs' trotters) is cropping up in sophisticated dishes on upmarket menus, simple traditional Irish fare can be remarkably hard to find. This is much remarked upon by visitors to the country who may well leave after a fortnight's holiday without so much as seeing a plate of bacon and cabbage or having the slightest idea what a Dublin Coddle is. Slow service is another frequent complaint and even some establishments which aspire to high standards overall fail to understand the crucial nature of reception, whether in a restaurant or accommodation – first impressions are never forgotten and those first few minutes are vital. Although we are pleased to note that the season is extending, the vagaries of the Irish climate must be faced. While there is nothing more delightful than arriving at a welcoming country house with blazing fires, generous use of central heating and a genial host offering hot whiskies, the frugal approach, where a hot water bottle is regarded as a reasonable alternative to proper heating and the host family huddles around the fire watching television while guests freeze in the upper regions of their house, does the reputation of Irish hospitality no good at all. Then there is that old chestnut, the restaurant service charge: confusion continues in this most contentious area and the Guide would like to see an all-inclusive policy adopted, with no extra charges added on. Many hotels continue the by-no-means-usual practice of adding an automatic service charge to hotel bills; once again, we would like to see hotel tariffs that include all service charges.

How to Use this Guide

This Guide includes not only our recommended establishments but many
other interesting features and a wealth of useful quick reference lists
designed to help you select the hotel, restaurant or pub that best suits your
requirements. A list of all establishments in county order, with key statistics
and prices, lets you see at a glance what is available in the area where you
intend to stay or eat. Conference and banqueting capacities are included – a
boon to organisers of business meetings or functions. Places of interest are
listed under the nearest relevant location throughout the Guide.

Order of Entries

Republic of Ireland appears first, in alphabetical order by **location**; Northern
Ireland locations come after those in the Republic. See contents page for
specific page numbers and the index at the back of the Guide for individual
entries by establishment name.

Map References

Map references alongside each hotel, restaurant or pub entry are to the
maps at the back of the Guide. Use this section in conjunction with the
county listings to select establishments in areas you wish to visit. Dublin has
its own city maps, and references alongside Dublin entries refer to those
maps. Entries under Blackrock (Dublin not Co Louth), Dun Laoghaire,
Monkstown (Dublin not Co Cork) and Stillorgan are also plotted on the Dublin
maps.

Accommodation

Accommodation entries are identified by the category '**HR**', '**H**', '**AR**' or **A**
The latter two categories include many superior guest houses where the
public rooms are limited (apart, perhaps, from a drawing room) and the
restaurant may only be open to residents; these 'Private House Hotels' are
ungraded; you will find them easily in the County Round-up. '**HR**' and '**AR**'
indicate a hotel with a recommended restaurant open to the public; Private
House Hotels that offer good food will still be categorised as '**H**' if their
restaurant is not open to the public; the entry will indicate where this is the
case. '**AR**' and '**A**' entries are not classified by Bord Fáilte as 'hotels'.

Accommodation Prices

These are based on current high-season rates at the time of going to press
and include VAT, for a *double room for two occupants with private bath and
two cooked breakfasts*. Wherever possible we have included the service
charge that many Irish hotels add on to accommodation as well as food bills;
this can be up to 15%.

The Percentage shown on a hotel entry is an individual rating arrived at
after careful testing, inspection and calculation according to our unique
grading system. **We assess** hotels on 23 factors, which include the quality
of service and the public rooms – their cleanliness, comfort, state of repair

and general impression. Bedrooms are looked at for size, comfort, cleanliness and decor. The exterior of the building, efficiency of reception, conduct and appearance of the staff, room service and leisure facilities are among other factors. The percentage is arrived at by comparing the total marks given for the 23 factors with the maximum the hotel *could* have achieved.

Percentage ratings

Hotels rating 80% or over are classified 'De Luxe'. A map showing these hotels is on page 13. **The Size** of a hotel and the prices charged are not considered in the grading, but the food is, and **if we recommend meals in a hotel a separate entry is made for its restaurant.**

Lodge-style chain hotels are ungraded and offer cheap, practical accommodation in convenient locations for one-night stop-overs (see Index entries for Forte Travelodges). Private House Hotels, categorised either as an '**A**' (if not classified by Bord Fáilte as a 'hotel') or as an ungraded '**H**' in other cases, are de luxe 'bed and breakfast' establishments offering comfortable (often luxurious) accommodation and personal service. For our purposes, an inn ('**I**' and '**IR**') is normally either a pub with hotel-style accommodation or a small hotel with a bar and the atmosphere of a pub. Any hotel undergoing major construction or refurbishment programme at the time of research is also ungraded.

Bargain breaks. Almost all hotels now offer bargain breaks of some kind. Specific details regarding the availability and price of such breaks should be checked with individual establishments. In addition to bargain breaks many hotels regularly offer price reductions across their range; seasonal changes, late availability, single rooms, room upgrades – remember the price quoted in this guide is for high season. Phone the hotels in the area you're visiting and see what they have to offer.

Restaurants

Restaurants open to the public (as opposed to many of those in private house hotels that are not) are identified by the letter '**R**'. We award one to three stars [★] for excellence of cooking. One star represents cooking much above average, two outstanding cooking, and three the best in the British Isles. ↑ beside stars indicates a restaurant at the top of its star range; an upward arrow by itself indicates a restaurant approaching star status. A map of starred restaurants throughout Ireland is on page 13.

The category '**RR**' denotes a restaurant with rooms, a category based on *restaurants avec chambres* in France. Food is the main attraction, but overnight accommodation is also available. A list of these restaurants appears at the back of the Guide.

We only include restaurants where the cooking comes up to our minimum standards, however attractive the place may be in other respects. We take into account how well the restaurant achieves what it sets out to do as reflected in the menu, decor, prices, publicity, atmosphere – factors that add up to some sort of expectation. Restaurants categorised '**JaB**' are listed in our *Just a Bite* Guide 1995 and recommended for eating out on a budget of £15 or less per head.

Symbols

**All symbols are judged and awarded by Egon Ronay's Guides'
inspection team.** Crowns are awarded to restaurants offering a degree of
traditional luxury [👑] or some striking modern features [👑]. They have
nothing to do with the quality of the cooking.

- 🍺 Awarded a star in our *Pubs & Inns* Guide for its **Bar Food** (not restaurant)
- 🎵)) Outstanding table presentation – sponsored by The National Dairy Council
- ☺ Good home-made bread – sponsored by Bord Fáilte
- 🍶 Outstanding wine list
- 🍷 Good range of wines served by the glass
- 🐟 Quality seafood – sponsored by Bord Iascaigh Mhara
- 🥩 Good Irish meat dishes – sponsored by Bord Bía
- 🍰 Notable desserts – sponsored by Wedgwood
- 🧀 Good selection of Irish cheeses – sponsored by The National Dairy Council
- ☕ Good-quality coffee – sponsored by Robt. Roberts Ltd
- 👪 Family-friendly establishments
- Ⅴ Vegetarian options on the menu – sponsored by Bord Glas

Restaurant prices, correct at the time of going to press, are for a **three-
course meal for two including one of the least expensive bottles of
wine, coffee, VAT and service.**

Set-price menus. Prices quoted will often not include service and usually
exclude wine. They are not necessarily of three courses. Where two prices
are given thus – £14.50/£17.75 – it indicates that there is a 2- or 3-course
option; prices given thus – £17.95 & £24.95 – indicate that there are two
different set-price menus. A growing number of restaurants offer *only* a set-
price menu (although this will usually include a choice).

Many restaurants offer at least one main course for vegetarians; tell them
your requirements when you book. There are lists of no-smoking restaurants
and those offering a serious vegetarian menu in the quick reference list
section, as well as those establishments that we consider to be family-
friendly.

Pubs

Pubs, identified by the letter '**P**', are recommended primarily for their **bar
food** and/or atmosphere. They vary from establishments that are more 'Inn'
or modest restaurant to much simpler local bars that not only serve a good
pint of stout but might also act as the village shop and general meeting
place. *Only where bar food is specifically mentioned in the entry (and Bar
Food stats given at the end of the entry) is it positively recommended.*
Gaming machines are forbidden by law in the Republic.

De Luxe Hotels

Republic of Ireland

88%	**Cong** Ashford Castle	
87%	**Kenmare** Park Hotel	
	Kenmare Sheen Falls Lodge	
	Straffan Kildare Hotel	
84%	**Thomastown** Mount Juliet Hotel	
81%	**Adare** Adare Manor	
	Gorey Marlfield House	

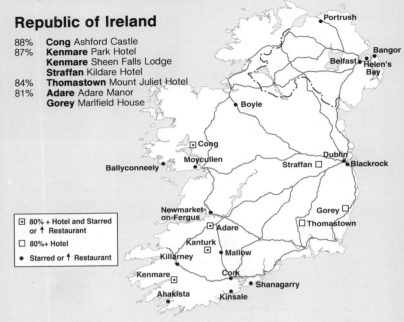

⊡ 80% + Hotel and Starred
or ↑ Restaurant

☐ 80%+ Hotel

● Starred or ↑ Restaurant

Starred Restaurants

Republic of Ireland ★ ↑

Dublin Patrick Guilbaud

Republic of Ireland ★

Ahakista Shiro
Ballyconneely Erriseask House
Boyle Cromleach Lodge
Cork Arbutus Lodge
Cork Cliffords
Dublin Le Coq Hardi
Dublin Le Mistral
Kanturk Assolas Country House
Kenmare Park Hotel
Kenmare Sheen Falls Lodge
Moycullen Drimcong House
Shanagarry Ballymaloe House

Republic of Ireland ↑

Adare Adare Manor
Adare The Mustard Seed
Blackrock Clarets
Cong Ashford Castle
Dublin Roly's Bistro
Dublin La Stampa
Dublin Zen
Killarney Aghadoe Heights Hotel
Kinsale Chez Jean-Marc
Mallow Longueville House
Newmarket-on-Fergus
   Dromoland Castle

Northern Ireland ★

Belfast Roscoff
Portrush Ramore

Northern Ireland ↑

Bangor Shanks
Helen's Bay Deanes on the Square

DRINKING THE BEST OF IRISH

BY JOHN CLEMENT RYAN
AUTHOR OF "IRISH WHISKEY"

Health and long life to you
Land without rent to you
The woman (or man) of your choice to you
A child every year to you
and may you be half an hour in heaven before
the devil knows you're dead!

Soldiers of Henry II and Elizabeth I appreciated Irish Whiskey

The art of distilling whisk(e)y has been around almost as long as people have enjoyed fine food, and Irish Whiskey is the world's oldest whisk(e)y

Finest barley

type. Nobody really knows where the story of whisk(e)y began or who began it. However we do know that the secret of distillation was brought to Ireland, probably from the Middle East, by missionary monks around the 6th century AD. They discovered the *alembic* being used for distilling perfume – they invented *whiskey* and called their version of the alembic a *Pot Still.*

Even the word whiskey comes from the Irish words *Uisce Beatha* (phonetically "isk'ke-ba'ha"). How the name came into the English language was when the soldiers of King Henry II paid what turned out to be the first of several uninvited visits to Ireland in 1170, they found the native Irish consuming their *Uisce Beatha.* Henry's soldiers soon got the hang of it, but never learned to pronounce the word *Uisce Beatha* and so, during the following centuries, the word was gradually anglicised, first to *Uisce,* then to *Fuisce,* and then finally to the word *Whiskey* that we know today.

Purest water

The Old Bushmills Distillery, the world's oldest licensed whiskey distillery is located in Co. Antrim. They first received their license to distil in 1608 and so have nearly 400 years of tradition behind them. Look for Black Bush as a digestif or with a little plain water, and for Bushmills Malt, the only single malt brand of Irish whiskey.

John Jameson founded his distillery in Dublin in 1780 and Jameson

Triple Distillation

soon became the best-known Irish Whiskey in the world, a position it still holds today. A glass of Jameson is particularly appreciated as an aperitif, either on the rocks with a little plain water, and as an accompaniment to a raw or smoked fish dish, and as a digestif try twelve year old *Jameson 1780.*

Matured in Oak Casks

The taste difference between Scotch and Irish is not something that words can convey, and stems largely from the difference in production methods. Both Scotch and Irish are based on barley, part of which is malted, and here comes the first difference: Malt for Irish is dried in a closed kiln, and not over open peat fires which gives the smoky flavour that is typical of Scotch – that smoky flavour is deliberately absent from Irish, and some of the subtleties and delicacies of taste can be appreciated because of the absence of the smoky taste.

John Jameson Distillery, founded in 1780

Secondly, Irish Whiskey is distilled three times in the old-fashioned copper Pot Stills to ensure the maximum purity of the spirit, and no other whisk(e)y category in the world is distilled more than twice.

Finally, Irish is matured in oak casks for a minimum of three years by law, but in practice between five and eight years, and in the case of some of the premium brands ten, and twelve years. As well as the brands from the Jameson and Bushmills stables, other brands that will be encountered are Powers Gold Label, the favourite in Ireland.

If you are travelling around Ireland, be sure to call in to learn the Story of Irish Whiskey. If you are in the North, visit the Bushmills Distillery, located in the village of Bushmills in Co. Antrim. This is open to visitors throughout the year (Mondays to Thursdays 9.00-12.00, 13.30-15.30 and Fridays 9.00-11.45, no reservations necessary). When in Dublin, go to the old Jameson distillery at Bow Street to see the *Irish Whiskey Corner* a museum to the history of Irish Whiskey where visitors are welcome. Here there is a tour daily (Mon-Fri) at 15.30 sharp. Finally *The Jameson Heritage Centre* in Midleton, Co. Cork, just 13 miles east of Cork City, is open to visitors throughout the

summer months during each day including weekends from 10.00-16.00. Visitors enjoy a guided tour through the Old Distillery, a whisk(e)y tasting, an audio-visual show, coffee shop, souvenir shop, and craft shops on the site.

After a fine meal, lift your glass of Jameson or Bushmills and wish an old Irish Toast to your companions:

> *May the road rise to meet you*
> *May the wind be always at your back*
> *May the sun shine warm upon your face*
> *And the rain fall soft upon your fields*
> *And until we meet again*
> *May God hold you in the hollow*
> *of His Hand.*

Matured to Perfection

THE IRISH
WHISKEY
TRAIL

Irish Whiskey is part of the rich
heritage of Ireland and its people.
Visitors can relive this fascinating story
by visiting the historic distilleries that
have made Irish Whiskey famous
throughout the world.

In Dublin, at the old Jameson distillery
at Bow Street, is *The Irish Whiskey
Corner*, a museum to the history
of Irish Whiskey where visitors
are welcome. Here there is a tour

daily (Mon to Fri) at 15h30 sharp,
and in summer an extra tour at
11h00 May-Oct. There is a charge of
£3 per person, and the tour includes
an audio-visual film, the opportunity
to do a whisk(e)y tasting and to visit
the museum. There is a very fine gift
shop at the Irish Whiskey Corner,
where souvenirs, including bottles of
all brands of Irish Whiskey are

available for sale. The *Midleton Very Rare* Book
which records the name and signature of the
owner of each bottle of Ireland's finest whiskey is
kept there.

At the Old Distillery in Midleton, Co. Cork, just
13 miles east of Cork City, the buildings on the 10
acre site have been refurbished

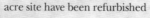

and opened as a major new tourist attraction called *The Jameson Heritage Centre.* Here we tell the story of Irish Whiskey to visitors with the aid of some magnificent artefacts, including a 40' Water Wheel, an original stationary Steam Engine, a charming steam-powered fire engine, and best of all the largest Pot Still in the world!

Open every day from 17 March to end October including weekends from 10h00 to 18h00 (last tour commences at 16h00), the entrance fee is £3.50 (£1.50 for children, and group & family rates are also available), which will permit visitors to enjoy an audio-visual show, a guided tour through the Old Distillery, a whisk(e)y tasting, a coffee shop, a large gift shop selling all brands of Irish Whiskey, and craft shops on the site. During winter, groups can visit by prior arrangement.

Bushmills Distillery, located in the village of Bushmills in Co. Antrim, is open to visitors throughout the year on Mondays to Thursdays 9h-12h, 13h30-15h30, and Fridays 9h-11h45, and Friday and Saturday opening 15h in summer (July-Sept), Bushmills is a jewel on the Tourist Trail known as the "Causeway Coast", which includes

the Giant's Causeway, one of the great natural wonders of the world. Visitors are welcome (£2 entry), and have a guided tour of the distillery, a 'dram' of Bushmills, and the opportunity to shop in two delightful souvenir shops, one of which sells whiskey!

IRISH WHISKEY

CONGRATULATIONS
TO
THE HOTEL OF THE YEAR

·

If travel broadens the mind then it also
tires the body. One step inside an Irish
hotel however, and your rest is completely
assured. There's something about our
friendly atmosphere that puts people at
their ease straight away.

Jameson Irish Whiskey is another
welcoming feature of Irish hotels. A taste of
its warmth is like tasting the authentic spirit
of Ireland and her people. Sláinte.

John Jameson&Son

JAMESON The Spirit of Ireland

Ireland 1995
Hotel of the Year

Kelly's Resort Hotel
Rosslare, Co Wexford

1995 is the centenary year for Kelly's Resort Hotel and thus a very appropriate time for marking the achievement of a century of service from the Kelly family, in whose hands the hotel has been nurtured for four generations. They have taken immense pride in building up their business and have invested an enormous amount of time, energy and money in improvements over the years; the last four years have seen improvements that range right from the new entrance foyer through to upgraded bedrooms and a new Health and Beauty Centre. Our revised grading this year (a rise of 5%) and new listing for Executive Chef Jim Aherne's restaurant reflect the improvements that are continuously being made. Managing Director William Kelly "strives for excellence" and we have to say it shows: the restful gardens make the most of the seashore setting and if the weather should be inclement the superb leisure centre, complete with two pools and beauty treatments, is a welcome retreat. "Failte Uí Cheallaigh" – the Welcome of the Kellys goes from strength to strength.

Last Year's Winner

Ashford Castle
Cong, Co Mayo

Sponsored by

JAMESON
IRISH WHISKEY
HERITAGE
CENTRE

L EGEND has it that Irish monks invented whiskey, learning of distillation from the perfumers of the Orient. They called their discovery *Uisce Beatha* (the water of life) and to this day the finest of whiskey is distilled by the Irish.

A visit to the Jameson Heritage Centre in Midleton, Co.

Cork will take you right to the heart of this cherished tradition. You are invited to take a two-hour tour of the Centre – it's a beautifully restored 18th

century, self-contained industrial complex, unique in Britain and Ireland. Delight in the fully-operational water wheel and be amazed by the copper pot still of 32,000 gallons, the largest in the world.

An audio-visual presentation, available in six languages, breathes life into the Irish whiskey legend.

After the history comes the tasting. Relax in the atmosphere of a traditional Irish pub and sample Ireland's finest whiskey. *Sláinte.*

Lose yourself in the charm of another age – the Jameson Heritage Centre with its craft and coffee shops is located on the main Cork-Waterford road which links the ferry terminals of Rosslare and Ringaskiddy. We're open from 10.00am to 4.00pm, May to October. Telephone John Callely at 021-613594 or fax 021-613642 for information.

JAMESON The Spirit of Ireland

"Serve good food, and your dinner guests will finish every mouthful. Open a good brandy and, regrettably, the same is true."

ARNOLD SORENSON,
VEGAN FOOD CRITIC, CALIFORNIA.

INTRODUCE SOME CALIFORNIAN INTO
THE CONVERSATION.

E&J

SINGLE CASK MATURED BRANDY.

Ireland 1995
Restaurant of the Year

La Stampa
35 Dawson Street, Dublin

A relative newcomer to the Dublin firmament and perhaps not in the category of 'luxury' eateries, but it's a breath of fresh air and exactly where the current restaurant scene is at. Eating here is a hugely enjoyable experience, doesn't burn too deep a hole in your pocket, and delivers what it sets out to do: real value for money, good food, cheerful and efficient service in fabulous surroundings. Above all, it's fun eating here, and whether you're clad in a pin-striped suit or jeans and sneakers you'll be treated and looked after the same. Dine alone or with friends, on business or for pleasure, the end result is the same: absolute satisfaction and the wish to return – the 'crack' is here!

Last Year's Winner

Cliffords
Cork, Co Cork

Sponsored by

THE WINE CELLARS OF
Ernest & Julio Gallo.

The city he loved. The cafe she remembered. California's best loved wine

Memories await. The Wines of Ernest & Julio Gallo, California.

WINE MAKER'S NOTES: Aged in oak, cork matured. Very dry and well balanced. Classi

Across the bay to San Francisco.

Cabernet character with hints of berry, plum and spice. Superb with red meat and pasta.

JAMESON

Established · *Since 1780*

SINE METU

IRISH WHISKEY

CONGRATULATIONS
TO
THE HOST OF THE YEAR

*"May the roof above us never fall in and may
we friends below never fall out."*

Only in Ireland are there so many old
sayings to greet a new friend. When a smile
and a handshake come as naturally as the
next breath, you know you've arrived in
good company.

Jameson Irish Whiskey is part of this great
welcome. Sip it slowly and you'll realise
you're tasting the spirit of Ireland – smooth
and friendly and always inviting.

John Jameson+Son

Ireland 1995
Host of the Year

Mary Bowe
Marlfield House, Gorey, Co Wexford

For 17 years Mary Bowe has reigned supreme at her Regency mansion, one of Ireland's very finest country house hotels. Her attention to detail at Marlfield House extends to the upkeep of the stylish interior and to overseeing chef Kevin Arundel's kitchen, vegetable and herb garden and the 14 hectares of woodlands and landscaped gardens that surround the house. Her stated aim is to "meet the demands of the more discerning guest in a country house atmosphere, providing a home from home in which one would like to remain"; this she achieves with considerable aplomb. Mary Bowe is the perfect hostess – personable and dignified but never dull – and her dedication is to be admired.

Last Year's Winner

Francis Brennan
Park Hotel Kenmare, Co Kerry

Sponsored by

Out of Africa...

The Father of South African Wine

Wine making in the Cape began over 350 years ago when, soon after the thirty year war, an expedition under the command of Jan Van Riebeeck (pronounced Ree-bee-ek) ended their four month voyage from Holland to South Africa.

The small fleet of three ships, led by the 200-ton Drommedaris, was sent by the Dutch East India Company to set up a food supplies station and arrived at their destination on 6th April, 1652.

On a four month sea journey at that time, a death rate of up to forty percent was not unusual, but this small fleet had just lost 2 of their company.

The 33 year old Van Riebeeck had been a ship's surgeon and noted that the Portuguese and Spanish losses at sea were less than those of the Dutch. The only difference seemed to be in their diet, the Mediterranean based fleets included wine in their on-board rations.

On arrival, Van Riebeeck quickly determined that the Cape had a Mediterranean climate and soon convinced his council of seventeen back home in Holland to send him some vine cuttings.

There are few countries that have been growing grapes as long as South Africa that can pin-point their exact winemaking beginnings.

Jan Van Riebeeck, however, kept a meticulous diary and on the 2nd of February 1659 he wrote;

"Today, God be Praised, Wine was pressed for the first time from Cape Grapes."

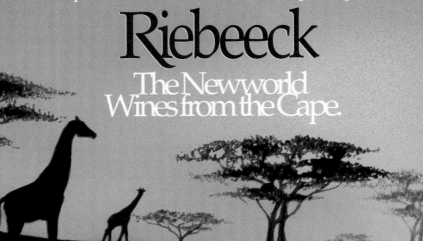

Riebeeck
The Newworld Wines from the Cape.

Ireland 1995
Chef of the Year

Stefan Matz
Erriseask House, Ballyconneely, Co Galway

Stefan Matz and his brother Christian have been running Erriseask House in
Connemara since 1988. Ballyconneely may be almost as far west as you can go
in Ireland but intrepid travellers' efforts are well rewarded with comforts and
a superb table. Thoroughly deserving of his new star this year, Stefan is
passionate about his cooking art; from perfectly crafted *amuse-bouche* and
moreish hot bread basket to cleverly balanced *menu dégustation*, his careful
hand and keen eye are much to be admired. His imagination is only tempered
by a complete understanding of when and when not to let the simplicity of
tip-top ingredients speak for itself. Add Christian's natural hospitality to
Stefan's fine culinary skills and you have one of the very best restaurants in
Ireland – as one of our inspectors laconically reported: "sheer magic".

Last Year's Winner

Gerry Galvin
Drimcong House, Moycullen, Co Galway

Sponsored by

TO THE

connoisseur

IT'S THE

purist

WATER

IT'S NOT WHAT IS IN A MINERAL WATER

THAT DETERMINES ITS QUALITY,

IT'S WHAT IS ABSENT. IN THAT RESPECT,

TIPPERARY NATURAL MINERAL WATER

IS OF THE HIGHEST QUALITY.

IT HAS THE LOWEST MINERALISATION

OF ANY IRISH MINERAL WATER

AND A PERFECT PH BALANCE.

—

FROM THE PUREST ENVIRONMENT,

THE PURIST'S WATER.

TIPPERARY
= *Irish* =
NATURAL
MINERAL WATER

BY APPOINTMENT TO MOTHER NATURE

Ireland 1995
Bar Food Award

Roundwood Inn
Roundwood, Co Wicklow

Jürgen and Aine Schwalm's 17th-century inn is traditional within, while
outside the beauty of the Wicklow Hills is all around. Both the comfortable
pub and restaurant operations make the very best use of local produce like
Wicklow lamb, and chef Paul Taube combines German and Irish influences
in tremendous bar food dishes like a modern version of Irish stew (although
described as traditional, theirs is a distinctly fat-free and boneless version),
goulash with red cabbage, Sunday roast suckling pig, hearty venison ragout,
braised oxtail, oysters, smoked salmon or trout and lobster. Home-made soups
(served with home-made bread) and sandwiches are also served. Definitely
leave room for the handful of desserts – the triple liqueur parfait alone is well
worth withdrawing from waistline worship. The outstanding wine list is also
suitably geared for indulgence, though hillwalkers might find their more
humble (and perhaps equally satisfying) glühwein more warming.

Last Year's Winner

Moone High Cross Inn
Moone, Co Kildare

Sponsored by

Premium
TASTE

Anvil is a vintage, cold filtered cider
which will appeal to the discerning palate.
Long on flavour, it has been specially
fermented using age old techniques to
guarantee an extra special clear dry taste.
Always serve cold or with ice.

CIDER MADE IN THE TRADITIONAL
WAY, GUARANTEEING THE
NATURAL GOODNESS & REFRESHING
FLAVOUR OF ITS HERITAGE.

M. J. Gleeson

How long does it take to read the ingredients on a butter wrapper?

As long as it takes to say 100% natural.

Butter.
Often copied, never equalled.

Ireland 1995
Best Table Presentation

Fredrick's Restaurant
Aghadoe Heights Hotel, Killarney, Co Kerry

Breathtaking views of the island-filled lakes and mountains of Killarney
compete strongly for diners' attention in the first-floor, split-level Fredrick's
restaurant at Aghadoe Heights. This is surely one of the most dramatic settings
in the whole of Ireland and the formal style within is equally praiseworthy:
panelled walls, crisply-clothed tables, monogrammed, crystal-clear glassware
and sparkling silverware set an elegant tone. Portraits of famous Irishmen
grace the walls. Staff are smart, friendly and attentive.

Last Year's Winner

The Motte
Inistioge, Co Kilkenny

Sponsored by

taste that will not be overlooked

The natural and appetising appearance of butter complements any table setting, just as its pure, delicious taste enhances any dish. It's always full marks for butter ... for taste.

NATIONAL DAIRY COUNCIL

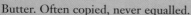

Butter. Often copied, never equalled.

Just a flavour

It's impossible to show all the appeal of Ireland in one picture.

The freshness of the food ... the friendliness of the people ... the variety of places to stay and things to do.

Explore a different restaurant round every corner – no matter how simple or how gastronomic your taste.

Contact your nearest Irish Tourist Board office or travel agent and whet your appetite for the real Ireland.

Bord Fáilte
Irish Tourist Board

Bord Fáilte – Irish Tourist Board. Baggot Street Bridge, Dublin 2.
Tel: 01 6024000

Irish Tourist Board, 150 New Bond Street,
London W1Y 0AQ. Tel: 0171 493 3201.

Irish Tourist Board, 345 Park Avenue, New York NY 10154.
Tel: 212 418 0800.

Ireland 1995
Best Traditional Irish Bread

Mary Ann's Bar & Restaurant
Castletownshend, Co Cork

Fergus and Patricia O'Mahoney's 150-year-old, cosy, low-ceilinged bar is on a steep hill over the little harbour. It's a delightful, wonderfully old-fashioned little place in which to sample the joys of Ireland's fine tradition for bread baking. Home-made brown bread is prepared every day for both bar snacks and the Contented Sole restaurant upstairs; almost every bar food dish – from straightforward sandwiches to chicken liver and herb paté and smoked salmon platter – includes a taste of Patricia's handiwork. In good weather the back garden and shaded patio come into their own – just the place to try oysters or an open crab sandwich.

Last Year's Winner

Strawberry Tree
Killarney, Co Kerry

Sponsored by

Enjoy the colour and beauty of Ireland six times a year…

Meet the Irish people and listen to their stories.

Share in the mouth-watering recipes.

Be entranced by the cream of Irish literature and poetry.

Learn of our culture and history.

Delight in the craftsmanship of traditional arts and crafts.

Read of family history and genealogy.

All this by simply subscribing to 'Ireland of the Welcomes'.

Ireland
OF THE WELCOMES
VOL. 43 NO. 1 JANUARY-FEBRUARY 1994

RATES

	1 year 6 issues	2 years 12 issues	3 years 18 issues
Ireland:	Ir£11.00	Ir£19.00	Ir£26.00
Britain:	Stg£11.00	Stg£19.00	Stg£26.00
USA:	US$21.00	US$37.00	US$49.00

Send your name, address and cheque or credit card details to:
Ireland of the Welcomes, PO Box 84, Limerick, Ireland.
North American orders to:
Ireland of the Welcomes, PO Box 54161, Boulder,
CO 80322-4161

Ireland of the Welcomes, is a bi-monthly magazine published by Bord Fáilte - Irish Tourist Board.
Please allow six weeks for delivery.

JACOB'S CREEK®

Ireland 1995
Wine Cellar of the Year

Le Coq Hardi
Ballsbridge, Dublin 4

John and Catherine Howard's classic restaurant is in a classic Georgian building. Their wine list is definitely a classic, too, a perfect match for John's cooking, which is based on sound classical principles! It is truly a connoisseur's list to drool over, with exceptional depth in Bordeaux that extends to several dozen vintages. Four dozen or so '70s, two dozen '78s, a dozen '71s – the range goes on down through '66, '61, '59 and '45 right back to 19th-century Mouton Rothschilds at collectors' prices. There are, in fact, at least three dozen Mouton Rothschilds, the complete spread of Beaujolais vineyards from Georges Duboeuf, and dozens of top-rated Burgundies. Interesting and unusual wines like Chateau Grillet, Condrieu, a rare 1929 Anjou Rablay, Dr Lungarotti's wines from Umbria, and Vega Sicilia are little seen in Ireland, and the choice of vintage ports and armagnacs is unmatched. A lone Chateau Musar from Lebanon, two dozen champagnes, Chardonnays from around the world, a fine choice of Riojas, and a small, carefully selected New World selection complete the picture (Germany doesn't get a look in). Long pockets may be required by those tempted to indulge.

Last Year's Winner

Arbutus Lodge
Cork, Co Cork

Sponsored by

Orlando. Australia's Award Winning Wines.

In 1847 Johann Gramp, a German immigrant and founder of Orlando Wines, planted his first vineyards at Jacob's Creek in South Australia's Barossa Valley. Within three years Johann had crushed his first grapes and made around eight gallons (36 litres) of white wine.

He later became the Barossa Valley's first commercial winemaker and named the company 'Orlando' a German derivation of the name Roland (now Rowland) Flat, the site of his first winery. Orlando expanded rapidly and by 1971 had become one of the leaders of the Australian wine industry.

Since then Orlando have carefully grown and selected premium grapes from a wide variety of cooler climate vineyard areas throughout South East Australia often many miles from their original vineyards in the Barossa Valley.

These areas such as Coonawarra and Padthaway, south of Adelaide, are becoming internationally famous for the production of some of Australia's finest wines.

BAROSSA VALLEY
EDEN VALLEY
ADELAIDE
COONAWARRA
PADTHAWAY
SYDNEY
MELBOURNE

Carrington.

CARRINGTON EXTRA BRUT AND CARRINGTON ROSE

Carrington Extra Brut is produced from early-harvested fruit to ensure delicacy and elegance. A small amount of carefully selected red wine is added to produce the Rosé. Complex in aroma and delicate fruit flavour, extended yeast contact adds richness to these top quality sparkling wines.

ORLANDO "RF" CABERNET SAUVIGNON

An excellent example of a premium, full-flavoured Cabernet Sauvignon. A rich, medium-bodied wine with minty Cabernet characters balanced by integrated soft oak flavours from 12 months maturation in French and American oak.

ORLANDO "RF" CHARDONNAY

This full-flavoured premium white is a complex blend of grapes from a large spectrum of warm and cooler regions. Aged in French and American casks this Chardonnay has distinctive oak character.

JACOB'S CREEK

With its first vintage in 1973 Jacob's Creek broke new ground in establishing a benchmark for quality Australian red wine and became the most popular brand in Australia. With 1992 being celebrated as the twentieth vintage of Jacob's Creek, it is now one of Australia's most successful wine exports being shipped to over forty international markets.

ST. HUGO COONAWARRA CABERNET SAUVIGNON

Coonawarra is regarded as the best region for Australian red wines. St. Hugo is traditionally vinified using selected premium fruit and is matured in oak for up to two years giving depth of colour and excellent fruit structure.

ST. HILARY PADTHAWAY CHARDONNAY

From Padthaway in South Australia, the components are fermented and aged in new and one year old oak for a period of six months. It is a fine elegant Chardonnay with attractive complexity on the nose and rich, round fruit flavours.

BIM
Congratulates
The Red Bank
Restaurant
Winner of the
Seafood
Restaurant
of the Year 1995

Ireland 1995 Seafood Restaurant of the Year

Red Bank Restaurant
Skerries, Co Dublin

Terry & Margaret McCoy's restaurant in a converted bank is well appointed in pleasingly restrained style. Its well-spaced tables, fresh flowers and generous wine glasses invite anticipation of the unpretentious, often adventurous culinary delights to come. The main attraction is the ultra-fresh fish that comes straight from the harbour – Skerries is one of the principal landing ports for the famous Dublin Bay prawns. The choice of shellfish dishes is extensive: Rossmore rock oysters, cockle and mussel consommé (or seafood chowder), baked crab, 'sizzling shellfish' (with Dublin Bay prawns and crab claws), and lobster (thermidor, ragout or à la nage) all appear on the à la carte, along with seafood tagliatelle and hot smoked salmon stuffed with salmon and hake mousse. Even the good-value, fixed-price menu might include cod with a herb crust, Creole-style haddock or horseradish-stuffed hake fillets. To complete the picture, Lambay Island scallops may be simply cooked in butter, white wine and cream, black sole may be plainly cooked on the bone and skate wings could be steamed with spring onions. The choice is yours – just hope the boat comes in!

Last Year's Winner

Chez Youen
Baltimore, Co Cork

Sponsored by

BIM
An Bord Iascaigh Mhara
Irish Sea Fisheries Board
is responsible for
developing and expanding
markets at home
and abroad
for Irish Seafood

For information contact:

Market Development Division,
BIM/Irish Sea Fisheries Board/
An Bord Iascaigh Mhara,
Crofton Road,
Dun Laoghaire,
Co.Dublin,
Ireland.

Tel: 353 1 2841544
Fax: 353 1 2841123

IRISH SEAFOOD

...*Nature's Best*

BIM
Congratulates
The King Sitric
Restaurant
Winner of the
Seafood Dish
of the Year 1995

Ireland 1995
Seafood Dish of the Year

King Sitric
Howth, Co Dublin

One of the largest fishing fleets in Ireland lands the freshest of fish supplies right on the pier and harbourside over which King Sitric (once the home of a harbourmaster) looks out. A new fish auction hall opened last August and has made the restaurant's supply of fresh fish and shellfish even better; brill and black sole make daily appearances, while turbot, monkfish, skate and John Dory all feature when the boat comes in. Our Seafood Dish of the Year – King Sitric Catch – is always on the menu and changes according to whatever chef-proprietor Aidan MacManus feels is best from the daily catch: five or more pieces of seafood are then simply grilled and attractively presented, perhaps with a béarnaise sauce. The superb wine list offers many perfect matches for seafood. Incidentally, the restaurant is named after the apparently jolly Viking, King Sitric III, who established the first Catholic Church in Howth; he was a son-in-law of the famous Irish warrior Brian Boru.

Last Year's Winner

Aherne's Seafood Restaurant
Youghal, Co Cork

Sponsored by

IRELAND
A Seafood Isle

We are an island people and much of what made us, including our remotest ancestry came to us from the sea. It has shaped our history; it has found its way into

the lives and minds of the people; it is a source of potential wealth, a source of the most wondrous variety of food - Seafood.

An island with 2,000 miles of beautiful indented coast and surrounded by clear, unpolluted waters on the edge of Europe with the vast Atlantic off the western coast means "Superb Seafood". Its lucrative fishing grounds produce an abundance of fish. Varieties are amazing and amount to 74 in all.

THE CHOICEST FISH

They include cod, haddock, whiting, hake, plaice, sole, brill and turbot. On the menu too you can taste seafish like monkfish, gurnard, John Dory...

Oily fish like herring, mackerel, salmon and trout. Shellfish like prawns, mussels, oysters, lobsters and scallops, so eating should be an ever-changing adventure.

NEW TASTES IN SEAFOOD

At sea the search for new species goes on and BIM's fishing technologists have been successfully pursuing new deepwater species for markets at home and abroad.

Available in the future will be species such as orange roughy, redfish, grenadier, black scabbard, blue ling, siki, shark and argentine.

Aquaculture has made available mussels, oysters, clams, scallops and abalone. Already salmon and trout are our most successful new product developments in the seafood industry and are famous throughout the world. The farming of novel finfish species means that we can choose to eat in the future such delicacies as turbot, arctic char and European eel.

EXPORT MARKETS

Having a small population we export most of our fishing catch to some 30 countries around the globe. The export market is currently valued at £200 million and with consumption increasing in the major markets worldwide this figure is set to grow.

A FEAST OF SEAFOOD

Our visitors perceive Ireland as an island where seafood abounds and so the choice of seafood is favoured by most of them.

If you're looking for seafood in the hotels, restaurants and pubs in Ireland then it's good to know that of late we are acting like an island should. Two thirds of most menus are now seafood and this is probably because seafood cooking is not a popular feature in Irish homes, so people like to eat it when dining out.

Ireland is a perfect island for the traveller who wants to discover countryside and coast in a short time. Discover too that you can eat at least 10 different varieties of oysters from Carlingford to Galway, mussels from Bantry to Lough Foyle, salmon from almost every port and river and fresh catches of fish from just about everywhere!

The fact that seafood is now recognised as a health food, good for the heart and good if you need to keep slim and trim, means it's the 'in' food of the 90's.

If that doesn't tempt you to eat a little more of this food while in Ireland, can I share with you my favourite set of slogans which go - eat fish, live longer, eat clams, last longer, eat oysters, love longer and eat mussels, laugh longer!

Now, how about choosing some of this wonderful food when dining at your favourite table.

Happy eating!

BIM

**An Bord Iascaigh Mhara
Irish Sea Fisheries Board**
Crofton Road, Dun Laoghaire,
Co. Dublin, Ireland.
*Telephone: 353 1 2841544
Fax: 353 1 2841123*

A Message from

Michael Duffy

Chief Executive

An Bord Bia

The Irish Food

Board

The Irish Food Board

Welcome to the world of Irish Food. This guide will bring you to the best tables in Ireland. Our objective in the Irish Food Board is to bring this same quality to tables world-wide.

The Irish Food Board has been established to develop and implement a co-ordinated and comprehensive marketing strategy for Irish Food. We recognise that the first taste of the product is critical and that for many potential consumers, their first taste of Irish food will take place in a hotel or restaurant.

This gives restaurants and hotels a key role in the promotion of Irish food products. The Board appreciates the standards that are being achieved throughout the country and the valuable work being done by Egon Ronay's Guides in monitoring excellence in food preparation.

Our success requires that Irish Food becomes synonymous with high quality in all of our target markets. In the meantime, the standards shown in this guide will continue to provide the benchmark.

Bon appétit.

The Irish *f*OOD AWARD

An Bord Bia

The Irish Food Board congratulates

The Irish Food Award Winner

Michael Clifford

Cliffords Restaurant and

Michael's Bistro, Cork

for his outstanding contribution

to the innovative use of Irish Food

An Bord Bia

The Irish Food Board

Ireland 1995
Irish Food Award

Michael's Bistro
4 Mardyke Street, Cork

A new award this year for creative use of all Irish food products, particularly lamb. Michael Clifford opened the bistro offshoot of his renowned restaurant only last year and offers a sensibly short menu that makes the most of traditional Irish ingredients, however humble. Michael's skill in sourcing and using local meat (in particular) is clearly evident in the bistro dishes. Sirloin steaks or a simple hamburger use carefully chosen, prime Irish beef; a casserole may use home-made sausages, Clonakilty black pudding and flageolet beans; ravioli might be stuffed with chicken and Milleens cheese (from West Cork); finally, pride of place goes to a magnificent Irish lamb stew served with boiled potatoes – and you can't get more quintessentially Irish than that!

The Irish Food
Award Winner

*Michael
Clifford*

An Bord Bia
The Irish Food Board

Michael Clifford of Cliffords
Restaurant and Michael's Bistro, Cork
is this year honoured with the first
Irish Food Award for his innovative
use of indigenous produce. Michael
is a wonderful promoter of Irish food.
Simplicity and quality raw materials are
the essential ingredients. His versatile
selection of Irish Food includes top
quality Irish beef, lamb, pork, poultry,
fish, venison and game. Michael makes
full use of local foods including the
extensive range of cheese produced in
the area. West Cork is rich in natural food
sources, and Cliffords Restaurant and
Michael's Bistro are the ideal venues in
which to sample Irish food at its very best.

Recipes for Success

Cliffords Gourmet Stew

One of the great successes in Cliffords, made with tender lamb. The flavour of the stew is softened with just a drop of delicious cream!

Gateau of Clonakilty Black Pudding

Traditional black pudding made in West Cork, combined with other local products - apples, potatoes and smoked bacon, is another example of simple food at its best.

Warm Smoked Haddock Salad

Thinly sliced oak smoked haddock brushed with olive oil and lemon, grilled and served with mixed salad leaves - delicious.

The Irish
Meat Awards

An Bord Bía
The Irish Food Board

An Bord Bia

The Irish Food Board congratulates

The Irish Meat Award Winners

Rathsallagh House,

Dunlavin, Co Wicklow

for the consistent quality of Irish Beef

and Lamb served in their restaurant and

The China-Sichuan Restaurant,

Stillorgan, Co. Dublin

for their innovative use of Irish Pork

Ireland 1995
Irish Beef & Lamb Award

Rathsallagh House
Dunlavin, Co Wicklow

A regional winner last year, freshness and quality continue to be the bywords in the kitchen at Joe and Kay O'Flynn's Rathsallagh House. The warm, low-ceilinged dining room is graced with carefully chosen antique pieces and chef Owen Sherry ensures that prime local produce is equally carefully selected. The short menu offers quality rather than any great depth, as is evident in straightforward dishes like roast rib of beef with fresh horseradish sauce or sirloin steaks. After a hard-fought 18 holes on the new golf course a dish of fillet of beef with béarnaise sauce is likely to hit the right spot. Wicklow lamb and game in season also feature strongly.

Last Year's Winner

Dunraven Arms
Adare, Co Limerick

Sponsored by

An Bord Bía

The Irish Food Board

Ireland 1995
Irish Pork Award

China-Sichuan Restaurant
Stillorgan, Co Dublin

Self-styled as the "first of its kind in Ireland and the UK", China-Sichuan claims to serve the most authentic Sichuan dishes in the British Isles. Owner David Hui's claim is based on the fact that special spices, seasonings and raw materials are imported directly (along with government-rated chefs) from China in co-operation with the state-run China Sichuan Catering Service Company. The attraction of the dishes that make good use of Irish pork, however, is the choice of different flavours and textures: sweet and sour-style, diced with cashew nuts, shredded with garlic sauce (or pickled vegetables), or fried pork fillet with assorted Chinese vegetables. 'Zousiu' or 'Guoqui' dumplings are served in a hot, spicy sauce, in soup or pan-fried.

Irish Meat Award Winners

Rathsallagh's Team: Brian McParland, Eamon O'Reilly, Owen Sherry

Rathsallagh House, Dunlavin, Co. Wicklow, winner of the **Irish Beef and Lamb Award**. Kay O'Flynn attributes much of her culinary success to the wonderful food which surrounds Rathsallagh, and a first rate local butcher. Top quality grass fed Wicklow lamb is a speciality with Kay, which might be presented as a Rack of Lamb with a Crust of Fresh Herbs and Garlic Sauce, or Barbecued Leg of Lamb with Mustard and Ginger. The aged ribs of beef are always cooked on the bone for maximum flavour and served with home-made Horseradish Sauce - horseradish and fresh herbs grown in her own walled kitchen garden.

Recipes for Success

The China-Sichuan Restaurant, Stillorgan, Co. Dublin, winner of the **Irish Pork Award,** chooses the best Irish Food for this superb cooking style which originated in Western China. Selected here for their innovative use of Irish Pork. David Hui, the proprietor, complements the best of Irish Meat with Fresh Irish Vegetables such as beans, broccoli, beansprouts, as well as a blend of traditional Chinese ingredients.

The Irish Food Board

Congratulations

to the winner of

DESSERT OF THE YEAR

from

Serving the finest hotels and restaurants

around the world

Hotel and Restaurant Division
represented by
G. Duke & Co Ltd
Unit K, Greenmount Industrial Estate,
Harolds Cross, Dublin 6

Tel: 01-454 7877
Fax: 01-454 7879

Geoff Duke
Director

Ireland 1995
Dessert of the Year

Cromleach Lodge
Boyle, Co Sligo

The relaxed air of the restaurant at Cromleach Lodge belies the supreme efforts made in chef-joint proprietor Moira Tighe's kitchen. Pastry chef Sheila Sharpe's creative touch is clearly evident in her *florentina cone of marinated tropical fruits on a passion fruit coulis*: it's simply a matter of taking a little butter, castor sugar, liquid glucose, cream, sliced almonds, porridge oatlets and lemon juice, along with some apricot brandy, mango, papaya, pear, peach, strawberry, raspberry, pineapple, passion fruit, vanilla ice cream and icing sugar, and turning it all into a mouthwatering creation. The finished dish appears deceptively simple and invitingly colourful.

Last Year's Winners

MacNean Bistro
Blacklion, Co Cavan

**MacDuff's Restaurant,
Blackheath House**
Garvagh, Co Londonderry

Sponsored by

England   Est 1759
WEDGWOOD

Irish Farmhouse Cheeses

- Ryefield Boilie
- Abbey Blue Brie
- Lavistown
- St Tola
- Cratloe Hills
- Cooleeney
- Liathmore
- St Martins
- Cashel Blue
- St Killian
- St Brendan Brie
- Kerry
- Bay Lough
- Croghan
- Ardrahan
- Knockanore
- Ring
- Coolea
- Knockalora
- Round Tower
- Glen O'Sheen
- Durrus
- Chetwynd Blue
- Milleens
- Carrigaline
- Gubeen

Congratulations to the Irish Cheeseboard of the Year Award Winners from Cáis.

FOR FURTHER INFORMATION CONTACT:
J. BEECHINOR, CÁIS, CASTLEWHITE HOUSE, WATERFALL, CORK. TEL: 021-543502.
OR THE NATIONAL DAIRY COUNCIL, GRATTAN HOUSE, LOWER MOUNT STREET, DUBLIN 2. TEL: 01-661 9599.

Ireland 1995 Irish Cheeseboard of the Year

Assolas Country House
Kanturk, Co Cork

From the Atlantic coastline of West Cork and Kerry to the Lakelands of County Cavan, Irish farmhouse dairies produce a distinguished range of delicious hand-finished cheeses. The Bourke family's creeper-clad Assolas Country House in Kanturk is right in the heart of one of the finest dairying areas of Ireland and offers a particularly fine selection on its farmhouse cheeseboard; the quality is typified by *Ardrahan*, a semi-soft Gouda-style cheese made right on the doorstep of the hotel from cow's milk with a vegetarian rennet. The 'rather traditional' cheese trolley offers appropriate accompaniments such as a selection of biscuits (or home-baked yeast and soda breads), grapes and celery. Other carefully chosen and lovingly nurtured cheeses might include ripe and runny *Milleens* from the Beara Peninsula; *St Tola* (soft) and *Lough Caum* (hard) goat's cheeses from Inagh, Co Clare; Camembert-style *Cooleeney* and soft, usually mild *Cashel Blue*, both made with milk from Friesian cows in Co Tipperary; and *Glen O'Sheen* – a traditional, mature Cheddar – from Ballinacourty, Co Limerick. A magnificent selection that demonstrates the flourishing art of Irish cheesemakers.

Last Year's Winner
Blairs Cove House Restaurant
Durrus, Co Cork

Sponsored by

Farm Made Cheeses From Ireland

I RISH FARMHOUSE CHEESE
IS AS RICHLY VARIED AS THE NATIONAL LANDSCAPE.
IT'S ALSO AS RICH IN TRADITION,
WITH MORE THAN 40 VARIETIES MADE BY FARMERS WHOSE
FAMILIES HAVE LIVED AND WORKED ON THE SAME FARMS FOR
GENERATIONS. TIME-HONOURED METHODS HAVE NOW
COMBINED WITH CONTINENTAL SKILLS TO BRING A FRESH
DIMENSION TO THEIR TRADITIONAL CRAFT. FROM THE
ATLANTIC COASTLINE OF WEST CORK AND KERRY TO THE
LAKELANDS OF COUNTY CAVAN, IRISH FARMHOUSE DAIRIES
PRODUCE A DISTINGUISHED RANGE OF
DELICIOUS HAND-FINISHED CHEESES – BRINGING
CHARACTER TO YOUR CHEESEBOARD.

CÁIS

1. Cooleeney
2. St. Martin's
3. Durrus
4. Coolea
5. Cashel blue
6. Chetwynd
7. Smoked Gubbeen
8. Gubbeen
9. Kerry Farmhouse
10. Cratloe Hills Sheeps' Cheese
11. Ardrahan
12. Knockanore
13. Boilie
14. Liathmore Lite Cream Cheese
15. St. Tola Goats' Cheese
16. Lavistown
17. Carrigaline
18. Glen O Sheen
19. Ryefield
20. Croghan Goats' Cheese
21. Liathmore Full Fat Cream Cheese
22. Milleens
23. Bay Lough
24. Ring
25. Knockalora Sheeps' Cheese
26. Knockanore Smoked
27. St. Brendan Brie
28. Round Tower
29. St. Killian
30. Abbey Blue Brie

KEN MAGUIRE'S GUIDE TO SERVING GOOD COFFEE.

Robt. Roberts, sponsors of the Coffee Award of Excellence, would like to extend their congratulations to this year's winner, who has achieved an outstanding degree of excellence in their service and presentation of coffee. For other establishments who would like to improve their own standards of coffee service, Ken Maguire, Robt. Roberts' Chief Coffee and Tea Taster, has compiled some suggestions.

This checklist is not a definitive guide, as ambience, good service and friendly, helpful staff are also vital for creating the perfect setting for customers to enjoy their cup of coffee, and to leave your premises with a good, lasting impression.

By following a few simple rules you can ensure your customers are rewarded with an aromatic, consistently fresh, high quality and rewarding beverage on every occasion:

1. Always start with a good quality coffee and fresh, cold water.
2. Water should be heated to 92 – 96°C, never boiled. Each coffee machine requires an individual setting.
3. Be generous with coffee (90 – 113 gm per 3 pint jug).
4. Serve as soon as possible after brewing. Do not hold coffee too long on the heat (max 30 mins), and do not reheat.
5. All coffee equipment should be thoroughly cleaned on a regular basis and ensure that all cleaning agents are thoroughly rinsed off.

It is recommended that whole roasted coffee beans and ground coffee be kept in an airtight container in a cold, dry atmosphere well away from any strong odours. The flavour and aroma of beans and ground coffee deteriorate when they are exposed to air.

Filter papers should also be stored away from strong-smelling foods.

Staff training, coffee audits and full details of our blends and coffee equipment can be obtained by contacting Terry Pennington, Catering Sales Director, Robt. Roberts at (01) 459 9000.

Good luck!

K. Maguire

KEN MAGUIRE
Chief Coffee & Tea Taster

ROBT. ROBERTS

BLENDERS OF THE FINEST COFFEE SINCE 1905

Ireland 1995
Coffee Award of Excellence

Buzz's Bar
Carlow, Co Carlow

Carlow's first Continental-style café-pub is stylishly up to date, right from
the dark glass and contemporary lettering of the frontage down to the hard-
worked espresso machine behind the curved bar. Cappuccino and espresso are
very much the order of the day in brother and sister Joe and Geraldine Tully's
bar, which opened in May last year, giving Carlow a much-needed centre of
exellence for lovers of freshly-ground coffee. Danish pastries help complete the
cosmopolitan air.

Last Year's Winner

The Mustard Seed
Adare, Co Limerick

Sponsored by

WHY NOT TAKE IN A LITTLE
ARABIC AFTER DINNER...

...OR KENYAN
...OR COLOMBIAN
...OR COSTA RICAN.

Only the best beans, carefully chosen, dried roaster
and blended to perfection go into
Robt. Roberts fresh, ground coffee. That's why
you'll find it in fine restaurants everywhere.

ROBT ROBERTS

TEA & COFFEE

79 Broomhill Road, Tallaght, Dublin 24.
Tel: (01) 459 9000. Fax: (01) 459 9342.

SHARWOOD'S - REGIONAL COOKING IN CHINA

We often forget that mainland China is as big as Europe and that its climate is just as varied.

For example, Canton in the South, enjoys almost tropical weather for much of the year. No surprise then that fresh fruit, vegetables and rice are abundant.

In Cantonese villages, cooking is often done in the courtyard, over a charcoal brazier. Thus the food tends to be quick, light and almost vegetarian - ideal for today's life-style.

In contrast, the North of China is too cool for rice to grow well. Wheat is the preferred staple and so noodles, steamed buns and all manner of pancakes and breads are popular.

Aromatic and Crispy Duck is a typical Northern dish. Here shreds of full flavoured duck meat with morsels of crisp skin are coated in a sweet, rich sauce before being rolled in doily-like pancakes.

In the West of China the climate is quite cool and damp. The Szechuanese love to use special tiny red chillies, called 'To the Sky', which they believe ward off aches and pains.

Finally there is Shanghai in the East. Being more European in outlook, stews, hearty soups and casseroles abound, but as in all Chinese cooking, the seasonings are based on the eight essential flavours - sweet, sour, salty, bland, aromatic, pungent, fragrant and bitter.

These classic flavours are achieved by using ginger, spring onion, garlic, sugar, soy sauce, sesame oil, bean paste and five spice powder.

Ireland 1995 Oriental Restaurant of the Year

Langkawi Malaysian Restaurant
46 Upper Baggot Street, Dublin 4

Malaysian cuisine accurately mirrors the diverse influences of the country, incorporating Malay, Chinese and Indian dishes. Spices feature prominently, reflecting the country's former position as one of the key stopovers for spices being shipped to India, the Middle East and Europe. Langkawi's chef-proprietor Alexander Hosey is Malaysian himself and refuses to compromise in his cooking and, even after four years, his menu continues to evolve. Malaccan devil's chicken curry will sort the strong out from the weak; however, for those with milder palates, there is still much to enjoy like satay, 'kurma' curries and 'masak lemak udang' (a mild-flavoured coconut 'santan' dish with prawns, turmeric, lemon grass, ginger, garlic and Chinese leaves). The restaurant is as popular at lunchtime with local office workers as it is in the evening with diners from further afield searching for new culinary tastes.

Last Year's Winner
Zen
Upper Rathmines Road, Dublin 6

Sponsored by

With Sharwood's you can create this authentic Chinese stir-fry in minutes......

FROM RUSSIA WITH LOVE

WITH GREAT CARE, FROM THE GREAT BEAR.

DHL WORLDWIDE EXPRESS ®

Ireland 1995
Business Hotel of the Year

Castletroy Park Hotel
Limerick, Co Limerick

Where better to hold a business conference than lovely Limerick? General
Manager Patrick Curran and his staff offer a genuinely warm welcome,
up-to-date conference facilities – purpose-built rooms cover a range from
small boardroom size to 300 delegates theatre-style in the Barrington Suite –
and spacious bedrooms with large desks, two phones and fax and computer
point (in both standard and Executive rooms). An elegant ballroom seats up
to 450 theatre-style and 250 for a sit-down banquet supervised by head chef
Pat O'Sullivan. A well-equipped business centre with full secretarial support
(24hr copying and fax transmission plus no charge for incoming faxes), a new
Executive lounge, 24hr room service, regular stay incentives, conservatory bar
and coffee dock are nice touches for the busy business executive. When all the
hard work has finished guests can relax in the superbly equipped leisure centre
(try an exercise bicycle with a video screen, a skiing machine or the running
track) and later enjoy traditional Irish hospitality in the 'Merry Pedlar' pub or
more formal food from restaurant chef Serge Coustrain in McLaughlin's
restaurant (named after the man who first brought electricity
to Ireland). The new Limerick County Golf and Country Club is in nearby
Ballyneety; the University of Limerick Concert Hall is nearby; Shannon
International Airport is 15 miles away and a hotel limousine service is
available.

Last Year's Winner

Hotel Conrad
Earlsfort Terrace, Dublin 2

Sponsored by

DHL – BRINGING EXCELLENCE TO IRISH BUSINESS

"Since 1979, DHL Ireland has enjoyed considerable growth to the point where we now employ over 170 people, each one of whom is dedicated to giving you the best possible service. By sponsoring the DHL Business Hotel of the Year Category in the Egon Ronay Guide, we know we will find the same standards of excellence that we offer our customers."

John McCarthy, Managing Director DHL Ireland

THE DHL SERVICE

DHL have shown commitment to the growth of Irish industry by investing heavily in Cork, Dublin and Shannon Airports. Single minded commitment to anticipating and to meeting our customers changing needs has led to the development of an unrivalled range of services. Each service is designed to get packages or documents to where they're going, with minimum fuss, the lowest cost, securely and on time.

IF YOU'RE IN BUSINESS, THEN DHL IS IN PARTNERSHIP WITH YOU

To be the best we must give our customers that competitive edge. We must be able to meet customers needs and to take an active part in helping to build their business. If you're in manufacturing, our professionals will work side-by-side with you to develop comprehensive air express programmes and take a little of your work load off you.

If you are in a service industry, DHL has to help you keep your promises and get your deliveries where they need to go on time and within your budget. Our global network is at your disposal. From pick-up to final delivery, DHL provide the most comprehensive door-to-door service for documents, packages and air freight available today.

DHL can expediate shipments overnight, clearing customs with the electronic transfer of shipping documents. Our staff in 200 countries are all working to make sure your shipment arrives securely and full automation means we can trace, book pick-ups and order supplies faster than ever before.

OUR NETWORK WORKING FOR YOU

There are over 32,000 DHL air express professionals working for you. DHL has offices in over 200 countries around the world, giving a unique local on-the-ground expertise and back-up. There's a fleet of aircraft and literally thousands of trucks and vans, at your disposal.

You have unrivalled access to anywhere in the world.

Every year, over 1 million customers choose DHL. For you too, all of these resources are just a 'phone call away.

DHL ARE COMMITTED TO IRELAND. TO THE PEOPLE, TO YOUR BUSINESS.

Since setting up in Ireland, DHL has invested millions of pounds in warehousing, offices and training, employing nearly 200 people and now have offices at Dublin, Cork and Shannon Airports.

DHL understands that exports are the basis of economic growth. New markets mean new opportunities and new jobs. DHL can help our customers to gain access to these new markets. DHL will help you to create those new jobs, because you know that goods assembled here today can be shipped tonight directly to your customers wherever they are. And because you can meet the tightest deadlines, delivering your products as quickly as any other supplier, you know you can compete in the toughest market.

JAMESON

Established · SINE METU · *Since 1780*

IRISH WHISKEY

CONGRATULATIONS
TO
THE PUB OF THE YEAR

———— • ————

Step into an Irish Pub and you've stepped
into an integral part of life in Ireland.
Try a Jameson Irish Whiskey,
it's warm and welcoming like the
people you'll meet.
Ireland is unique, here people have time
for people.
Jameson is the Spirit of Ireland
part of its heritage and its
enduring charm.

John Jameson & Son

JAMESON The Spirit of Ireland

Ireland 1995
Pub of the Year

The Hillside
Hillsborough, Co Down

Dating from 1777 (if not earlier), The Hillside is a fine old town pub-bar-restaurant with a gently rustic decor. Food plays an important part, with all-day offerings ranging from brunch on Sundays through Devon cream teas in the afternoon to an eclectic evening menu of wholesome pub bar food (and fancier offerings in the restaurant). The carefully chosen wine list offers at least 10 good wines by the glass and there's both room-temperature (or chilled) Guinness and real ale (Hilden, brewed in Lisburn) on tap at the bar. Cosy, intimate atmosphere, fine fare and a good choice of liquid sustenance – what more can you ask of a well-run bar such as this?

Last Year's Winner

Smugglers Creek Inn
Rossnowlagh, Co Donegal

Sponsored by

LEGEND has it that Irish monks invented whiskey, learning of distillation from the perfumers of the Orient. They called their discovery *Uisce Beatha* (the water of life) and to this day the finest of whiskey is distilled by the Irish.

A visit to the Jameson Heritage Centre in Midleton, Co.  Cork will take you right to the heart of this cherished tradition. You are invited to take a two-hour tour of the Centre – it's a beautifully restored 18th century, self-contained industrial complex, unique in Britain and Ireland. Delight in the fully-operational water wheel and be amazed by the copper pot still of 32,000 gallons, the largest in the world.

An audio-visual presentation, available in six languages, breathes life into the Irish whiskey legend.

After the history comes the tasting. Relax in the atmosphere of a traditional Irish pub and sample Ireland's finest whiskey. *Sláinte.*

Lose yourself in the charm of another age – the Jameson Heritage Centre with its craft and coffee shops is located on the main Cork-Waterford road which links the ferry terminals of Rosslare and Ringaskiddy. We're open from 10.00am to 4.00pm, May to October. Telephone John Callely at 021-613594 or fax 021-613642 for information.

JAMESON The Spirit of Ireland

Seek Protection Under Our Wing

" We are delighted to sponsor the 'Newcomer of the Year Award'. In fact we are no strangers to winning awards ourselves. For example, following a recent Micropal award, Eagle Star is now recognised as the best personal pension fund manager over five years. When we receive an award like this it's our customers who are the real winners!

Successful newcomers are marked by key people with key ideas. But all new ventures carry an element of risk - the last thing you need to worry about as you start up in business.

Sound financial planning for new businesses is essential to survival. For example, businesses need to protect their key people against serious illness, disability, and death. Partners need to protect their interests in each other. And pensions are a sound and tax-efficient way to secure the future. Fledgling businesses should talk to their financial consultant about the difference Eagle Star can make to their future. **"**

John Caslin, General Manager Marketing
Eagle Star

EAGLE STAR

EAGLE STAR HOUSE FRASCATI ROAD BLACKROCK CO DUBLIN FAX 01 283 1578 TELEPHONE 01 283 1301

Ireland 1995
Newcomer of the Year

Shanks
Bangor, Co Down

Robbie and Shirley Millar obviously learned more than a few tricks of the trade during their time with the Rankins at Belfast's *Roscoff*. They set up their new venture at the Blackwood Golf Centre in October last year and immediately got into the swing of things. Robbie keeps his dinner menus sensibly short and makes good use of local Clandeboye estate venison, game and Angus beef in dishes like rare beef salad with rocket, fried polenta and Roquefort; émincé of pheasant with Jerusalem artichokes and creamed lentils; or venison with potato rösti, red cabbage, port and green peppercorn jus. Meanwhile, at front of house, Shirley marshals service from a smart, keen team. An eclectic wine list helps find a suitable match for the diverse range of ingredients that appear on the menus (you might have to ask for a recommendation to go with seared scallops with salsify, coriander butter and Chinese five spice!). The interior design of the restaurant is modern, with clean lines and contemporary styling – a perfect stage for the team's culinary performances.

Last Year's Joint Winners

Le Mistral
Harcourt Street, Dublin 2
Sullivans
Holywood, Co Down

Sponsored by

EAGLE STAR

CHOOSING...

1989

EAGLE STAR

PERSONAL
PENSION PLAN

GRAND CRU CLASSÉ

EAGLE STAR

APPELLATION EAGLE STAR CONTROLÉE

13% VOL   75CL

AN EAGLE STAR PENSION WILL SHOW MORE THAN JUST GOOD TASTE...

An eye for detail...
A fine ageing wine made with a delicate blend of three top performing fund varieties, Dynamic, Performance and Balanced.

A nose for investment management...

An excellent start to Eagle Star Pension Funds in 1989. All varieties yielded well in this vintage. Careful fund management has provided the best results over frosty conditions in the equity market. A hint of pronounced fruit in the future.

A taste for quality...
Well rounded & full bodied performance. Underlying fruit is very evident and should improve with age, giving an excellent finish.

Conclusions...
Excellent quality, showing good promise for the future. Now talk to your financial consultant about the difference an Eagle Star personal pension can make to your future.

EAGLE STAR
There are pensions. *And Eagle Star Pensions.*

AGLE STAR HOUSE FRASCATI ROAD BLACKROCK CO DUBLIN FAX 01 283 1578 TELEPHONE 01 283 1301

Fly Aer Lingus to Ireland

The Cliffs of Moher, County Clare, West Coast of Ireland.

and send a postcard from the edge.

Perched on the westernmost edge of Europe,
Ireland is undoubtedly one of the most beautiful
countries in the world.
It is also one of the friendliest.
So much so that your welcome to Ireland begins
before you've even left home. Because when
you step on board your Aer Lingus flight you step
into a little piece of Ireland. And there you'll enjoy
all the warmth and hospitality for which the Irish
and Aer Lingus are renowned.

Ireland 1995 International Hospitality Award

Jurys Hotel Group
Peter Malone, Managing Director
Jurys Hotel & Towers, Dublin

The expanding Jurys Hotel group is at the forefront of tourism in Ireland, with group hotels in Cork, Dublin, Limerick and Waterford and their newly-built, more price-conscious inns in Cork, Dublin and Galway. Jurys Hotel & Towers in Dublin is their flagship, where Jurys' managing director, Peter Malone, leads the way by running a tight ship; 300 rooms in the main hotel building offer a high level of comfort and facilities, while the hotel-within-a-hotel Towers has 100 superior bedrooms and suites, an even higher level of comfort, and exclusive amenities that offer a quieter environment for guests. International visitors can enjoy a taste of traditional Irish musical entertainment at Jurys Cabaret (May-Oct) or a taste of the famous stout in the Dubliner Pub, both without leaving the hotel. Banqueting and conference facilities cater for up to 600 (for a sit-down banquet) in the Grand Ballroom, plus there are several medium-sized rooms and five syndicate suites. Situated on a 4½-acre site in Ballsbridge (near Lansdowne Road rugby ground), the hotel is 8 miles from Dublin Airport.

Last Year's Winner

Ballymaloe House
Shanagarry, Co Cork

Sponsored by

Business & Finance Magazine.
Published weekly by Belenos Publications Ltd.,
50 Fitzwilliam Square, Dublin 2.
Telephone: 01-6764587. Fax: 6619781.

Strictly Business

In Ireland, when it comes to business, only one publication handles the affairs of the nation with flair and in-depth accuracy.

Business&Finance

24th NOVEMBER 1994

PRICE £2.00 INCLUDING TAX

EU Fraud
Europe on the Fiddle

Take it

Mussenden Temple, Downhill

all in.

A cruise on the Fermanagh Lakes. A hill walk in the Sperrins. Breathe in the beauty of the Giant's Causeway. The Mountains of Mourne. The green Glens of Antrim.

Touch the history of Derry. Of Armagh's Cathedral city. And the warmth of the people.

Golf. Fishing. Sailing. Horse-riding. Activities awaiting discovery in idyllic surroundings. Superb restaurants. Pubs and live entertainment. You're really spoilt for choice.

And don't forget to visit Belfast. A city steeped in history with a fine tradition of culture, crafts, sports and business.

For further information on holidaying in Northern Ireland or to obtain 'A Taste of Ulster Guide' contact the Northern Ireland Tourist Board at any of the numbers below.

 Northern Ireland Tourist Board

Belfast
St. Anne's Court, 59 North Street,
Belfast BT11NB Tel: (01232) 246609

Dublin
16 Nassau Street, Dublin 2
Tel: (003531) 6791977

London
11 Berkeley Street, London W1X 5AD
Freephone: (0800) 282 662

Glasgow
135 Buchanan Street, 1st Floor,
Glasgow G1 2JA Tel: (0141) 204 4454

Recommended by
EGON RONAY'S GUIDES
1995

YOUR GUARANTEE
OF
QUALITY AND INDEPENDENCE

- Establishment inspections are anonymous

- Inspections are undertaken by qualified
  Egon Ronay's Guides inspectors

- The Guides are completely independent
  in their editorial selection

- The Guides do not accept advertising,
  hospitality or payment from listed
  establishments

Hotels & Restaurants   Pubs & Inns
Europe   Just a Bite
Family Hotels & Restaurants   Paris
Oriental Restaurants   Ireland
New Zealand & South Pacific   Australia

Egon Ronay's Guides are available from all good bookshops or can be
ordered from Leading Guides, 35 Tadema Road, London SW10 0PZ
Tel: 071-352 2485 / 352 0019   Fax: 071-376 5071

Ireland in Focus

Rosslare (Co Wexford), Kelly's Resort Hotel

Boyle (Co Sligo), Cromleach Lodge

Newport (Co Mayo), Newport House

Rossnowlagh (Co Donegal), Sand House Hotel

Adare (Co Limerick), Adare Manor

Moycullen (Co Galway), Cloonabinnia House Hotel

Galway, Brennan's Yard

Dublin, Hotel Conrad

Youghal (Co Cork), Aherne's

Skibbereen (Co Cork), Liss Ard Lake Lodge

Dundrum (Co Tipperary), Dundrum House

Recess (Co Galway), Lough Inagh Lodge

Newmarket-on-Fergus (Co Clare), Dromoland Castle

Wicklow (Co Wicklow), Old Rectory

Tahilla (Co Kerry), Long Lake

Killarney (Co Kerry), Aghadoe Heights Hotel

Cork (Co Cork), Dan Lowrey's

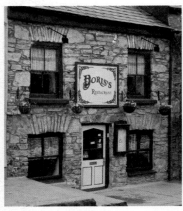

Clifden (Co Galway), Doris's Restaurant

Dingle (Co Kerry), Doyle's Seafood Bar and Townhouse

Republic of Ireland

Abbeyfeale   The Cellar

Tel 068 31085	**P**
The Square Abbeyfeale Co Limerick	Map 2 B5

Easily spotted as you drive through Abbeyfeale by the rows
of bottles of every shape and size displayed in the end window,
Padraig and Mary Fitzgerald's very pleasant "olde-style traditional"
pub will not disappoint – the locals are friendly and the open fire
and piano are not just for show, so sessions can get going at the
drop of a hat (Padraig is a fine musician himself). Traditional Irish
music (Thursday nights) is not exclusive, with rock music
on Saturday nights and sing-a-long on Sunday nights. The antique
decor includes original timber floors and ceiling, stone walls, pub
mirrors, gas lamps, church pews, pine dressers and old prints.
Snooker and pool room (plus a large-screen TV) on the second
storey. Nice walled garden at the back for sheltered summer
drinking. *Open 10.30am-11.30pm (11 in winter), Sun 12.30-2 &
4-11. No credit cards.*

Abbeyleix   Morrissey's

Tel 0502 31233 Fax 0502 31357	**P**
Main Street Abbeyleix Co Laois	Map 2 C4

A discreet black and gold sign singles out Morrissey's from its
neighbours in this handsome village; inside the lofty shelf-lined
grocery-bar, old-fashioned shades of black and brown
predominate, relieved here and there by a little cream. Mundane
groceries change hands along with their special blend of tea
(packed on the premises) and an unusually wide selection of loose
sweets like aniseed balls, pineapple chunks and bull's eyes, kept
in rows of big glass jars and sold by the 1/4lb in paper pokes.
On cold days customers reflect on their pints around an ancient
pot-bellied stove while reading the paper or exchanging the news
of the day – but card-playing and singing are not allowed. A good
place to take a break on the Dublin-Cork road but, although a cup
of tea or coffee will be served with charm, don't expect any food,
other than a sandwich. The landlord, Paddy Mulhall, is also
undertaker, travel agent and newsagent – typically Irish!
Open 10.30am-11.30pm, Sun 4-11. No credit cards.

Adare   Adare Manor   81%   £220

Tel 061 396566 Fax 061 396124	**HR**
Adare Co Limerick	Map 2 B5

Home, for two centuries, of the Dunraven family, this magnificent
neo-Gothic mansion is set in 900 acres on the banks of the River
Maigue. Its splendid chandeliered drawing room and the glazed
cloister of the dining room look over formal box-hedged gardens
towards the Robert Trent Jones golf course (currently still being
developed and not available for play, although arrangements are
made with a club nearby). Other grand public areas include the
gallery, modelled after the Palace of Versailles, with its Flemish
choir stalls, fine stained-glass windows and hand-carved
bookshelves. Gracious bedrooms have individual hand-crafted
fireplaces, fine locally-made mahogany furniture, cut-glass table
lamps and impressive marble bathrooms with strong showers over
huge bathtubs. Children under 12 are accommodated free in their

parents' room. No dogs. *Rooms 64. Garden, gymnasium, sauna, games room, snooker, golf driving range, riding, fishing, clay-pigeon shooting.* AMERICAN EXPRESS *Access, Diners, Visa.*

Restaurant   ↑   £85

Dining in style comes easy at Adare: after taking an aperitif in the drawing room overlooking the parterre gardens and developing golf course beyond, move through to the elegant panelled dining room with views of the River Maigue and consider chef de cuisine Gerard Costelloe's imaginative fare on a choice of table d'hote or à la carte menus. Local produce, including vegetables from the estate's own gardens, features in dishes like garden leaf salad, a colourful piquant combination of mixed leaves tossed in a creamy blue cheese dressing and scattered with crisp deep-fried beetroot 'chips', or a main course like baked fillet of sole and oysters topped with sesame seeds and red wine sauce. Desserts range from homely (individual blackberry and apple crumble, crème anglaise) to the richly exotic (chocolate marquise on a marmalade sauce). Tempting selection of home-made breads; excellent service. *Seats 65. Private Room 25. L 12.30-2.30 D 7-9. Set L & D £32.*

Adare	Dunraven Arms Hotel	72%	£127
Tel 061 396633 Fax 061 396541			**HR**
Adare Co Limerick			Map 2 B5

Sporting activities, including golf, fishing and especially hunting and all things equestrian, are a particular attraction here at 'the fox-hunting centre of Ireland' but the Dunraven Arms also attracts a wide range of guests, including business clients and many travellers who are tempted by imaginative bar food to break a journey here. Meticulously maintained public areas have a timeless, traditional atmosphere with old furniture lifted by classical colour combinations in the decor in everything from the busy, pubby bar to the serenity of the residents' drawing room, known as 'the library'. Bedrooms are individually furnished to a high standard with excellent bathrooms, antiques and many thoughtful extras, like fresh flowers, fruit and mineral water. The turn-down service includes fresh towels and chocolates on the pillow. No tea/coffee-making facilities, but room service is prompt. Frequent functions create a buzz around the hotel, but newer rooms away from public areas are quiet. Children up to 4 may stay free in their parents' room. 24hr room service. The hotel is presently building 22 additional en-suite 'de luxe' rooms – due for completion in May 1995. *Rooms 44. Garden, tennis, riding centre.* AMERICAN EXPRESS *Access, Diners, Visa.*

The Maigue Room   £55

Banqueting and dining are kept separate at the Dunraven Arms and head chef Mark Phelan is building up an excellent reputation for his elegant restaurant, named after the local river. Table d'hote or à la carte menus might typically start with a variation on a traditional local dish like black pudding, pan-fried and imaginatively served with featherlight apple fritters and a colourful red onion confit, or a stunningly pretty warm terrine of trout and fresh prawn tails in a vermouth-scented beurre blanc with dill. Main courses also highlight the quality of local produce, including the finest roast beef (carved from a trolley in the

evening). Delicious desserts like good old lemon meringue pie,
lightly baked and served with an orange sauce. Lovely brown soda
bread, aromatic coffee. **Seats** 70. Parties 20. Private Room 30.
L 12.30-2.30 D 7.30-9.30. Bar Food 12-6pm. Set L £11.50
Set D £21.50. Closed Good Friday.

Adare   The Inn Between   £45

Tel 061 396633   Fax 061 396541   **R**

Adare Co Limerick   Map 2 B5

In common ownership with *The Dunraven Arms* (see entry),
an informal restaurant in one of the village's old thatched cottages.
It retains the original style of the building, although it has been
sympathetically renovated and extended to provide extra space.
The atmosphere is cheerful (red and white tablecloths) and,
in contrast to other comparable restaurants nearby, The Inn
Between (as its name suggests) aims to provide good, reasonably
priced food. An à la carte lunch menu offers starters from £2.25
to £3.50 – typically home-made soup and warm lamb's kidney
salad – and main courses (under £7) such as tagliatelle of smoked
salmon and cream with a side salad. Desserts range from the
homely (apple pie and cream) to the sophisticated – double
chocolate terrine, orange and vanilla sauce, all £2.25. A la carte
dinner menus are slightly dressier, but also reasonably priced.
Outside eating area. **Seats** 65. Parties 12. L 12.30-2.30 D 6.30-9.30.
Closed Mon, Tues, 1 Nov-mid Mar. AMERICAN EXPRESS Access,
Diners, Visa.

If we recommend meals in a hotel or inn a **separate**
entry is made for its restaurant.

Adare   The Mustard Seed   ↑   £60

Tel 061 396451   **R**

Main Street Adare Co Limerick   Map 2 B5

Picturesque surroundings in this olde-worlde thatched cottage and
a warm welcome from the proprietor, Dan Mullane, provide the
perfect ambience for Michael Weir's confident, creative cooking.
Four-course dinner menus based firmly on the best of local and
seasonal produce present difficult choices but, once the decisions
are made, the cosy little reception/bar makes an enjoyable place
to anticipate the pleasures ahead: an Oriental terrine of layered
pork, leeks and spinach is a sight to behold on a bed of puréed
apples sharpened with balsamic vinegar, while a salad of crisp
green beans, with quail's eggs, slivers of parmesan and black olives
in a chive nut oil is, quite simply, moreish. Smoked haddock
chowder comes with a spicy rouille and irresistible home-baked
breads, while main courses feature game in season, local free-range
duck and elegant fish dishes such as trio of fish – baked escalope
of salmon with steamed sole and pan-fried scallops on a chive and
spring onion sauce. Good farmhouse cheeses and imaginative
variations on homely desserts, like delicious banoffi pie with
caramel sauce and banana coulis. To finish, home-made petits fours
and fragrant coffee. No smoking. As we went to press we heard
that the restaurant was moving premises at the end of 1995.
Seats 50. Parties 18. D only 7-10. Set D £25. Closed Sun & Mon,
Bank Holidays & 23 Jan-1 Mar. AMERICAN EXPRESS Access, Diners, Visa.

Adare   Woodlands House Hotel   60%   £50

H

Tel 061 396118   Fax 061 396073

Adare Co Limerick   Map 2 B5

From small beginnings in 1983 the Fitzgerald family have developed their hotel to its present stage, with facilities for weddings, banquets and conferences for up to 400. Roomy public areas include two bars and a strikingly decorated lobby/lounge with comfortable seating and a colourful mural, while both banqueting suites and the restaurant overlook well-maintained gardens and countryside. Bedrooms, including two suites and most with a pleasant outlook, vary in age and amenities but are all well maintained. No dogs. *Rooms 57. Garden, spa bath. Closed 24 & 25 Dec.* AMERICAN EXPRESS *Access, Diners, Visa.*

Adare   Place of Interest

Castle Matrix Rathkeale Tel 069 64284

Aghadoe   Killeen House Hotel   64%   £73

H

Tel 064 31711   Fax 064 31811

Aghadoe Killarney Co Kerry   Map 2 A5

This attractive, recently renovated early 19th-century house has been run as a small hotel by the present owners, Michael and Geraldine Rosney, since 1992. Popular with golfers, holidaymakers and business guests alike, it has a welcoming atmosphere which is especially noticeable in the pubby little bar, where locals mingle with residents. Rooms vary somewhat in size but are all en suite and freshly decorated, with phone and satellite TV, and there's a pretty drawing room furnished with a mixture of antiques and newer furniture and an open fire, where guests can relax. Ample parking. *Rooms 15. Garden, tennis. Closed early Dec-mid Mar.* AMERICAN EXPRESS *Access, Diners, Visa.*

Ahakista   Ahakista Bar

No Telephone   **P**

Ahakista nr Bantry Co Cork   Map 2 A6

Unchanged for as long as anyone can remember, and in the same family ownership for three generations, Margareta and Anthony Whooley's little bar is just opposite the entrance to the *Shiro Japanese Dinner House* and its corrugated iron roof conceals as pleasant an old-fashioned dart-playing pub as is to be found. Beyond the unspoilt bar lies another treasure – a delightfully ungroomed, rambling garden reaching right down to the sandy beach, with a big lawn where children can let off steam. *Open 3.30-11 (winter), 1-11.30 (summer) (12.30-2 & 4-11 Sun all year). Garden. No credit cards.*

Ahakista   Hillcrest House   £33

A

Tel 027 67045

Ahakista Durrus Co Cork   Map 2 A6

Comfortable accommodation and home-cooked food are the main attractions at this neat farmhouse, situated on a working farm overlooking Dunmanus Bay. Of the four rooms, three are upstairs and en suite while one double (with bath) is on the ground floor

with direct access to parking facilities. Suitable for families.
*Rooms 4. Garden, indoor & outdoor play areas. Closed Nov-Apr.
No credit cards.*

Ahakista	**Shiro**	★	**£80**

Tel 027 67030	**R**
Ahakista nr Bantry Co Cork	**Map 2 A6**

A visit to the remote Shiro Japanese Dinner House, situated in
a fine, meticulously maintained Georgian house overlooking
Dunmanus Bay, is likely to be both unique and unforgettable.
The dining room may only accommodate small numbers, but
both the welcome and the food are big-hearted. Often referred
to as an experience which defies description, Kei Pilz's authentic
Japanese food is so exquisite in both preparation and presentation
that it remains in the mind as a finely detailed patchwork,
an impressionistic mirage of culinary delights. With great charm
Werner Pilz guides newcomers through the menu, which changes
daily and may consist of three short courses – perhaps *zensai*
(flower-decked appetisers), *moriawase* (delicate egg dishes and
sushi) and *suimono* (a seasonal soup), followed by a choice of eight
main courses including a selection of lightly-battered deep-fried
tempura dishes, *sashimi* (seasonal raw fish, served with soy sauce
and *wasabi* – hot green mustard) and *shiyoyaki* (lightly salted
salmon and mackerel filets grilled with lemon). Several dishes are
suitable for vegetarians. A selection of home-made ices, including
green tea, dramatically arranged with some colourful fruit against
a black plate and followed by a choice of teas and coffees, rounds
off the experience. There's a pleasant, short wine list that lists
French classics alongside the *sake*. 5% supplement for paying
by credit card. Bookings only. No children under 12. A charming
traditional cottage (sleeping two) in the grounds is available for
self-catering. *Seats 18. Private Room 5. D only 7-9. Set D £34.
Closed 25 & 26 December.* AMERICAN EXPRESS *Access, Diners, Visa.*

> Any person using our name to obtain free hospitality is
> a fraud. Proprietors, please inform the police and us.

Annascaul	**Dan Foley's**

Tel 066 57252	**P**
Annascaul Co Kerry	**Map 2 A5**

Dan Foley's pub owes its colourful, much-photographed exterior
to the theatrical personality of the man himself – farmer, expert
on local history and magician. Inside, it's a great, unspoilt bar
in the rural tradition, made special by Dan's particular interest
in people and chat – and an unexpected collection of about fifty
liqueurs. Food is not the thing here although 'emergency rations'
of sandwiches, sausage rolls and the like will be served (11am-
8pm) to those who resist directions to the proper restaurant next
door. Children during daylight hours only. One of Ireland's most
famous pubs. *Open 11-11 (to 11.30 Mon-Sat in Summer), Sun
12.30-2.30 & 4-11. No credit cards.*

Ardee   The Gables

£60

Tel & Fax 041 53789

RR

Dundalk Road Ardee Co Louth

Map 1 C3

In what might still seem, relative to other areas which have developed so dramatically over the last few years, something of a culinary desert, this bourgeois restaurant is enormously popular. Owner-chef Michael Caine uses the best of local ingredients without allowing the forces of fashion to intrude on a French menu distinctly reminiscent of the 60s, with huge servings and rich sauces, typically in dishes like wild pigeon in Madeira sauce, fresh Clogherhead prawns thermidor, honey-roast duckling with raspberry sauce and breast of chicken stuffed with smoked salmon and crab, finished with butter, cream and Chablis – to the evident satisfaction of an appreciative local clientele who like things just the way they are. *Seats 34. D only 7-9.30. Set D £19.95. Closed Sun, Mon & Tues, 2 weeks Jun, 2 weeks Nov, Good Friday & 25/26 Dec.* AMERICANEXPRESS *Access, Diners, Visa.*

Rooms

£34

Accommodation is offered in five rooms, 3 en suite. *Garden.*

Ardee   Red House

£60

Tel 041 53523

A

Ardee Co Louth

Map 1 C3

Linda Connolly gives guests a warm welcome at her lovely Georgian house, which is impeccably run and furnished with a level of comfort bordering on opulence, yet loses none of its rural charm. The traditional huge log fire in the library is just that, burning logs from the grounds, and when there are only a few guests Linda sets up a cosy dining table there in preference to the formal dining room, with its long mahogany table. Beautifully furnished bedrooms are very comfortable – and, although two share a communal bathroom in true country tradition, the corridor is far from draughty. Delicious breakfasts are served at a brightly colourful table in the morning room. Small conferences (20), weddings (50). Not suitable for children except babies under 1 year. *Rooms 3. Garden, swimming pool, sauna (summer months only), tennis, stables. Closed 20 Dec-1 Mar.*

Ardmore   Cliff House Hotel   59%

£68

Tel 024 94106   Fax 024 94496

H

Ardmore Co Waterford

Map 2 C6

Eddie and Eileen Irwin took over this dramatically situated, unpretentious, family-friendly hotel in 1992 and are steadily working on improvements and refurbishment – most (15) of the bedrooms are now en suite and, along with the restaurant bar and lounge, have lovely sea views. The garden reaches down to the clifftop, making a lovely spot for afternoon tea. Under-14s may share their parents' room free of charge (4 family rooms); cots, extra beds, high-chairs and early evening meal available by arrangement. *Rooms 20. Closed Nov-Mar except weekends.* AMERICANEXPRESS *Access, Diners, Visa.*

Athleague Fitzmaurice's Tavern

Tel 0903 63383 **P**

Athleague Co Roscommon Map 1 B3

This award-winning, seriously olde-worlde pub could take prizes as an agricultural museum, but it's a very real place when it comes to efficient, cheerful service and a good local, judging by the gathering likely to be found around the open fire on a winter evening. "Whether or not everybody likes the clutter, it's always a great conversation piece" – which is fair enough and, anyway, it is interesting rather than twee. There's been a new landlord, Hugh Mitchell, recently. Food here is basically generous sandwiches of home-cooked meats, although you might get soup in winter (but don't bank on it!). *Open 12-11.30, Sun 12.30-2 & 4-11. Garden. No credit cards.*

Athlone Higgins's

Tel 0902 92519 **P**

2 Pearce Street Athlone Co Westmeath Map 1 C3

West of the river, in the interesting old part of the town near the Norman castle (which has a particularly good visitor's centre for history – siege of Athlone 1691 – and information on the area, including flora and fauna of the Shannon), the Higginses run a nice hospitable pub with accommodation in four recently-refurbished rooms upstairs. Rooms vary from a single to a family room with three single beds (also an extra child's bed available), but all have secondary glazing, neat shower rooms, television and hairdryer and there are communal tea/coffee-making facilities in the dining room where breakfast is served. There's also a cosy residents' lounge, with television and comfortable armchairs. No evening meals (soup and sandwiches only in the bar), but there's a good evening restaurant nearby and also a middle-market restaurant recommended by the Higginses for family meals. *Pub open 10.30am-11pm (Sun 12.30-2, 4-11).* **Accommodation** *4 bedrooms, all en suite, from £28 (single £15). Children welcome overnight (under-10s stay free in parents' room), additional beds & cots supplied. Pub closed 25 Dec, Good Fri, 2 weeks January. No dogs. No credit cards.*

Athlone Restaurant Le Chateau £55

Tel 0902 94517 **R**

Abbey Lane Athlone Co Westmeath Map 1 C3

Tucked into a lane close to the castle from which it takes its name, this well-appointed first-floor restaurant takes character from the old building in which it is located but it is owner-chef Steven Linehan's consistently creative approach which has earned its reputation locally. A typical dinner menu might include distinctive home-made soups (accompanied by irresistible dark, malty bread), an unusual combination of hot and cold oysters, main-course fish, such as fillets of brill with a white wine/dill sauce, midland meats – pork, perhaps, with a zippy blue cheese and mushroom sauce – and game in season (accompanied by imaginatively presented vegetables), typically rounded off with a tangy lemon tart and home-made chocolates with the coffee. Reflecting the numbers of Continental visitors holidaying on the

Shannon (which is only yards away), Le Chateau also features
an unusual "Euro-Menu" in four languages. *Seats 40. D only 6-
10.15. Closed Sun in winter, 3 weeks Jan. Set D £13.50 (6-7.15
only)/£18.* [AMERICAN EXPRESS] *Access, Diners, Visa.*

Athlone   Sean's Bar

Tel 0902 92358	**A**
13 Main Street Athlone Co Westmeath	Map 1 C3

Sean Fitzsimons's seriously historic west bank bar in the oldest,
most characteful part of Athlone lays claim to being the pub with
the longest continuing use in Ireland – quite reasonably, it seems,
as all of the owners since 1630 are on record. On entering from
the street, the sloping floor is the first of many interesting features
to strike the first-time visitor; now strikingly covered in bold
black and white tiles, the floor is cleverly constructed to ensure
that flood water drained back down to the river again as the
waters subsided. A handy watering hole for visitors cruising the
Shannon – there's still direct access to the river through the back
bar and beer garden – the bar has some nice old pieces, including
a mahogany counter and mirrored mahogany shelving as well as a
very large settle bed, which seems particularly appropriate to the
soothing, dimly-lit ambience. A glass case containing a section
of old wattle wall original to the building and a letter about
it from the National Museum highlights the age of the bar, but it's
far from being a museum piece. Food is restricted to sandwiches
and coffee, but the proper priorities are observed and they serve
a good pint. Music most nights. *Pub open 10.30am-11.30pm Mon-
Sat (to 11 in winter), Sun 12.30-2, 4-11. Garden. Closed 25 Dec,
Good Fri. No credit cards.*

Athy   Tonlegee House

	£55
Tel & Fax 0507 31473	**RR**
Athy Co Kildare	Map 2 C4

Just outside town, Mark and Marjorie Molloy's restored Georgian
home offers good cooking, a warm welcome, excellent bedrooms
and a favourable price/quality ratio. Dinner is a five-course affair
(priced according to the choice of main dish), or six if opting for
the selection of four Irish farmhouse cheeses (the small extra
charge includes a glass of port). The likes of duck liver parfait with
toasted brioche and onion confit, venison pithiviers, and ravioli
of crab with grain mustard and shellfish sauce are among the
starters, and guinea fowl with wild mushroom sauce or breast
of Barbary duck with a confit of its leg and a port and caper sauce
might be included in the main-course options. All are prepared
with a skill and care that extends to a choice of home-baked
breads and desserts like pear and almond tart cooked to order. The
day's fish and seasonal game dishes are recited when the menu
is offered. Diners and overnight guests share a comfortable period
sitting room. *Seats 40. L by arrangement D 7-9.30 (to 10.30 Fri &
Sat). 24-27 Dec and Good Friday. Access, Visa.*

Rooms

£60

Five spacious, antique-furnished bedrooms have been individually
decorated with attractive fabrics and offer various homely

comforts in addition to remote-control TV, direct-dial telephones and good, large en-suite bathrooms. Breakfast, using free-range eggs, makes an excellent start to the day.

Aughrim	Aughrim Schoolhouse Restaurant	£45
Tel 0905 73936		**R**
Aughrim nr Ballinasloe Co Galway		Map 2 B4

The work of conversion from schoolhouse to charming country restaurant can be followed in a scrapbook kept by the fire in the reception area. Geraldine Dolan and Mícheál Harrison produce intelligent menus of interesting modern dishes which have quickly won a fair following. Boneless quail stuffed with mushrooms, Indian spiced vegetables and fresh crab ravioli are typical starters, followed perhaps by poached salmon with a basil white wine sauce, guinea fowl with pork sauce or sirloin steak with green peppercorn or béarnaise sauce. Good vegetables; 'bonnofie' pie a speciality dessert. *Seats* 60. *L 12.30-3 (Sun only) D 5.30-9.30. Closed D Sun & all Mon Oct-May, 25 & 26 Dec. Set Sun L £10 Set D £16.95.* AMERICAN EXPRESS *Access, Visa.*

Aughrim   Place of Interest

Battle of Aughrim Centre Tel 0905 73939

Bagenalstown	Lorum Old Rectory	£45
Tel 0503 75282 Fax 0503 75455		**A**
Bagenalstown Co Carlow		Map 2 C4

Don and Bobbie Smith have built up a great reputation for good food and hospitality at their delightful Victorian rectory over the last decade. Elegance and comfort receive equal priority in spacious, well-proportioned rooms furnished in period style, including a lovely drawing room for guests, four thoughtfully furnished, en-suite bedrooms (one with a four-poster, £5 supplement) and an extra single room which has the use of a big old-fashioned bathroom with generous ball and claw cast-iron bath along the corridor; all rooms are non-smoking. A lovely place for families – there are swings (and a pony to ride under supervision) in the orchard, room for cots and extra beds in parents' rooms, baby-sitting, high-chairs, videos and children's teas all available. Bobbie's renowned dinner for residents is served communally at a long mahogany table (book by 3pm). Private parties and small conferences for up to 10. *Rooms* 5. *Garden, croquet. Closed Christmas week. Access, Visa.*

Ballina	Downhill Hotel	65%	£86
Tel 096 21033 Fax 096 21338			**H**
Ballina Co Mayo			Map 1 B3

Set in landscaped gardens overlooking the River Brosna, with extensive leisure and conference facilities and good fishing nearby as major attractions. The purpose-built conference centre and hospitality rooms accommodate groups from 10 to 450 and the leisure centre has a 50ft oval swimming pool with a children's pool being developed for early 1995; nightly entertainment in Frog's Pavilion piano bar. Good facilities for families include cots, high-chairs, playroom and a supervised creche. Easy parking for 300. **Rooms** *50. Garden, indoor swimming pool, keep-fit equipment, squash, sauna, spa bath, solarium, tennis, games room, snooker. Closed 3 days Christmas.* AMERICAN EXPRESS *Access, Diners, Visa.*

Ballina	Mount Falcon Castle	60%	£88
Tel 096 70811 Fax 096 71517			**AR**
Ballina Co Mayo			Map 1 B3

The castle was built in neo-Gothic style in 1876, and the 100 acres of grounds extend to the banks of the River Moy (fishing is available either here or on Lough Conn). Woodland walks unfold the beauty of the surroundings, while back inside huge log fires and convivial company make for instant relaxation. Simple bedrooms are furnished with antiques. Constance Aldridge, who has owned the castle and greeted visitors for over 50 years, is an indispensible part of the charm of the place. **Rooms** *10. Garden, tennis, game fishing. Closed Christmas week and Feb.* AMERICAN EXPRESS *Access, Diners, Visa.*

Restaurant   £50

Local produce, much of it from the estate farm and walled gardens, is the basis of confident, uncomplicated country house cooking. Soup, salmon, leg of lamb, spicy chicken, crème caramel and bread-and-butter pudding typify the menu. Guests gather around one table in the dining room. Lunch available by arrangement. **Seats** *28. D only at 8. Set D £22.*

Ballisodare	The Thatch	
Tel 071 67288		**P**
Ballisodare Co Sligo		Map 1 B2

This attractive, low-ceilinged thatched pub just south of Sligo town is very much a local and its open fire is as welcoming on a winter evening as the tables outdoors on a fine summer day. Whatever the weather the welcome from Brian and Denise Fitzpatrick (long-standing owners for 23 years of this family business) is warm and the pint is good. Traditional music is played 3 or 4 nights a week. No children under 15 inside. *Open 11am-11.30pm, Sun 12.30-2 & 4-11. Garden. No credit cards.*

Ballybofey   Kee's Hotel   62%   £65

`Tel 074 31018   Fax 074 31917`   **H**

Stranorlar Ballybofey Co Donegal   Map 1 C2

Originally a coaching inn, Claire and Arthur Kee's attractive hotel
has continued the family tradition of hospitality for four
generations and now has not only bustling public rooms –
including Scenes traditional bar with stone floor and open fire,
where bar food is served – but good leisure facilities, available free
to hotel guests, who have direct access from their rooms. All
rooms are comfortably furnished, with neat, en-suite bathrooms,
phone, TV, trouser press, hairdryer and tea/coffee facilities and the
14 recently refurbished Executive rooms have views of the
Bluestack Mountains. Children welcome, under-3s stay free
in parents' room; cots, baby-listening/sitting and high-chairs
available; creche some mornings in leisure centre; children's
portions on bar menu. Banqueting/conferences for 250/300. 60 car
parking spaces. **Rooms** 37. *Indoor swimming pool, gym, solarium,
sauna, spa bath, steam room.* AMERICAN EXPRESS *Access, Diners, Visa.*

Ballyconneely   Erriseask House Hotel   66%   £72

`Tel 095 23553   Fax 095 23639`   **HR**

Ballyconneely Clifden Co Galway   Map 2 A4

Since 1988 brothers Christian and Stefan Matz have been quietly
building up a reputation for excellence at their stunningly located
shoreside hotel and restaurant, seven miles south of Clifden.
There's a deceptively low-key atmosphere about the place,
especially in the foyer and lounge/bar areas, which have
a distinctly Continental feel with a lot of light wood (but the dark
stuff on draught) and (with the notable exception of Gertrude
Degenhardt's pictures) a generally understated approach which
is also carried through to the original bedrooms, which are neatly
decorated in rather neutral colours with compact shower rooms
and tea/coffee trays. The five new rooms, added in 1994, display
a different side to the Matz personality, however, a flamboyance
hitherto unsuspected – designed as two-storey suites, they have
luxurious ground-floor accommodation and en-suite bathrooms
with romantic spiral staircases leading up to the mezzanine sitting
room and dramatic drapes, which fall the whole height from
ceiling to floor but take nothing from the wild land and seascape
beyond. Its wildness and the raw beauty of the surroundings are
perhaps the main strength of the magnet that draws people back
to Erriseask, but the hosts' gentle cosseting also play a major,
if discreet, role. They even lend guests two ever-willing dogs
to enhance their walks along the white coral strands. Sheer magic.
Rooms 13. *Garden. Closed 1 Nov-1 Apr.* AMERICAN EXPRESS *Access,
Diners, Visa.*

Restaurant   ★   £75

Well appointed in every detail, with some magnificent Villeroy &
Boch plates, the restaurant provides a fitting backdrop for Stefan
Matz's dedicated, passionate cooking – for which he wins our
Ireland 1995 Chef of the Year award (see page 31). Four menus
are offered – a 4-course Dinner Menu, a slightly simpler 3-course
residents' dinner (changed daily), à la carte and Stefan's *pièce
de résistance*, a 7-course *menu dégustation*, in which the balance

of dishes is so carefully worked out that it results in a perfect no-choice menu. Starting with an *amuse-bouche* – a creamy miniature soufflé of turbot perhaps – complemented by one of the country's best bread baskets, then, perhaps, a carpaccio of scallops and turbot – the raw fish oh so finely sliced, a small masterpiece – contrasting with much chunkier little slices, delicately smoked and set on a bed of julienne vegetables. Next there might be ravioli of lobster, plump little pasta parcels on a rich sauce dotted with oyster mushrooms, and a sorbet such as buttermilk and lime, which will restore the most jaded palate and, with it, faith in this now clichéd course as it prepares the diner to launch into a meat course such as roast rack and fillet of Connemara lamb with unexpected enthusiasm. Vegetables will be small, carefully judged for colour, flavour and overall balance. After a short break, a magnificent board of French and Irish cheeses is served with big fat black grapes and – a touch of genius this – Stefan's close-textured fruit bread, very thinly sliced. Then to the grand finale, which might be a hot soufflé – of rhubarb, perhaps, served with a little egg of creamy vanilla ice cream and a compote of red fruits, gleaming jewel-like in their juices. Aromatic black coffee brings the chance to savour Stefan's irresistible petits fours – tiny palmiers, white and dark chocolate truffles, and more. The diner might get lost in admiration of Stefan's skill and precision, the perfectly judged portions, the balance of imagination and simplicity. Add to this Christian Matz's natural, unassuming hospitality – he pampers without intrusion and excellent service is provided by well-trained local staff under his supervision – and it becomes clear that this has become one of Ireland's finest restaurants. Light lunches only, unless by arrangement. A fair and decently-priced wine list, though there's little from the New World; the varietal section allows you to choose by the glass. No smoking. *Seats 36. Parties 8. D only 6.30-9.30. Set D £17.50/£21.90 & £29.*

Many hotels offer reduced rates for weekend or out-of-season bookings. Always ask about special deals.

Ballyconnell   Slieve Russell Hotel   75%   £140

Tel 049 26444   Fax 049 26474   **H**

Ballyconnell Co Cavan   Map 1 C3

Hotel, golf and country club and major conference venue, Slieve Russell stands in a lovely fishing area and takes its name from a nearby mountain. A marbled colonnade and grand central staircase set a tone of subdued luxury in the day rooms, where guests have a good choice of eating and drinking outlets. Spacious bedrooms have extra-large beds, with good amenities including trouser press as standard and large marble bathrooms, all with jacuzzi air baths. The championship golf course is in full swing and excellent leisure facilities adjoining the hotel include a 20 metre pool. On a recent visit management and staff motivation did not appear to be at the high standard of previous years. *Rooms 150. Garden, indoor swimming pool, children's pool, gymnasium, squash, sauna, spa bath, steam room, tennis, golf (18), snooker, creche, hair & beauty salon).* AMERICAN EXPRESS *Access, Diners, Visa.*

Ballycotton   Bayview Hotel   67%   £80

Tel 021 646746   Fax 021 646824   **H**

Ballycotton Co Cork   Map 2 B6

Although in the present ownership since 1974, this hotel has
recently been completely re-built. It now combines a unique
seafront location beside Ballycotton harbour with a carefully
judged design that retains traditional features like human
proportions and open fires, and also incorporates modern
conveniences and up-to-date bathrooms. Built to take full
advantage of the wonderful location, all rooms have lovely
sea/harbour views and well-designed bathrooms while suites,
which occupy corner sites on two floors, have especially good
views on two sides, and all the top floor has a pleasingly cosy
'cottage attic' feeling. All rooms have space for a cot (no charge)
or extra bed. Public areas are spacious and, although not
ostentatious, quality is evident in the furnishing throughout; the
dining room, which can be divided if required, is particularly
attractive and, like the rest of the hotel, also enjoys the magnificent
views. Facilities for small conferences (up to 50, theatre-style) and
plenty of parking. Tennis facilities available at a nearby hotel.
No dogs. **Rooms** 35. *Garden. Closed Nov-Easter.*
Access, Visa.

Ballydehob   Annie's Bookshop and Café

Tel 028 37292   **JaB**

Main Street Balydehob Co Cork   Map 2 A6

Just up the street from her famous little evening restaurant, Annie
Barry opened this daytime bookshop and café in 1994 to offer
informal daytime food in summer. The atmosphere is lovely – old
pine, oilcloths, blackboard menu alongside the books – and prices,
for undemanding home-cooked snacks, refreshingly low. Seafood
soup with home-baked brown soda bread is £2.25, for instance,
fresh crab open sandwich £3.50, while 'ordinary' sandwiches are
only £1.50/£1.60. Home bakes are tempting: gateau of the day,
£1.50, hot chocolate fudge cake and cream, £1.20, carrot cake
90p. There's a good choice of teas and coffees too – and home-
made scones with butter and jam only 55p. **Seats** 25. *Open 10am-
6pm. Closed Sun, 1 Nov-30 Apr (but a phone call is worthwhile to
check). No credit cards.*

Ballydehob   Annie's Restaurant   £55

Tel 028 37292   **R**

Main Street Balydehob Co Cork   Map 2 A6

Faces light up when Annie Barry's tiny restaurant is mentioned.
It's all so laid back: the way Levis' old grocery/bar across the road
serves aperitifs while you wait for your table and, quite likely,
digestifs afterwards, to relieve pressure on space. Set 4-course
dinners change regularly and, although understandably leaning
towards local seafood, give a wide range of choices at each course,
including a vegetarian dish of the day. Lamb kidneys in filo, baked
fresh wild salmon with lemon and fresh herb sauce, followed
by roasted almonds and Baileys ice cream or local Gubbeen cheese
typify the style. Booking essential. **Seats** 24. *D only 6.30-9.30.*

*Set D £20. Closed Sun, Mon, first three weeks Oct + ring in winter
to check opening times. Access, Visa.*

Ballydehob   Levis Bar

Tel 028 37118	**P**
Corner House Main Street Ballydehob Co Cork	Map 2 A6

A friendly welcome awaits visitors to this 150-year-old grocery
store and bar, which sisters Julia and Nell Levis have run for
"years and years". The bar is not only host to 'resident' drinkers
but also serves as a reception and aperitif area for the tiny *Annie's*
restaurant over the road. *Open 10.30am-11.30pm (Sun 12.30-2 &
4-11). No credit cards.*

Ballyferriter   Long's Pub

Tel 066 56344	**P**
Ballyferriter Village Ballyferriter Co Kerry	Map 2 A5

Right next door to the Well House in Ballyferriter Village, this
colourful little Irish-speaking pub has probably changed little since
it first opened in 1854. A good spot for a quiet pint during the
day, or traditional music sessions, held nightly in summer. Just
open sandwiches available from 11 to 6. En-suite accommodation
promised from Easter 1995 onwards. *Open 10.30am-11.30pm,
Sun 12.30-2 & 4-11. Garden. No credit cards.*

Ballyferriter   Tigh an Tobair (The Well House)   £35

Tel 066 56404	**R**
Ballyferriter Co Kerry	Map 2 A5

In an area otherwise surprisingly badly served, this pleasant,
informal restaurant is an oasis for parched travellers. Walk
through the grocery shop at the front and you will find
an unpretentious little restaurant arranged, quite literally, around
a deep well (glass-topped for safety but still clearly visible) and
furnished with the unmistakable tiled tables and chunky wares
of Louis Mulcahy's nearby pottery. The emphasis is very much
on simple home cooking in traditional dishes like Irish stew and
Dublin coddle, good thick soups and big, wholesome salads and
sandwiches made with home-made bread. From March 1995 local
seafood will be the main feature of a new formal dinner menu
served from 6pm. ***Seats** 52. Parties 8. L 12-4 D 6-10.
Closed Mon plus Jan & Feb. Access, Visa.*

Ballyhack   Neptune Restaurant   £50

Tel 051 389284 Fax 051 389284	**R**
Ballyhack New Ross Co Wexford	Map 2 C5

Pierce and Valerie McAuliffe's charming rust-red restaurant just
under the castle near the Ballyhack car ferry continues to charm,
with Valerie's welcome and sunny Mediterranean colour scheme
(enriched of late by touches of gold replacing white) a fitting
foil to Pierce's delicious food. Local seafood takes centre stage
in starters such as a superb bisque-like creamy Neptune fish soup,
or bouchée of fat Bannow mussels with a richly garlicky sauce,
followed perhaps by an excellent, generous fresh crab platter with
garlic mayonnaise or hot crab brehat, a house speciality that never

palls. Round off with local cheeses, or a homely dessert like
Valerie's fresh peach crumble with crunchy almonds, or a pretty
poached pear in red wine and a cup of aromatic coffee. BYO
encouraged. *Seats 36. Private rooms 14/30. L during Opera festival
only (or by special arrangement) D 6.30-9.30. Closed Mon (except
Bank Holidays), Sun-Wed mid Nov-mid Mar. Set D £12.50 (6.30-
8.30).* AMERICAN EXPRESS *Access, Diners, Visa.*

Ballylickey	Ballylickey Manor House	67%	£99
Tel 027 50071 Fax 027 50124			**A**
Ballylickey Bantry Co Cork			**Map 2 A6**

Ballylickey has been the Graves' family home for four generations
and a hotel for over four decades. The main house, which
is impressively furnished with antiques, has views over Bantry
Bay and five spacious suites with well-appointed bathrooms. Ten
acres of award-winning gardens afford a splendid setting for
an outdoor swimming pool and garden restaurant, in addition
to simpler accommodation in seven chalets, all with en-suite
rooms. *Rooms 5 in main house. Garden, outdoor swimming pool,
fishing, croquet. Closed 1 Nov-30 Mar.* AMERICAN EXPRESS *Access, Visa.*

Ballylickey	Larchwood House		£60
Tel 027 66181			**R**
Pearsons Bridge Ballylickey Bantry Co Cork			**Map 2 A6**

Owner-chef Sheila Vaughan and her husband Aidan have
been steadily building up a reputation for good food and
accommodation at Larchwood since they opened in 1990. Located
in a private home, the restaurant is cleverly designed to take full
advantage of views over garden and river to the mountains
beyond and also to allow maximum privacy in a limited space.
Five-course, fixed-price-only menus offer a wide selection, priced
according to the choice of main course and highlighting the best
of local produce, particularly a good range of fish: seafood mousse,
rhubarb sorbet, paupiettes of sole with mustard sauce and duckling
breast with kumquats are typical, followed by warm chocolate
cake with caramel sauce, perhaps, or local farmhouse cheeses.
Excellent breakfasts also offer an unusual range of options,
including several fish choices. Accommodation is offered in four
comfortable en-suite rooms, including two family rooms. Rooms
at the back have lovely views. No dogs. *Garden. Seats 20.
Parties 13. D only 6.30-9.30. Set D from £18. Closed Sun, 1 week
Christmas.* AMERICAN EXPRESS *Access, Diners, Visa.*

Ballylickey	Seaview House Hotel	70%	£100
Tel 027 50462 Fax 027 51555			**HR**
Ballylickey Bantry Co Cork			**Map 2 A6**

Since converting her family home to a hotel in the mid-70s, Miss
Kathleen O'Sullivan has built up an impressive reputation – not
only for consistently high standards of essentials like comfort and
housekeeping, but also for her personal supervision and warmth
of welcome. Spacious, well-proportioned public rooms include
a graciously decorated drawing room, a library and comfortable

television room, while generously-sized bedrooms are all
individually decorated and some have sea views. Family furniture
and antiques enhance the hotel throughout and a ground-floor
room has been thoughtfully equipped for disabled guests.
Rooms 17. *Garden. Closed mid Nov-mid Mar.* AMERICAN EXPRESS
Access, Visa.

Restaurant   £55

Overlooking the garden, with views over Bantry Bay, several
well-appointed rooms linked by arches and furnished with
antiques and fresh flowers combine to make an elegant restaurant
with plenty of privacy. Set five-course dinner menus change daily
and offer a wide choice on all courses, with the emphasis firmly
on local produce, especially seafood, in dishes ranging from fresh
crab lasagne or scallop mousse with vermouth sauce to turbot
in wild herb sauce. No children under 5 in dining room; separate
arrangements are made for them. *Seats* 60. *L (Sun only) D 7-9.
Set Sun L £12.50 Set D £22.*

Ballymote	Temple House	61%	£70
Tel 071 83329 Fax 071 83808			**A**
Ballymote Co Sligo			Map 1 B3

Temple House is a magnificent Georgian mansion set in 1000
acres of parkland with terraced gardens, a working farm and
a lake well known for the size of its pike. Imposing, even austere
externally, the house is warm and welcoming behind its front
door, in spite of the grand scale of the outer hall (note the trophies
of outdoor pursuits) and the elegant inner hall. There are four
centrally heated double bedrooms – two of them very large, all
very comfortable – and a single with shower. Deb Perceval does
the cooking, using home-grown or home-reared produce to good
effect in her no-choice dinners (residents only). Guests gather for
drinks in a cosy sitting room with an open fire, and coffee
is served in the drawing room afterwards. The day starts with the
double delight of marvellous views and a super breakfast. High tea
for kiddies is served at 6.30 – children's room rates are negotiable.
No perfumes or aerosols, please, owing to Mr Perceval's chemical
sensitivity. No dogs. *Rooms* 5. *Garden, coarse fishing, snooker, lake
boats (3). Closed Dec-Mar (except shooting parties Dec & Jan).*
AMERICAN EXPRESS *Access, Visa.*

Ballymurn	Ballinkeele House	£60
Tel 053 38105 Fax 053 38468		**A**
Ballymurn nr Enniscorthy Co Wexford		Map 2 D5

John and Margaret Maher's substantial early Victorian house has
been in the family since it was built in 1840 and is remarkable
because, with the exception of obvious additions like central
heating and en-suite bathrooms, so little has changed. Very much
the family centre of a working farm, it is grand in an unusually
matter-of-fact way: large, high-ceilinged rooms are furnished
in style with their original antiques and paintings (the billiards
room is especially impressive), yet there is no sense of the house
being dressed up for guests. Aside from private bathrooms, the
spacious bedrooms are also remarkable period pieces and have

sweeping country views. *Rooms* 5. *Garden, tennis, snooker.*
Closed 12 Nov-1 Mar (parties by arrangement in winter). Access, Visa.

Ballynahinch	Ballynahinch Castle	71%	£104
Tel 095 31006 Fax 095 31085			**H**
Recess Ballynahinch Co Galway			Map 1 A3

Renowned as a fishing hotel, this crenellated Victorian mansion
can be both more impressive and more relaxed than expected –
the fish, the grandeur and the wonderful setting may attract the
first-time visitor, but it is the unstuffy atmosphere combined with
a high level of comfort, friendliness and an invigorating mixture
of residents and locals at the bar at night that brings people back.
Under the present management, renovations and extensions have
been completed with unusual attention to period detail, a policy
also generally carried through successfully in furnishing both
public areas and bedrooms. Most bedrooms and some reception
rooms – notably the dining room – have lovely romantic views
down through ancient woodland to the Ballynahinch River
below. *Rooms* 28. *Garden, croquet, tennis, fishing, shooting, bicycles.*
Closed Feb. AMERICAN EXPRESS *Access, Diners, Visa.*

Our inspectors **never** book in the name of Egon Ronay's
Guides. They disclose their identity only if they are
considering an establishment for inclusion in the next
edition of the Guide.

Ballyneety	Croker's Bistro		£55
Tel 061 351881 Fax 061 351384			**R**
Limerick County Golf & Country Club Ballyneety Co Limerick			Map 2 B5

Located in a very pleasing new clubhouse at the country golf club,
with sweeping views over the course and countryside from both
the bar and dining room. Bright and stylishly decorated
throughout with colourful quality fabrics and lots of natural
wood, the restaurant is well appointed with soft yellow cloths
over ivory, fine glassware, chunky modern cutlery, white
Villeroy & Boch china, fresh flowers and striking modern chairs.
Acoustics are surprisingly good (considering the predominantly
hard surfaces), contributing to a very positive atmosphere for the
enjoyment of chef Rose Brannock's confident cooking. From
a choice of four or five dishes for each course, typical starters
might include an unusual presentation of Clonakilty black
pudding on a bed of apple purée with a piquant red sauce
or roulade of fresh salmon mousse with seasonal salad and spring
onions, followed perhaps by baked monkfish tail with a fennel
butter sauce or pan-fried loin of pork with an onion compote and
a garlic and rosemary sauce. Finish with a delicious and unusual
poached pear with ice cream and caramel sauce or an Irish
farmhouse cheese selection and a cup of freshly brewed coffee.
Excellent service under Daniel Jannière (ex-*Adare Manor*).
Seats 70. *Parties* 12. *Private Room* 25. *Bar Food 11am-10pm.*
L 12.30-2 D 7-9.30. Set Sun L £10.50 Set D £19.50.
AMERICAN EXPRESS *Access, Diners, Visa.*

Ballyvaughan   An Féar Gorta (The Tea Rooms)

Tel 065 77023   **JaB**

Ballyvaughan Co Clare   Map 2 B4

The twin strengths of this charming old harbourside stone
building are Catherine O'Donoghue's skills in the kitchen –
particularly baking – and her lovely garden. Inside, homely
groups of mismatched old tables, chairs and sofas are arranged
in front of the black cast-iron range and a display of home-baked
goodies. All kinds of scones, breads, cakes and tarts and home-
made preserves (also to take away) are on offer, along with light
savoury specialities such as salads with baked ham, Irish cheeses
or local crab – all at very reasonable prices, starting at 50-60p for
tea (choice of four), a mere 50p for scone, butter and home-made
jam, through to £6.90 for smoked salmon salad. Cakes and
desserts are a snip, from 50p. The *féar gorta* is a kind of fairy grass:
if one passes it on the road it brings pangs of hunger and the limbs
refuse to move (so the legend goes) – but The Tea Rooms are the
perfect antidote. *Seats 25 (+20 in conservatory & 16 in garden).
Open 11am-5pm. Closed 1 Oct-1 Jun. No credit cards.*

We do not accept free meals or hospitality – our inspectors
pay their own bills.

Ballyvaughan   Gregans Castle Hotel   73%   £112

Tel 065 77005   Fax 065 77111   **HR**

Ballyvaughan Co Clare   Map 2 B4

In a magnificently isolated location on the edge of the Burren,
at the foot of the aptly-named Corkscrew Hill (which provides
the most scenic approach to Ballyvaughan), the grey mass of Peter
and Moira Haden's substantial country house hotel may disconcert
the first-time visitor, but its uncompromising exterior only serves
to contrast with – and highlight – the warmth and elegance
inside. A welcoming fire in the foyer sets the tone and well-
appointed public areas include the characterful Corkscrew bar
(where light lunches are served from 12-3), a lovely drawing
room furnished with antiques and comfortable sofas, and a well-
appointed dining room (under the management of Simon Haden)
with views towards the Burren. Spacious, individually decorated
rooms are all furnished to a high standard and have private
bathrooms; there are four magnificent suites with wonderful
views over the Burren. Suitable for small conferences of up to 16
delegates. Ample parking. ***Rooms** 22. Garden, croquet.
Closed end Oct-1 Apr.* AMERICAN EXPRESS *Access, Diners, Visa.*

Restaurant   £80

Relax in the bar and place your order before settling into the
elegant dining room. Five-course, daily-changing menus are
carefully constructed and are always based on the best of local
ingredients, notably lamb and seafood. Good, locally-made Irish
farmhouse cheeses. Light meals are served all day in the bar.
Seats 60. Private Room 40. D 7-8.30. Set D £27.

Ballyvaughan   Hyland's Hotel   65%   £66

Tel 065 77037   Fax 065 77131   H

Ballyvaughan Co Clare   Map 2 B4

Dating back to the early 18th century and still in the same family
ownership, genuine hospitality is central to the charm of this
warm, relaxed hotel currently under the able management of
8th-generation owner Maire Greene. Public areas are appealing
and well maintained, with comfortable furniture, pleasant lighting
and open fires and the recently renovated bedrooms are now all
en suite, with phone, tea/coffee facilities and TV as standard;
hairdryer, iron and ironing board are available on request.
Unusually attractive conference/banqueting facilities for 150.
Ample free parking. *Rooms 20. Patio. Closed 5 Jan-5 Feb.*
AMERICAN EXPRESS *Access, Visa.*

Ballyvaughan   Monks Pub

Tel 065 77059   P

The Quay Ballyvaughan Co Clare   Map 2 B4

In 1983 Bernadette and Michael Monks took over this away-
from-it-all quayside pub, modernised it sensitively so that it has
retained its cottagey character, then set about acquiring
a reputation for good, simple bar food, especially local seafood.
There are several smallish, low-ceilinged, white-walled
interconnecting rooms with wooden country-kitchen furniture.
Open fires give a cosy atmosphere. Interest in food is emphasised
by a cluster of sturdy family-sized tables at the far end of the main
bar and in summer the pier provides a sunny overspill. Everything
is home-made by Bernadette, or under her supervision – and she
has the wisdom to keep it simple. Regulars include fish cakes with
salad (£4.50), mussels steamed in garlic (£4.50), a big bowl
of seafood chowder served with home-made brown soda bread
(£2.25), and a seafood platter (£9) which varies with the catch
but might typically include salmon, crab, Dublin Bay prawns,
mussels and oysters; home-made apple pie is always popular and
there may be daily specials added to the short bar menu. Open
(crab, prawn or smoked salmon £4.75) and toasted sandwiches
(£1.50) complete the picture. Baby-changing facilities and a toilet
for the disabled have recently been added. *Bar Food 12-9 (to 6
Oct-end Apr). Children's portions. Access, Visa.*

Ballyvaughan   Whitehorn Restaurant

Tel 065 77044   Fax 065 77155   JaB

Ballyvaughan Co Clare   Map 2 B4

In a dramatic location right on the edge of the sea, this
imaginatively designed craft shop/restaurant offers lovely homely
fare through the day – soup of the day, served with freshly-baked
bread (£1.20) seafood pie (£4.95) crab or smoked salmon salad
(£6.95) and desserts like apple or rhubarb pie, pavlova or éclairs
(all at £1.50). Vegetarian dishes are always available and in the
evening tables are set more formally for dinner, when a lovely   V
summer sunset can highlight the beauty of the location. Outdoor
eating. *Seats 100. Parties 10. Private Room 30. Meals 10am-5pm +*   🗋
D 6.30-9.30 Wed-Sat high season, Fri & Sat low season.
Closed 16 Oct-13 Mar. Access, Visa.   ♣

Ballyvaughan   Places of Interest

Tourist Information Tel 065 81171
Aillwee Cave Tel 065 77036
Cliffs of Moher
The Burren
Dunguaire Castle Kinvara Tel 091 37108
Thoor Ballylee by Gort. W B Yeats' home. Tel 091 31436

Baltimore   Bushe's Bar

Tel 028 20125	
Baltimore Co Cork	Map 2 B6

Richard and Eileen Bushe have run their famous old bar
overlooking the harbour for over 20 years; it has a remarkable
collection of maritime artefacts in the public bar, including
admiralty charts, tide tables, ships' clocks, compasses, lanterns,
pennants – all of real interest and guaranteed to make those
arriving in Baltimore under sail feel at home. Eileen's homely bar
food includes a choice of soups – always a fish one and something
vegetable-based, changed daily in summer – and open or closed
sandwiches with fresh or smoked salmon, smoked mackerel and
a choice of meats such as turkey, ham, roast beef and corned beef,
all home-cooked. Three large en-suite rooms have television,
comfortable armchairs and kitchenette facilities (with food
provided) for making Continental breakfast. Children welcome "if
controlled"; each room has both a double and single bed. Showers
in the bar for sailors and fishermen – could this be anywhere else
but Ireland? No dogs. *Open 9.30am-11pm (11.30 in summer, Sun
12-3 & 4-11). Garden.* **Accommodation** *3 bedrooms, all en suite, £25
(single £20). Outdoor eating. Visa.*

Baltimore   Chez Youen   £70

Tel 028 20136	R
Baltimore Co Cork	Map 2 B6

In his little restaurant overlooking Baltimore harbour, Youen
Jacob has for many years run an uncompromisingly Breton
establishment, using only the very best of local fish and seafood –
notably crustaceans – and presenting them with masterly
simplicity. The 1994 season saw some new developments,
however, with the arrival of a new young chef, Michel Philippot,
who has extended the repertoire to include a wider range of sauces
and more sophisticated, composed dishes: carefully prepared and
neatly presented scallops provençale, a richly flavoured
complement to the hearty shellfish platters and specialities like
Youen's superb poached lobster, served absolutely plain with
a little pan of melted butter and some fresh lemon. Vegetables are
not a big thing here – except, perhaps, a pot of local potatoes
boiled in their jackets – but what better to round off the seafood
feast than a platter of mixed French and local Irish cheeses
or another house speciality, a magnificent tarte tatin? *Seats 40.
L 12.30-2.30 (summer only) D 6.30-11. Closed L Sun, all Nov &
Feb. Set L £12.50 Set D £21.50/£32.* AMERICAN EXPRESS *Access,
Diners, Visa.*

Baltimore   McCarthy's Bar

Tel 028 20159   **P**

The Square Baltimore Co Cork   **Map 2 B6**

A lively bar, next door to the restaurant *Chez Youen*, overlooking
the harbour. Decor takes two main themes, one nautical
(including a map of sea disasters in the area), the other musical,
with a wall of photographs relating to the music business back
in the '60s. The bar food *only* is recommended and covers a good
range of dishes, from garlic mussels and crab claws via spaghetti
bolognese and lasagne (beef or vegetarian with garlic bread and
salad £5.45) to Irish stew (£5.45), seafood casserole and garlic
mussels (£6.95). These dishes are available only in the summer –
at other times the choice is limited to soup, sandwiches and a daily
hot dish. *Open 10.30am-11.30pm (12-11 in winter), Sun 12.30-2 &
4-9.30. Bar Food (1 Apr-end Oct only) 12-9.30, Sun 12-2 & 4-11).
Outdoor eating in the square. Access, Diners, Visa.*

Banagher   Brosna Lodge Hotel   56%   £44

Tel 0509 51350   Fax 0509 51521   **H**

Banagher Co Offaly   **Map 2 B4**

Although some rooms at this friendly hotel are distinctly cramped,
all have en-suite facilities, TV, direct-dial phones and a hair dryer
on request at reception – and there are two larger rooms, sleeping
three. Cot available free, baby-listening/sitting, high-chair and
children's early evening meal. Children under 5 may stay free
in their parents' room. Wholesome breakfast, cheerful service.
*Rooms 14. Garden. Own parking. Closed Feb, Christmas week.
Access, Visa.*

Banagher   JJ Hough's

No Telephone   **P**

Main Street Banagher Co Offaly   **Map 2 B4**

Vines abound in Banagher – in summer the colourful red and
white frontage of this atmospheric 250-year-old pub almost
disappears behind the luxuriant vine that grows around the door,
making it instantly recognisable from anywhere along the main
street. Inside, all is dim, especially in the small side and back rooms
off the front bar – well-suited to the cheerful eccentricity of the
current owner, Michael Hough, and equally well-liked by the
locals and groups on cruising holidays, both Irish and visitors, who
come up from the harbour for the 'crack' and the music. *Open
10.30-11.30 Mon-Sat (to 11 in winter), Sun 12.30-2, 4-11.
Closed 25 Dec, Good Fri. No credit cards.*

Banagher   The Old Forge   £32

Tel 0509 51504   **A**

Westend Banagher Co Offaly   **Map 2 B4**

A few minutes walk from the harbour and under a distinctive old
archway, the Crean family provide a warm welcome and
exceptionally comfortable accommodation. Public areas include
a cosy sitting room with an open fire and plenty of books and
an attractive dining room overlooking a courtyard at the back,

but many guests succumb to the lure of Mac Crean's immaculate but friendly kitchen. Rooms are not big, but are thoughtfully furnished and very comfortable, with neat en-suite shower rooms and the use of a large and well-appointed communal bathroom. Ex-restaurateur Mac cooks a 4-course dinner for residents by arrangement. **Rooms** *4. Garden, courtyard (shed available for dogs). Access, Visa.*

Banagher   The Vine House

Tel & Fax 0509 51463   **P**

Westend Banagher Co Offaly   **Map 2 B4**

At the bottom of the village in an almost-waterside location, this is a bar with a history; the original restaurant area at Vine House was once Cromwell's refectory – the barracks and a house providing accommodation for his generals are next door – and the bar itself is in the stables. More recently (and in considerable contrast), there is a literary connection – with the Brontë sisters, who also lived here. The interior is very attractive, with indoor vines a major feature, and the current owner (who, despite going by the anglicised name, Julian Barry, is actually Italian) continues the Continental feeling through to the menu in authentic renditions of popular pasta dishes like lasagne, tagliatelle napolitana or bolognese, which take their place quite comfortably alongside local favourites such as Irish stew and steaks. *Open 10.30-11 (Sun 12.30-2, 4-11).* **Bar Food** *12-8pm. No bar food Sun. Garden, outdoor eating. Closed 25 Dec, Good Fri. Access, Visa.*

> When telephoning establishments in the Republic from *outside* the Republic, dial 00-353 then the number we print less the initial zero: eg The Strawberry Tree in Killarney is 00-353 64 32688.

Bantry   Anchor Tavern

Tel 027 50012   **P**

New Street Bantry Co Cork   **Map 2 A6**

A town-centre pub with a history going back 130 years, run since 1962 by William E O'Donnell (the third generation of his family to hold the reins) with his son Michael. Pubs are for intelligent conversation and the exchange of ideas, says William, who sees the family's vast collection of mainly nautical memorabilia displayed around the two bars as a talking point most of all – although he does admit to a special fondness for one item, an original 'croppy pike' from the rising of 1798 which will go with him if he ever leaves. There's also a morning crossword club (dictionaries provided) and soup and sandwiches are offered as sustenance throughout opening hours. Well-behaved children are welcome "if a small bit of control is exercised ... if not we'll help the parents." at reasonable hours (not after 9pm). "Old-fashioned in every sense ... everybody who comes into us leaves with a better understanding of Ireland and the Irish." Consult the pub's Red Book for places of local interest. *Open 10.30am-11 (11.30pm in season, Sun 12.30-2 & 4-11). No credit cards.*

Bantry Westlodge Hotel 66% £68

Tel 027 50360 Fax 027 50438 **H**

Bantry Co Cork Map 2 A6

Once inside this 1970 concrete-and-glass structure it is pleasanter than first impressions might suggest. Spacious public areas are bright and comfortably furnished and the dining room, especially, is cleverly designed to allow a clear view of countryside over the road. Bedrooms are on the small side and somewhat dated, but all en-suite (some shower only), quiet and comfortable, with tea/coffee facilities and phone; some rooms have TV, otherwise available on request. Children under 3 are free in their parents' room and cots, baby-sitting, high-chairs and early evening meals can be arranged. 24hr room service. No dogs. *Rooms 104 (5 non-smoking, 4 equipped for disabled). Garden, indoor swimming pool, gym, sauna, solarium, squash, tennis, pitch & putt, bowling, billiards. Banqueting/conferences 400/550. Closed 24-26 Dec.* AMERICAN EXPRESS® *Access, Diners, Visa.*

Set menu prices may not always include service or wine.
Our quoted price for two does.

Barna Donnelly's of Barna

Tel 091 592487 Fax 091 64379 **P**

Barna Co Galway Map 2 B4

Seafood is the thing at Donnelly's (it's only 100yds from the sea), built as a thatched cottage and extended at the turn of the century. In the cosy, cottagey bar-rooms the menu choices run from smoked fish and potato cakes, seafood pancakes and crab claws for starters ('bait') to grilled trout, salmon and mushrooms with white wine sauce and a festival of seafood and pasta as main courses ('the catch'). Also a few meat dishes and an evening menu in the restaurant at the back: Donnelly trio of monkfish, scallops and salmon (£12.95), deep-fried plaice stuffed with salmon mousse (£8.95), salmon stuffed with prawns, cod and spinach (£11.50). Traditional roast Sunday lunch (£6.95). *Open 12-11.30 (to 11 in winter)*, Sun 12.30-2 & 4-11. *Bar Food* 12-10. *Patio, outdoor eating.* AMERICAN EXPRESS® *Access, Diners, Visa.*

Barna Ty Ar Mor £60

Tel 091 592223 **R**

The Pier Barna Co Galway Map 2 B4

Close your eyes and imagine you're in Brittany when you visit this little seafood restaurant, last in a row of cottages on the quay at Barna (*Ty Ar Mor* means The House of the Sea). In summer Hervé Mahé puts a few tables out on the terrace so guests can enjoy the view – on colder days sitting by the cosy turf fire contemplating the pleasures ahead, as read off a large and scrupulously legible blackboard menu, has more appeal. The place has natural charm with its stone walls and flagstones, narrow winding stairs to an upper room with bigger windows, home-laundered linen and haunting background jazz. All this and good food too, with even the simplest of dishes executed with Gallic flair – a wonderful *salade*, zesty with radishes, grated carrot, a punchy dressing and a basket of hot baguettes and butter, perhaps, or six fat oysters nestling on a bed of cracked ice and glistening seaweed; lobster is fresh from the sea and cooked to order. Look out for the typically French 'prix-fixe' value in limited choice 3-course menus (lunch, £8.50; dinner £12.50 – *crepe nordique*, *coq au vin*, daily tart). A wide variety of Breton crepes are a lunchtime speciality (served from 1 to 4, to 5 Sun). Short wine list of French favourites. ***Seats** 50. Parties 20. Private Room 30. Open 12.30-11 L 12.30-3.30 D 7-11. Closed 15 Jan-15 Feb, Sun Nov-Mar. Set L £8.50 Set D £12.50.* AMERICAN EXPRESS *Access, Diners, Visa.*

Beaufort	Dunloe Castle	71%	£96
Tel 064 44111 Fax 064 44583			H
Beaufort nr Killarney Co Kerry			Map 2 A5

In a glorious, verdant setting of parkland, only the empty shell of the keep from the original 13th-century castle remains at this modern hotel. Nevertheless, the building gives a good first impression and all public areas, including the cocktail bar and restaurant, have been refurbished. The main public room is a spacious, comfortably furnished first-floor drawing room with some well-chosen antiques and lovely views of the Gap of Dunloe. All bedrooms have good bathrooms; twenty new junior suites were recently created. 24hr room service. Sister hotel to *Hotel Europe* (Killarney, 2½ miles away) and *Ard-na-Sidhe* (Caragh Lake). Banqueting/conference facilities for 200/600. ***Rooms** 120. Garden, indoor swimming pool, sauna, tennis, riding, game fishing, cycling. Closed Oct-Apr.* AMERICAN EXPRESS *Access, Diners, Visa.*

When telephoning establishments in the Republic from *outside* the Republic, dial 00-353 then the number we print less the initial zero: eg The Strawberry Tree in Killarney is 00-353 64 32688.

Bennettsbridge	Millstone Café	
Tel 056 27644		JaB
Bennettsbridge nr Kilkenny Co Kilkenny		Map 2 C5

Appealing café-cum-craft gallery opposite Nicholas Mosse's pottery in a charming riverside village. Run by Eavan Kenny and Gail Johnson (both Ballymaloe-trained), who take turns in the kitchen, producing a lively short menu with welcome emphasis on wholesomeness and eye-appeal. Expect simple, attractively presented light meals like bruschetta with goat's cheese, basil and sun-dried tomatoes (£4), seafood vol au vent (£3.50), home-made quiches (£3.50) and open sandwiches (from £1.50), all attractively presented. Warm salads (*salade tiède* of duck's liver

with caramelised onions and garlic potatoes is considered
a speciality), stuffed pancakes, fresh pasta and farmhouse cheese,
with lovely freshly-baked brown bread and butter, generous
glasses of wine and individual cafetières of coffee complete the
picture. *Seats 30 (+ 12 outdoor). L 12-5.15 D 7.30-9.30 (Thu-Sat
only). Closed D Wed & Sun, all Mon & Tue (Mon only in summer),
Bank Holidays, 2 weeks Nov, 4/6 weeks Jan-Feb. Access, Visa.*

Bettystown	The Coastguard Restaurant	£55
Tel 041 28251		**R**
Bettystown Co Meath		Map 1 D3

Although their menus are well balanced to make the most of local
meat and poultry, the fact that Michael and Maureen Hassett get
their Atlantic fish and shellfish direct from a family business
on Achill island is bound to influence most visitors to this
charming cottagey beachside restaurant in favour of seafood.
Dishes such as crab cocktail, or real old-fashioned scampi –
"Galway Bay prawns deep-fried in a light batter" – turn out to be
an all-but-forgotten treat and prettily presented too, on mixed
lettuce and in a crisp filo basket, respectively. Freshly-baked bread,
good vegetables, seasonal desserts, friendly service and a patio with
direct access to miles of golden strand all add to the equation.
*Seats 40. Parties 25. Meals from 12.30 in summer, D 7-9.30.
Closed D Sun, all Mon (except Bank Holidays or by arrangement),
24-26 Dec. Set L £12.50 Set D from £12.95.* AMERICAN EXPRESS *Access,
Diners, Visa.*

Birdhill	Matt the Thresher	
Tel 061 379227		**P**
Birdhill Co Tipperary		Map 2 B4

On the main Dublin road a few miles outside Limerick, this pub
has succeeded in becoming one of Ireland's best-known inns since
Ted and Kay Moynihan took over in 1987. It's as reliable for its
food as for its foolproof location overlooking the Shannon estuary
and makes a perfect meeting place. Characterful in the modern
mode – red-tiled floors, country-kitchen furniture (including some
settles, thankfully cushioned) and bar stools made from old tractor
seats – chintzy curtains and gas coal-effect fires introduce a slightly
suburban note. But the agricultural theme is developed to its
logical conclusion in an unexpected way – home-grown, stone-
ground flour is used in the brown soda bread, which is baked
on the premises and served with a wide variety of home-made
soups and bar snacks on the 'Snug Menu'. Seafood is a speciality,
with West Cork mussels and crab claws, or salmon from local
rivers served hot, or cold in salads (smoked salmon £9.50) and
open sandwiches, while carnivores may prefer home-baked ham,
a good steak, cheese and bacon burger (£6) or steak and kidney
pie (£4.50). 10% service charge is added to 'After Six' dishes
(served 6-10pm, to 9pm Sun) such as avocado with crab and
grilled fresh salmon. Ample parking in the yard, which backs
on to a quality craft shop. "Children must remain seated and under
parental control at all times." *Open 10am-11.30pm, Sun 12.30-11.
Bar Food 11am-10pm (Fri & Sat to 10.30, Sun 12-9). Garden.*
AMERICAN EXPRESS *Access, Visa.*

Birr   Dooly's Hotel   60%   £55

Tel 0509 20032   Fax 0509 21332   **H**

Birr Co Offaly   **Map 2 C4**

Right on Emmet Square, in the centre of Georgian Birr, this
attractively old-fashioned hotel is one of Ireland's oldest coaching
inns, dating back to 1747. It's a good holiday centre with plenty
to do locally – Birr Castle gardens are very near, also golfing,
fishing, riding and river excursions. Public rooms include
a characterful bar and a newly furbished function room. Pleasant,
modest bedrooms are all en suite; some may be noisy when there's
a function in the night-club. Children up to 4 share parents' room
at no charge (under-12s £10). *Rooms 18. Garden, coffee shop
(9am-9.30pm), night club, coarse fishing. Closed 25 Dec.*
AMERICAN EXPRESS *Access, Diners, Visa.*

Birr   Tullanisk   £76

Tel 0509 20572   Fax 0509 21783   **A**

Birr Co Offaly   **Map 2 C4**

George and Susie Gossip have run their carefully restored 18th-
century Dower House in the demesne of the Earls of Rosse (still
resident at Birr Castle) as a delightful country house hotel since
1989. The house is beautiful, interesting and comfortable, the
surrounding gardens and parkland lovely and full of wildlife,
of which a fair cross-section may make an appearance while you
watch from the big mahogany dining table at dinner. George
is an excellent chef and enjoys producing memorable no-choice
dinners (£22 per head for non-residents) and breakfasts live up to
the promise of the night before and more. *Rooms 7. Garden,
croquet, table tennis. D only 8.30. Closed 4 days at Christmas.*
Access, Visa.

Birr   Places of Interest

Birr Castle Tel 0509 20056
Charleville Forest Castle Tullamore Tel 0506 21279 *20 miles*

Blacklion   MacNean Bistro   £40

Tel 072 53022   **R**

Blacklion Co Cavan   **Map 1 C2**

A modest little room on Blacklion's main street is the setting for
some excellent and imaginative cooking by Vera Maguire and her
son Nevan. Pithiviers of duck liver in puff pastry on a tomato and
leek butter sauce is a typical starter, which could precede fried
fillet of lamb with a scallop mousse, steamed monkfish with
saffron chervil sauce, or even saddle of kangaroo. Splendid desserts
(typically roast pear with caramel sauce, passion fruit ice cream
and a compote of berries) finish the meal in fine style. *Seats 40.
L (Sun only) 12.30-3.30 light meals 3-6 D 5-9. D Tue-Sun (winter
Thu-Sun only). Closed Mon, 25 & 26 Dec. Set L (Sun) £10.
Set D from £18.90. Access, Visa.*

Blacklion   Places of Interest

Enniskillen Keep *10 miles*
Castle Coole Tel 0365 322690 *15 miles*
Florence Court Tel 0365 348249 *5 miles*

Blackrock   Ayumi-Ya   £40
`Tel 01 283 1767   Fax 01 662 0221`   **R**
Newpark Centre Newtownpark Avenue Blackrock Co Dublin   **Map 2 D4**

Situated in a small shopping centre, Ayumi-Ya opened in 1983
and offers a wide range of authentic Japanese dishes. Diners are
given the choice of Western or Japanese-style seating when
booking – also the time to opt for a teppanyaki table if you want
food cooked in front of you. In addition to teppanyaki and an
à la carte menu for old hands, set menus ranging from vegetarian,
through the Ayumi-Ya dinner course to a special seasonal dinner
make the choices easier. Staff are very ready with advice, and
owner Akiko Hoashi uses the menu to impart a few tips on how
to order and even how to eat ('Japanese customers tend to make
noise when sipping soup'). No children after 8.30. The Dublin
Ayumi-Ya (qv) is slightly more geared to Western tastes. There
are plans for the addition of a sushi bar by March '95. *Seats 65.
Private Room 25. D only 6-11. Closed 24-26 Dec, Good Friday,
1/2 Jan. Set D £14.95.* AMERICAN EXPRESS *Access, Diners, Visa.*

Blackrock   Clarets   ↑   £70
`Tel 01 288 2008   Fax 01 283 3273`   **R**
63 Main Street Blackrock Co Dublin   **Map 2 D4**

An unpretentious, comfortable and welcoming restaurant where
Alan O'Reilly offers creative, interesting cooking. There may be a
special tasting menu one week, or a theme menu based on a
specific cuisine another, but there will always be imaginative,
carefully cooked food at fair prices. Mousseline of seafood in a
ginger sauce, lemon sole with ragout of leek and green
peppercorn, crispy duck confit on a bed of hot and sour cabbage
and roast rack of lamb in a mustard and herb crust show the style.
Game is a speciality in season; breads are good. *Seats 50.
L 12.30-2.15 D 7.30-9.45. Closed, all Sun & Mon, 1 week
Christmas. Set L £13.95 Set D £22.95.* AMERICAN EXPRESS *Access, Visa.*

Please note there are two places named Blackrock,
one in Co Dublin and one in Co Louth.

Blackrock   The Brake Tavern
`Tel 042 21393`   **P**
Main Street Blackrock nr Dundalk Co Louth   **Map 1 D3**

A warm, bustling seafront pub with a characterful wooden
interior and mountains of fascinating local memorabilia. The bar
is broken up into several room-sized areas, with unpretentious but
comfortable arrangements of country furniture in welcoming

groups and – increasingly unusual these days – a real open fire
to settle round. The Brake is especially well known for the quality
and variety of food, served only in the evenings. Seafood is a
speciality – Dublin Bay prawns (£8.95), lobster (when available,
as a starter course £5.50), fish platters, fresh sea trout (£8.95),
salmon mayonnaise, crab claws in garlic butter – but there's also
a good choice for carnivores, including a range of steaks, casseroles
and the like. Everything is home-made and very wholesome.
No children under 10 allowed. *Open 2-11.30, Sat 12.30-11.30,
Sun 12.30-2 & 6-11. **Bar Food** 6.30-10.30 (Sun to 9.30).
Access, Visa*

Blarney	**Blarney Park Hotel**	**63%**	**£110**
Tel 021 385281 Fax 021 381506			**H**
Blarney Co Cork			**Map 2 B6**

About half an hour's drive out of Cork city, this modern, low-rise
hotel has good conference and family facilities, including
a particularly well-equipped leisure centre with a high and
winding 40-metre water slide. Bright, spacious public areas
include a recently refurbished lounge on two levels, each with its
own open fire, with a pleasant outlook over extensive grounds
at the back of the hotel. Bedrooms are organised along the
corridors with good-sized doubles on one side and smallish twins
(especially suitable for children) opposite. Children under two stay
free (no charge for cots – reserve when booking), extra beds are
available by arrangement; there are fun-packs provided
in children's rooms, a creche operates all year round and children's
entertainment can be arranged at any time when five or more
children are resident. Conference facilities for 350, with
an efficient secretarial service. Nearby attractions include Blarney
Castle, with its famous Blarney Stone, and Blarney Woollen Mills.
24hr room service. No dogs. ***Rooms** 76. Garden, indoor swimming
pool, children's splash pool & 40m water slide, gym, sauna, steam room,
tennis, games room, pool table, children's play room.* AMERICAN EXPRESS®
Access, Diners, Visa.

Blessington	**Downshire House**	**59%**	**£66**
Tel 045 65199 Fax 045 65335			**H**
Downshire House Blessington Co Wicklow			**Map 2 C4**

It's difficult not to be charmed by the friendly atmosphere and
unpretentious comfort of this substantial village hotel built
in 1800 and run by Rhoda Byrne since 1959. One enters into the
recently refurbished bar-lounge, where all the seats are small
armchairs, before finding the reception desk at the head of a broad
flight of stairs leading down to the function room – a modern
addition. Decoratively modest bedrooms – plain white walls,
candlewick bedspreads, functional fitted furniture – nevertheless
offer all the modern comforts including remote-control TV,
hairdryer, direct-dial phones and beverage kit plus crisp, pure
cotton bedding. Bathrooms are a little dated and boast only
unwrapped soap on the toiletries front but, like the whole hotel,
are immaculately kept. ***Rooms** 25. Garden, croquet, tennis.
Closed mid Dec-early Jan. Access, Visa.*

Blessington   **Place of Interest**

Russborough Tel 045 65239

Boyle	**Cromleach Lodge**	**78%**	**£120**
Tel 071 65155 Fax 071 65455			**HR**
Ballindoon Castlebaldwin nr Boyle Co Sligo			Map 1 B3

The views over Lough Arrow from Christy and Moira Tighe's
modern, purpose-built small hotel are almost heart-breakingly
beautiful and it has been designed to make the most of them.
Spacious, thoughtfully furnished rooms all share the wonderful
views and are individually decorated and finished to the highest
of international standards, each with queen-size and single bed,
safe, mini-bar, tray with tea/coffee-making facilities (including
a teapot) and fresh milk always in the fridge, remote-control TV,
comfortable armchairs, and writing and dressing areas. In addition
to the usual hairdryer in the room there's a trouser press, ironing
board and ice machine on the landing (a full laundry/ironing
service is also offered). Large, well-lit and thoughtfully appointed,
tiled bathrooms have full-size bath with strong over-bath shower,
efficient extraction, piles of big, warm towels on heated rails and
quality toiletries. Standards of housekeeping are exceptional. Not
really suitable for children – Cromleach is really a carefully honed
adult preserve (and all the better for it). **Rooms** 10. *Garden, game
fishing, boating. Closed 15 Dec-28 Jan.* AMERICAN EXPRESS *Diners,
Access, Visa.*

Restaurant   ★   **£75**

The excellent restaurant continues to develop, with a more relaxed
air of confidence now adding to the enjoyment of Moira Tighe's
talents in the kitchen. In addition to the 5-course set dinner menu,
an 8-course tasting menu is prepared daily for residents at the same
price, reinforcing this establishment's well-earned reputation for
providing not only excellence, but also outstanding value for
money. The dining areas are beautifully appointed and
immaculately maintained, with crisp linen, elegantly understated
china, silver and modern crystal, while fresh flowers on the table
provide a single, striking splash of colour. Moira Tighe's real love
of cooking shines through in her impeccably sourced ingredients
and talented renditions of great modern classics; she has a rare
lightness of touch – notably in excellent saucing – also seen in the
work of pastry chef Sheila Sharpe, who is producing outstanding
results in dishes like tartlet of quail breasts on armagnac cream –
boneless, tender, pink-cooked quail breasts in a little wisp of a
featherlight pastry case, set in a pool of pale, interesting sauce.
Simplicity goes gourmet in, for example, a tasting trio of soups,
served in tiny cups and accompanied by a selection of four home-
made breads, and local meat is seen to advantage in creative main
courses like medallions of venison in vintage port sauce or fillet
of beef with a piquant sauce of Cashel blue cheese. Organically
grown vegetables and side salads, served separately, are treated
with imagination and respect. But Moira's meals are designed
to end on a triumphant note: her desserts are renowned and the
Tasting Selection is specially recommended; *florentina cone of
marinated tropical fruits on a passion fruit coulis* wins our 1995
Ireland Dessert of the Year Award (see page 71). Over twenty

wines under £20 on an otherwise humdrum wine list.
No smoking. *Seats 40. Parties 20. Private Room 20. L by
arrangement D 7-9 (Sun 6.30-8). Set D £29.50.*

Boyle   Place of Interest

Clonalis House Castlerea Tel 0907 20014 *15 miles*

Bray   Tree of Idleness   £65

Tel 01 286 3498	**R**
Seafront Bray Co Wicklow	Map 2 D4

The original Tree of Idleness was situated in Bellapais, Cyprus,
with views of the coastline and the hillside citrus groves. This one,
on the seafront at Bray, continues the Greek-Cypriot tradition and
in the capable hands of owner Susan Courtellas and chef Ismail
Basaran is firmly established among Ireland's favourite restaurants.
Dips and dolmades, moussaka and souvlaki, halloumi and
calamares account for only part of the menu, and other choices
include spinach ravioli filled with crab mousse served with
a carrot sauce, chicken saffron, roast pheasant with grapes and
chestnuts and fillet steak with a red wine sauce and truffles.
Supplementing the à la carte menu is a table d'hote (not available
Saturday) whose price depends on the main course. A stupendous
wine list has a terrific all-round balance, both in Europe and the
New World. Alongside the classic red Bordeaux collection are
superb burgundies and Rhones. Those with deep pockets will
enjoy the Massandra collection of ports. *Seats 50. Parties 20.
D only 7.30-11 (Sun to 10). Closed Mon, 2 weeks Sep, 1 week
Christmas. Set D from £15.50.* AMERICAN EXPRESS *Access, Diners, Visa.*

Bray   Place of Interest

Killruddery House and Gardens Tel 01 286 3405

See the County Listings section (highlighted by colour
pages) at the back of the Guide for instant comparison
of establishments in a particular area.

Bruckless   Bruckless House   £40

Tel 073 37071 Fax 073 37070	**A**
Bruckless Co Donegal	Map 1 B2

Although the family home on a working farm, 'farmhouse' is not
the term for Clive and Joan Evans' lovely classically proportioned
18th-century house. Set in 19 acres of woodland gardens and
overlooking Bruckless Bay through meadows grazed by Irish
draught-horses and Connemara ponies. Spacious reception rooms
are furnished with an interesting variation on the Irish country
house style, enlivened by furnishings and ornaments brought back
by the family from Hong Kong. Good-sized, comfortable
bedrooms are attractively furnished; those not en suite share
a large, well-fitted bathroom. The one en suite attracts a £5
supplement. Woodland walks. *Rooms 4. Garden, fishing.
Closed 1 Oct-31 Mar. Access, Visa.*

Bunclody	**Clohamon House**	£80
Tel 054 77253 Fax 054 77956		**A**
Bunclody Co Wexford		Map 2 C5

Set in 180 acres of rolling farmland in the scenic Slaney valley,
with a wonderful view across the River Slaney to Mount Leinster,
Sir Richard and Lady Levinge's enchanting 18th-century family
home is a haven backed by beechwoods and gardens with many
rare trees and shrubs. Graciously proportioned rooms are enhanced
by family furniture and portraits going back over 250 years, but
there is a lovely family atmosphere as guests gather at the fireside
in the chintzy drawing room for drinks, knowing that Maria
Levinge is in the kitchen whipping up one of her wonderfully
imaginative dinners, to be served at an elegant, polished table lit
by candles. Thoughtfully decorated rooms vary, but have a full
complement of antiques and characterful bathrooms complete
with toiletries; comfortable beds are turned down as you dine and
a very good chocolate left on the pillow. On the premises,
Connemara ponies are a major interest – Maria manages
an internationally renowned stud – and there is a private stretch
of salmon and trout fishing on the Slaney. Self-catering
accommodation in converted outbuildings includes a barn which
is suitable for the disabled. Dogs welcome – kennels provided.
Busy around the time of the Wexford Opera Festival in late
Oct/early Nov. *Rooms* 4. *Garden, riding, fishing.*
Closed mid Nov-1 Mar. Access, Visa.

Bundoran	**Le Chateaubrianne**	£55
Tel 072 42160		**R**
Sligo Road Bundoran Co Donegal		Map 1 B2

Since opening in 1993, Brian and Anne Loughlin's correct,
impeccably furnished yet warm, welcoming and family-friendly
restaurant has made quite an impact on the north-west dining
scene. Well-trained staff ensure that everything runs smoothly
and Anne makes an excellent hostess, keeping a close eye on the
comfort of guests from the moment they are shown into the
bar and presented with daily-changing menus to the moment
of reluctant departure. Comfortable chairs and well-appointed
tables – white linen over a colourful undercloth, linen napkins,
quality cutlery and fine, plain glasses – provide an appropriate
setting for Brian Loughlin's fine food. Typically, a tartlet of baby
mushroom and smoked bacon in a creamy garlic sauce might see
a light, crisp pastry case piled high with lightly-cooked mushroom
quarters and crunchy diced smoked bacon in a sauce with a good
bite of garlic in it. Local ingredients predominate, cooked with
a nicely judged balance of simplicity and imagination, as in
Donegal lamb on a bed of wild mushrooms with a rosemary jus –
a thick slice, served pink and juicy with a light, herby stuffing, the
piquancy of rosemary and the richness of the mushrooms
complementing the meat without dominating. Seafood is handled
with similar flair, and imaginatively cooked, plentiful vegetables
are left on the table in their serving dishes. Good desserts range
from homely puddings (such as an individual, steamed dark
chocolate pudding set in a pool of orange chocolate sauce)
to classic crème brulée served on a fruit compote.

Delicious cafetière coffee and petits fours. *Seats 45. Parties 14. Private Room 20. L 12.30-2.30 D 6.30-10. Closed Tues in winter, 1st two weeks Nov. Set L £10 Set D £17.50. Access, Visa.*

Bunratty   Fitzpatricks Bunratty Shamrock Hotel   60%   £137

Tel 061 361177   Fax 061 471252

Bunratty Co Clare   Map 2 B4

A low-rise modern hotel alongside Bunratty Castle with a leisure centre and banqueting facilities for up to 180. Only four miles from Shannon airport, this would make a good base for touring Clare and the Burren; children under 12 charged £5 (but babies free) if sharing parents' room. *Rooms 115. Indoor swimming pool, sauna, steam room. Closed 24 & 25 Dec.* AMERICAN EXPRESS *Access, Diners, Visa.*

Bunratty   MacCloskey's   £70

Tel 061 364082   **R**

Bunratty House Mews Bunratty Co Clare   Map 2 B4

The MacCloskeys established a successful formula over a dozen years at this atmospheric restaurant in the cellars of 17th-century Bunratty House. A five-course fixed-price menu offers straightforward dishes such as asparagus beurre blanc, grilled kidneys on a bed of braised onions, cod with parsley and lemon butter, duck with orange sauce and steak with green peppercorns. Icky sticky pudding, passion fruit mousse or honey and lime cheesecake to finish. *Seats 60. Private Room 20. D only 7-9.30. Closed Sun & Mon, 20 Dec-20 Jan. Set D £26. Access, Visa.*

Bunratty   Place of Interest

Bunratty Castle and Folk Park Tel 061 361511

Butlersbridge   Derragarra Inn

Tel 049 31003   Fax 043 83327   **P**

Butlersbridge Co Cavan   Map 1 C3

A few miles north of Cavan, on the N3, the Derragarra Inn is well situated to break a journey and is easily recognised by its thatched roof and the old agricultural implements and rural artefacts at the door. The agricultural theme is developed inside with items of local interest as well as curiosities from further afield such as a wall covered with currencies from different countries. The inn's riverside location means freshwater fish will be on the menu, as well as ever-popular seafood like smoked salmon (£4.35), garlic mussels (£3.95) and fish pie (£3.95), but carnivores are also well catered for with the likes of burgers (£3.75), dressed pork chop in sweet and sour sauce (£3.95), steaks, mixed grill (£5.95) and beef and Guinness casserole (£3.95). The restaurant menu is also available in the bar, extending to stuffed whiting, chicken curry and surf and turf. Music is also an attraction, with traditional Irish music on Friday nights from June to September. *Open 10.30am-11.30pm, Sun 12.30-11. Breakfast 10.30-12 (6 days). Bar Food 12-11.30 (Sun 12.30-11). Restaurant Meals 12.30-3 (Sun only), 7-10. Riverside terrace, outdoor eating. Closed Good Friday, 25 Dec. Access, Visa.*

Butlerstown · Atlantic Sunset · £30

Tel 023 40115 **A**

Butlerstown Co Cork **Map 2 B6**

Comfortable accommodation and exceptional hospitality in a neat
modern house that lives up to its name – the breakfast room and
some bedroom windows have lovely views down to the sea
at Dunworley. *Rooms 4. Garden. No credit cards.*

When telephoning establishments in the Republic from *outside*
the Republic, dial 00-353 then the number we print less the
initial zero: eg The Strawberry Tree in Killarney is
00-353 64 32688.

Butlerstown · Dunworley Cottage · £60

Tel 023 40314 **R**

Dunworley Butlerstown Clonakilty Co Cork **Map 2 B6**

This legendary restaurant is in a neat assembly of buildings
huddled together against the elements in a uniquely wild and
remote coast with a western aspect that can be dramatic at sunset.
Guests are greeted by an extended family of ducks which roam
free and contribute to Katherine Norén's organic gardening
methods by consuming slugs. A set-price Gourmet Menu offers
four courses, often including specialities such as the famous nettle
soup, and home-grown globe artichokes – served with a trio
of piquant sauces – or an unusual chunky home-made salami
which, like the artichokes, can be bought to take home. True
to her origins, Katherine serves West Cork black and white
puddings with her native lingonberries and Swedish meatballs
feature too – originally starring on the children's menu, but
proving so popular that adult portions are now on offer too.
Apfelstrudel sits easily on the dessert menu alongside home-made
ice creams and local cheeses, served with fresh fruit and a glass
of port. Lovely home-baked yeast breads and big, colourful
organic salads underline the attention to detail which makes
Dunworley special, and special diets, whether vegetarian, vegan,
diabetic, gluten-free, or low-cholesterol, present no problem.
Take-away meals also available for self-catering. *Seats 50. L 1-5
D 6.30-10. Closed Mon & Tue, Nov, Jan-Feb. Set D £20.*
AMERICAN EXPRESS *Access, Diners, Visa.*

Butlerstown · O'Neill's

Tel 023 40228 **P**

Butlerstown Bancon Co Cork **Map 2 B6**

A nice old-fashioned pub in a pretty terrace with views over
farmland that slopes away down towards the sea at Dunworley; its
gleaming mahogany bar counter and fresh paintwork in pinks and
lilacs (somewhat unexpectedly echoing the 'West Cork pastels'
exterior theme so familiar throughout the area) create a pleasingly
cared-for setting for friendly locals and visitors alike. *Open
10.30am-11.30pm Mon-Fri (to 11pm Sat & in winter), Sun 12.30-
2.30, 4-11. Garden. Closed 25 Dec, Good Fri. No credit cards.*

Butlerstown	Sea Court	£40
Tel 023 40151		**A**
Butlerstown Co Cork		Map 2 B6

Just outside the colourful village of Butlerstown, American academic David Elder opens his Georgian mansion to guests for the summer months, meanwhile advancing his ambitious restoration programme a little further each year. Expect American priorities tempered by an agreeable element of eccentricity and you will not be disappointed – large, graciously proportioned rooms are furnished with an eclectic collection of old and antique furniture acquired at auctions with a reassuring emphasis on comfort, as in the bedrooms, which all have private bathrooms of varying vintages, all but one en-suite. Candle-lit dinners are available to residents by reservation and hearty breakfasts with home-baked fruit and nut scones are a feature. The house and surrounding parkland are open to the public, free, from 10 June to 20 August. *Rooms* 6. *Garden, tennis. Closed Sep-May. No credit cards.*

Caherciveen	Brennan's Restaurant	£55
Tel 066 72021		**R**
13 Main Street Caherciveen Co Kerry		Map 2 A6

The Brennans are now well established in their stylish new premises on the main street, offering interesting daytime food in addition to owner-chef Conor Brennan's imaginative dinner menus, which now include a popular early option that represents exceptionally good value with most main courses under £5. Creative use of local ingredients remains their hallmark on wide-ranging menus including dishes like sauté of crab claws with garlic and herbs, breast of chicken stuffed with wild salmon with a Cashel Blue cheese sauce, loin of Kerry lamb with rosemary and garlic and medallions of monkfish with a herb crust and saffron sauce. Good tarts and home-made ices for dessert. Early Bird dinner (served 6-7.30) offers good value. *Seats* 36. *Parties* 16. *Snacks served 10-5 (except Sun), L 12-2.30 D 6-9.30 (Sun 6-9). Closed D Feb & Nov, all Sun Oct-Nov, 1 Jan, Good Friday, 24-26 Dec. Access, Visa.*

Caherciveen	Old Schoolhouse Restaurant	£55
Tel 066 72426 Fax 066 72861		**R**
Caherciveen Co Kerry		Map 2 A6

Visitors often have difficulty finding a good place to stop on the scenic Ring of Kerry and it is worth noting that Anne O'Kane's deceptively small restaurant is open for lunch throughout the tourist season, when limited menus are offered to coaches, and it is worth asking about other choices from the blackboard à la carte. Start either meal with Anne's excellent, richly-flavoured chowder – almost a bisque – or big fat mussels in garlic butter, both served with freshly-baked crusty brown soda scones followed, perhaps, by perfectly cooked fillet of wild salmon, served with a sorrel sauce Kerry potatoes and a crisp mixed leaf salad tossed in hazelnut oil dressing, or a sizzling portion of juicy crab meat au gratin. Desserts range from homely apple sponge and custard or Guinness fruit cake on the lunch menu, to rich chocolate mousse cake with

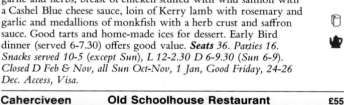

raspberry coulis, made to a secret recipe. *Seats 80. Parties 14.
Private Rooms 20 & 50. L 1-3 D 6.30-9.30. Closed Nov-mid Mar,
also L Thur & D Sun offpeak season Access, Diners, Visa.*

Caherdaniel	Derrynane Hotel	62%	£60
Tel 066 75136 Fax 066 75160			**HR**
Caherdaniel Co Kerry			Map 2 A6

In a spectacular location on the southern stretch of the Ring
of Kerry, this unprepossessing 1960s' hotel offers a warm welcome
and good facilities for family holidays. Accommodation is simple
but a high standard of housekeeping, good value for money and
lovely sea views ensure satisfaction. Eight family rooms have bunk
beds; supervised creche in the evenings during July and August.
*Rooms 75. Garden, tennis, outdoor swimming pool, indoor play area.
Closed Nov-Apr.* AMERICAN EXPRESS *Access, Diners, Visa.*

Restaurant   £45

The bar and restaurant overlook the open-air swimming pool and
are well placed to take advantage of the magnificent sea views.
Good, fresh ingredients are used to produce enjoyable home-
cooked food and attractive desserts at very reasonable prices.
Children's menu; high-chairs provided. No smoking. Sunday bar
lunches Jul/Aug. *Seats 100. D 7-9. Set D £18.50.*

Caherdaniel	Loaves & Fishes	£55
Tel 066 75273		**R**
Caherdaniel nr Derrynane Co Kerry		Map 2 A6

Helen Mullane and Armel Whyte set up this charming little
restaurant in 1990. The style is comfortably cottagey, with an old
range, low ceilings and random plate collection and an interesting
little bar/reception area at the back with light filtering through
a stained-glass skylight. Armel's imaginative, shortish à la carte
menu offers plenty of interest, starting, perhaps, with a platter
of smoked wild fish with a cucumber pickle or country terrine
of pork with garlic and a tomato and mustard-seed relish (for
serious garlic-lovers). Well-balanced main courses include
favourites like crab claws on a beurre blanc, sirloin steak and local
Kerry lamb, with a rosemary-scented potato stuffing and port jus,
perhaps, and fish, typically darne of salmon with a creamed Noilly
Prat sauce. Good desserts include a tangy lemon tart. *Seats 32.
Private Room 12. D only 7-9.30. Closed Mon Jun-Aug, Mon & Tues
Sep, all Halloween to Easter. Access, Visa.*

Cahir	Kilcoran Lodge Hotel	62%	£68
Tel 052 41288 Fax 052 41994			**H**
Kilcoran Cahir Co Tipperary			Map 2 C5

Set in 20 acres of grounds but easily spotted from the N8, on the
Cork side of Cahir, this former hunting lodge overlooking the
Suir Valley still retains an air of graciousness which, together with
the friendliness of the staff and old-fashioned comforts including
big chairs and log fires, creates a welcoming ambience. Public
rooms are well appointed in a relaxed style and comfortable
bedrooms, which vary considerably according to age and location
within the building, are all en suite, with TV, video, radio,

phone, tea and coffee-making, trouser press and hairdryer. Conference/banqueting facilities for 300. Children under 12 may stay free in their parents' room (three family rooms); cots, high-chairs and early evening meals by arrangement. *Rooms 23. Indoor swimming pool, keep-fit equipment, sauna, spa bath, solarium, riding, coarse & game fishing.* *Access, Diners, Visa.*

Cahir   Place of Interest

Cahir Castle Cahir Tel 052 41011

Caherciveen   The Point Bar

| Tel 066 72165 | **P** |
| Renard Point Caherciveen Co Kerry | Map 2 A6 |

In the same family for many generations (at least 150 years), this magical little place, at what was until 1960 the final stop on the Great Southern & Western Railway line, overlooks Valentia Island and harbour and has been sympathetically modernised to retain its charm without gimmicks. During the summer Michael and Bridie O'Neill serve ultra-fresh fish and seafood in simple, wholesome dishes ranging from plain and toasted sandwiches (£1.25-£1.75) to fresh lobster salad (£11.95 per pound). Other dishes might include monkfish (Point Special £7.95) or Roman-style hake pan-fried with garlic and olive oil (£6.95). For fine weather there's a very pleasant patio with tubs and tables looking past the old terminal to the sea. Children must be supervised – the bar can get very busy. *Open 10.30-11.30, Sun 5-11.* **Bar Food** *10.30-9.30 (Sun from 5). Garden, outdoor eating area. No credit cards.*

Caragh Lake   Hotel Ard-na-Sidhe   70%   £98

| Tel 066 69105   Fax 066 69282 | **H** |
| Caragh Lake nr Killorglin Co Kerry | Map 2 A5 |

The beautiful lakeside setting and the peace and quiet are major pluses at this splendid Victorian mansion on the edge of Caragh Lake. In the house there are 12 good-sized bedrooms furnished with antiques and a further eight rooms with private patios are available in the garden house (recently refurbished). Sister hotel to *Hotel Europe* (Killarney) and *Dunloe Castle* (Beaufort), whose sporting facilities are available to Ard-na-Sidhe guests. *Rooms 20. Garden, game fishing. Closed Oct-Apr.* AMERICAN EXPRESS *Access, Diners, Visa.*

Caragh Lake   Caragh Lodge   65%   £88

| Tel 066 69115   Fax 066 69316 | **A** |
| Caragh Lake nr Killorglin Co Kerry | Map 2 A5 |

Owner Mary Gaunt is in personal charge at this Victorian fishing lodge, which stands in delightful gardens on the shore of Caragh Lake. Boating, fishing and swimming are favourite pastimes, there's a tennis court in the grounds and five championship golf courses are a short drive away. Peaceful antique-furnished day rooms. Bedrooms in main house or garden cottages. *Rooms 10. Garden, sauna, tennis, game fishing, rowing boat, bicycles. Closed 14 Oct-14 Apr. Access, Visa.*

Carlingford   Carlingford House   £30

Tel 042 73118

A

Carlingford Co Louth

Map 1 D3

Hospitable Peter and Irene Finegan provide guests with a real
home-from-home at their lovely old house, conveniently located
near the centre of Carlingford yet backing on to the Mountains
of Mourne. Comfortably furnished rooms are all en suite and
children are welcome; there's a cot and high-chair available.
*Rooms 5. Garden. Closed 1 Nov–mid Mar (unless by arrangement).
No credit cards.*

Carlingford   Jordan's Bar & Restaurant   £55

Tel 042 73223

R

Carlingford Co Louth

Map 1 D3

Harry and Marian Jordan take turns in the kitchen of their
warmly decorated restaurant, but the day always starts with
a baking session to produce their delicious brown soda bread and
white yeast rolls. Menus are nicely balanced between the
traditional and modern, and local produce is used wherever
possible. They grow their own herbs and even produce their own
butter. A typical five-course meal might be lamb kidneys in red
wine sauce or natural or baked oysters, followed by soup of the
day, breast of wild pigeon with apple and red cabbage or fillet
of salmon in white wine for main course, with lemon mousse
with a raspberry coulis or pear, chocolate and almond tart
to finish. Half the wines are priced at under £13. Seven letting
bedrooms are available (£55 for 2) with period-style pine
furniture, lough views and business facilities. No smoking.
*Seats 34. Private Room 16. L (Sun only) 12.30–2 D 7–9.45 (Sun
from 6.30). Closed 25 & 26 Dec, 3 weeks mid Jan, Good Fri.
Set L (Sun) £12.50 Set D £20.* AMERICAN EXPRESS *Access, Diners, Visa.*

Hotel sporting facilities are highlighted in the Quick Reference
lists for easy comparison.

Carlingford   McKevitt's Village Hotel   59%   £59

Tel 042 73116   Fax 042 73144

H

Carlingford Co Louth

Map 1 D3

A happy family atmosphere prevails at this bustling establishment
and the emphasis is firmly on enjoyment and relaxation for all
age groups. Public areas include a comfortable bar and restaurant
and a residents' sitting room is available for quieter moments.
Bedrooms vary considerably in size, but all are comfortably
furnished and en suite, with phones and TV. Banqueting/
conferences for 120. Children welcome: under-12s may stay free
in their parents' room; cots and high-chairs available; children's
entertainment (details on enquiry); children's menu and early
evening meals. Limited parking (8 residents' spaces). *Rooms 13.
Closed 25 Dec.* AMERICAN EXPRESS *Access, Diners, Visa.*

Carlingford   Magee's Bistro   £35

Tel 042 73751   **R**

D'Arcy Magee Centre Carlingford Co Louth   Map 1 D3

Hugh Finnegan and Sheila Keiro's minuscule, tightly packed
restaurant is in a lovely old cut-stone building and looks out on to
the foothills of the Mournes – almost reason in itself to visit
perhaps, but it's Sheila's wholesome cooking – prepared on site
in an open kitchen despite limitations of space – that has attracted
a following. Eclectic menus range from classic home-made soups
and chicken liver paté through guacamole and corn chips and
pineapple coconut cream to main courses like Cajun-style chicken
or Mexican hotpot, a range of pasta dishes and vegetarian options
like cheese parcels with fresh herbs and tomato or Chinese
vegetable curry. Interesting salads are arranged as a buffet, breads
are home-baked and you can round off with carrot cake or a juicy
apple pie. *Seats 26 (+16 in courtyard). Parties 4. L 1-6 (Sun only)
D 7-10. Closed Mon-Wed in winter, 1 week at Christmas, 2 weeks
Jan. Access, Visa.*

Carlingford   PJ O'Hare's Anchor Bar

Tel 042 73106   **P**

Carlingford Co Louth   Map 1 D3

Grocer's shop and bar share the same premises at PJs, which stands
right in the heart of a picturesque medieval village. Carlingford
oysters are the speciality on the bar menu (£3 for 6), with
smoked salmon and the day's soup (65p) among the rival
attractions. It's a favourite spot with the local sailing community,
and the walls are covered with items of nautical interest. The
enclosed yard by the bar is a popular summer rendezvous.
*Open 10.30am-11.30pm (Sun 12.30-2 & 4-11). Bar Food 10.30am-
10.30pm (Sun 12.30-2 & 4-10.30). No credit cards.*

Carlingford   Place of Interest

Carlingford Castle

Carlow   Barrowville Townhouse   £39

Tel 0503 43324   Fax 0503 41953   **A**

Kilkenny Road Carlow Co Carlow   Map 2 C4

Ex-hoteliers Marie and Randal Dempsey run a tidy ship at this
attractive and exceptionally comfortable guesthouse within easy
walking distance of the town centre. Public areas include not only
a cosy sitting room with open fire but also a conservatory
(complete with vine) and, when weather permits, outdoor seating
in a well-kept and secluded back garden. Rooms vary in size and
outlook but all are furnished and decorated to a high standard
with phone, radio, TV and neat, thoughtfully planned en-suite
bath/shower rooms. Delicious breakfasts – served at antique tables
in a delightful dining room overlooking the garden – include
a choice of fresh juices and fruit and a buffet with smoked salmon
and farmhouse cheeses. *Rooms 7. Garden. Access, Visa.*

Carlow   The Beams Restaurant   £60

Tel 0503 31824   **R**

59 Dublin Street Carlow Co Carlow   **Map 2 C4**

Situated in premises which have held a full licence since 1760, it is appropriate that this restored coaching inn should now be run by a member of the Guild of Sommeliers. It's a characterful building, notable for the massive wooden beams it is named after, and has a welcoming, cosy atmosphere in the well-appointed dining room, which has direct access to The Wine Tavern off-licence and specialist food shop (under common ownership) next door. The dinner menu offers some choices more likely to be restricted to the à la carte in other establishments, including game in season and seafood such as scallops and sole, available at only £1 supplement. Starters may be pleasant rather than inspiring, but French chef Romain Chall gets into his stride with main courses like roast duck – good gamey wild duck, semi-boned and served with a rich calvados sauce – game pie, or excellent seafood dishes such as monkfish medallions with a delicious fresh-tasting Provençal sauce. Finish, perhaps, with chocolate marquise – from a verbally recited choice – or a plated selection of farmhouse cheeses. *Seats 40. Parties 8. D only 7-9.30 (L by arrangement). Closed Sun, Mon & 3 days Christmas. Set D £18.50. Access, Visa.*

Carlow   Buzz's Bar

Tel 0503 43307   **P**

7 Tullow Street Carlow Co Carlow   **Map 2 C4**

Carlow's first café-pub is noticeably different from the street, with its darkened glass and contemporary lettering – an impression emphasised by a multi-level interior in a mixture of styles – yellow ragged walls and black metal furniture here, tented ceiling and sofas there and a curvaceous bar with wooden stools in the middle. But its real difference runs deep – down to the basement in fact, where the Bridewell Lane Theatre (Carlow's only permanent live auditorium) has its home. Although students from the local technical college will find greater sustenance at lunchtime, cappuccino and espresso with light bites like Danish pastries are the fashionable thing here, creating a distinctly cosmopolitan air. Winner of our 1995 Coffee Award of Excellence (see page 77).*Open 10.30-11.30 (to 11 in winter), Sun 4-11. Closed Good Fri, 25 Dec. No credit cards.*

Carlow   Royal Hotel   60%   £55

Tel & Fax 0503 31621   **H**

Dublin Street Carlow Co Carlow   **Map 2 C4**

Conveniently situated on the main street, this unassuming hotel originated as a coaching inn in the early 18th century and, although the age of the building tends to limit improvements, it has a pleasant atmosphere and helpful staff. Public areas include a thriving, well-run bar and attractive dining room and, while bedrooms vary a good deal, all have en-suite bath or shower, TV, clock/radio, phone, hairdryer and tea/coffee facilities. Banqueting/conference facilities for 200/300. Children welcome;

cots, baby-sitting, high-chairs available; under-5s stay free
in parents' room. **Rooms** *34. Garden. Closed 25 Dec.* AMERICAN EXPRESS
Access, Diners, Visa.

Carlow   Tully's

Tel 0503 31862	**P**
149 Tullow Street Carlow Co Carlow	Map 2 C4

They do things differently in Carlow – anywhere else this unspoilt
old pub would be likely to provide a serene retreat for mature
citizens, but here the young crowd from the technical college
seem to call the shots and the place is bursting with youth and
vigour. Music is the big thing – they built up their reputation
with live performances from the likes of Mary Black and Sharon
Shannon. CDs have taken over, but they're always right up to the
minute and there are no complaints. At quieter times Tully's is a
nice old-fashioned pub with broader appeal (television is banned
from the bar). Light snacks only. *Open 10.30am-11.30pm (Sun 4-
11). Closed Good Friday, 25 Dec. No credit cards.*

Carne   Lobster Pot   £50

Tel 053 31110 Fax 053 31401	**R**
Carne Co Wexford	Map 2 D5

Pub, seafood bar and restaurant – Ciaran and Anne Hearne's
Lobster Pot has it all and attracts a loyal clientele. In a prime
roadside location, the long, low building is typical of traditional
houses in the area; inside several small, cosy interconnecting bar
areas are furnished in simple, practical style with sturdy furniture
designed for comfortable eating – augmented, in fine weather,
by an ample supply of picnic tables out at the front. One smallish
room is given over to a slightly more formal restaurant area, but
the atmosphere throughout is very relaxed and the emphasis is on
providing good value and efficient service. The bar menu offers
seafood chowder (£2.50), daily home-made soup (£1.20),
Wexford mussels in garlic (£3.50), oven-baked crab mornay
(£4.95), crab claws in garlic (£6.95) and a pasta dish (£5.50)
as its hot dishes plus a plethora of cold plates (from £2.25 for egg
mayonnaise to £10.50 for generous seafood platters; also
sandwiches and a handful of homely puddings (hot apple sponge
and cream £1.50, Harvey's sherry trifle £1.50). More substantial
evening-only à la carte offerings in the recommended restaurant
might include prawn cocktail (£5.95), Barrow Bay or Rossmore
oysters (£5.95 for half a dozen), wild salmon either smoked
(£5.95), grilled or poached (£9.95), scallops (£11.50), grilled
Dover sole (£12.95), seafood mornay (£10.95) and lobster from
the tank (from £13 per pound). Also a 'landlubber's choice'
of chicken Kiev (£8.95), crispy duckling (£9.90) and various
steaks (from £11). 4-course Sunday lunch in winter only £8.95
(children £5) – but usual bar menu in summer; winter
Wednesday evening table d'hote £12.95. Smoking is discouraged.
Tables outside in the summer. No children under 10 after 8.30pm.
Parents are requested to keep an eye on their children and children
are requested to keep an eye on their parents – best behaviour all
round! *Open 10.30-11.30 (to 11 in winter) & Sun 12.30-2, 4-11;
January bar only open (no food): Mon-Thur 6-11 only, Fri 3-11 only,
Sat 10.30-11 & Sun 12.30-2, 4-11.* **Bar Meals** *12-10, Sun 12.30-2,*

*4-10 (to 9 in winter). **Restaurant Meals** 6-9 (not Mon or Sun in winter Sep-May, except Bank Holiday weekends) & Sun Lunch (12.30-2.30 Sep-May). Paved fourcourt with ten tables. Closed Good Friday, 25 & 26 Dec.* AMERICAN EXPRESS *Access, Visa.*

Carrick-on-Shannon	Hollywell House	£50
Tel & Fax 078 21124		**A**
Liberty Hill Carrick-on-Shannon Co Leitrim		Map 1 B3

Just across the bridge at Carrick-on-Shannon, with lovely views down through the garden to the river, this fine period house offers comfortable en-suite rooms (one with shower only) furnished with antiques (two with river views), but it is Tom and Rosaleen Maher's hospitality which makes Hollywell outstanding. Good breakfasts, with home-made bread and preserves, but no evening meals except by special arrangement. No dogs. *Rooms 4. Garden, fishing. Closed 16 Dec-10 Jan. Access, Visa.*

Carrick-on-Shannon   Places of Interest

Lough Rynn Estate and Gardens Mohill Tel 078 31427 *10 miles*
Strokestown Park House Strokestown Tel 078 33013 *12 miles*

Carrickmacross	Nuremore Hotel	72%	£105
Tel 042 61438 Fax 042 61853			**H**
Carrickmacross Co Monaghan			Map 1 C3

Just off the N2 south of town, 50 miles north-west of Dublin on the way to Monaghan and Donegal, a modern, low-rise hotel that creates a good impression on arrival. The approach, through 100 acres of golf course and lake-studded parkland ('please drive slowly – look out for ducks'), is pleasant and the exterior of the hotel building not only spick and span but brightened and softened by imaginative planting and generous use of tubs. There's a high standard of furnishing throughout the large, well-appointed public areas and the comfortable, airy bedrooms, many of which overlook the lake. Five family rooms accommodate up to six people; five mini-suites. Banqueting facilities for 200, conferences up to 400. Self-styled as a hotel and country club, the 18-hole golf course (new pavilion with bistro snacks; resident PGA professional), good leisure club (18m pool) and trout fishing on the lake are all major attractions. No dogs. *Rooms 69. Garden, indoor swimming pool, sauna, solarium, spa bath, gym, tennis, squash, games room, golf (18).* AMERICAN EXPRESS *Access, Diners, Visa.*

Carrigaline	Gregory's	£50
Tel 021 371512		**R**
Main Street Carrigaline Co Cork		Map 2 B6

In the premises previously occupied by Pews Bistro, chef Gregory Dawson and partner Rachelle Harley opened their buzzy little restaurant in 1994 and quickly attracted a following. A long, narrow room has been transformed with low key green and cream decor enlivened by some startling modern pictures, providing an appropriate setting for Gregory's imaginative, well-judged cooking. Shortish, keenly-priced and carefully portioned à la carte lunch menus might typically include an exemplary warm salad of bacon, blue cheese and croutons or juicy garlic

mussels, with richly flavoursome stir-fried chicken or kidney and mushroom fricassee, then imaginatively presented local cheeses or dessert – a light meringue roulade with fresh strawberries, perhaps – to follow. Evening menus are a little more elaborate and offer more choice, but the same light touch is evident throughout, teamed with a clear desire to give value for money. Admirable attention to detail includes lovely breads, good coffee and charming service. **Seats** 45. L 12.30-2.30 D 6.30-10.
Closed D Sun (except high season & Christmas), all Mon (except Bank Holidays). Set Sun L £9.95. Access, Visa.

Cashel	Cashel House	76%	£149
Tel 095 31001 Fax 095 31077			**HR**
Cashel Co Galway			Map 2 A4

Standing in secluded beauty at the head of Cashel Bay, the Victorian house is set in award-winning gardens running down to a private beach. Dermot and Kay McEvilly have been the welcoming, professional hosts since 1968, and their hotel won instant renown a year later when General and Madame de Gaulle stayed for two weeks. Turf and log fires add a cosy glow to the gracious day rooms, where antiques and fresh flowers take the eye. Bedrooms are individually decorated, and the Garden Suite rooms are particularly stylish, with separate seating areas and access to the patio. Service is excellent and breakfast includes a wide range of home-made produce, from soda bread and marmalade to black pudding. **Rooms** 32. *Garden, tennis, sea & game fishing, boating, horse riding (inc dressage). Closed 10-31 Jan.* AMERICAN EXPRESS *Access, Diners, Visa.*

Restaurant   £70

Fixed-price five-course dinners in the sunny restaurant feature the best of home-grown and local produce prepared without undue elaboration or fuss. From a typical winter menu you might choose warm salmon mousse, feuilleté of scallops or seafood terrine, then one of two soups, a sorbet, and filo chicken parcels, tournedos of wild salmon, lobster (£7.20 per pound supplement) or roast sirloin of beef with pepper sauce. Home-made ice cream and tarte tatin are sweet alternatives to a selection of Irish cheeses. Lunch in the bar. **Seats** 75. *Private Room 8. L 1-2 (in the bar) D 7.30-8.45 (Sun 7.30-9). Set D from £29.*

Cashel	Zetland House	65%	£109
Tel 095 31111 Fax 095 31117			**H**
Cashel Co Galway			Map 2 A4

On the edge of Cashel Bay, Zetland House was a sporting lodge when built in the early 19th century. It's still a favoured base for outdoor pursuits, notably fishing and rough shooting. Cosy sitting rooms; most bedrooms have spectacular sea views. **Rooms** 20. *Garden, croquet, tennis, fishing, snooker. Closed Nov-March.* AMERICAN EXPRESS *Access, Diners, Visa.*

Please note there are two places named **Cashel**, one in Co Galway (see Map 2 A4), the other in Co Tipperary (see Map 2 C5).

Cashel   Chez Hans   £70

Tel 062 61177   **R**

Rockside Cashel Co Tipperary   **Map 2 C5**

First-time visitors are amazed by the sheer size and style of Hans-Peter Matthiä's converted Wesleyan chapel which is tucked behind the town right under the Rock of Cashel – and the concept which has stood the test of time so well was way ahead of its time when he established the restaurant in 1968. Also surprising, perhaps, considering the location, is the strength of seafood throughout the well-balanced carte – escalope of turbot with Dublin Bay prawns, for example, is an exceptional dish of enormous langoustines, a very large fillet of turbot and a garnish of mussels served with dramatic simplicity on a huge, deep, white plate. Classics – updated perhaps with a contemporary garnish – still claim the limelight and carnivores looking forward to rack of Tipperary lamb will not be disappointed. Finish with a dessert tasting plate, perhaps, or a selection of Continental and Irish farmhouse chesses. *Seats 60. Parties 8. D only 6.30-10. Closed Sun, Mon, 3 weeks Jan, Good Friday, 24-27 Dec. Access, Visa.*

Cashel   Dowling's

Tel 062 62130   **P**

Cashel Co Tipperary   **Map 2 C5**

Pat and Helen Dowling have changed the name of their pub from Meaney's, but that's about the only change. It stands handily on the main street and its attractions include traditional decor, a cosy open fire and good simple snacks ("soup, sandwiches and toasties"). But above all this is a place for music: there are traditional Irish sessions organised on Friday and Sunday nights (also Wednesday in summer) as often as they can, but anyone with an instrument is always welcome and impromptu sessions can get going at any time. *Open 10.30-11.30 (Sun 12.30-2, 4-11). No credit cards.*

Cashel   The Spearman   £55

Tel 062 61143   **R**

Main Street Cashel Co Tipperary   **Map 2 C5**

Tucked in a slip road just off the main thoroughfare, a few steps from the Cashel Palace Hotel, this family-run restaurant has a restrained atmosphere that belies the hearty wholesomeness and sheer generosity of David Spearman's food. Swiftly served lunchtime specials – a homely no-choice, three-course meal for under a fiver – offer exceptional value, while more imaginative à la carte menus might typically include dishes like goujons of monkfish with a red pepper sauce or tagliatelle with smoked salmon in a parmesan sauce. Sundays are special at The Spearman: not only a full traditional Sunday lunch, but a regular pasta menu

on Sunday nights rounded off with tiramisu or an Italian
cheeseplate. *Seats 36. Parties 10. L 12-2.30 D 6-10.*
Closed D 24 Dec, all 25 & 26 Dec. Set Sun L £10.95. Access, Visa.

Cashel   Places of Interest

GPA Bolton Library Tel 062 61944
Thurles Racecourse Tel 0504 22253 *16 miles*

Castleconnell   Bradshaw's Bar

Tel 061 377724	**P**
Castleconnell Co Limerick	Map 2 B4

The Bradshaw family bought this atmospheric 19th-century
village pub in the 1920s and since the current owner, Ger
Bradshaw, took over in 1992 he has worked hard to make
improvements while remaining true to the old traditions – so,
although an extra room has been opened up to increase space,
it has retained the authentic feeling, with bare floor, fairly spartan
furniture and an open fire. Traditional acoustic music midweek.
*Open 5-11.30pm weekdays, usual pub hours at weekends (Sat
10.30am-11.30pm, Sun & Bank Holidays 12.30-2, 4-11).*
Closed 25 Dec & Good Friday. Garden. No credit cards.

Castleconnell   Castle Oaks House Hotel   64%   £72

Tel 061 377666 Fax 061 377717	**H**
Castleconnell Co Limerick	Map 2 B4

In the picturesque waterside village of Castleconnell, six miles
from Limerick off the Dublin road, this attractive, well-located
hotel makes an excellent venue for local functions, but is of special
interest to fisherfolk as it has its own stretch of the River Shannon
that runs alongside well-maintained woodland paths in the
grounds. Public areas in the hotel are nicely proportioned –
notably the pretty blue and yellow dining room, a pleasant
breakfast location. Bedrooms vary considerably in size and
appointments, ranging from elegant and spacious with half-tester
bed and garden view to a rather cramped double with a dated
bathroom and overlooking a flat roof, but it is generally
a comfortable hotel, with helpful staff and a family-friendly
attitude. There's an exceptionally well-equipped leisure centre
(creche Mon-Fri 10-2) in the large wooded grounds, plus a large
complex of 24 self-catering holiday houses. Banqueting/conference
for 300/350; parking for 200. 24hr room service. No dogs.
*Rooms 11. Garden, indoor swimming pool, solarium, sauna, spa bath,
steam room, beauty salon, tennis, pitch & putt, fishing. Closed 25 Dec.*
AMERICAN EXPRESS® *Access, Diners, Visa.*

Castledermot   Kilkea Castle   70%   £214

Tel 0503 45156 Fax 0503 45187	**HR**
Kilkea Castledermot Co Kildare	Map 2 C4

The oldest inhabited castle in Ireland, Kilkea was built in 1180
by Hugh de Lacy. Steeped in history, it has been renovated and
converted with skill and sensitivity that allow it to retain its
inherent elegance and grandeur. Rooms, many with wonderful
views over the formal gardens and surrounding countryside, are

splendidly furnished to incorporate modern comforts in a manner appropriate to their age and style and the adjoining leisure centre, although architecturally discreet, offers state-of-the-art facilities. Outdoor sports include clay-pigeon shooting, archery, tennis and fishing on the nearby River Greese. An 18-hole championship golf course was due to open in April 1995. *Rooms 39. Garden, tennis, indoor swimming pool, sauna, jacuzzi, steam room, solarium, gymnasium, clay-pigeon shooting, archery, fishing.*
Closed 4-5 days Christmas. AMERICAN EXPRESS *Access, Diners, Visa.*

De Lacy's   £75

The first-floor restaurant is appropriately grand with magnificent views over the countryside and a bright, airy atmosphere. Scottish chef George Smith has a distinctive style and the lengthy descriptions on the menu give an indication of the complexity of what is to follow. But the quality of ingredients shines through and, in specialities such as the roast of the day, there are excellent simpler alternatives available. Local produce features strongly, much of it taken from the gardens below, where guests can take coffee in summer and wander around to see the old fruit trees, vegetables and herbs. Salads and vegetables are a speciality and desserts are beautiful and sophisticated, to match their surroundings. Typical main-course dishes include supreme of salmon brushed with lemon and lime butter and served with a fresh lobster sauce, or haunch of venison pan-fried with herbs, carved on rösti glazed with game essence and served with poached grapes. *Seats 60. L 12.30-2.30 D 7-9.30. Closed Christmas week. Set L £15 Set D £28.*

Castlelyons   Ballyvolane House   £80

Tel 025 36349 Fax 025 36781	**A**
Castlelyons Co Cork	Map 2 B5

This gracious house, set in lovely wooded grounds and surrounded by its own farmland, dates back to 1728 and was modified to its present Italianate style in the mid-19th century. The impressive pillared hall with its baby grand piano sets the tone but, despite the formal elegance of the house and its period furnishings, the owners, Jeremy and Merrie Green, are well known for their special brand of relaxed hospitality. Well-proportioned reception rooms are warmed by huge log fires, and residents' dinner is cooked by Merrie and taken communally around a lovely mahogany table, with stories relating to the house abounding. Bedrooms vary in size and outlook but all are warm and comfortable, furnished with antiques and with roomy bathrooms en suite – one has an original Edwardian bath reached by mahogany steps. No dogs. *Rooms 7. Garden, croquet, fishing.* AMERICAN EXPRESS *Access, Visa.*

Castletownbere   MacCarthy's

Tel 027 70014	**P**
Town Square Castletownbere Co Cork	Map 2 A6

One of the first drinking places to be granted a licence in Ireland, MacCarthy's has been in the same family for 150 years (Adrienne MacCarthy is the fourth generation). It's not only a pub, but also a grocery which provisions the trawlers that are based in the harbour. In the front – the grocery section – one of the last remaining match-making booths (traditionally used by the match-maker and the bride's and groom's parents to arrange marriage terms) is now used as a snug, while in the back bar darts and live music make for a very sociable ambience. Live music Thu-Sun. *Open 10.30-11.30, Sun 12-2 & 4-11. Closed Good Friday & 25 Dec. No credit cards.*

Castletownshend	Bow Hall	£56
Tel 028 36114		**A**
Castletownshend Co Cork		**Map 2 B6**

Americans Barbara amd Dick Vickery have been running this delighful 17th-century house overlooking the anchorage at Castle Haven as a home-from-home for discerning guests since 1977, but there is no sign of their enthusiasm flagging and it is not just the high level of comfort but the warmth of their welcome that makes a visit to their characterful and thoughtfully furnished home memorable. Barbara is also a dab hand in the kitchen, using produce from their lovely garden (open to the public once a year) in imaginative meals for residents – and be sure to allow time in the schedule for full enjoyment of a lengthy breakfast, which includes freshly-baked muffins, pancakes and home-made sausages. No dogs. **Rooms** *3. Garden. Closed for several days at Christmas; advance bookings only in winter. No credit cards.*

Castletownshend	Mary Ann's Bar & Restaurant	£50
Tel 028 36146 Fax 028 36377		**R**
Castletownshend nr Skibbereen Co Cork		**Map 2 B6**

This famous, low-ceilinged haven from the 'soft' West Cork weather has been in the capable hands of Fergus and Patricia O'Mahony since 1983 and celebrated its 150th birthday last year. Mary Ann's offers particularly good bar food, most of which is served with tip-top home-made bread and which wins our Ireland 1995 Best Traditional Bread award. Home-made soup, seafood chowder, chicken liver and herb paté, crab cocktail or prawn cocktail; sandwiches, a few lunch dishes (scallops Mary Ann, steaks, chicken Kiev or a daily special), and salads (smoked salmon or crab, seafood platter) served with that wonderful bread also feature. However, Patricia's good home-cooking is also on offer in The Contented Sole restaurant (separately recommended) upstairs, where you'll find excellent, super-fresh local seafood and also lamb and good steaks. On the 4-course dinner menu (£19.95) you might commence with tagliatelle of seafood, baked avocado and crab, home-made seafood soup and bread, grilled black sole on the bone, roast duckling on a sauce of grapes and oranges, herb-crusted rack of West Cork lamb with a red wine jus, coquilles St Jacques au gratin, and pan-fried medallions of monkfish in a light prawn and white wine sauce. Desserts lean towards homely favourites like lemon meringue pie or strawberry shortcake and the farmhouse cheese plate is as generous as it is good. No children under 4 after 7.30pm. Plenty of room in the garden for open-air eating and a back bar area with TV that is popular with visitors in holiday homes locally. *Bar open 12.30-11.30 (to 11 in winter), Sun 12-2, 4-11.* **Bar Food** *12.30-*

2.30, 6-8.30. **Restaurant Meals** *Tue-Sat 6.30-9.30 & Sun lunch in winter (12-2). Restaurant closed Mon Nov-Mar (except Christmas period), 24-26 Dec, Good Friday. Set L £13 Set D £19.95. Children allowed in bar to eat. Access, Visa.*

Castlewarren   Langton's

Tel 0503 26123   **P**

Castlewarren Co Kilkenny   **Map 2 C4**

A bit of a curiosity – not a real pub at all but a relic of what used to be so common in rural Ireland – the kitchen-cum-grocery-cum-bar. A visit here will take the traveller away from main roads through the pleasant countryside of a little-known corner of Ireland and back in time. A row of high stools beside the bacon slicer at the counter and a good shelf of bottles over it are the only real clues to the nature of the premises but, once you're ensconced, Josie Langton, here for 25 years, will put the world to rights with you and rustle up a bit of a sandwich in the kitchen on demand. *Open 10.30am-11.30pm (Sun 12.30-4). Closed Sun eve. Garden. No credit cards.*

Ceanannas Mor (Kells)   O'Shaughnessy's

Tel 046 41110   **P**

Market Street Ceanannas Mor (Kells) Co Meath   **Map 1 C3**

A reasonably new pub, comfortably and pleasantly decorated on an old-style theme. Unpretentious, fairly-priced bar food is the main attraction – food like Irish stew, chicken or beef curry, lasagne, quiches and pizzas, but better and cheaper than most. You'll find O'Shaughnessy's just behind St Columba's Church (where a copy of the *Book of Kells* is kept). Now under new ownership. *Open 10.30am-11.30pm (Sun 12-11).* **Bar Food** *all day from 12). Closed Good Friday & 25 Dec. Access, Visa.*

Cheekpoint   McAlpin's Suir Inn

Tel 051 38220   **P**

Cheekpoint nr Waterford Co Waterford   **Map 2 C5**

When this tiny black-and-white pub was built in 1750 Cheekpoint was the main port for the boats from England. Today it's a quiet little backwater, although much of the seafood which forms the bulk of the bar menu here is still landed at the quay opposite the inn. Inside, the single bar is as neat as a new pin with old photos and plates decorating the red walls, around which are thinly upholstered banquettes and varnished rustic tables. The menu offers about eight starters – shrimp cocktail (£3.95), grilled smoked mackerel (£2.95), crab claws in garlic butter (£3.95) – and eight main dishes – wild salmon mayonnaise (£8.95), king scallops in cheese and white wine sauce (£8.95), curried chicken breasts (£7.50). There's always a fruit pie made with Mrs McAlpin's excellent pastry. *Open evenings only 6-11.30 (6-11 in winter), Sun 12-2, 7-11. Closed Mon (except July & Aug).* **Bar Food** *6-9.30 Tue-Sat (& Mon in July & Aug). No food Tue Oct-Easter.* *Access, Visa.*

Clarecastle   Carnelly House   £146

Tel 065 28442   Fax 065 29222   **A**

Clarecastle Co Clare   Map 2 B4

Conveniently located close to Shannon airport and nicely
positioned for touring the west of Ireland, this impressive
Georgian residence offers accommodation to rival the most
luxurious of hotels. Spacious bedrooms, overlooking lawns planted
with spreading trees, are furnished with antiques and individually
decorated to the highest standard, with elegantly draped king-size
or twin beds and luxuriously appointed private bathrooms.
Magnificent reception rooms include a beautifully proportioned
drawing room, with Corinthian pillars, Francini ceiling and grand
piano. Communal dinners (prepared by a Ballymaloe-trained
cook) are taken in a striking, panelled dining room. Hospitality
is a priority and the atmosphere at Carnelly is warm and homely
in the true Irish country house tradition. *Rooms 5. Garden.
Closed 22 Dec-early Jan.* AMERICAN EXPRESS *Access, Visa.*

Clarenbridge   Paddy Burke's

Tel 091 96226   Fax 091 96016   **P**

Clarenbridge Co Galway   Map 2 B4

Synonymous with Clarenbridge, a steady stream of the great and
famous have made their way to Paddy Burke's ("The Oyster Inn")
– and there's been plenty of time to do it in, as the history of the
pub goes right back to 1650. Especially famous for their oysters
(£4.50 for 6, £9 for 12) – "The world is your oyster at Paddy
Burke's" – they also offer a wide range of bar food including
an excellent Galway Bay chowder (£2.20), served with home-
made brown bread, or chicken and broccoli bake (£6.95);
sandwiches as well (£1.50-£4.50). Lunchtime carvery (£4.75);
more formal restaurant meals (£15.50 3-course or long à la carte)
are served in the evening. September 1995 sees proprietor Norbert
Fallon's fifth oyster festival. *Pub open 10.30am-11.30pm Mon-Sat
(to 11 in winter) Sun 12-2, 4-11.* **Bar Food** *11am-10.30pm (Sun &
Bank Holidays from 12, to 9.30). Garden. Pub closed Good Friday, 24
& 25 Dec.* AMERICAN EXPRESS *Access, Diners, Visa.*

Clifden   Abbeyglen Castle   60%   £92

Tel 095 21201   Fax 095 21797   **H**

Sky Road Clifden Co Galway   Map 1 A3

Take the N59 from Galway City to Clifden, then Sky Road out
of Clifden to find the hotel, 300 yards on the left in 12 acres
of grounds. Owner Paul Hughes personally welcomes guests,
many of whom return year after year, to his crenellated hotel.
Steps lead down from the hotel to landscaped gardens and
an outdoor pool and tennis court. Public areas include a spacious
drawing room for residents and a relaxing pubby bar with open
peat fire. Refurbishment continues in the good-sized bedrooms.
No children under 10. Local fishing facilities are a major
attraction. *Rooms 40. Garden, outdoor swimming pool, sauna,
tennis, pitch and putt, snooker, table tennis, riding, fishing.
Closed 8 Jan-1 Feb.* AMERICAN EXPRESS *Access, Diners, Visa.*

Clifden   Ardagh Hotel   60%   £84

Tel 095 21384   Fax 095 21314   **HR**

Ballyconneely Road Clifden Co Galway   Map 1 A3

Quiet family-run hotel on the edge of Ardbear Bay, a couple
of miles south of Clifden. Day rooms include a roomy and
comfortable bar, two lounges and a top-floor sun room. Golf,
fishing and riding can be arranged. No dogs. *Rooms 21.*
Closed Nov-end Mar. AMERICAN EXPRESS *Access, Diners, Visa.*

Restaurant   £55

The first-floor restaurant has lovely views to add to the enjoyment
of Monique Bauvet's imaginative way with local produce. Lamb
sweetbreads in puff pastry, seafood chowder, saffron-sauced brill,
lobster (grilled fresh from the tank) and pot-roasted rack of spring
lamb show their style. Lighter meals in the bar. *Seats 50.*
Parties 30. D only 7.15-9.30. Set D from £23.

Clifden   Destry Rides Again   £40

Tel 095 21722   Fax 095 41168   **R**

Clifden Co Galway   Map 1 A3

Decor at the Foyles' entertaining little restaurant (named after
a Marlene Dietrich film) is predictably wacky – an old Georgian
fanlight decorates one wall and has a real skull balanced on top,
a collection of silver food domes and a variety of 'boys in the
backroom' memorabilia all create atmosphere. Dishes on the
shortish menu have a modern ring, exemplified by vermicelli
with smoked chicken and mozzarella, chargrilled halibut with
black olives and horseradish, roast Barbary duck with raspberry
and ginger, and grilled pork fillet coated in spices with hot and
sour sauce. Desserts include good home-made ices and a rich
'Lethal Chocolate Pud', made to a secret recipe. Confident, classy
cooking and great fun. Short, user-friendly, keenly-priced wine
list, with plenty available by the glass. *Seats 40. L 12-3 D 6-10
(in winter open only for dinner Thu-Sat 7-9).*
Access, Visa.

Clifden   Doris's Restaurant

Tel 095 21427   Fax 095 21054   **JaB**

Market Street Clifden Co Galway   Map 1 A3

An attractive, cottagey house in the middle of town, Doris's has
small rooms on three floors and is a handy place for an informal
bite. The overlong menu may set off alarms, but they do a tasty
meal-in-a-bowl chowder (£2.50), delivered with a particularly
good home-baked brown bread, albeit with mini-butter packs.
Bearing in mind that one of the chefs is Burmese, the Asian
specials (Burmese pork curry, with tomatoes, ginger and garlic,
£7.50) look less out of place and may reward investigation.
Seats 62. Private Room 30. Parties 8. Meals noon-10pm.
Closed Sun 1 Nov-end Feb, 24-26 Dec. *Access,
Diners, Visa.*

Clifden   E J King's

Tel 095 21330

The Square Clifden Co Galway   Map 1 A3

On the square in the centre of town, a lively old bar on two
floors, retaining an essentially traditional character despite modern
touches in its atrium and striking primary colour schemes on the
upper floors. Menus lean towards local seafood, especially oysters,
crab and smoked salmon but typical blackboard specials might
include bacon and cabbage or roast beef or rack of lamb, plus
there's a choice of farmhouse cheeses. Trenchermen should head
for the fisherman's platter, complete with smoked salmon, prawns,
crab, mussels, salmon, cod, smoked trout and mackerel and salad!
Live music, mainly traditional folk and ballads, features nightly
in season, 2 or 3 times a week in winter. *Open 10.30am-11.30pm*
(Sun 12.30-11). **Bar Food** *10.30-9 (Sun from 12.30). Terrace.*
AMERICAN EXPRESS *Access, Diners, Visa.*

Clifden   Foyles Hotel   61%   £79

Tel 095 21801   Fax 095 21458   **H**

The Square Clifden Co Galway   Map 1 A3

Formerly known as the Clifden Bay Hotel Edmund Foyle (twin
brother of Paddy, see *Quay House*) decided to change the name
recently when a German visitor complained that he could not see
the bay from his window – and high time, too, as it's been owned
by, managed by and lived in by the Foyle family since 1917. It's
a comfortable, friendly, undemanding, old-fashioned hotel with
rooms which are all en suite but vary considerably in size and
appointments, rather grand corridors and public areas which were
in the process of re-arrangement at the time of going to press – the
bar (where food is available all day) is moving to the back of the
hotel and a new upmarket restaurant is to take its place beside the
front door. The residents' dining room, which opens on to
a sheltered, private courtyard, will remain. **Rooms** *30.*
Closed 1 Nov-Easter weekend. AMERICAN EXPRESS *Access, Diners, Visa.*

Clifden   O'Grady's Seafood Restaurant   £50

Tel 095 21450   **R**

Market Street Clifden Co Galway   Map 1 A3

Mike O'Grady's traditional seafood restaurant has well-spaced
tables, some in alcoves but all with a degree of privacy. Try
starting with a speciality like Jack's smoked fish bisque – smooth,
creamy but with just the right amount of texture and smokiness
to be interesting, served with a choice of good home-made white
yeast bread or wholemeal soda. Sophisticated main courses from
a wide choice, predominantly but not exclusively seafood, on the
à la carte dinner menu might include grilled fillet of turbot with
a compote of rhubarb and champagne butter cream or best end
of lamb on a jus of wild mushrooms with a hint of pesto, while
lunch offerings are simpler – marinière-style mussels, perhaps,
or braised kidneys with a creamy mushroom and pink peppercorn
sauce. Follow with 'sinful desserts' or farmhouse cheese.
An informal piano bistro serves one-plate specialities. No children
under 5. **Seats** *50. Parties 21. Private Room 12. L 12.30-2.30*
D 6.30-10. Closed Sun (Mar-Jun), Feb-mid Mar. Set L £6/£8.95
Set D £12/£18. AMERICAN EXPRESS *Access, Visa.*

Clifden   The Quay House   £50

Tel 095 21369   **RR**

Beach Road Clifden Co Galway   Map 1 A3

Paddy and Julia Foyle (*Rosleague Manor, Destry Rides Again*) seem
finally to have put down roots at this lovely quayside restaurant
with rooms. Simultaneously elegant and delightfully wacky (who
else would hang one of an otherwise sobre set of prints upside
down?), it has a comfortable drawing room for aperitifs and chat,
with newly-added conservatory off it for afternoon teas and such,
while the restaurant itself comprises two rooms across the hall
which can be opened up or separate, but is nicest as one space
so that the unusual triangular fireplace halfway up the far end wall
can be enjoyed by all (a thoughtfully placed mirror makes this
possible from most angles). Paddy and Julia supervise service,
while Dermot Gannon, who moved down with them from
Destry, turns out little gems like deep-fried calamari with chili and
grilled pepper salad or sautéed lamb's kidneys and sweetbreads
with red onion confit, served with a choice of wholemeal yeast
bread and focaccia, fresh from the Aga. Seafood is the main
attraction, of course, as in chargrilled halibut with tarragon and
garlic butter, but local meats are not overlooked – Connemara
lamb is always a winner, typically roasted with wild thyme and
garlic, but also beef, which is carefully sourced from a Midland
farmer and transformed into something like 'prime steer beef
fillet, flame-grilled, with Italian potato cakes'. Finish, perhaps, with
a dessert such as Lethal Chocolate Pudding, a secret invention
imported from *Destry*. **Seats** *70. Parties 10. Private Room 30.
L 12-3 D 7-9.30. Closed 2 weeks Christmas, Sun & Mon Oct-Apr.
Set D £19.50 ('Highdays & Holidays only'). Access, Visa.*

Rooms   £50

Six lovely airy, stylishly decorated rooms with large
individualistic bathrooms are available for weary diners to retire
to. Front ones enjoy a quayside outlook, with or without water
depending on the tide, while others overlook gardens. Children
under 7 may stay free in their parents' room and an early evening
meal is available by arrangement.

Set menu prices may not always include service or wine.
Our quoted price for two does.

Clifden   Rock Glen Manor   67%   £90

Tel 095 21035   Fax 095 21737   **HR**

Ballyconneely Road Clifden Co Galway   Map 1 A3

A mile and a half from Clifden on the Ballyconneely road, this
lovely, restful, 19th-century shooting lodge is tucked away over
a secluded anchorage in what must surely be one of the most
beautiful hotel locations in Ireland. John and Evangeline Roche,
who have owned Rock Glen for over 20 years, describe it as "an
oasis of tranquillity" and they are right. Comfortable, chintz-
covered sofas and chairs in front of a welcoming turf fire tempt
guests into a drawing room which, along with the bar and

conservatory area beside it, enjoys lovely hill and sea views. Fourteen of the rooms, all in a regular ongoing programme of improvement and refurbishment, are on the ground floor and the standard of comfort is high throughout. Golf, horse riding, fishing, mountain climbing and beaches are all available nearby. Children welcome "if well behaved". No dogs. **Rooms** 29. *Garden, croquet, tennis, putting green. Closed Nov-mid Mar.* AMERICAN EXPRESS *Access, Diners, Visa.*

Restaurant   £60

Clever use of mirrors creates a feeling of spaciousness in this pleasant, traditionally decorated room and uniformed staff move swiftly to ensure that every comfort has been anticipated. Meanwhile, John Roche prepares local produce such as oak-smoked salmon salad followed by freshly caught fish, perhaps turbot, served in a tomato, onion and caper sauce, or medallions of venison on a redcurrant jus. Finish off with a warm pear and almond sponge or a plate of farmhouse cheeses. Next morning's breakfast sees the room transformed, with fresh juice and freshly baked brown bread on the table and a very fine breakfast menu to choose from, including a selection of fish and a vegetarian breakfast. Informal bar snacks served from 12 to 5. No smoking. **Seats** 60. *Parties 10. D only 7-9. Set D £22. Closed Nov-mid Mar.*

Clifden   Place of Interest

Connemara National Park Tel 095 41054

Clonakilty   An Súgán   £50
Tel 023 33498   **R**
41 Strand Road Clonakilty Co Cork   **Map 2 B6**

On a corner site, reassuringly easy to find on the way into town after leaving the N71, a colourful, characterful pub that sums up everything that now makes Clonakilty such a delightful place to visit. Above the famous bar (where excellent bar food is served), a more formal restaurant – adorned with pictorial tributes to many of the musical greats of Ireland's past – provides a fine setting for hearty fare, especially local seafood in fresh-flavoured renderings of popular dishes including starters such as crab cocktail, garlicky stuffed mussels, oak-smoked salmon and fresh oysters, typically followed by scallops, sole on the bone or lobster, served perhaps in a brandy, cream and tomato sauce with mushrooms and shallots. Steaks, lamb and duckling are on offer for carnivores, with generosity the keyword throughout. "Ní béile bí bia gan deoch" (Food without drink is not a meal). **Seats** 45. *L (Sun only) 12.30-2.30 D 7-9.45. Closed Wed, Good Fri, 25 Dec. Set Sun L £8.50 Set D £18.90. Access, Visa.*

Clonakilty   Fionnula's   £35
Tel 023 34355   **R**
30 Ashe Street Clonakilty Co Cork   **Map 2 B6**

Known affectionately as 'Fionnula's little Italian Restaurant', this laid-back place charms with its mis-matched chairs, tables and cloths in warm colours, walls covered with pictures and personal memorabilia. Lunch is served in the soothingly dim atmosphere

on the ground floor, while equally characterful rooms up the
narrow stairs on the first floor come into their own in candle-lit
evening meals. Menus offer zappy, colourful food with bags
of flavour: memorable soups – tomato and fennel, perhaps – pasta
with piquant, spicy sauces, richly flavoured olive oil and colourful
salads and, in the evening, main-course specials such as chicken
cacciatora (with red wine, garlic, fresh herbs and tomatoes).
Snazzy snacks include half a pizza of your choice and vegetarian
choices like houmus with garlic bread, and spinach and cream
cheese lasagne. Finish off with a pleasingly gooey tiramisu.
*Seats 34. Parties 14. Private Room 14. L 12.30-2.30 D 6-10. Closed
Mon & Tues in winter (except Bank Holidays), 24-26 Dec.
Access, Visa.*

Clondalkin Kingswood Country House	£60
Tel 01 459 2428/459 2207	**RR**
Old Kingswood Naas Road Clondalkin Dublin 22	Map 2 D4

Within its old stone-walled garden and surrounded by mature
trees, a remarkable country house atmosphere prevails
at Kingswood, despite its location within the city limits and just
yards from the Naas dual carriageway. The restaurant is divided
between a series of rooms of pleasingly domestic proportions, one
with an open fire and all overlooking the garden. The welcome
is warm and service is uniformed and efficient, befitting chef
Jaswant Samra's delicious, well-balanced meals. Start, perhaps, with
a country salad of mixed leaves, with a zesty citrus vinaigrette and
crunchy croutons, toasted pine nuts and crispy bacon dice, or an
unusual first course like baked codling on lightly nutmeg-
flavoured spinach and julienne vegetables, all gratinated with
a herbed parmesan. Main courses might include a traditional roast,
or breast of chicken stuffed with a tarragon mousse and served
on a mushroom sauce, or even the house version of Irish stew.
Good desserts include well-made ices and homely fruit crumbles,
served with *crème anglaise.* Popular for Sunday lunch (£11.95).
*Seats 60. Private Room 50. L 12.30-2.30 D 6.30-10.30.
Closed L Sat, D Sun, Good Friday, 25-27 Dec. Set L £12.95
Set D £19.95.* AMERICAN EXPRESS *Access, Diners, Visa.*

Rooms   £80

Seven en-suite rooms are individually decorated to a high
standard. Tariff reductions at weekends.

Clonmel Clonmel Arms 61%	£86
Tel 052 21233 Fax 052 21526	**H**
Sarsfield Street Conmel Co Tipperary	Map 2 C5

Some of the bedrooms at the town-centre Clonmel Arms are
suitable for family occupation, and children under 10 can stay
free in their parents' room. There are extensive banqueting and
conference facilities (for up to 600), two restaurants and two bars.
Rooms 31. Terrace, coffee shop (9-6). Closed 25 Dec. AMERICAN EXPRESS
Access, Diners, Visa.

Clonmel   Places of Interest

Ormond Castle Carrick-on-Suir Tel 051 40787
Clonmel Racecourse Powerstown Park Tel 052 22611

Cobh   Mansworth's

Tel 021 811965	**P**
Midleton Street Cobh Co Cork	**Map 2 B6**

Well up the hill, a hundred yards from St Colman's Cathedral,
Mansworth's is Cobh's oldest-established pub (est. 1895) and has
been run by the same family for as long as anyone can remember.
A warm, welcoming place by any standards, this unspoilt,
traditional bar is especially worth visiting for its fascinating
collection of memorabilia connected with the naval history of the
port, both past and present – many of the more recent
photographs feature the present owner, John Mansworth,
an enthusiastic promoter of Cobh in general and its maritime
characteristics in particular. Not really a food place, although light
snacks (soup, sandwiches, pizzas) are available, but there's
an unusually good choice of non-alcoholic drinks, including wines.
*Open 10.30am-11.30pm Mon-Sat (to 11pm in winter), Sun 12.30-2,
4-11. Closed 25 Dec, Good Friday. No credit cards.*

Collon   Forge Gallery Restaurant   £65

Tel 041 26272	**R**
Collon Co Louth	**Map 1 D3**

This stylish, meticulously appointed two-storey restaurant – the
upper half is an elegant galleried bar/reception area overlooking
the dining room below – provides a fitting setting for Des
Carroll's bounteous fare and Conor Phelan's hospitality.
Frequently changed menus feature local seasonal produce –
seafood, game in season, vegetables, fruit – in first courses such
as Thai-style pork kebabs with summer fruit or, as experienced
on a recent visit, memorable Dublin Bay prawns in garlic butter:
simple and magnificent, with home-made breads – white yeast
bread, scones or brown bread with thyme – to mop up the juices.
Typical main courses include a special vegetarian dish as well
as local meat and fish such as rack of Cooley lamb, salmon from
the Boyne or, perhaps, a delicious matelote of seafood, including
lobster and served in a filo basket. Outstanding vegetables –
a plentiful selection of about five, imaginatively presented – and
lovely seasonal desserts, such as mouthwatering rhubarb and
raspberry fool, all rounded off by freshly brewed coffee or tea
(including herbal teas) and petits fours. *Seats 65. Parties 20. Outside
seating 25. D only 7-9.30. Closed Sun & Mon, Christmas, 2 weeks
in Jan. Set D £22. Access, Diners, Visa.*

Collooney   Glebe House   £45

Tel 071 67787	**RR**
Collooney Co Sligo	**Map 1 B2**

Marc and Brid Torrades rescued Glebe House from dereliction
to open it as a restaurant in 1990 and, while it does not yet have
the level of sophistication that many of the established country
houses have achieved, their warmth of hospitality and willingness

to please are likely to win the hearts of many a guest. Judging
by their performance to date, each passing year will see big
improvements. Chef Brid uses the best of local produce in hearty,
generous dishes such as braised duck breast with olives or smoked
salmon in a dill sauce topped by a featherlight fleuron of puff
pastry followed, perhaps, by trio of seafood with a pink
peppercorn sauce or a filo of vegetables in a light mustard sauce.
Good vegetables are served up in dishes left on the table for guests
to help themselves. Classic desserts include a surprise dessert plate;
balanced selection of French and Irish farmhouse cheeses. *Seats 40.
Parties 20. L by arrangement D 6.30-9.30. Set D £15. Closed Sun,
Mon in winter, all Nov & 25/26 Dec.* AMERICAN EXPRESS® *Access, Visa.*

Rooms   £30

Accommodation is available in four spacious, individually
decorated rooms, all en suite, two with baths. Room 5 is planned
to open in the spring. *Garden.*

Collooney	Markree Castle	60%	£97
Tel 071 67800 Fax 071 67840			**H**
Collooney Co Sligo			Map 1 B2

Charles Cooper, the tenth generation of his family to live
in Markree, has made a fine job of restoring pride and splendour
to a castle which had for some years been empty and neglected.
Space and character both abound, the place is well heated (huge
fires everywhere) and there's a beautiful dining room with some
exquisite Italian plasterwork. The views are superb, and the
setting, in meadows, woods and gardens reaching to the River
Unsin, guarantees peace and quiet. They serve an excellent
afternoon tea. *Rooms 14. Garden, fishing, riding. Closed Feb-Mar.*
AMERICAN EXPRESS® *Access, Diners, Visa.*

Cong	Ashford Castle	88%	£265
Tel 092 46003 Fax 092 46260			**H R**
Cong Co Mayo			Map 1 B3

With its origins dating back to the early 13th century and set
amid 350 acres of magnificent parkland (including a golf course)
on the northern shores of Lough Corrib, this splendid castle has
been lovingly restored – its recent history is depicted for all to see
by photographic and written memorabilia displayed in various
parts of the building. Throughout, there's rich panelling,
intricately carved balustrades, suits of armour and fine paintings.
Whether you wish to relax in the elegant drawing room, wander
around the halls and galleries, or retire to the Dungeon Bar after
dinner and listen to the delightful Annette Griffin singing
traditional Irish folk songs and playing the harp to the
accompaniment of Carol Coleman's piano, there's a unique
atmosphere throughout. Managing Director Rory Murphy has
been in situ for over 20 years and, with the assistance of William
(Bill) Buckley, runs a truly fine hotel, backed up by excellent
professional and committed staff. Spacious bedrooms (including
several suites) offer attractive views and every conceivable luxury,
from flowers and fresh fruit on arrival to slippers, bathrobes and
Molton Brown toiletries in the splendid bathrooms; in all the
rooms you'll find period furniture, fine fabrics and superb
housekeeping that includes a turn-down service. Discreet

conference facilities (several EEC ministerial conferences have been held here) accommodate up to 140 theatre-style and 150 for banquets. The hotel is committed to excellence in standards of both service and ambience. Scheduled for April 1995 is the completion of a new leisure centre to include gym, spa bath and steam room. *Dromoland Castle* in Newmarket-on-Fergus (see entry) is a sister hotel. **Rooms** *83. Garden, croquet, golf (9), tennis, equestrian centre, jaunting-car, fishing, lake cruising, bicycles, boutique, snooker.* AMERICAN EXPRESS *Access, Diners, Visa.*

Connaught Room   ↑   £110

Part of the original Georgian House built in 1715, the handsome, panelled dining room with chandeliers and vast windows is only open at night and is sometimes used for theme evenings. Executive chef Denis Lenihan presides over both restaurants (see George V below) and here presents an à la carte menu with supplementary daily specials. Meat and poultry are sourced from local farms, so you can rely on the quality of raw materials, and fish comes from the West Coast. A typical meal might include tartare of lightly smoked lamb fillet served with tapénade, fillet of turbot with scallops on a parsley dressing and a plate of assorted chocolate desserts. Fine selection of breads, cheeses and good coffee. Service is both caring and supremely professional. There are a few French wines quite reasonably priced for a hotel of this class, though look outside France for the best value. 15% service charge. **Seats** *40. D only 7-9.30.*

George V Room   £100

A much larger room also with handsome panelling and chandeliers. Service is again outstanding, and here fixed-price menus with several choices in each course are offered. Dinner is usually a five-course affair. Start with poached Cleggan lobster served on a truffle oil dressing, followed by carrot soup, roast rack of Connemara hill lamb and a confit of shallots, finishing with local farmhouse cheeses and a lightly frozen prune and armagnac soufflé. 15% service is added to all prices. **Seats** *135. L 1-2.15 D 7-9.30. Set L £19 Set D £34.*

Cong   Place of Interest

Ballinroe Racecourse Tel 092 41052

Cork   An Spailpín Fánac

Tel 021 277949   **P**

28/29 South Main Street Cork Co Cork   **Map 2 B6**

Food at John and Deirdre O'Connor's pleasant pub is of the simple, wholesome variety: freshly-cut sandwiches, toasted Kiev and doorstep special with fries, lasagne, shepherd's pie, bacon and cabbage, Irish stew, minced beef and onion pie, a fish special. Low ceilings, open brickwork, soft natural colours, a siimple wooden bar with rush-seated stools and dim natural light create a soothing atmosphere emphasised by the friendliness of the proprietor; a growing collection of postcards from regulars bears witness to the local popularity of the premises. The name of the pub (pronounced 'an spawlpeen fawnoc') translates roughly as 'the jobbing traveller', recalling a once-familiar Irish character who used to keep on the move around the country in search of work.

No children after 6.30pm, but they are welcome during the day.
The Beamish brewery is opposite the pub and the River Lee
is 40 yards away. Music six nights a week Jul & Aug (not Sat);
Tue, Wed, Thu & Sun Sep-Jun; Fri bluegrass, Thu folk and
balads. *Open 12-11 (to 11.30 in summer), Sun 12.30-2, 4-11.*
Bar Food *12-3. No credit cards.*

Cork	**Arbutus Lodge**	70%	£80
Tel 021 501237 Fax 021 502893			**HR**
Montenotte Cork Co Cork			**Map 2 B6**

Considerable improvements and refurbishment have taken place
in all the bedrooms at this former home of a Lord Mayor of Cork,
high above the city with views of the River Lee and the
surrounding hills. The hotel gets its name from the Arbutus tree,
one of the many rare trees and shrubs growing in the spectacular
terraced gardens. The house is full of genuine antique furniture
(note the four-poster in the Blue Room) and some marvellous art,
both old and new, the modern paintings by Irish artists much
in demand by galleries and museums. Declan and Patsy Ryan, here
since 1962, extend a warm welcome to all their guests, ably
backed up by charming staff. Whether you choose to relax in the
cosy lounge or the panoramic bar with its own terrace, you'll feel
at home and the cleverly designed and smartly decorated
bedrooms, utilising all possible space, provide both comfort
and tranquillity. Bathrooms boast quality towels, bathrobes
and toiletries and you'll start the day with as good a breakfast
as you'll find anywhere. Conference facilities for up to 150.
Rooms *20. Garden, tennis. Closed 24-29 Dec.* AMERICAN EXPRESS *Access,
Diners, Visa.*

Restaurant   ★   £80

Alongside Myrtle Allen (see entry for *Ballymaloe House*), Declan
Ryan has trained and brought on more chefs in this country than
anyone. His restaurant has remained loyal to its roots – no slavish
copying of French trends but a reliance on local produce including
herbs and soft fruit from the hotel's own garden and traditional
Cork dishes. Game in season and the freshest of fish are also
a feature (inspect the seafood tank in the bar) and always a fine
example of the kitchen's style is the nightly-changing, seven-course
tasting menu – no mini-portions, but enough to satisfy the
hungriest of souls – spiced beef and mushroom filo parcels, nage
of fresh prawns tails, medallions of monkfish with mussels and
saffron, very tender roast mallard with elderberry sauce, finishing
with chocolate and rum log or gargantuan floating islands. Ask
for the ingredients of the 'fence reducer sorbet', sometimes served
as a palate cleanser! Service is as caring and professional as you'll
find anywhere, the cheeseboard promotes Irish cheeses in tip-top
condition, and the sweet trolley will tempt even the faint-hearted.
The wine list is not the easieast to find your way around, but what
quality! Every wine has been carefully chosen, many personally
by Declan himself. Prices are very fair, the choice vast in both
France and the New World. A variety of breads is baked on the
premises daily. **Seats** *50. Parties 30. Private Room 25. L 1-2
D 7-9.30. Closed Sun, 1 week Christmas. Set L £12.50
Set D £21.50/£27.75.*

Cork	Bully's		£25

Tel 021 273555   Fax 021 273427   **R**

40 Paul Street Cork Co Cork   **Map 2 B6**

Pizzas from the wood-burning oven are one of the specialities
of Eugene Buckley's popular little place. They come in a dozen
varieties, top of the range being Bully's special – a half-folded
version with bolognese sauce, ham, onion and mushrooms. Also
home-made pasta, grills, omelettes and seafood dishes. Also
at Douglas Village, Co Cork Tel 021 892415; and Bishops Town
Tel 021 546838. *Seats 40. Meals 12-11.30. No credit cards.*

Cork	Cliffords ★		£70

Tel 021 275333   **R**

18 Dyke Parade Cork Co Cork   **Map 2 B6**

Style and quality are the keynotes here, in terms not only
of cooking but also of service and decor. The building itself,
once the civic library, is Georgian, but the whole place has been
elegantly modernised, and Michael and Deirdre Clifford's
collection of contemporary Irish art adorns the walls. The dining
area is striking in its simplicity, with comfortable high-back chairs,
high-quality linen and single flowers floating in glass bowls.
Michael's cooking is controlled and confident, with inventive use
of the best of local produce (he wins our 1995 Iriish Food Award –
see page 61). The dinner menu changes monthly, though some
specialities put in regular appearances. Typifying his style are pan-
fried scallops with lemon grass jus, Clonakilty black pudding with
poached free-range egg, cabbage and smoked kassler, loin of venison
in light cream sauce and medallions of monkfish in white wine sauce.
There's always a fresh fish of the day, plus game in season and
hard-to-resist chocolate desserts. The wine list is relatively short,
but writ large! There are inexpensive house wines, but few half
bottles. *Seats 45. Parties 10. Private Room 35. L 12.30-2.30
D 7-10.30. Closed L Sat, all Sun & Mon, Bank Holidays, 1 week
Aug, 1 week Christmas. Set L £13.50 Set D £29.* AMERICAN EXPRESS
Access, Diners, Visa.

Changes in data sometimes occur in establishments
after the Guide goes to press. Prices should be taken
as indications rather than firm quotes.

Cork	Crawford Gallery Café		£45

Tel 021 274415   **R**

Emmet Place Cork Co Cork   **Map 2 B6**

In the city centre next to the Opera House, this is an offshoot
of the renowned *Ballymaloe House* at Shanagarry. Ballymaloe
desserts, ice cream or petits fours round off a meal whose
centrepiece could be roast loin of pork, duck legs with honey and
rosemary or the day's catch from Ballycotton. Snackier items
include tartine of the day and open sandwiches. Also open for
breakfast. *Seats 70. Private Room 200. Meals 9-5. Closed Sun, Bank
Holidays, 1 week Christmas. Access, Visa.*

Cork   Dan Lowrey's Seafood Tavern

Tel 021 505071

13 MacCurtain Street Cork Co Cork

P

Map 2 B6

A delightfully old-fashioned pub – a perfect place to meet and eat. It's small, with two interconnecting rooms (the one in the back with an open fire) and is now named after a much-lamented local theatre. The pub's history goes back to 1875 and many of the original tavern features have been retained, including the wooden floor and a remarkable mahogany bar unit with unusual shelving and antique bevelled mirrors. The stained-glass windows on the street are also of special interest, as they come from Kilkenny Cathedral. The food is the source of justifiable pride: the bar menu offers an above-average choice of simple soups served with home-made bread (£1.40), salads, seafood or meat platters (£4.50 for ham to £8 for prawn) and a wide selection of sandwiches – fresh, toasted or open (£1.40-£1.60) – but it is the emphasis on the home-made and attention to detail (such as the freshest prawns, served only when available, and home-made cocktail sauce) which make this place special. Apple pie with cream (95p) completes the picture. Directly opposite *Isaacs* restaurant. *Open 10.30am-11.30pm, Sun 12.30-2, 5-11.* **Bar Food** *12-3 (not Sun).* *No credit cards.*

Cork   Fitzpatrick Silver Springs   65%

£109

Tel 021 507533   Fax 021 507641

Tivoli Cork Co Cork

H

Map 2 B6

On the side of a steep hill overlooking the river and the main Dublin road, about 2 miles out of town, the modern Silver Springs is also a major convention centre with a large, up-to-date facility built in 1990 a little further up the hill above the hotel (banqueting for 750, conferences up to 850). Even further up the hill are an extensive leisure centre and nine-hole golf course. Within, the public areas are spacious and include a large public bar with live music from Thursday to Sunday evenings. Recently refurbished bedrooms, all double-glazed, have lightwood fitted furniture, good easy chairs and practical bathrooms. 'Club' rooms are larger and there are two 'full' and three 'junior' antique-furnished suites. 24hr room service. Children under 5 share their parents' room at no charge – 5-12s £5. No dogs. *Rooms 109.* *Garden, indoor swimming pool, gymnasium, aerobic studio, solarium, sauna, spa bath, steam room, 9-hole golf course, squash, indoor & outdoor tennis, snooker, helipad, courtesy coach, creche, indoor children's play area. Closed 24 & 25 Dec.* AMERICAN EXPRESS *Access, Diners, Visa.*

Cork   Flemings

£55

Tel 021 821621   Fax 021 821800

Silver Grange House Tivoli Cork Co Cork

RR

Map 2 B6

Just a short drive from Cork on the Dublin road, Flemings is a large Georgian family house standing in five acres of gardens. Those acres include a kitchen garden which provides much of the fruit, vegetables and herbs needed in the restaurant, a light, handsome double room with marble fireplaces, comfortably upholstered chairs and well-dressed waiters. Michael Fleming's

cooking is French, his menus sometimes fractured French with
English translations: poached salmon in filo pastry with
champagne sauce, smoked duck confit with herbs and nuts, pan-
fried fillets of pork with a mushroom mousseline and a symphony
of seafood with chive sauce. Always a roast at Sunday lunchtime.
Not a lengthy wine list, but it's full of choice bottles and the best
growers. *Seats 50. Parties 22. Private Room 36. L 12.30-2.30
D 6.30-10.30. Set L £12.50 Set D £20. Closed Good Friday, 24-26
Dec.* AMERICAN EXPRESS® *Access, Diners, Visa.*

Rooms   £55

Accommodation is available in four spacious rooms, comfortably
furnished in a style appropriate to the age and graciousness of the
house. All have en-suite bathrooms. *Garden.*

Cork   **Forte Travelodge**   £45

Tel 021 310722 Fax 021 310707	**H**

Jct South Ring Road/Kinsale Road Cork Airport Blackash Co Cork   **Map 2 B6**

Spacious accommodation for two or adequate space for a family
of five at a room rate of £31.95 (without breakfast) 1½ miles
south of Cork city centre on the main airport road and 1 mile
from it. Well-maintained, scrupulously clean pre-paid rooms have
neat bathrooms, tea/coffee-making facilities, TV and radio/alarm.
Pay phones in foyer. *Rooms 40.* AMERICAN EXPRESS® *Access, Visa.*

JAMESON®
IRISH WHISKEY

Cork   **The Gingerbread House**

Tel 021 276411 Fax 021 646147	**JaB**

Paul Street Cork Co Cork   **Map 2 B6**

Recently resited from their previous location in Frenchurch Street,
Barnaby and Colleen Blacker's Gingerbread House has moved
up several gears at once and now offers barbecue and casserole
meals in the evening. Nevertheless, our current recommendation
is for their home-baked cakes like carrot, French chocolate, praline
and lemon (all at £1 a slice), sausage rolls (£1.80 for two), soup,
quiche (£2.60) and Cornish pasties (baked fresh every morning
£2.60). Home-made jams and preserves to take away. Good
cafetière coffee. Ideal for taking a break from a hectic day's
shopping. They may or may not open on Sundays according
to trade. *Seats 75. Open 9-6.30 for snacks, 6.30-10pm for meals.
Closed Bank Holidays. No credit cards.*

Cork	Harolds Restaurant	£55

Tel 021 361613 **R**

Douglas Cork Co Cork   **Map 2 B6**

When chef Harold Lynch and front-of-house partner Beth
Haughton opened this stylish little place just off the busiest
shopping area of Douglas, in August 1993, it was an instant hit.
The interesting modern interior – unusual paintings by a local
artist, clever lighting, striking mirrors, arty floral arrangements
and well-furnished tables with cloths, fine glasses, pottery butter
dishes but bentwood chairs and paper napkins – sets the right tone
for Harold's lively Cal Ital-influenced food. On a sensibly limited,
moderately priced à la carte menu, old favourites like twice-baked
cheese soufflé jostle for space with starters like warm salad
of smoked chicken with sun-dried tomatoes, pine nuts, parmesan
shavings and balsamic dressing or tapas. Likewise main courses
range from reassuringly familiar, perfectly cooked noisettes
of spring lamb with warm mint dressing through fish of the day –
a gleaming white fillet of John Dory, perhaps, on a light buttery
sauce – to a vegetarian option like fettucine with wild and fresh
mushrooms. Desserts favour classics with a modern twist – crème
brulée with plum salad, perhaps – and there's always a selection
of Irish farmhouse cheeses. Delicious brown soda bread, good
coffee by the cup. *Seats 51. D only 6-10. Closed 24 & 25 Dec.
Access, Visa.*

Cork	Imperial Hotel	66%	£121

Tel 021 274040   Fax ext 2507 **H**

South Mall Cork Co Cork   **Map 2 B6**

On the main commercial and banking street of town the
Imperial's neo-classical facade conceals something of a mixture
of styles. The marble-floored lobby and some of the bedroom
corridors, which feature a number of fine antiques, retain their
original 19th-century grandeur, the cocktail bar (with nightly
pianist) and restaurant have been given a 1930s' theme and the
public bar remembers Cork's history as a shipbuilding centre.
Bedrooms, apart from a few that are furnished with antiques
in traditional style, are determinedly modern with white fitted
units, glass and chrome coffee tables and contemporary lights.
About half the rooms have novel wall-mounted 'clothes grooming
cabinets' that are designed to deodorise and dewrinkle garments.
12 of the bathrooms have shower and WC only. Room service
is available but not advertised. Secure covered parking for about
80 cars, three minutes' walk from the hotel. *Rooms 100.
Closed 1 week at Christmas.* AMERICAN EXPRESS *Access, Diners, Visa.*

Cork	Isaacs	£35

Tel 021 503805 **R**

48 MacCurtain Street Cork Co Cork   **Map 2 B6**

An 18th-century warehouse has been carefully adapted into a fine
restaurant serving an eclectic menu conceived by chef Canice
Sharkey. Lunchtime brings some snacky items (French bread with
ham, cheese and pickle, bruschetta or selection of salads) but
otherwise a fairly similar selection to the evening, including
perhaps grilled chicken with tomatoes cream and basil, salmon

and potato cakes, grilled king prawns and sirloin steak with
rosemary and garlic potatoes. Sauternes and olive oil cake with
winter fruit salad is an intriguing dessert. Short vegetarian menu.
Seats 100. *Parties 30. L 12-2.30 D 6.30-10.30. Closed L Sun, 5 days
Christmas.* AMERICAN EXPRESS *Access, Diners, Visa.*

Cork	**Ivory Tower Restaurant**	£55
Tel 021 274665		**R**
35 Princes Street Cork Co Cork		Map 2 B6

Situated in the first-floor front of a period office building just off
one of Cork's main shopping streets. The atmosphere is friendly
and informal – bare-board floor, unclothed tables, work of local
artists on the walls – and chef-patron Seamus O'Connell's cooking
is certainly individualistic. Try skate and spinach gratin with
lemon and caper nut butter or mussel walnut and pepper chowder
to start and conger eel boudin, scallops and prawns in saffron sauce
or breast of wild duck with a white peach glaze for main course.
There are always several vegetarian options – vegetable sushi and
Korean pickled cabbage. Lunch prices are lower than in the
evening. Two or three home-made breads vary from day to day.
5% 'plastic charge'. *Seats 35. L 12-4 D 6.30-11. Set D varies, from
£15. Closed Sun & Mon (except Bank Holidays), 25-29 Dec.
Access, Visa.*

Cork	**Jacques**	£55
Tel 021 277387 Fax 021 270634		**R**
9 Phoenix Street Cork Co Cork		Map 2 B6

Jacqueline and Eithne Barry have transformed their popular,
centrally located restaurant from a comfortable but unremarkable
place to a dashing modern bistro, vibrant and colourful – lovely
deep pumpkin oranges and yellows, sweeping curvaceous lines and
contemporary art. Along with the obvious, this change of style
brought table service to replace the lunchtime self-service – but
they haven't abandoned their successful formula on the food side:
bruschetta with green salad, warm salads – of lamb's kidneys,
crispy bacon, orange and croutons perhaps – or chicken breast
with lemon, garlic, ginger, potato and greens are still typical fare.
*Seats 60. Parties 20. L 11.30-3 D 6-10.30. Closed D Mon, all Sun,
Bank Holidays, 10 days Christmas.* AMERICAN EXPRESS *Access,
Diners, Visa.*

Cork	**Jurys Cork Inn**	60%	£55
Tel 021 276444			**H**
Anderson's Quay Cork Co Cork			Map 2 B6

The latest Jurys budget hotel opened in 1994 in a central riverside
site. Like the other inns, room prices include accommodation for
up to four (including a sofa bed) and there is space for a cot.
Although there are no frills, simple design and good-quality
furnishings combine to provide maximum comfort at the
minimum price: not only ample open wardrobe and
writing/dressing space, well-placed mirrors and lighting but also
phone, TV, cleverly designed built-in tea/coffee facilities and neat,
well-lit bathrooms with full (if unusually small) bath, shower and
the necessary toiletries. No room service. Cots, extra beds and

high-chairs available by arrangement. Seven rooms are equipped for disabled guests. Limited parking (27 spaces), but there is an arrangement with a nearby car park. *Rooms 133. Café/restaurant 7-10am, 6-9.30pm. Closed 24-28 Dec.* AMERICAN EXPRESS *Access, Diners, Visa.*

Cork	Jurys Hotel	66%	£140
Tel 021 276622 Fax 021 274477			H
Western Road Cork Co Cork			Map 2 B6

Modern low-rise riverside hotel about half a mile from the centre of town on the Killarney road. Public areas include a choice of two bars, both with live music nightly: the convivial, pubby Corks Bar that is popular with locals and a cocktail bar with waterfall feature in the open-plan, split-level restaurant area. Decor in the well-kept bedrooms is gradually being changed from abstract to more appealing floral patterns with matching curtains and quilted bedcovers. TVs are multi-channel with the remote controls rather annoyingly wired to the bedside units. Extras include fruit and mineral water. Good, well-lit bathrooms all have vanity units, sometimes in white marble, offering good shelf space. Room service is 24hr and beds are turned down at night. Conference/banqueting facilities for 700/520. No dogs. *Rooms 185. Garden, indoor & outdoor swimming pool, children's splash pool, keep-fit equipment, sauna, spa bath, squash. Coffee shop (7am-11pm). Closed 24-26 Dec.* AMERICAN EXPRESS *Access, Diners, Visa.*

Cork	Lotamore House	60%	£48
Tel 021 822344			A
Tivoli Cork Co Cork			Map 2 B6

Once the home of the Cudmore family, a large house only a few minutes' drive from the city centre, set in mature gardens which soften the view over what is now a commercial harbour. Although not grand, the house was built on a large scale with airy bedrooms that have slightly dated but well-maintained bathrooms and are comfortably furnished to sleep three, with room for an extra bed or cot (no extra charge). A large drawing room has plenty of armchairs and an open fire and, although only breakfast and light meals are offered, *Fleming's Restaurant* (see entry) is next door. Conference facilities for up to 20. *Rooms 20. Garden. Closed 2 weeks Christmas.* AMERICAN EXPRESS *Access, Diners, Visa.*

Cork	Lovetts		£75
Tel 021 294909 Fax 021 508568			R
Churchyard Lane off Well Road Douglas Cork Co Cork			Map 2 B6

Dermod Lovett continues to make guests feel welcome in the cosy bar and reception area of this well-established restaurant and to keep a close eye on proceedings throughout and, while Margaret Lovett and Marie Harding's extensive and carefully sourced menus for the main restaurant remain, their new brasserie was just opening on our most recent visit and understandably claiming the limelight. Chargrills are the speciality there, with limited but carefully selected regulars – chicken, gammon, steak and salmon – cooked in front of diners and served with salad and potatoes; limited starters/soups and desserts, plus a keen pricing policy complete the formula. Bar lunches (soups, pasta, stir-fries, quiches, casseroles); times as restaurant. *Seats 45. Parties 14. Private Room 25. L 12.30-2 D 7-9.45. Closed L Sat, all Sun, Bank Holidays, 23-30 Dec. Set L £14.50 Set D £21.* AMERICAN EXPRESS® *Access, Diners, Visa.*

Cork	**Metropole Hotel**	58%	£85
Tel 021 508122 Fax 021 506450			**H**
MacCurtain Street Cork Co Cork			Map 2 B6

Recent refurbishment has given the 100-year-old 'Met' a new lease of life. That the hotel is the epicentre of Cork's annual jazz festival is reflected in the numerous photos and sketches of the stars who have performed here displayed in the bar. On the bedroom front it is only those on the top two floors that we recommend, those being the ones that have been refurbished, partly with dark stained pine furniture (some retain the old units revamped); they all have good bathrooms that although brand new are given a period feel by the tiling, wood-panelled tub and generously sized, chunky wash basins. Bedroom size and shape varies considerably and the view from some is a bit grim. The best have views over the River Lee as it flows through the centre of town. 24hr room service. Banqueting for 320, conference facilities for 550. The latest addition is a leisure centre with swimming pool, gym and sauna. No dogs. *Rooms 108. Indoor swimming pool, gym, sauna.* AMERICAN EXPRESS® *Access, Diners, Visa.*

Cork	**Michael's Bistro**		£45
Tel 021 276887			**R**
4 Mardyke Street Cork Co Cork			Map 2 B6

Situated next door to Michael Clifford's eponymous restaurant (see entry), with its entrance around the corner and its own separate (but communicating) kitchen under the supervision of Michael, the new bistro's colour scheme alone, with its violets, pinks and black, would alert afficionados to the common ownership. The air-conditioned Bistro is smaller and more intimate, however, seating a couple of dozen on smart black chairs at rather small tables plus an extra four on stools at a little bar by the door (better for a drink while waiting for a table); prints of food photographs from Michael's cookery book line the walls and the menu is much more informal, incorporating starters like casserole of wood pigeon, shallots and bacon, a stew of Clonakilty black pudding, flageolet beans and home-made sausages or a daily soup. Main courses are homely, typically Michael's 'gourmet' Irish stew (Michael wins our 1995 Irish Food Award for his creative use of all Irish food products) served with boiled potatoes, or braised chicken with cabbage and onions on a puréed potato bed, home-made hamburger or good steaks; seafood and game feature when they're at their best. Desserts might include a nicely gooey caramelised banana *c*repe with butterscotch sauce, chocolate roulade with fresh fruit or an Irish cheese plate. *Seats 25. L 12-3 D 6-10.30. Closed Sun, Mon, Bank Holidays, 1 week Aug, 1 week Christmas. Access, Visa.*

Cork   Morrisons Island Hotel   68%   £123
Tel 021 275858   Fax 021 275833   **H**
Morrisons Quay Cork Co Cork   **Map 2 B6**

Overlooking the River Lee, in Cork's business district, this 'all-suite' hotel – in France it would be called a *hotel résidence* – is designed for the business person with each suite having a separate lounge (with kitchenette): ideal for meeting or entertaining. Actually four are junior suites (large rooms with separate sitting area) without the kitchenette and there are four larger penthouse suites with balconies and completely separate kitchens, two with two bedrooms. Decorwise it's fairly simple with lightwood units in the bedrooms and darkwood in the sitting rooms with tweedy soft furnishings. Downstairs there's a smart marble-floored lobby and cosy bar that with several sofas doubles as a lounge area. Room service is 24hr, as is porterage, and there is free secure parking. No dogs. **Rooms** 40. *Closed 4 days at Christmas.*
 Access, Diners, Visa.

Cork   Quay Co-op
Tel 021 317660   **JaB**
24 Sullivan's Quay Cork Co Cork   **Map 2 B6**

A former priest house by the River Lee near the city centre, this vegetarian restaurant occupies several period rooms on the two floors above a wholefood shop – the stairway walls acting as a notice-board for events and organisations in the city. Work by local artists features on the peach-coloured walls and there are bare board floors. From opening there's tea, coffee (including espresso), cakes and croissants until 12.30 when the self-service lunch counter opens. This features a selection of pizzas (£3.40), lasagne (£3.90) and daily specials like Thai chili and rice (£3.90). Soups might include lentil and apricot or drunken mushroom (both £1.40) and come with organic wholemeal bread. For the sweet-toothed there's chocolate cake, lemon sponge, apple pie and the like. From 6pm the mood changes and there is table service from a printed menu – tempura vegetables (£2.70), nachos (£2.50), traditional nut roast with chestnut stuffing and gravy (£5.90), spinach and ricotta cannelloni (£4.90) and pear and almond tart with coconut-ginger cream (£2) demonstrate the range. Children can have smaller portions at reduced prices – there is just a single high-chair. About a dozen wines are offered (just the house wine by the glass) or you can bring your own for a corkage charge (£1.80). Two of the three rooms are no-smoking. **Seats** 80. *Meals 9.30am-10.30pm (from 1pm Sun). Closed 25 & 26 Dec, Good Friday, Easter Sunday. Access, Visa.*

Cork   Reidy's Wine Vaults
Tel 021 275751   **P**
Lancaster Quay Western Road Cork Co Cork   **Map 2 B6**

Imaginatively converted from a wine warehouse (and conveniently situated just opposite the entrance to *Jurys Hotel*), Reidy's is quite large and stylish, with vaulted ceilings, a minstrel's gallery housing country antiques, dark green and terracotta paintwork, traditional black-and-white tiles and a pleasing mixture

of old and new furnishings. The focal point is the main bar fixture
– a massive mahogany piece, complete with a London clock,
bevelled mirrors, stained glass and all the original Victorian
details. Bar food is prepared to a high standard by Noelle Reidy,
starting with bread and quiches baked on the premises in the early
morning and with choices noted on the blackboard as the day
progresses. The menu dishes might typically include steak and
kidney pie, Irish stew (£4.95), chicken curry (£4.95), steak and
kidney pie or lasagne (both £4.95), savoury pancakes (chicken and
mushroom £3.95) and seafood platter (£8). Sandwiches and
home-made soup (£1.50) also available. Children are welcome "as
long as they are well behaved" (but not after 7pm). *Open 10.30am-
11.30pm (winter to 11), Sun 12.30-2 & 4-11.* **Bar Food** *10.30am-
10.30pm. Closed 25 Dec, Good Friday.* AMERICAN EXPRESS *Access,
Diners, Visa.*

Cork	Rochestown Park Hotel	67%	£85
Tel 021 892233 Fax 021 892178			**H**
Rochestown Road Douglas Cork Co Cork			Map 2 B6

Take the south ring road to Douglas and keep a sharp lookout for
the hotel's signs (they're small and brown) to find the bright
yellow building. Public rooms are in the original Georgian house,
formerly a seminary for trainee priests and once home to the Lord
Mayors of Cork, with bedrooms in modern extensions. Standard
bedrooms have been designed with the business person very much
in mind and have practical fitted furniture including a well-lit
desk with a second phone. Extras include mineral water, bowl
of fruit, mints and towelling robes in bathrooms that all boast
bidets. Twenty Executive rooms are very large and have spa
baths. Public areas include comfortable sitting areas off the
marble-floored lobby, a bar with rattan-furnished conservatory
and a snug residents' bar for late-night drinkers. The hotel's pride
and joy is a most impressive leisure centre. Seven acres of mature
gardens are open to residents. No dogs. **Rooms** *63. Garden, indoor
swimming pool, children's splash pool, gymnasium, solarium, sauna, spa
bath, steam room, hydro-massage pool, aerobics studio, thalassotherapy
clinic.* AMERICAN EXPRESS *Access, Diners, Visa.*

Cork	Seven North Mall		£60
Tel 021 397191 Fax 021 300811			**A**
7 North Mall Cork Co Cork			Map 2 B6

This elegant house dating from 1750 belongs to the family
of Cork city architect Neil Hegarty and is run by his wife,
Angela, who offers guests tea on arrival. It's centrally situated on a
tree-lined south-facing mall overlooking the River Lee. Rooms are
all spacious, individually furnished in a pleasingly restrained style
in keeping with the house itself and with bathrooms cleverly
added to look as if they have always been there. Some rooms have
river views and there is a ground-floor room especially designed
for disabled guests. Excellent breakfasts. A nice touch is the
provision for each guest personalised map of the city centre, which
shows clearly all the best restaurants, pubs, museums, galleries and
theatres, mostly conveniently near. **Rooms** *5. Closed 9 Dec-15 Jan.
Access, Visa.*

Cork   Places of Interest

Tourist Information Tel 021 273251
Bus Eirann (Irish Bus) Booking Information Tel 021 508188
Jazz Festival (end Oct) Tel 021 270463
The Queenstown Story Cobh Tel 021 813591
Jameson Heritage Centre Midleton Tel 021 613594
Triskell Arts Centre off South Main Street Tel 021 272022
Crawford School of Art and Gallery Emmet Place Tel 021 966777
GAA Athletic Grounds Pairc Chaoimh Tel 021 963311
Cork City Gaol Tel 021 542478
Church of St Francis Liberty Street
St Finbarre's Cathedral Sharman Crawford Street
St Colman's Cathedral Cobh
Everyman Palace MacCurtain Street Tel 021 501673
Opera House Emmet Place Tel 021 270022
  Historic Houses, Castles and Gardens
Blarney Castle House and Gardens Tel 021 385252
Dunkathel Glanmire Tel 021 821014 *4 miles*
Riverstown House Glanmire Tel 021 821205 *4 miles*
Fota Wildlife Park Carrigtwohill nr Cobh Tel 021 812678

Courtmacsherry   Courtmacsherry Hotel   £65
Tel 023 46198   **H**
Courtmacsherry Co Cork   Map 2 B6

Family-run by Terry and Carole Adams since 1973, this
unpretentious, homely hotel offers simple comfort and a relaxed
atmosphere. Public areas are quite spacious, if somewhat dated,
and, although on the small side, all bedrooms have TV and direct-
dial phones and most are now en-suite. Traditional family holiday
activities are well catered for, with boats and bikes available
nearby, lawn tennis in the grounds and also Carole's riding school
where many children happily spend most of their holiday time.
Accommodation is also available in new on-site self-catering
cottages, furnished to a high standard. **Rooms** 14. *Garden, tennis.
Closed end Oct-Easter. Access, Visa.*

Crookhaven   O'Sullivan's
Tel 028 35200   **P**
Crookhaven Co Cork   Map 2 A6

One of the most popular traditional pubs in Ireland, sited beside
the delightful little sandy-beached harbour at 'Crook'. O'Sullivan's
has been family-run for 20 years and nowadays it's run by Billie
and Angela O'Sullivan, who somehow successfully combine the
function of providing a proper local for the lobster fishermen and
the kind of pub dreams are made of for families on holiday. The
stone-flagged bar is practical for sandy feet and parents can easily
keep an eye on castle-builders when the tide is right. Angela looks
after the food herself, making soups and chowders, bread and
good, simple dishes based on local seafood – fresh and smoked
salmon, smoked mackerel, crab or shrimps – and moreish home-
made ices or apple crumble. Six tables are almost on the water's
edge. Live solo music every night in summer. Next door, the
Welcome Inn, under the same ownership, has a restaurant
in summer (July & August) and two self-contained apartments

to let (not inspected). *Open 10.30am-11.30pm, Sun 12-2 & 4-11.*
*Bar Food 10.30-9 (Sun 12-2 & 4-9). Closed Monday afternoons
in winter (Nov-May). No credit cards.*

Crosshaven   Cronin's Bar
Tel 021 831207   Fax 021 832243   **P**

Crosshaven Co Cork   **Map 2 B6**

Lots of wood, soft furnishings in country prints and selected bric-
a-brac create a homely atmosphere at this welcoming bar
overlooking the marina, but the real point of interest is a great
collection of pictures, prints and photographs of local interest,
notably maritime history. Excellent food is made on the premises
by owner Sean Cronin's Dutch wife, Thecla, from snacky
sandwiches (£1.30-£3.50, open brown sandwiches made with
soda bread are a speciality – try the rare roast beef or 'rasher
special') and salads (ploughman's £2.95, wild smoked salmon
£6.25) to evening seafood specials (large 'Dublin Bay' prawns are
very popular – they're actually caught off the west and south
Cork coast!) and steaks (£9/£12). Children are welcome and
there's a dining area at the back especially suitable for family
meals. A self-catering cottage is available (not inspected). *Open
10.30am-11.30pm, Sun 12.30-2 & 4-11. Bar Food 11-3 & 6-8 (3-6
soup and sandwiches only, summer bar food to 6). Sunday coffee and
scones only. Access, Visa.*

Crossmolina   Enniscoe House   63%   £88
Tel 096 31112   Fax 096 31773   **A**

Castlehill nr Crossmolina Ballina Co Mayo   **Map 1 B3**

Generations of the same family have lived here on the shores
of Lough Conn since the 17th century and the mature woodland,
antique furniture and family portraits all contribute to today's
enjoyment of Irish hospitality and country house life. The current
owner, Susan Kellett, has established a Research and Heritage
Centre in converted yard buildings behind the house. One service
offered by the Centre is tracing family histories. The main
bedrooms have four-posters or canopied beds and fine views
of park and lake. *Rooms 6. Garden, game fishing.*
Closed mid Oct-end Mar. AMERICAN EXPRESS *Access, Visa.*

Culdaff   McGuinness's
Tel 077 79116   **P**

Culdaff Inish Owen Co Donegal   **Map 1 C1**

Just the kind of place the traveller might hope to happen upon,
this traditional country pub has been in the McGuinness family
for generations (albeit some under different names) and always has
a welcoming turf fire burning in the public bar. This is simply
furnished in a pleasant way with plain furniture, old prints, plates
and notices of local interest. Next door, a comfortable lounge bar
has great appeal, with homely, chintzy sofas, cushioned chairs and
a nice old-fashioned conservatory on the back of the pub with
a few more tables leading on to the small back garden. Food
requirements other than very simple snacks are dealt with in a
practical way – by telephoning orders to the village restaurant,
which is under the same ownership. The bar also acts as an off-

licence, so a variety of wines can be served by the glass. Well-behaved children are welcome during the day, but they "must be kept under control". *Open 10.30am-11.30pm, Sun 12.30-2, 4-11. Garden. Visa.*

Dalkey   The Queens

Tel 01 285 4569   Fax 01 285 8345

Castle Street Dalkey Co Dublin

P

Map 2 D4

One of South Dublin's most famous pubs, The Queens is a characterful and extremely professionally run operation, with open fires, old pine and whiskey jars creating atmosphere and friendly, efficient staff dispensing good food and drink.The bar menu features sandwiches (closed or open), ploughman's salads, paté and a very popular seafood chowder and garlicky mussels. Sunday brunch fry-up is £4.95. There's also an Italian restaurant, La Romana (and a sister pub in Budapest!). *Open 10.30am-11.30pm, Sun 12-11.* **Bar Food** *12-6 (Sun brunch menu 12-3).* **Restaurant Meals** *5.30-11. Children allowed in bar to eat until 6.30pm only. Front and back patios. Closed Good Friday, 25 & 26 Dec. Access, Visa.*

Delgany   Glenview Hotel   63%   £90

Tel 01 287 3399   Fax 01 287 7511

Glen o' the Downs Delgany Co Wicklow

H

Map 2 D4

The glen in the name is Glen o' the Downs, and the views of it are dramatic from this hotel standing in 30 acres of gardens beneath Sugarloaf Mountain. The building encompasses a conference area with state-of-the-art facilities (catering for up to 300) at one end and extra bedrooms at the other. Well-equipped bedrooms have tea and coffee-making facilities, hairdryer and trouser press as standard and children under 5 stay free in parents' room. A new leisure centre with swimming pool, gymnasium, steam room and jacuzzi was due to be finished by March 1995. **Rooms** *37. Garden.* AMERICAN EXPRESS *Access, Diners, Visa.*

Delgany   The Wicklow Arms

Tel 01 287 4611   Fax 01 287 3878

Delgany Co Wicklow

P

Map 2 D4

A friendly, well-maintained pub that's a popular weekend spot with Dubliners and visitors alike. Practicalities are well thought out, with a sensibly designed car park backing on to an attractively planted seating area which leads down to the back bar. Inside, the atmosphere is comfortable no-nonsense, with plenty of space to relax and enjoy generous, unpretentious food from the lounge menu, such as open sandwiches served with salad (from £5.48), paté, seafood chowder, garlicky mussels or breaded mushrooms (£2.98), and hot main courses served with chips (boiled potatoes or side salad for calorie-counters): grilled salmon (£8.78), chicken Kiev (£5.18). Finish with a lemon cheesecake or home-made ice cream (£2.25). A long wine list includes 40 half bottles. *Pub hours 6-11.30 (Sat from 2, Sun 12-11).* **Bar Food** *7-10.15 (Sat from 6, Sun & Bank Hols 12.30-9). Children allowed in bar to eat. Garden. Closed Good Friday, 25 & 26 Dec.* AMERICAN EXPRESS *Access, Diners, Visa.*

Dingle   Beginish Restaurant   £55

Tel 066 51588   Fax 066 51591   **R**

Green Street Dingle Co Kerry   Map 2 A5

Two lofty rooms provide the main seating here, while a small
conservatory overlooking the lovely garden can be used as a
private room. The restaurant takes its name from one of the
Blasket islands and is a comfortable spot for enjoying the talents
of Pat Moore. Her menu leans heavily towards seafood, the final
choice depending on the day's catch and her own inspiration.
Typical items on the dinner carte run from smoked mackerel paté
and mussels beurre blanc to grilled wild salmon, turbot with olive
oil-scented potato purée and a chive sauce, and pan-fried
medallions of monkfish with herb crust and fennel sauce. Some
meat choices, too, and delicious desserts like choux puff with fresh
fruit or rhubarb soufflé tart. Good farmhouse cheese selection.
Seats 34. L 12.30-2.15 D 6-10. Closed Mon and all mid Nov-mid
Mar. Access, Visa.

Dingle   Dick Mack's

No Telephone   **P**

Green Lane Dingle Co Kerry   Map 2 A5

Amazingly unspoilt shop-bar, once a cobbler's, now selling
modern leather items and wellington boots. Basic bar,
no pretensions. The cashier's booth remains as a snug and
all is as it should be. *No credit cards.*

Dingle   Dingle Skellig Hotel   61%   £109

Tel 066 51144   Fax 066 51501   **H**

Dingle Co Kerry   Map 2 A5

Pleasant, practical and comfortable behind its unprepossessing
60s' facade, the Dingle Skellig is a popular place with families
on holiday. Children are very well looked after, and there's also
plenty to keep grown-ups active and amused. The sea views
are quite a feature, and there's special anti-glare glass in the
conservatory restaurant. Bedrooms are of a reasonable size, with
several designated for family occupation. No dogs. *Rooms 110.*
Garden, indoor swimming pool, sauna, tennis, games room, snooker,
deep-sea fishing. Closed mid Nov-mid Mar. *Access,*
Diners, Visa.

Dingle   Doyle's Seafood Bar   £65

Tel 066 51174   Fax 066 51816   **RR**

4 John Street Dingle Co Kerry   Map 2 A5

Established in the 70s, before Dingle became fashionable (or,
indeed, very profitable) John and Stella Doyle's delightfully
informal seafood restaurant has lost none of its charm or freshness
– John is still a lively host with a knack for anticipating his guests'
every need, while Stella continues to cook the wonderful dishes
that are the basis of their undiminished reputation. Start, perhaps,
with a house speciality like millefeuille of warm oysters in a

Guinness sauce – an inspired dish of gently heated oysters resting in a silky sauce of wonderfully rich yeasty tones topped with a featherlight cap of golden-brown puff pastry. Then hot poached lobster would be hard to resist, perfectly cooked and served with magnificent simplicity, with just a hot butter sauce; or, perhaps, a platter of seafood – not only a selection of mixed seafood – crab claws, sole, salmon etc – but including half a lobster as its centrepiece. There's much else besides, including roast rack of Kerry lamb as a gesture to carnivores (vegetarian dishes by arrangement at time of booking). Round off with Irish farmhouse cheeses, or a lovely dessert such as deliciously simple meringue with raspberry purée and some freshly brewed coffee. Carefully selected list of interesting wines. *Seats 50. Parties 8. D only 6-9. Closed Sun, mid Nov-mid Mar. Set D (6-7pm) £13.50. Access, Diners, Visa.*

Rooms £62

Excellent accommodation is offered in eight stylishly decorated rooms furnished with antiques (and luxurious bathrooms) and a residents' sitting room. John Doyle takes personal pride in preparing breakfasts including the restaurant's own smoked salmon (also available to take away) served with scrambled free-range eggs.

Dingle	Greenmount House	£40
Tel 066 51414 Fax 066 51974		A
Greenmount Dingle Co Kerry		Map 2 A5

John and Mary Curran's neat modern guesthouse views over Dingle enjoys an enviable reputation for hospitality, comfort, excellent housekeeping and outstanding breakfasts, which are served in a stylish conservatory overlooking the harbour. Individually decorated rooms all have new bathrooms (shower only), direct-dial telephones and many thoughtful touches including electric blankets, TVs, clock radios, hairdryers, fresh fruit and flowers. Six luxury suites are scheduled for completion before May 1995. No children under 8 years. No dogs. Own parking. *Rooms 8. Garden. Closed 20-28 Dec. Access, Visa.*

Dingle	The Half Door	£55
Tel 066 51600 Fax 066 51206		R
John Street Dingle Co Kerry		Map 2 A5

Cosy and welcoming, with a genuine cottage atmosphere enhanced by exposed stone walls, copper pots and original white tiles around the chimney breast. There's a sunny conservatory area to the rear. Denis O'Connor's menu majors on seafood, so the choice varies with the season and the catch. Shellfish cocktail, steamed mussels, or sautéed oysters masked with a chive sauce could be your starter, followed perhaps by grilled brill, boiled lobster or fillet of plaice with mustard sauce. Good simple sweets. *Seats 50. Parties 14. Private Room 20. L 12.30-2.30 D 6-10. Set L £8, Set D £17. Closed Tue, also mid Nov-mid Dec & early Jan-Easter.* *Access, Diners, Visa.*

Dingle   James Flahive

Tel 066 51634   **P**

The Quay Dingle Co Kerry   Map 2 A5

Down by the harbour near the marina, this comfortable,
welcoming and most friendly of pubs has been run by James and
Peggy Flahive (Gregory Peck is her cousin, but don't tell anyone,
now will you?) for 30 years. It's a great favourite of sailing people.
Photographs of distinguished visitors adorn the walls but none
is more proudly displayed than that of Dingle's best-loved resident,
Fungie the dolphin. No food, but you're assured of a good pint
of Guinness. *Open 10.30am-11.30pm, Sun 12-2 & 4-11.*
No credit cards.

Dingle   Lord Baker's Bar & Restaurant   £60

Tel 066 51277   **R**

Main Street Dingle Co Kerry   Map 2 A5

Tom Baker – businessman, councillor, auctioneer and poet, and
affectionately known as Lord Baker – acquired these premises
in 1890 and they've gradually developed from general supplier
and function caterer to a popular and thriving restaurant and bar.
Locally made tapestries are an eye-catching display in the main
eating area, beyond which is a conservatory extension leading into
the garden. The full restaurant menu and the less formal bar menu
offer similar choices from seafood soup, garlic prawns and chicken
liver paté to seafood mornay and steaks. Particularly favoured for
Sunday lunch. *Seats 65. Parties 20. L 12.30-2.30 D 6-9.30.*
Closed 24 & 25 Dec. Set D £16.50. AMERICAN EXPRESS *Access,*
Diners, Visa.

Dingle   O'Flaherty's

Tel 066 51461   **P**

Bridge Street Dingle Co Kerry   Map 2 A5

Large square room, high-ceilinged, with flagstones, a stove, barrel
tables, an old piano and masses of old shelving for a collection
of antique signs and local bric-a-brac. Traditional Irish music is the
main attraction, with regular sessions in summer (nightly May-
Sep), other impromptu sessions and occasional bursts on any
instrument you can imagine by landlord Fergus O'Flaherty.
Access to the harbour from the back of the bar. No food.
Open 10.30am-11.30pm, Sun 12-2 & 4-11. Closed Good Friday,
25 Dec. No credit cards.

Dingle   Tigh Mhaire de Barra

Tel 066 51215   **P**

The Pier Head Dingle Co Kerry   Map 2 A5

Since 1989, when Dubliners Mhaire de Barra and Pat Leahy opted
out of the rat race for the "easy" life in Dingle, they've hardly had
a day off between them, but have built up a great reputation with
this harbourside pub. It's unpretentiously comfortable, without the
olde-world charm of some other establishments in the area but
with, instead, the solid attractions of real hospitality, good food

and music. Home-made soups with freshly-baked bread, local
seafood specials, traditional dishes like boiled bacon and cabbage
and Kerry porter cake are typical lunchtime fare, while evening
meals include a range of hot main courses, mostly around £5.
Visit off-season if you can – once the tourists start to disappear, the
famous Dingle Pies return to the menu, much to the delight
of hungry locals. *Open 10.30am-11.30pm. L 12.30-3 D 6.30-8.30.
Closed Good Fri, 25 Dec. No credit cards.*

Dingle   Place of Interest

Great Blasket Island Tel 066 13111

Donegal   St Ernan's House Hotel   70%   £130

Tel 073 21065   Fax 073 22098   **HR**
St Ernan's Island nr Donegal Town Co Donegal   Map 1 B2

Utter tranquillity is the main attraction of Brian and Carmel
O'Dowd's secluded hotel on its own wooded tidal island across
a causeway just two miles from Donegal town. Arriving up the
covered stone entrance steps, with original Victorian glazing and
lots of pot plants, is rather like going through a time capsule –
once inside the foyer at the top, the pressures of modern life fall
away and the deep peacefulness of the island and the gentle
hospitality of its owners begins to work its magic. Well-
proportioned rooms have log fires and antique furniture and each
of the spacious, individually decorated bedrooms has en-suite bath
and shower, telephone and television, while most also have
beautiful views of the sea and surrounding countryside. Not
suitable for children under six. No dogs. ***Rooms** 12. Garden.
Closed 1 Nov-mid April. Access, Visa.*

Restaurant   £65

Although mainly intended for resident guests, Gabrielle Doyle's
5-course country house-style dinner menu is available to non-
residents if there is room. Local produce is used to good effect
on well-balanced menus offering a choice of five dishes for each
course; vegetarian dishes on request. ***Seats** 28. Parties 6. D only
6.30-8.30. Set D £23.50.*

Donegal Town   Ardnamona House   £60

Tel 073 22650   Fax 073 22819   **A**
Lough Eske Donegal Town Co Donegal   Map 1 B2

Beautifully situated in outstanding gardens overlooking Lough
Eske, the secluded position of this attractive, rambling house belies
its close proximity to Donegal town. Front rooms are most
desirable, with lovely views over the lough to the mountains
beyond, but all are individual, with private bathrooms and
a peaceful outlook through rhododendrons and azaleas which have
received international acclaim. It is, in fact, a gardener's paradise
(with a garden trail, guide leaflet and all plants labelled) but this
serene place also offers miles of walks through ancient oak forests
full of mosses and ferns, private boating and fishing on the lake.
No smoking. ***Rooms** 5. Garden, fishing. Closed Christmas &
New Year. Access, Visa.*

Donegal Town   Harvey's Point Country Hotel   63%   £99

Tel 073 22208   Fax 073 22352   **H**

Lough Eske Donegal Town Co Donegal   **Map 1 B2**

Situated in a marvellous location close to Donegal town on the
shores of Lough Eske, Jody Gysling's low-rise, purpose-built hotel
has a predictably Swiss-German atmosphere. The chalet-style
buildings make good use of wood, with pergolas and covered
walkways joining the residential area to the main bars and
restaurants. Views over the lough are lovely and the waterside
location brings an atmosphere of serenity which is emphasised
by the good nature of everybody involved in this family-run
business, ranging from the host himself down to his trusty dogs.
Continental-style rooms, all on the ground floor with direct access
to verandah and gardens, feature show-wood furniture and are
well equipped with satellite TV, video and mini-bars as well
as direct-dial phones, hairdryers, tea/coffee facilities and,
in Executive rooms, four-poster beds and trouser presses.
Banqueting and conference facilities for 200/300. No children
under 10. Easy parking. *Rooms 20. Garden, tennis, fishing.
Closed end Nov-Easter.* AMERICAN EXPRESS *Access, Diners, Visa.*

Dromahair   Stanford's Village Inn

Tel 071 64140   Fax 071 64770   **P**

Dromahair Co Leitrim   **Map 1 B2**

Situated just south of Lough Gill (eleven miles from Sligo) on the
ever beautiful Yeats country route, Stanford's has been in the
McGowan family for five generations and the front bar remains
as a testament to the Irish country pub of yesteryear – not
a sentimental reconstruction, but the real thing. Elsewhere in this
fisherman's hideaway, there are comfortable bars with fires and
good, simple fare (home-made soup £1, Irish stew £3.50, salads
from £6.50, sandwiches from 80p) and a 36-seat restaurant
(straightforward 3-course lunches £6.50, 4-course dinners £12)
for those who prefer to sit at a table. Sunday lunch £6.50. Our
recommendation is currently only for bar food. Live music
on summer Saturday or Monday nights. Modest accommodation
is also offered in five rooms (£28, one family room £45, not
inspected, but Bord Fáilte Irish Tourist Board approved). *Open
10.30am-11.30pm, Sun 12.30-2 & 4-11. **Bar Food** 11am-10pm,
Sun 11-2 & 4-10. Children allowed in bar to eat, children's menu, one
high-chair provided. Garden, outdoor eating, private fishing.
Closed 25 Dec, bar closed Good Friday. Access, Visa.*

Drumcliff   Yeats Tavern & Davis's Pub

Tel 071 63117   **P**

Drumcliff Co Sligo   **Map 1 B2**

Efficiently run, sympathetically modernised Yeats country pub
beside Drumcliffe River. The bar menu holds few surprises, but
there's plenty of variety, from vegetable soup, garlic mushrooms
and barbecue ribs to home-made burgers, omelettes, chicken
(breaded, Kiev, Maryland, curry), cod, plaice, salads and omelettes;
poached salmon hollandaise (£4.95), bacon and cabbage (£4) and
braised steak (£4.50) might also be on offer. Also snacks

of sandwiches and filled baked potatoes. Children's menu. A new
80-seater restaurant was completed towards the end of last year,
but it's the bar food that we recommend here. Country and
Western music every weekend. *Open (& **Bar Food** served) 12.30-
10. Children allowed in bar to eat, children's menu. Closed 25 Dec,
Good Friday.* AMERICAN EXPRESS® *Access, Diners, Visa.*

Dublin **Aberdeen Lodge**	**£66**
Tel 01 283 8155 Fax 01 283 7877	**A**
53 Park Avenue off Ailesbury Road Dublin 4	Map 4 C2

Located in a smart, peaceful south Dublin suburb, Aberdeen Lodge
stands on an avenue lined with well-established trees. The Halpins
have converted two substantial Edwardian properties to create
a discreet, comfortable private hotel. There's a simple lounge
on the ground floor along with an attractive and spacious
breakfast/dining room (dinner is available to residents by prior
arrangement). Bedrooms, their windows double-glazed, are
identically furnished, each with custom-built modern pieces; rear
ones overlook a cricket and rugby ground. The usual comforts
like trouser presses and hairdryers are provided and bathrooms
have full facilities, showers being quite powerful. Enjoyable
breakfasts include the likes of scrambled eggs and smoked salmon.
No dogs. **Rooms** *16. Gym, spa bath.* AMERICAN EXPRESS® *Access,
Diners, Visa.*

Dublin **Anglesea Town House**	**£90**
Tel 01 668 3877 Fax 01 668 3461	**A**
63 Anglesea Road Dublin 4	Map 3 B2

A fine, creeper-clad south Dublin Edwardian residence run with
enormous dedication and flair by Helen Kirrane with the help
of her charming daughters. The minute you enter, the heady
perfume of pot pourri greets and all around are beautiful
ornaments and furnishings. A drawing room is the epitome
of cosy homeliness with its fine, comfortable seating, numerous
books and yet more tasteful ornaments. Bedrooms feature
lacework, heavy drapes and a comforting, motherly decor.
Bathrooms, some with shower only, are spotless, like the rest
of the house. Bedding has a wonderful 'all-through' freshly
laundered smell. In the mornings guests are treated to what
is without doubt the most stunning breakfast in the British Isles.
To begin, a large bowl of fresh fruit salad is brought, then a bowl
of dried fruit compote and one of baked fruit in creamy yoghurt.
Next comes a bowl of warm baked cereal (oats, fruits, nuts soaked
in orange juice overnight then freshly baked with cream). You
help yourself to all these along with a glass of freshly squeezed
orange juice. The main course follows – specialities are kedgeree
and Anglesea omelette (a soufflé omelette with smoked salmon
and three different cheeses). Other options include kidneys, sole,
plaice, salmon or trout as well as more usual offerings.
To accompany, hot buttered toast, home-baked breads and
limitless amounts of good tea or coffee. To finish, a selection
of small dainty cakes such as a moist frangipane tart. A quite
extraordinary place. No dogs. **Rooms** *7. Garden.*
Closed 22 Dec-3 Jan. AMERICAN EXPRESS® *Access, Diners, Visa.*

Dublin   Ariel House   £100

Tel 01 668 5512   Fax 01 668 5845   **A**

52 Lansdowne Road Ballsbridge Dublin 4   **Map 6 H2**

A substantial listed Victorian mansion, built in 1850, has for the past 35 years been home to the O'Brien family. It has also been one of Dublin's most charming private house hotels. Unusually for such premises there's a cosy 'wine bar' close to the reception desk where a selection of wines can be enjoyed. The drawing room, in the original house, is furnished with beautiful pieces of Victorian furniture. Rooms, all completely refurbished this year, are spacious and well equipped and each has its own character. There is, however, a wing of ten standard bedrooms at rear which are more functional in style and overlook the neat, well-tended garden. All bedrooms have full tub facilities (both bath and shower). Each also has a trouser press with iron and board, a hairdryer and an array of useful extras. Breakfast is served in a pretty conservatory on highly polished mahogany tables. Smoking discouraged. Free parking. No dogs. *Rooms 28.*
AMERICAN EXPRESS *Access, Visa.*

We welcome bona fide complaints and recommendations on the tear-out pages at the back of the Guide for readers' comments. They are followed up by our professional team.

Dublin   Ashtons

Tel 01 283 0045   **P**

Clonskeagh Dublin 6   **Map 3 B2**

Behind a frontage which can only be described as a cross between those old country garages with facades disguising Nissen huts and a glossy Chinese restaurant, all shiny marble, black and gold, lies a large pub on a number of levels – one of Dublin's most surprising pubs. It descends down to the River Dodder and as many tables as possible are positioned to take advantage of the river view with its ducks and waterfowl, the occasional swan foraging among the reeds and locals pottering along the banks. Inexpensive bar snacks include excellent home-made soups and brown bread with walnuts and hazelnuts, but it is the lunchtime buffet for which they are famous. There's always a roast joint (£5.95) and a selection of hot dishes (stuffed trout with scallop and monkfish £6.25, stuffed aubergine £5.75) plus an imaginative cold buffet and salad bar, where a whole dressed salmon takes pride of place surrounded by dressed crab, crab claws, prawns and other freshly cooked seafood as available. Sunday lunch is £5.95. From a varied choice of desserts try, perhaps, their banoffi cheesecake (£1.90). After the lunchtime buffet is cleared a separate bar snack menu operates until 8pm: burgers (£4.75), minute steaks (£4.75), crab claws (£4.75) and open sandwiches (£2.50). A full à la carte dinner menu is served downstairs in the restaurant. *Open 10.30am-11.30pm, Sun 12.30-2.30 & 4-11. Bar Meals lunch 12.30-2.30, snacks 3.30-8. Restaurant Meals 6-10. Children allowed to eat in the bar. Outdoor eating. Closed Good Friday, 25 Dec.* AMERICAN EXPRESS *Access, Diners, Visa.*

Dublin   **Ayumi-Ya Japanese Steakhouse**   £40

Tel 01 662 2233   Fax 01 662 0221   R

132 Lower Baggot Street Dublin 2   Map 6 G2

One section of the menu at this informal basement restaurant,
an offshoot of the Blackrock original, is given over to teppanyaki
– beef, chicken, salmon, prawns, tofu, Tokyo burger – griddled
and served with a choice of sauces. Other favourites include
tonkatsu (deep-fried breadcrumbed pork), mixed vegetable stir-fry
and egg noodles with meat, seafood or vegetables. The evening
selection is more extensive. Japanese-style seating for 8. *Seats 45.
L 12.30-2.30 D 6-11.30. Closed Sun, 24 Dec-2 Jan. Set L £8.95,
Set D £12.95.* AMERICAN EXPRESS *Access, Diners, Visa.*

Dublin   **Berkeley Court**   **76%**   £180

Tel 01 660 1711   Fax 01 661 7238   H

Lansdowne Road Dublin 4   Map 6 H1

The flagship of the Doyle Hotel Group, the luxurious Berkeley
Court has an impressively large split-level lobby-lounge with
mirrored columns, brass-potted parlour palms and reproduction
furniture in a mixture of styles. There are two bars – the Royal
Court and the popular Conservatory – and two restaurants. The
Court Lounge is a civilised spot for afternoon tea. Ballroom,
boardroom and several suites provide function facilities for up to
300 (banquet) and 400 (conference) people. All bedrooms have
been refurbished this year – they include a proportion of spacious
Executive suites with classic furnishings and the sumptuously
appointed Penthouse Suite. One floor of rooms (29) is designated
non-smoking. *Rooms 207. Keep-fit equipment, hair salon, news
kiosk, boutique.* AMERICAN EXPRESS *Access, Diners, Visa.*

Dublin   **The Bleeding Horse**

Tel 01 475 2705   P

24 Upper Camden Street Dublin 2   Map 5 F1

Family-owned and partly family-run on sound, traditional
principles of service and efficiency, the Bleeding Horse is lofty and
impressive, with vast dark timbers and a huge fireplace in the
smaller bar. A balcony runs right around the centre, giving
an almost medieval feel. Trendy young staff serve a simple
selection of food, basically soup (chicken and sweetcorn), home-
made bread sandwiches, salads and desserts such as banoffi pie,
meringues, apple tart and gateaux. Sunday brunch. *Open 12-11.30,
Sun 12-2 & 4-11. Bar Food from 12.30. Children allowed in bar
to eat. Beer garden. No credit cards.*

Dublin   **Blooms Hotel**   **60%**   £140

Tel 01 671 5622   Fax 01 671 5997   H

6 Anglesea Street Temple Bar Dublin 2   Map 5 F3

Modern city-centre hotel near Trinity College and Dublin Castle.
Bedrooms are pleasant and well kept with triple-glazed windows
and extras like a complimentary quarter bottle of wine and
evening newspaper. Bathrooms are a little dated but generally
of good size and quite adequate; all have low stools and telephone
extensions and some have bidets. An improvement this year has

been the complete refurbishment of the pubby bar and lobby area. No dogs. **Rooms** 86. *Night club. Closed 24, 25 & 26 Dec.* AMERICAN EXPRESS *Access, Diners, Visa.*

Dublin   The Brazen Head

Tel 01 677 9549	**P**
20 Lower Bridge Street Dublin 8	**Map 5 E3**

Dublin's oldest pub is worth a visit out of curiosity alone (and was a real curiosity until a few years ago when they finally got electricity) but, although it is undoubtedly ancient, with a series of thick-walled, low-ceilinged, rather dark rooms, it isn't caught in a time-warp and does a thriving trade with locals as well as visitors. Handy for the law courts just across the bridge and a lot of offices around Christchurch, so the lunchtime carvery is especially popular (latecomers must expect to queue). But it's a pleasant place for a quiet drink at other times, either beside the fire in the back bar in winter, or in the yard on a fine summer day. *Open 10.30-11 (Sun 12-11).* **Bar Food** *Carvery to 2pm, bar menu to 6.30/7, (sandwiches only at weekends). Closed Good Friday, 25 & 26 Dec. Access, Visa.*

Dublin   Burlington Hotel   70%

	£154
Tel 01 660 5222 Fax 01 660 8496	**H**
Upper Leeson Street Dublin 4	**Map 6 G1**

Part of the Doyle Hotel Group, the Burlington is Ireland's largest hotel and always bustles with commercial business. Public rooms are on a grand scale, with large chandeliers in the main lobby/lounge area, a convivial bar (Buck Mulligan's) and a disco. Bedrooms are thoughtfully designed and well equipped, with good working space for the business guest and neat tiled bathrooms with ample shelf space and bathrobes. The Burlington has a good reputation for banquets and has conference facilities for up to 1000. No dogs. **Rooms** 450. *Hair salon, kiosk, boutique.* AMERICAN EXPRESS *Access, Diners, Visa.*

Dublin   Café En Seine

Tel 01 677 4369	**P**
40 Dawson Street Dublin 2	**Map 5 F2**

A seriously trendy, high-ceilinged European café-style bar (and pub of sorts) whose long, narrow copper-topped bar is reminiscent of *La Stampa* just a few doors away at number 35. Bottled lagers, cappuccino and people-watching are the order of the day and in summer the fashionable clientele spill out on to the pavement under its distinctive green awning. Food is of secondary importance to the crack. *Open 10.30-11.30pm, Sun 4-11. Closed Good Friday, 25 Dec.* AMERICAN EXPRESS *Access, Diners, Visa.*

Dublin   Canaletto's

	£35
Tel 01 678 5084	**R**
69 Mespil Road Dublin 4	**Map 6 G1**

Just beside the canal near Baggot Street Bridge, this atmospheric little restaurant has built up quite a following for imaginative all-day self-service food and keenly-priced short à la carte menus, served by candle-light in the evening. Chef Terry Sheeran's zesty style comes through in moreish details like 'his own unique garlic bread', with sun-dried tomatoes and basil and warm goat's cheese, served with mixed leaf salad, toasted hazelnuts and a nut oil vinaigrette. Steamed mussels are given the pep treatment too, with stem ginger, garlic, scallions, white wine and cream and main courses burst with Cal-Ital flavours and the occasional spicy piece, as in Terry's own special chicken salad, hot and spicy with chilis, garlic, ginger, coriander and Indonesian *Ajam Pawgang* seasoning. ***Seats*** *55. Parties 8. Meals served 8am (9am Sat)-11.15pm. L 12.15-4.30 D 7-11.15 Sun brunch 10.30-4.30 (Bank Holidays as Sun). Closed Good Friday, 3 days at Christmas.* AMERICAN EXPRESS *Access, Diners, Visa.*

Dublin	Central Hotel	57%	£139
Tel 01 679 7302 Fax 01 679 7303			H
1 Exchequer Street Dublin 2			Map 5 F3

Privately-owned hotel whose plus points include a central location, nightly live music in the Tavern, the owner's collection of contemporary Irish art around the walls and free use of a nearby office car park overnight (7.30pm-8.30am) and at weekends. Bedrooms vary widely in size and shape but all are furnished in similar style with functional lightwood units. About half the bathrooms have shower and WC only. No dogs. ***Rooms*** *70. Closed 25 & 26 Dec.* AMERICAN EXPRESS *Access, Diners, Visa.*

Dublin	Chapter One	£70
Tel 01 873 2266 Fax 01 873 2330		R
18/19 Parnell Square Dublin 1		Map 5 F4

A characterful vaulted cellar restaurant underneath the Dublin Writers Museum. A modern and eclectic menu offers starters like cream of leek soup with crispy fried oysters and truffle oil and risotto of Dublin Bay prawns with chargrilled spring onions; main dishes might include rabbit fillet with prawn tortellini and celery cream or roast loin of lamb with spiced spinach and mango stuffing. Good pastry dishes among the desserts. Concise wine list. The Museum Coffee Shop, upstairs, serves more informal food all day. Pre-theatre dining (6-7) £12.50. ***Seats*** *80. Private Rooms 20/12. L 12-3 D 6-11. Closed L Mon, all Sun, Bank Holidays (except coffee shop). Set L £12.50 Set D £15.50.* AMERICAN EXPRESS *Access, Diners, Visa.*

Dublin	Chicago Pizza Pie Factory	
Tel 01 478 1233 Fax 01 478 1550		JaB
St Stephen's Green Centre Dublin 2		Map 5 F2

In a dimly-lit basement with deep-red-painted walls, Chicago-related memorabilia – flags, road signs, pictures, number plates and what have you – create an entertaining backdrop to read while waiting for the delivery of your chosen deep-pan (from £6.75 for 2 persons) or thin-crust pizza, burger, chili, lasagne, salad or other delight. Cheerful American-style service, a genuinely friendly atmosphere and fresh, wholesome cosmopolitan food fast-cooked to order. Gooey desserts might undo all the good of what went before, but you don't see anyone complaining – it's fun. Special value weekday lunch menus and

family entertainment (balloons, face-painting and a magician)
on 'fun day' Sundays. *Seats 90. Meals 12-11.30 (Sun from 12.30).
Closed 25 & 26 Dec, Good Friday.* AMERICANEXPRESS *Access, Visa.*

Dublin	The Chili Club	£45
Tel 01 677 3721		**R**
1 Anne's Lane South Anne Street Dublin 2		**Map 5 F2**

Just off bustling South Anne Street, in Dublin's most fashionable
shopping area, this intimate, low-ceilinged restaurant provides
an oasis of serenity. Anna, the Thai chef, cooks the hot and spicy
food of her homeland to be 'as traditional as the market will
allow'. Satays, sweet and sours and even most of the curries are
easy on the palate, but the soups have the expected Thai kick.
*Seats 42. Parties 30. Private Room 20. L 12.30-2.30 D 7-11.
Closed L Sat & Bank Holidays, all Sun, Good Friday, 25 & 26 Dec.
Set L £7.95 Set D £17.50.* AMERICANEXPRESS *Access, Diners, Visa.*

Dublin	The Courtyard	£45
Tel 01 283 8815		**R**
Belmont Court 1 Belmont Avenue Donnybrook Dublin 4		**Map 3 B2**

Owned by Tom Williams, The Courtyard is a model of what
a successful middle-market restaurant can be. Literally built
around a courtyard, an attractively planted area with decorative
pool which makes a pleasant seating area and creates a feeling
of oasis in the city, the restaurant is deceptively small, as it
is broken up into quite intimate sections, including a separate bar.
Evenings are à la carte only and there's a no-bookings policy
which appears to work well without undue delay and is especially
appropriate for the popular carvery lunch which operates every
day except Sunday, when the traditional set lunch is good value
at £8.50. Unpretentious food is cooked well and based on good
ingredients, then served by well-trained and well-informed staff
who are invariably courteous and helpful. *Seats 180. L 12-2.30
D 5-12. Closed 25 & 26 Dec. Set Sun L £8.50.* AMERICANEXPRESS
Access, Diners, Visa.

Dublin	Hotel Conrad	78%	£230
Tel 01 676 5555 Fax 01 676 5424			**H**
Earlsfort Terrace Dublin 2			**Map 5 F2**

In the city's business district opposite the National Concert Hall,
yet just a short walk away from fashionable Grafton Street for
shopping and St Stephen's Green for a stroll in the park, the hotel
is blessed with wonderful staff, who are both courteous and
friendly, efficient and professional, an important asset to a hotel
of distinction. Our Irish Business Hotel of the Year last year,
it does indeed have an impressive array of facilities and a staffed
business centre, and thus caters largely to a corporate clientele,
though at weekends, when very attractive rates are available,
it serves as a good base to explore the delights of Dublin. Public
areas are contemporary in style, though you'll find all the
atmosphere of a traditional pub in Alfie Byrne's. Well-planned
bedrooms are models of good taste and offer all the necessary
comforts, from large beds and easy chairs to plenty of work space
and good lighting, as well as air-conditioning. There are three

telephones in each room (one in the bathroom), a fax socket, remote-control satellite TV and mini-bar, while the bathrooms have large tubs and good showers, decent toiletries and towelling, and generously-sized bathrobes. At night there's a full turn-down service with a bottle of mineral water and hand-made Irish chocolate left beside the bed. Full 24-hr room service. Free valet parking. Banqueting for 250, conference facilities for 300. No dogs. **Rooms 191.** *Patio, beauty/hair salon, gift shop/news kiosk, brasserie (7am-11.30pm).* AMERICAN EXPRESS *Access, Diners, Visa.*

Any person using our name to obtain free hospitality is a fraud. Proprietors, please inform the police and us.

Dublin	**Cooke's Café**	**£70**

Tel 01 679 0536   Fax 01 679 0546   **R**

14 South William Street Dublin 2   Map 5 F3

Major changes have taken place of late at Johnny Cooke's fashionable city centre restaurant, where the original tiny space has been expanded upwards and out, to make a big new private room upstairs; the main dining area on the groud floor has also been extended into the building next door to create a much more spacious atmosphere and eliminate the need for tightly-packed tables and over-booking. Much of the original, successful format has been reinstated, however: the 'distressed' classical Italianate style has been retained and the open kitchen is still a major feature. Apart from a brilliantly coloured mosaic floor in the reception area, the first thing that meets arriving diners is Johnny and his dedicated team hard at work on the meal ahead. The menu is essentially the same as before (new-wave cooking with the emphasis on Italian), typically beginning with fried calamari with a spicy arrabbiata sauce and roasted garlic, a magnificent Caesar salad – Romaine lettuce with Caesar-style dressing, croutons and Parmesan cheese – or grilled asparagus with arugula, roast peppers, Parmesan shavings and balsamic dressing, all served with Cooke's famous home-baked bread selection and an olive oil dip. Main courses are quite diverse, ranging from tortellini au gratin – with a gorgonzola cream, melted Appenzeller and parmesan cheese – through warm duck confit salad with Puy lentils, cherry tomato, fried celeriac and sherry dressing, to lobster, either grilled with a herb butter sauce or as lobster and prawn fettuccine with cream, tomato, basil and vodka; game also features in season. Desserts include good, home-made ice creams but it is for the baked goods that Cooke's has established an unrivalled reputation, so don't miss out on the likes of pear and almond tart, apple toffee tart or Cooke's chocolate cake; a choice of coffees or herb teas completes the picture. Service was somewhat disjointed on our most recent visit and, although presentation – on huge plain white plates that are rather too large for the tables – was clearly an important element of the meal, there were lapses in detail, as in a (still) frozen strawberry used to garnish a dessert. A few tables are set under a wide awning on the pavement for use in fine weather. **Seats 50.** *Parties 12. Private Room 60. Meals 12.30-3.30 & 6-11 (Sun to 9). Set L & D £13.50. Closed Bank Holidays.* AMERICAN EXPRESS *Access, Diners, Visa.*

Dublin   Le Coq Hardi   ★   £100

Tel 01 668 9070   Fax 01 668 9887   **R**

35 Pembroke Road Ballsbridge Dublin 4   Map 6 H1

John and Catherine Howard run a classic restaurant in a classic
Georgian building at the end of a terrace. Inside are high ceilings
and handsome mirrors, brasswork and ornate plasterwork, and the
immaculately set tables put the seal on a setting that's entirely
fitting for John's serious French-based cooking. Many of his dishes
are from the traditional repertoire – terrine of foie gras with
brioche, cod boulangère, Venetian-style lamb's liver, entrecote
with a shallot and bone marrow sauce. 'Le Coq Hardi' is a breast
of chicken filled with potato, wild mushrooms and herbs,
wrapped in bacon, oven-roasted and finished with Irish whiskey
sauce. Other dishes are more contemporary in style: Dover sole
fillets poached in rosé wine, paprika and cream, strudel
of vegetables on a light curry sauce with mint, or breast of duck
and fresh asparagus salad in a light truffle oil dressing. Bread-and-
butter pudding with Irish whiskey custard is a favourite dessert.
Winner of our Ireland 1995 Wine Cellar of the Year award (see
page 47 for comment). *Seats 50. Private Room 34. L 12-2.30
D 7-11. Closed L Sat, all Sun, 1 week Christmas, 2 weeks Aug.
Set L £17.50 Set D £30.* AMERICAN EXPRESS *Access, Diners, Visa.*

Dublin   The Commons Restaurant   £85

Tel 01 475 2597   Fax 01 478 0551   **R**

Newman House 85/86 St Stephen's Green Dublin 2   Map 5 F2

In the basement of Newman House, one of Dublin's most historic
buildings, this spacious restaurant is unique among city-centre
restaurants as it looks out on to mature trees in a large courtyard
(where tables are set out for aperitifs in fine weather) and has
access to a further five acres of private gardens beyond. Soothing
decor is in classic dark blues and creams, with stone floors warmed
by the earthy tones of oriental rugs, fresh flowers and
a stimulating collection of specially commissioned paintings
by Irish artists. Michael Bolster, second chef under Gerard Kirwan
until the spring of 1994, has taken on the mantle of chef de cuisine
and, on the basis of recent visits, is cooking confidently with
no great change of style. The best of local produce – notably fish
but also a good choice of meats and game in season – imaginative
use of offal (typically in fillet of veal with a ragout of sweetbreads,
red wine and roast garlic) and, occasionally, unusual offerings such
as kid provide a sound base for dishes which are generally
colourful and lively. A few minor lapses, as in a rather dull tomato
and fennel soup remarkable only for the unexpected addition
of saffron, are quickly forgotten in the context of the high
standard of cooking and presentation generally experienced
throughout a meal. A good choice of delicious, freshly-baked
breads starts a meal off on the right track. From a three-course
(five-course at dinner) table-d'hote and carte, typical first courses
might include a good mixed leaf salad with a judicious sprinkling
of mixed herbs and either lightly char grilled tender pieces
of lamb fillet (pink and juicy within) topped with substantial
shavings of fresh parmesan and a piquant dressing with whiskey
or, perhaps, grilled monkfish with a zappy lime and ginger pickle.

Imaginative, simply presented main courses might include
perfectly pan-fried halibut set on an emerald bed of finely slivered
mangetout surrounded by an artistic splash of lobster cream,
or firm-fleshed roast fillet of monkfish, sliced and fanned over
a bed of mixed lentils and finely diced vegetables in a pool of dark
red wine beurre blanc. An unfussy selection of accompanying
vegetables includes two styles of potato – typically new boiled
potatoes and 'marquise', a nest of puréed potato enclosing a tasty
spoonful of colourful finely diced mixed vegetables. Elegant,
refreshingly understated desserts could include a simple hazelnut
praline parfait with a dark chocolate sauce or lovely featherlight
puff pastry in a feuilleté of fresh fruit in a scented mango coulis;
in the evening there's also a selection of Irish cheeses. Delicious
Java coffee is served with a crunchy brandysnap. A functional
wine list only, but it scores with its helpful tasting notes; short on
half bottles. A fair sprinkling of wines under £20. 15% service
is automatically applied to the bill. *Seats 60. Parties 12.*
Private Room 20. L 12.30-2.15 D 7-10. Closed L Sat, all Sun, Bank
Holidays, 1 week Christmas. Set L £18 Set D £29.50.
AMERICAN EXPRESS *Access, Diners, Visa.*

Our inspectors **never** book in the name of Egon Ronay's
Guides. They disclose their identity only if they are
considering an establishment for inclusion in the next
edition of the Guide.

Dublin	**The Davenport Hotel**	**76%**	**£182**
Tel 01 661 6800 Fax 01 661 5663			**H**
Merrion Square Dublin 2			Map 6 G3

The original, imposing neo-classical facade of architect Alfred
G Jones's Merrion Hall fronts one of Dublin's most elegant hotels,
opened last year. Only a stone's throw from Trinity College and
the National Gallery, the impressive exterior of The Davenport
is carried through into the marble-pillared lobby, an atrium
encircled by Georgian windows which soars up through six
storeys to the domed roof and cupola. Rooms beyond are on a
more human scale, with relatively low ceilings creating
an unexpectedly intimate atmosphere throughout the hotel.
Colour schemes tend to be bold, giving each area a specific
character – the Presidents Bar is masculine, club-like, for example,
the restaurant lighter and more feminine – with stylish drapes and
quality materials, notably marble and a variety of woods, used
throughout. Although they are not individually decorated there
is considerable variety among the bedrooms (some Lady Executive
designated), which tend to have a homely, almost country
atmosphere which is emphasised by the irregular shapes in some
rooms and (well-furnished) bathrooms. Nice touches include a safe
as well as trouser press, air-conditioning, good American over-bath
showers, bathrobes, turn-down service and an attractive Irish-made
range of toiletries. 24hr room service. Private 24hr valet parking.
Banqueting/conference facilities for 400/300. Guests have use
of the private Riverview Racquets and Fitness Club at members'
rates. *Rooms 116.* AMERICAN EXPRESS *Access, Diners, Visa.*

Dublin   Davy Byrnes

Tel 01 677 5217   Fax 01 677 5849

P

21 Duke Street Dublin 2

Map 5 F3

At the heart of Dublin life (and immortalised in James Joyce's
Ulysses), Davy Byrnes is not only a mecca for literary-minded
tourists, but also a pleasant, well-run and conveniently central
place well used by Dubliners in town on business, shopping
in nearby Grafton Street or simply having a day out. Decor-wise,
it is in a 1920s' time-warp and is likely to remain so through
future redecorations as it has done in the past; however, for such
a famous pub, it is remarkably unselfconscious. It has always had
a good reputation for food. At its simplest, sandwiches (£1.60-
£3.75) are invariably fresh and there's a good choice of six or so
moderately-priced hot dishes (£4.25-£5.95) on a blackboard
every day. They take pride in seafood, particularly, with fresh crab
or king prawn open sandwiches (around £3.75) featuring among
the lunchtime dishes, and grilled salmon steak with hollandaise
(£6.95), Irish stew (£5.95), grilled sirloin steak with black pepper
sauce (£5.95) appearing among additional hot dishes in the
evening. Oysters (£4.50 in season), Irish cheeses and salads
complete the picture. Sunday brunch. No children under 7.
Open 10.30am-11.30pm, Sun 12.30-2 & 4-11. **Bar Food** *12-10
(Sun 12-2 & 4-10), to 9pm in winter. Closed Good Friday,
25 & 26 Dec. Access, Visa.*

Dublin   Dobbins Wine Bistro

£60

Tel 01 661 3321   Fax 01 661 3331

R

15 Stephen's Lane Dublin 2

Map 6 G2

Probably best visited in a group, this clubby, city-centre, air-
conditioned 'Nissen-hut' operates well under the close supervision
of owner John O'Byrne and has a dark, curved ceiling (offset
somewhat by the bright conservatory area at the far end, which
is very popular in summer), sawdust-strewn floor and a series
of tables for 2-4 in intimate booths along the wall; low lighting
and an abundance of bottles add to an away-from-it-all atmosphere
which means this is a place to approach with caution if you have
to go back to work after lunch. Chef Gary Flynn's tempting
menus might include starters such as marinated breast of chicken
with a salad of French beans and basil or fresh West Coast crab
with asparagus and smoked salmon, followed by pan-fried veal
kidneys in pastry with Pommery mustard sauce or roast crispy
duckling with a trio of sauces (apple, plum and balsamic).
Attention to detail is good: generous, plain wine glasses, lovely
home-baked brown bread and white rolls and lightly cooked
vegetables. Interesting desserts and particularly creamy,
flavoursome ice cream served with a brandy snap; good,
freshly-brewed coffee. Ten tables on a patio for outdoor eating.
*Seats 60. Parties 12. Private Room 40. L 12.30-3 D 7.30-11.30.
Closed D Mon, L Sat, all Sun, Bank Holidays, Christmas week.
Set L £14.50 Set D £21.50.* AMERICAN EXPRESS *Access, Diners, Visa.*

Dublin   Doheny & Nesbitt

Tel 01 676 2945   Fax 01 676 0655   **P**

5 Lower Baggot Street Dublin 2   Map 6 G2

Only a stone's throw across the road from *Toners*, Doheny &
Nesbitt is another great Dublin institution, but there the similarity
ends. Just around the corner from the Irish parliament, this solid
Victorian pub has traditionally attracted a wide spectrum
of Dublin society – politicians, economists, lawyers, business
names, political and financial journalists – all with a view to get
across, or some scandal to divulge, so a visit here can often
be unexpectedly rewarding. Like the *Shelbourne Hotel* down the
road, which has a similar reputation and shares the clientele, half
the fun of drinking at Nesbitt's is anticipation of 'someone'
arriving or 'something' happening, both more likely than
not. Apart from that it is an unspoilt, very professionally
run bar with an attractive Victorian ambience and a traditional
emphasis on drinking. Traditional Irish music on Sunday
nights. *Open 10.30-11.30 (winter to 11), Sun 12.30-2, 4-11.*
AMERICAN EXPRESS *Access, Visa.*

Dublin   Doyle Montrose Hotel   65%   £114

Tel 01 269 3311   Fax 01 269 1164   **H**

Stillorgan Road Dublin 4   Map 4 C2

A major facelift has given the Montrose a smart modern
appearance. Located alongside the N11, a few miles south of the
city centre, it now also has an attractive 'old Ireland' themed pub
with its own entrance. Spacious public areas include a large open-
plan bar and lounge. Bedrooms are furnished in an identical smart,
contemporary style with Executive rooms differing only in being
larger. A good selection of amenities includes an iron and ironing
board. Acceptable breakfasts are cooked to order – quite a rarity
in a large hotel. ***Rooms*** *179. Beauty salon, hair salon, news
kiosk/shop.* AMERICAN EXPRESS *Access, Diners, Visa.*

Dublin   Doyle Tara Hotel   61%   £108

Tel 01 269 4666   Fax 01 269 1027   **H**

Merrion Road Dublin 4   Map 4 C2

Formerly the *Tara Tower*, the hotel continues to undergo major
changes. On the ground floor, the spacious lobby and open-plan
bar are being refurbished, while at the rear there are now 32
splendid new Executive rooms decorated in a smart, modern style.
All rooms have the same amenities but the standard rooms at the
front enjoy the best views over Dublin Bay. The hotel is very
convenient for the Dun Laoghaire ferry. ***Rooms*** *114. News
kiosk/shop.* AMERICAN EXPRESS *Access, Diners, Visa.*

Dublin   Eamonn Doran

Tel 01 679 0100/679 9114   Fax 01 679 2692   **P**

3A Crown Alley Temple Bar Dublin 2   Map 5 F3

Just settling in as the guide went to press, this new Dublin cousin
of a well-known trio of New York Irish pub/bar/restaurants was
already looking very promising, with a lively bar menu and

a reputation established from the start of serving the best steaks in town. *Seats* 70. *Parties* 10. *Private Parties* 30/40. *Bar food served from* 11.30; *carvery L* 12.30-2; *D* 6-1.45. *Closed Good Friday, 25 Dec.* AMERICAN EXPRESS *Access, Diners, Visa.*

Dublin	L'Ecrivain	£70
Tel 01 661 1919 Fax 01 661 0617		**R**
112 Lower Baggot Street Dublin 2		**Map 6 G2**

L'Ecrivain is scheduled to have moved a door down to 109a Lower Baggot Street by February 1995 – but the address is all that is expected to change. The writer's theme, highlighted by portraits of famous Irish scribes by local artist Liam O'Neill will remain the background to some classical French cooking, expertly produced by chef-patron Derry Clarke and his small team in the kitchen. Fresh seasonal produce is a feature, notably the fish that comes from south and west Cork on the day the catch is landed; vegetarian and à la carte menus are supplemented by good-value set lunch and dinner offerings with a selection of five starters and main courses to choose from. Look out for dishes such as pan-fried black and white puddings with onion marmalade, apple and calvados sauce and West Coast mussels steamed with garlic and lemon followed by fresh Howth lobster with lemon butter or saddle of venison with a venison sausage and wild mushroom compote. Desserts, recited at the table, could include pear and almond tart, crème brulée and Paris-Brest. Excellent Irish farmhouse cheeses, generous cups of various coffees and intimate service from Sally-Anne Clarke and her team. The decent wine list has the added benefit of wines costing £20 or more not attracting the service charge – a commendable practice that more restaurants should follow. *Seats* 70. *Private Room* 14. *L* 12.30-2.15 *D* 7-11. *Closed L Sat, all Sun, Bank Holidays. Set L* £13.50 *Set D* £22.95. AMERICAN EXPRESS *Access, Diners, Visa.*

Dublin	Elephant & Castle	£50
Tel 01 679 3121 Fax 01 679 1366		**R**
18 Temple Bar Dublin 2		**Map 5 F3**

In a prime location in Dublin's 'Left Bank', this busy, buzzy New York-style restaurant specialises in informal food: pasta dishes (fettuccine, perhaps, with shrimps, sun-dried tomatoes and saffron), omelettes every which way (19, in fact), big, healthy salads served in huge glass bowls (their special Caesar salad is legendary), equally generous baskets of spicy chicken wings, New York sandwiches and hamburgers all kinds of ways. It's noisy and full of life – but don't drop in when you're in a hurry as service is distinctly leisurely. *Seats* 89. *Parties* 10. *Meals* 8am-11.30pm *Mon-Thu (Fri to* 12), *Sat* 10.30-12, *Sun* 12-11.30. *Closed Good Friday,* 25 & 26 *Dec.* AMERICAN EXPRESS *Access, Diners, Visa.*

Dublin	Ernie's	£80
Tel 01 269 3260 Fax 01 269 3969		**R**
Mulberry Gardens Donnybrook Dublin 4		**Map 2 D4**

The Evans family has owned this elegant south-city restaurant since 1984 and its most remarkable feature is the late Ernie Evans's personal collection of paintings (mostly of Irish interest and many

of his beloved Kerry), which take up every available inch of wall
space – closely followed by the pretty little central courtyard
garden which makes an especially attractive feature when floodlit
at night. The interior was extensively refurbished last year. Chef
Sandra Earl is very much in control in the kitchen, producing
refreshingly updated versions of the classics. Cassoulet of scallops
with wild mushroom risotto, fricassee of prawns with a julienne
of vegetables and tournedos of beef with lentils and red wine sauce
are typical of her style and desserts could include temptations
such as apple and prune tart with calvados ice cream. *Seats 60.
L 12.30-2.30 D 7.30-10.30. Closed L Sat, all Sun & Mon,
Bank Holidays, 1 week Christmas. Set L £13.95 Set D £25.*
AMERICAN EXPRESS *Access, Diners, Visa.*

Dublin	Fitzers Café Ballsbridge	£65
Tel 01 667 1301 Fax 01 667 1303		R
RDS Merrion Road Dublin 4		Map 3 B2

The dashing neo-classical interior in warm, bold colours makes the
most of the latest Fitzers location in the members' annexe of the
Regency-style Royal Dublin Society building – sculptures and old
paintings from the RDS archives look wonderful against deep-
orange walls. New and old meet very satisfactorily, providing
a high level of comfort with great style – a dramatic setting for
Vincent Wright's Cal-Ital-influenced menus which feature
ingredients like chili and lime, typically in first courses like satay
of skewered chicken breast on a deliciously crunchy peanut and
chili sauce or crisp, golden-fried mushrooms with lime, chili and
aïoli. Main courses, which always include at least one good
vegetarian option and game in season, are more balanced in terms
of basic ingredients than their execution. Service was very slow
in its early days, although it appears that this is a place where
people like to linger. There is a large, elegant and comfortably
furnished bar/reception at one end of the main dining area and the
Café Orchestra plays on Friday evenings – the acoustics are
excellent, making relaxed conversation possible even at very busy
times. Branches at Dawson Street (Tel 01 677 1155) and Upper
Baggot Street (Tel 01 660 0644). Private parking. *Seats 120.
Parties 15. Private Room 25. L 12-3 D 6-11.30. Closed 25-28 Dec.
Set L £10.50.* AMERICAN EXPRESS *Access, Visa.*

Dublin	Les Frères Jacques	£80
Tel 01 679 4555 Fax 01 679 4725		R
74 Dame Street Dublin 2		Map 5 E3

Situated opposite Dublin Castle, a stone's throw from Trinity
College, this discreet two-storey French restaurant has dark green
and cream decor, Parisian prints, pristine white table linen and
fine glasses full of promise. Although the menus are given
unstuffily in English, everything else is uncompromisingly French.
A well-balanced choice on the menus will always include well-
sourced local poultry and meat. Sample this in a starter of duck
confit on a bed of sautéed garlic potatoes, perhaps, or in main
courses such as roast lamb en croute with a minted béarnaise and
rosemary juices or roast pork steak with baby vegetables, potato
cake and sherry sauce. Lobster is a speciality, in starters like
cassolette of fresh lobster thermidor or, as a dramatic main course,

roast lobster with Irish whiskey. A la carte seafood suggestions given at the end of the lunch and dinner menus depend on daily market availability. Desserts are sophisticated – a trio of exotic fruit sorbets nestled in a brandysnap basket, perhaps, or a dark chocolate truffle cake laced with vanilla and coffee sauce; the French cheeseboard is a further temptation. Special house recommendations on the wine list are good value. *Seats 55. Private Rooms 15 (downstairs)/40 (upstairs). L 12.30-2.30 D 7.30-10.30 (Fri & Sat to 11). Closed L Sat, all Sun, Bank Holidays, 25-29 Dec. Set L £13 Set D £20.* AMERICAN EXPRESS *Access, Visa.*

Dublin	Furama Chinese Restaurant	£75
Tel 01 283 0522 Fax 01 668 7623		R
Anglesea House Donnybrook Main Road Donnybrook Dublin 4		Map 3 B2

Like eating inside a gleaming black lacquered box, with the dining area reached via a small wooden bridge over an ornamental pool with goldfish. Furama offers a selection of familiar Cantonese as well as a few Szechuan dishes, capably cooked and served by hardworking, very pleasant staff. There's a special fish menu offering oysters, black sole, squid and lobster (from a tank); many are available steamed with garlic and black bean sauce or ginger and scallions. Sweets – like much of the menu – are aimed at Western palates with various ices dominating the choice. *Seats 100. Parties 25. L 12.30-2 D 6-11.30. Set D £17.50. Closed L Sat, 24-26 Dec, Good Friday.* AMERICAN EXPRESS *Access, Diners, Visa.*

Dublin	George's Bistro & Piano Bar	£70
Tel 01 679 7000 Fax 01 679 7560		R
29 South Frederick Street Dublin 2		Map 5 F3

In a side street between the Dail and Trinity College, a bistro popular with the post-theatre crowd. Straightforward menu of dishes based on top-quality ingredients, correctly cooked. Steaks, racks of lamb and Dover sole are favourite main courses, with something like avocado with crab or garlic mushrooms to start. The other attraction is live music (piano with female vocal), which tends to inhibit conversation but fuels the late-night buzz. *Seats 90. Private Room 40. L 1.30-3.30 D 7-12.45am. Closed Sun & Mon, Bank Holidays, 1 week Christmas. Set L £9 Set D £22.* AMERICAN EXPRESS *Access, Diners, Visa.*

Dublin	Georgian House	56%	£94
Tel 01 661 8832 Fax 01 661 8834			H
20 Lower Baggot Street Dublin 2			Map 6 G2

Bedrooms in the original building have character and charm while those in the recently built separate bedroom extension at the rear are more modern and functional. Conveniently close to the city centre, the hotel also has direct access to its own pub, Maguire's, next door. Children up to 3 stay free in parents' room. 24hr room-service. No dogs. *Rooms 33.* AMERICAN EXPRESS *Access, Diners, Visa.*

Dublin   Glenveagh Town House   £60

Tel 01 668 4612   Fax 01 668 4559   **A**

31 Northumberland Road Ballsbridge Dublin 4   **Map 6 H2**

A large Georgian house within comfortable walking distance
of the city centre (it has off-street parking – a very useful feature).
Bedrooms are pleasantly decorated and sport duvets and remote-
control TVs. Bathrooms have excellent showers. Breakfasts are
available from 8am though earlier meals can be arranged. The
selection is a familiar one but includes black and white pudding
among its offerings. There's a comfortable drawing room at the
front. Friendly, caring staff. No dogs. **Rooms** 10. *Access, Visa.*

Dublin   The Goat

Tel 01 298 4145   Fax 01 298 4687   **P**

Goatstown Dublin 14   **Map 3 B1**

"Dublin's Sporting Pub" is a real city landmark. Big, with an even
bigger car park (complete with house mini-bus to ferry customers
home safely), it has its own clock tower and would be unmissable
even without its current coat of pink paint. Inside, despite its size,
it is a friendly sort of place where families are made especially
welcome. The lounge menu offers sandwiches, omelettes, steaks
and salads, and there's a more formal Anvil restaurant. **Bar Food**
*12-3 & 3.30-9. Children allowed in bar to eat, children's menu.
Patio & garden.* AMERICAN EXPRESS *Access, Diners, Visa.*

Dublin   Good World   £40

Tel 01 677 5373   **R**

18 South Great George's Street Dublin 2   **Map 5 F3**

A city-centre restaurant much favoured by Dublin's Chinese
community, who flock here at lunchtime for an excellent selection
of carefully prepared dim sum. These come in steamer baskets
of stainless steel rather than bamboo but this is no way affects their
quality. Mixed meat dumplings and char siu buns are noteworthy
as are the long, slippery rice-flour envelopes of the various cheung
funs. The regular menu features a standard selection of classic
Cantonese dishes, but it's the dim sum that are primarily
of interest here. No smoking in the downstairs dining room.
Seats *95. Parties 40. Private Room 20. Meals 12.30pm-3am.
Closed 25 & 26 Dec. Set L £5.50 Set D £13.50.* AMERICAN EXPRESS
Access, Diners, Visa.

Dublin   Gotham Café

Tel 01 679 5266   Fax 01 679 5280   **JaB**

8 South Anne Street Dublin 2   **Map 5 F3**

Right in the heart of the city, off Grafton Street, Gotham Café
is bright, buzzy and new. Walls are lined with framed Rolling
Stone magazine covers and the menu features "American-Italian"
pizza and pasta cooking. Thus penne come with a chili sauce
and Creole sausage (£6.50) and tagliatelle with chicken breast
and broccoli (£7.50). Excellent value is found in the selection
of gourmet pizzas, for example the Harlem (£4.85 regular, £7.50
large) with sun-dried tomatoes, roast peppers, garlic and a mix

of goat's and mozzarella cheeses. Wine licence only. *Seats 65.*
Parties 8. Meals 12-12 (to 12.30am Fri & Sat). Closed Good Friday,
3 days Christmas. Access, Visa.

Dublin	The Grafton Plaza Hotel	64%	£90

Tel 01 475 0888   Fax 01 475 0908   **H**

Johnsons Place Dublin 2   **Map 5 F2**

Modern, well-designed and not without a certain style, the
Grafton Plaza is located by Grafton Street and St Stephen's Green,
putting shopping areas, parks, museums and theatres within easy
walking distance. Decor is bright and stylish, and bedrooms
of various sizes are well appointed with Irish-made carpets and
furniture (except for some antiques) also of Irish origin.
Good shelf space in the bathrooms. A sometimes noisy setting, but
good value for its location. No private parking, but guests can use
a nearby multi-storey park. No dogs. *Rooms 75. Closed 24-26 Dec.*
AMERICAN EXPRESS® *Access, Diners.*

Dublin	Gresham Hotel	64%	£175

Tel 01 874 6881   Fax 01 878 7175   **H**

Upper O'Connell Street Dublin 1   **Map 5 F4**

A prime position on Upper O'Connell Street and free, secure valet
parking are major attractions of this famous north-city hotel. The
comfortably furnished, chandelier-lit lobby/lounge is a popular
meeting place, especially for morning coffee or afternoon tea, and
Toddy's Bar (named after an illustrious former manager) is an all-
day eating spot. Front bedrooms are best, with smart modern
bathrooms, and there are six full suites. Banqueting/conference
facilities for 250/350. *Rooms 202. Closed 25 Dec.* AMERICAN EXPRESS®
Access, Diners, Visa.

Dublin	Grey Door		£50

Tel 01 676 3286   Fax 01 676 3287   **RR**

22 Upper Pembroke Street Dublin 2   **Map 5 F2**

Conveniently close to the main south city-centre shopping and
business areas, the Grey Door is discreetly set in a fine Georgian
terrace near Fitzwilliam Square. North European (Russian/
Scandinavian) influences feature strongly, especially in the dinner
menu of the cosy, small-roomed ground-floor restaurant decorated
in classical pale grey and primrose yellow. Starters could include
spiced chicken 'satsivi' with walnut and coriander dressing,
gravlax, salmon 'solianka' (a traditional Finnish soup with onion,
cucumber and capers) or home-made chicken and pork liver paté.
Chicken Kiev, fillet of beef romanoff, fillets of sole 'katinka'
(garnished with diced mixed peppers, celery and herbs and topped
with toasted almonds and lemon juice) and the ever-popular rack
of lamb with a rosemary and garlic jus might complete the main-
course picture. Lunchtime sees a simple 3-course set menu;
in the basement the newly restyled *Pier 32* (see separate entry:
Tel 01 676 1494 closed L Sat & Sun, live music most nights)
pub-restaurant offers more traditionally Irish – but equally
recommendable – pub fare. *Seats 50. Private Rooms 14/20/46.*
L 12.30-2.30 D 7-10.45. Set L £11.50/£14.50 Set D £22.50.
Closed L Sat, all Sun & Bank Holidays. AMERICAN EXPRESS® *Access,*
Diners, Visa.   *See over*

Rooms   £99

Seven bedrooms are spacious and appointed to a high standard,
with mahogany furniture and fine fabrics in pale blues and reds;
thoughtfully designed bathrooms have powerful over-bath
showers and generous towels. There is an elegant, period drawing
room for residents' use, traditionally furnished with a marble
fireplace and antiques. A studio suite attracts a small supplement.
Staff are friendly and helpful.

Dublin   The Harbourmaster

| Tel 01 670 1688 | **P** |
| Custom House Docks Dublin 1 | Map 6 G4 |

Right in the middle of Dublin's ultra-modern financial services
centre this old Dock Offices building was retained and opened
in 1994 as a pub, with plans to start a restaurant (and probably
extend the current opening hours) in 1995. The location
is exceptional and the dock is to be re-filled to allow boats in once
more but, even as it stands, the set-up is attractive and has been
sensitively converted to its present use – the old two-storey hall
(once used to auction goods impounded for non-payment of taxes)
is now the main bar, a balcony area – containing a little look-out
corner where the Dock Manager used to keep an eye on things –
overlooks it and there's a pleasant new conservatory with a view
of the dock itself. Wooden floors and hard surfaces mean it gets
noisy when there's a crowd, but there's a great atmosphere.
Outside seating for 40 on a terrace. *Closed Sat, Sun,
Bank Holidays.* AMERICAN EXPRESS *Access, Diners, Visa.*

Dublin   Hibernian Hotel   70%   £135

| Tel 01 668 7666   Fax 01 660 2655 | **HR** |
| Eastmoreland Place Ballsbridge Dublin 4 | Map 6 G1 |

A Victorian redbrick building, once a nurses' home, tucked away
in a quiet residential area. Handy for the centre of Dublin, though
not quite as central as the fondly-remembered *Royal Hibernian*
(now the site of a shopping mall on Dawson Street). The public
areas, including two reception lounges, can double up to receive
small conferences/receptions; they are cosy, with open fireplaces
and well furnished with decent pictures and plenty of comfortable
seating as well as pretty floral arrangements; the perfect spot for
afternoon tea, offering a haven of peace and tranquillity. The
hotel's trademark is a huge glass bowl of liquorice allsorts and jelly
babies on the reception counter, a theme carried through to the
bedrooms, where it becomes a novel alternative to fresh fruit.
Bedrooms, by no means lavish but quite adequately furnished,
offer remote-control TV, trouser press, hairdryer, bathrobe,
slippers; quality Crabtree & Evelyn toiletries (plus emergency
shaving kit and dental care) are to be found in the compact
bathrooms, though the towels are on the small side. Super-friendly
staff provide just the right level of service, which includes
a nightly bed turn-down service; an added bonus is that of real
loose-leaf tea for a refreshing breakfast drink. Children under 12
stay free in their parents' room. Under the same ownership
as *Grey Door* (see entry). Secure parking. **Rooms** *29. Patio garden.*
AMERICAN EXPRESS *Access, Diners, Visa.*

Restaurant £55

Relaxing dining in an elegantly appointed room decorated in deep terracotta, dark green and cream or under stylish cream parasols on the terrace – an oasis of tranquillity in the city. New chef David Foley produces daily-changing à la carte and table d'hote menus; the former may offer a choice of about four starters, typically stir-fry of codling with soya butter sauce or baked avocado and blue cheese with spicy coulis followed by soup and sorbet at dinner. Main courses might include roast leg of spring lamb with creamed leeks and garlic jus or baked hake fillet with ratatouille and squid ink sauce. French cheeseboard. *Seats 40. Parties 15. Private Room 25. L 12.30-2.30 D 6.30-10 (Fri & Sat to 11). Set Sun L £12.95 Set D £21.95. Closed L Sat, Good Friday, 1 week Christmas.* AMERICAN EXPRESS *Access, Diners, Visa.*

Dublin **Imperial Chinese Restaurant** £40

Tel & Fax 01 677 2580 **R**
13 Wicklow Street Dublin 2 Map 5 F3

Smartly decorated Chinese restaurant with pink and gold marble effect walls and much polished brass in evidence, creating a smartly upmarket interior. An ornamental pool has golden carp (not on the menu). The regular menu features a familiar selection of mainly Cantonese dishes. Lunchtime and especially on Sundays there's a good selection of dim sum available. Standards of service are excellent. *Seats 180. Parties 50. Private Room 70. Meals 12.30pm-11.45pm. Set L £6 Set D £15.* AMERICAN EXPRESS *Access, Visa.*

Dublin **Ivy Court** £55

Tel 01 492 0633 Fax 01 492 0634 **R**
88 Rathgar Road Dublin 6 Map 3 A2

Swiss chef Joseph Frei cooks an eclectic and imaginative range of dishes in his delightful restaurant almost due south of the city centre. Walls have large Breughel-inspired murals while the menu offers such varied starters as tiger shrimp wrapped in bacon with pineapple peppers and piquant sauce, or traditional black pudding with venison sausage and onion jam. Main dishes include enjoyable pasta dishes as well as medallions of monkfish with pink peppercorn sauce; half a roast boned and stuffed duckling with stuffing and orange and honey glaze. There's an attractive courtyard, out front, used for fine-weather dining. No smoking in downstairs dining room. Children welcome before 8pm. Early bird set dinner (5.30-7, £11.25) Mon-Fri. *Seats 80. Parties 12. Private Room 34. D only 5.30-11.30 (Sun 5-9). Closed 24-28 Dec, Good Friday. Access, Diners, Visa.*

Dublin **Jurys Christchurch Inn** 60% £60

Tel 01 475 0111 Fax 01 475 0488 **H**
Christchurch Place Dublin 8 Map 5 E3

Budget hotel within walking distance of the city centre run on the same lines as sister hotel *Jurys Galway Inn* (see entry, Galway). Spacious rooms, some with views over Christchurch cathedral and its environs, accommodate up to four people for a flat-rate room tariff. Basic requirements are well provided for, with good-sized beds, neat bathrooms with over-bath showers, decent towels and toiletries, direct-dial phone and colour TV. One floor of rooms is designated non-smoking. Children up to 14 stay free in parents' room. No room service. No dogs. Multi-storey car park nearby. *Rooms 183. Closed 24-26 Dec.* AMERICAN EXPRESS *Access, Diners, Visa.*

Dublin	**Jurys Hotel and Towers**	76%	£168
Tel 01 660 5000 Fax 01 660 5540			**H**
Pembroke Road Ballsbridge Dublin 4			Map 6 H1

Flagship hotel of the Jurys Hotel group, winner of our 1995 International Hospitality Award (see page 97). With its close proximity to the Lansdowne Road (rugby and soccer) ground, the main hotel can get seriously busy on match days with fans clamouring to gain access to the bars. The traditional Dubliner Pub to the right of the bright and airy foyer has a comfortable raised seating area, while the other, the Pavilion Lounge, is to the rear under a glass pyramid with rockery, greenery and trickling water. In addition, the hotel has two restaurants, a long-hours Coffee Dock, and from May-October 2½ hours of sparkling Irish cabaret that has played to well over 2 million people during the last 30 years. Most of the bedrooms in the main hotel, including four rooms (two in each part of the hotel) specially adapted for the disabled, provide decent comfort and facilities. Away from all this hustle and bustle, The Towers is a separate hotel within a hotel! With its own security, hospitality lounge, boardroom and reading room you can escape the scrum and relax in total peace and tranquility. Here, the superior bedrooms (£225) and suites, with their own dressing room, and furnished to a high standard, even offer a modern rocking armchair, as well as fresh fruit and chocolates on arrival. There are well-stocked 'robo' bars that charge you at a touch, several telephone extensions, and a turn-down service at night. Smartly-tiled bathrooms have good toiletries, bathrobes and an overhead (and sometimes overpowering) shower above the bathtub. Children under 14 stay free in their parents' room. Extensive banqueting (600) and conference (850) facilities. Ample parking. No dogs. *Rooms 390. Garden, indoor and outdoor swimming pools, spa bath, beauty and hair salons, masseuse, shop, airline desk, coffee shop (6.30am-4.30am, to 10.45pm Sun).* AMERICAN EXPRESS *Access, Diners, Visa.*

Dublin	**Kapriol**		£65
Tel 01 475 1235			**R**
45 Lower Camden Street Dublin 2			Map 5 F1

A popular Italian restaurant near the famous *Bleeding Horse* pub and within walking distance of many of the main hotels. Egidia and Giuseppe Peruzzi provide a warm greeting, a very friendly atmosphere and a menu of traditional Italian dishes which has barely changed in 20 years. Pasta is all home-made, and main-course specialities include baked salmon with prawns and cream, chicken involtini, veal escalopes stuffed with chopped fillet steak and casseroled, and venison in a rich wine sauce (Oct-Mar). *Seats 30. D only 7.30-12. Closed Sun, 3 weeks Aug.* AMERICAN EXPRESS *Access, Diners, Visa.*

Dublin   Kavanagh's

No Telephone	**P**

Prospect Square Glasnevin Dublin 9   Map 3 A4

An entertaining, unselfconscious pub that's been in the Kavanagh
family since 1833. It's known locally as the 'Gravediggers Arms'
because of its location at the back of Dublin's largest cemetery.
It's a small place, with a stone floor, rather rickety woodwork
breaking up the bar, and fittings and decorations which are simple,
original and authentic. Pints of Guinness are the main liquid
sustenance. *No credit cards.*

Dublin   Kielys

Tel 01 283 0209	**P**

22/24 Donnybrook Road Donnybrook Dublin 4   Map 3 B2

Kielys is a Donnybrook landmark with its long, impressive
frontage. Inside, it's rather sober – a masculine image that does
nothing to prepare the first-time visitor for the contrast inside,
where art nouveau decorations writhe around the mirrors,
especially at the impressive mahogany bar area, creating a feminine
feeling. This unexpectedly fin de siècle atmosphere is reinforced
by the use of traditional mahogany tables on curvaceous wrought-
iron bases, stained-glass windows at the back (although clear glass
at the front lets in the midday sunshine and allows a refreshing
view of the little green across the road) and a semi-snug, the size
of a domestic sitting room, which creates the feeling of a club
within the pub. Typical lunchtime meals from the blackboard
might include a roast joint (£5.50), cod mornay, beef stroganoff
or lasagne verdi (£4.95), which, like lighter food (basket meals)
later in the day, is ordered from the bar and served to your table.
Sunday brunch £3.25. Another surprise awaits the curious –
at the back there is another pub, *Ciss Madden's,* a very traditional
old Dublin spit'n'sawdust kind of a place; it has a separate entrance
but can also be reached through Kielys bar. The locals clearly
think all this quite normal. Furthermore, there's an Italian
restaurant, *La Finezza,* upstairs (Tel 01 283 7166, open from
5.30pm, bar and restaurant menus). *Open 10.30am-11.30pm,
Sun 12.30-2, 4-11.* **Bar Food** *12.30-8 (Sun 12.30-2 & 4-8).
Children allowed in the bar to eat. Closed Good Friday, 25 Dec.*
AMERICAN EXPRESS® *Access, Visa.*

Dublin   Kilkenny Kitchen

Tel 01 677 7066	**JaB**

Nassau Street Dublin 2   Map 5 F3

Situated on the first floor of a modern, purpose-built shop, over
the famous Kilkenny Shop with its Irish crafts and woollens, this
self-service restaurant is a favourite spot for local workers and
shoppers alike, thanks to its wholesome, inexpensive all-day food.
Although the menu is quite wide-ranging (it includes a good
choice of hot and cold lunch dishes – fennel and blue cheese soup
(£1.15), seafood chowder (£2.50), salmon mayonnaise (£1.50),
lentil loaf (£3) and chicken satay), it is for refreshing salads and,
even more, home-made breads, cakes and biscuits (to eat or take
home), that the Kilkenny Kitchen is best known. Always busy,

so expect to share a table, the best of which overlook the playing
fields of Trinity College. *Seats 168. Open 9-5 Mon-Sat (lunch
dishes served 12-4). Closed Sun (except during Dec), Bank Holidays,
25-27 Dec.* ▰▰▰▰▰ *Access, Diners, Visa.*

Dublin   Kitty O'Shea's Bar

Tel 01 660 8050 Fax 01 668 3979	**P**
23/25 Upper Grand Canal Street Dublin 4	Map 6 G2

One of Dublin's best-known and best-loved pubs, a favourite
meeting place before or after a rugby match at Lansdowne Road
and a popular spot for a snack or a meal. Typical dishes on the
luncheon menu include chicken liver paté (£1.75), prawn
cocktail, lasagne, roast pork and devils on horseback (£4.75,
lamb's liver stuffed and wrapped in bacon). Similar evening
choice, with apple pie a dessert always in demand. Live traditional
Irish music each night. No small children after 5. Saturday and
Sunday brunch (£3.95) a speciality. *Open 10.30am-11.30pm
(winter to 11), Sun 12.30-2 & 4-11. Bar Food 12-10, Sun 12.30-2
& 4-11 (plus snacks at other times). Beer garden, outdoor eating. Closed
Good Friday, 25 & 26 Dec.* ▰▰▰▰▰ *Access, Visa.*

Dublin   Langkawi Malaysian Restaurant   £40

Tel 01 668 2760	**R**
46 Upper Baggot Street Dublin 4	Map 6 G1

Decorated throughout with a batik theme, Langkawi offers
a selection of Far-Eastern dishes with Malay, Chinese and Indian
influences. Chef Alexander Hosey brings street credibility to his
mee goreng 'hawker' style (£8.95) – the type of popular food sold
cheaply in outdoor markets in Malaysia and Singapore – as well
as subtlety to some of his more exotic dishes. Choose from mild
satay to 'devil's curries' for fireproof palates: ayam (chicken breast)
and daging babi (pork). The inspiration for the latter comes from
"a blending of locally produced spices and seasoning of Portuguese
influence in the region of the city of Malacca". Winner of our
Ireland 1995 Oriental Restaurant of the Year award (see page 81).
*Seats 60. L 12.30-2 D 6-11.45. Closed L Sat & Sun, 24-27 Dec,
Good Friday.* ▰▰▰▰▰ *Access, Diners, Visa.*

Dublin   Little Caesar's Pizza

Tel 01 671 8714	**JaB**
5 Chatham House Balfe Street Dublin 2	Map 5 F2

Well-placed opposite the entrance to the Westbury Hotel, this
great meeting place occupies a buzzy little ground-floor and
basement premises with considerable chic – mirrors and murals
work miracles in minuscule spaces. The menu may hold
no surprises but it is honest fare, cooked to order before your very
eyes, and its popularity bears witness to a high level of consistency.
Minestrone will be thick, rich and served with lots of crisp,
finger-licking garlic bread, thin, crisp-crusted pizza *ripiena* (pizzas
and pasta dishes around £5) comes laden with ham and bubbling
mozzarella, parmesan and ricotta cheeses while creamy spaghetti
carbonara is just dead-on classic and side salad is Sicilian style,
heady with olive oil. 'Caesar's Favourite Dishes' – *pollo alla diavolo,*

charcoal-grilled steak and fish on a skewer. *Seats 60. Meals Noon-12.30am. Closed 25 & 26 Dec and Good Friday.* AMERICAN EXPRESS® *Access, Diners, Visa.*

Dublin Lobster Pot   £70

Tel & Fax 01 668 0025   **R**

9 Ballsbridge Terrace Dublin 4   Map 6 H1

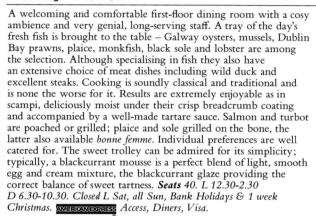

A welcoming and comfortable first-floor dining room with a cosy ambience and very genial, long-serving staff. A tray of the day's fresh fish is brought to the table – Galway oysters, mussels, Dublin Bay prawns, plaice, monkfish, black sole and lobster are among the selection. Although specialising in fish they also have an extensive choice of meat dishes including wild duck and excellent steaks. Cooking is soundly classical and traditional and is none the worse for it. Results are extremely enjoyable as in scampi, deliciously moist under their crisp breadcrumb coating and accompanied by a well-made tartare sauce. Salmon and turbot are poached or grilled; plaice and sole grilled on the bone, the latter also available *bonne femme*. Individual preferences are well catered for. The sweet trolley can be admired for its simplicity; typically, a blackcurrant mousse is a perfect blend of light, smooth egg and cream mixture, the blackcurrant glaze providing the correct balance of sweet tartness. *Seats 40. L 12.30-2.30 D 6.30-10.30. Closed L Sat, all Sun, Bank Holidays & 1 week Christmas.* AMERICAN EXPRESS® *Access, Diners, Visa.*

We endeavour to be as up-to-date as possible, but inevitably some changes to key personnel may occur at restaurants and hotels after the Guide goes to press.

Dublin Locks Restaurant   £65

Tel 01 454 3391   **R**

1 Windsor Terrace Portobello Dublin 8   Map 5 E1

Claire Douglas's relaxing canal-side restaurant has undergone some refurbishment of late, notably in the bar area, but aficionados need not fear any loss of charm – the antiques, interesting pictures, crisp linen and fine glasses are still in situ and Brian Buckley's tasty meals continue to be served on delightfully mis-matched old plates. Good soups come with a selection of home-made breads and well-judged starters – typically a smooth richly flavoured duck terrine with a piquant plum relish and crisp Melba toast – are followed by a moreish main courses such as tenderloin of pork filled with black pudding on a red wine and mustard sauce, or pretty pink and white fillets of sea trout and lemon sole with a Noilly Prat and lettuce sauce. Desserts, confidently presented on extra-large plates, might include a richly dark chocolate marquise and lighter options such as a compote of black cherries, served spilling out of a brandy snap cornet. Finish with a selection of Irish farmhouse cheeses, perhaps, and plenty of Cona coffee. *Seats 45. Parties 16. Private Room 30. L 12.30-2, D 7.15-11. Closed L Sat, all Sun, Bank Holidays, 1 week Christmas. Set L £13.95 Set D £22.* AMERICAN EXPRESS® *Access, Diners, Visa.*

Dublin   Longfield's Hotel   61%   £96

Tel 01 676 1367   Fax 01 676 1542   **HR**

Fitzwilliam Street Lower Dublin 2   Map 6 G2

Its situation, in a Georgian terrace previously staff headquarters for
the nearby Shelbourne Hotel, is crucial to the character of this
charming antique-furnished hotel: the location, right in the heart
of Georgian Dublin, is ideal and the human scale and sensitive
renovation give it a specially intimate atmosphere, like that of a
graciously proportioned and beautifully furnished private house.
Public areas are comfortable and bedrooms are individually
furnished, all with en-suite bath/shower, but they do vary
considerably in size as Georgian buildings become progressively
smaller in scale with each storey, so guests expecting rooms to be
neat rather than spacious will not be disappointed. Friendly staff
and 24-hour room service. Limited menus served in drawing
room – morning coffee 10-12.30; afternoon tea 1.30-5. Limited
private parking (4 spaces). Children welcome: under-12s may stay
free in parents' room; baby-listening/sitting by arrangement; cots
and high-chairs provided. ***Rooms** 26. Closed 24 Dec-3 Jan.*
AMERICAN EXPRESS *Access, Diners, Visa.*

No 10 Restaurant   £65

In the basement, with direct access from the hotel or the street, the
restaurant uses space with ingenuity (aperitifs are served in what
was once the coal bunker, now cleverly transformed with trompe
l'oeil) and, although tables are rather tightly packed, it is a popular
venue. Tommy Donovan's imaginative menus include a no-
nonsense, no-choice lunch, guaranteed to cut out the dithering.
Typical dishes might include spiced beef salad with horseradish
and gherkins (served with home-made brown bread), sautéed tuna
steak on a pink peppercorn sauce and chocolate terrine served on a
coffee bean sauce. French and Irish cheeses are offered, and a choice
of coffee/speciality teas. ***Seats** 40. Parties 10. Private Room 20.
L 12.30-2.30 D 6.30-10 (7-11 Fri & Sta). Closed L Sat & Sun.
Set L £12.50 Set D £17.50 (Sun only).*

Dublin   The Lord Edward   £60

Tel 01 454 2420   **R**

23 Christchurch Place Dublin 8   Map 5 E3

Billed as Dublin's oldest seafood restaurant, The Lord Edward
occupies three floors of a tall, narrow and appropriately ancient
building overlooking Christchurch Cathedral. The style is club-
like, traditional, downright old-fashioned in fact – which appears
to be just the way the loyal local following likes it. Minimal
concessions to carnivores, but the seafood can be excellent –
those in the know keep it simple, in sole goujons, perhaps, served
with a mountain of crisply fried chips, or a plain-grilled turbot
fillet. Lunchtime bar food in the traditional bar. ***Seats** 40. Parties
8. L 12.30-2.30 D 6-10.45. Closed L Sat & Sun, Bank Holidays,
Christmas week. Set L from £15.95 Set D £20.* AMERICAN EXPRESS
Access, Diners, Visa.

Dublin   McCormack's Merrion Inn

Tel 01 269 3816 Fax 01 269 6877	**P**
188 Merrion Road Dublin 4	**Map 4 C2**

They take their lunch and its comfortable consumption seriously
at this well-established pub. Despite its considerable age – and
more than a passing nod to tradition where serious matters such
as service, friendliness and efficiency are concerned – a modern
hand has been at work with the decor, but the unexpectedly
bright colours work surprisingly well to create a cheerful
atmosphere, with various styles of seating and a generous
distribution of tables and bar space to enjoy food and drink
in comfort. Soup and sandwiches are available at the bar and there
is a hot and cold buffet at the back. Choices on the blackboard
change daily, but there is always a roast, typically roast beef with
roast potatoes and a selection of five other vegetables (£5.95),
a traditional casserole such as beef and Guinness (£4.95), plus
perhaps pork Madras (£4.95), vegetable lasagne (£4.95)
or chicken Kiev (£5.45); there's also usually a range of salads and
good desserts (all £1.50) like pear and chocolate tart or banoffi
pie. Sunday brunch is the works (including black pudding) for
£4.95. Children "under control" are welcome at lunchtimes and
until 6pm on Sunday. No parking; use the hospital's car park over
the road. *Open 10.30am-11pm (Sun 12.30-2 & 4-11).* **Bar Food**
*12-2.30 (Sun to 2) & 3-9. Garden, outdoor eating. Closed
25 & 26 Dec, Good Friday.* AMERICAN EXPRESS *Access, Diners, Visa.*

Dublin   Marine Hotel   64%   £86

Tel 01 839 0000 Fax 01 839 0442	**H**
Sutton Cross Dublin 13	**Map 4 C4**

Standing right at Sutton Cross at the isthmus of Howth some
10kms from the city centre, the Marine has a large car park at the
front while at the rear lawns lead right down to the waters
of Dublin Bay. Public rooms include a delightful sun lounge
overlooking the lawns and a newly refurbished bar. Decor
is appealing with richly coloured floral fabrics and smart
darkwood furniture. All are well equipped (hairdryer, trouser
press, remote TV). Bathrooms, too, are neat, all with showers,
some with shower/WC only. Friendly and helpful staff.
Rooms *26. Garden, indoor swimming pool, sauna.
Closed 25 & 26 Dec.* AMERICAN EXPRESS *Access, Diners, Visa.*

Dublin   La Mère Zou   £45

Tel 01 661 6669	**R**
22 St Stephen's Green Dublin 2	**Map 5 F2**

Eric Tydgadt (ex *Frères Jacques*) and his wife Isabelle opened their
basement premises in the summer of '94, left the decor pretty
much as it was (as *The Ark*) and concentrated on providing real
French country cooking at surprisingly reasonable prices – which
may explain why, as we go to press, this unassuming little place
is poised to become fashionable. The three- or four-course set
menus give outstanding value (even though breads – baguette and
home-baked brown soda bread – are charged extra, French-style),
starting with soup – simple carrot and celery, perhaps – and

a choice of starters, such as piquant salad of goat's cheese mousse with balsamic dressing, or juicy garlic mussels, served on the half shell, followed by big, wholesome main-course specialities like *carbonnade flamande* or *pot au feu*, or lighter alternatives such as *blanquette* of chicken or fish – typically crisply grilled fillet of salmon. Finish off with French cheeses or classic desserts like tarte tatin or Belgian chocolate mousse and coffee by the cup. *Seats 55. Parties 12. L 12.30-2.30 D 6-11. Closed L Sat, all Sun, 25 & 26 Dec, 1-8 Jan. Set L £9.50 D from £12.50 (6-7.30).* AMERICAN EXPRESS ® *Access, Visa.*

Dublin	Merrion Hall	£70
Tel 01 668 1426 Fax 01 668 4280		**A**
56 Merrion Road Ballsbridge Dublin 4		Map 3 B3

The recent addition of the adjacent property has doubled the capacity of this charming, immaculately maintained, family-run guesthouse on the main ferry road just south of the city centre. The main sitting room is very comfortable, encapsulating perfectly the friendly and homely ambience generated by the Sheeran family. There's now an additional sitting room identical in size to the original one. It is used primarily in the busier summer months. Bedrooms are pretty and well equipped. Four are triple rooms while a further four have both a double and a single bed. The excellent breakfast selection features a self-service buffet including home-made yoghurt, poached fruits, fresh fruit salad and a cheeseboard. No dogs. **Rooms** *15. Closed 2 weeks from 21 Dec. Access, Visa.*

Dublin	Le Mistral ★	£80
Tel 01 478 1662 Fax 01 478 2853		**R**
16 Harcourt Street Dublin 2		Map 5 F2

Despite its cellar setting and other-worldly history – the restaurant is located in the now whitewashed basement of a house once inhabited by Bram Stoker (creator of Dracula) and still contains the old black range used in his kitchen – Le Mistral brings a touch of warm, herb-scented Provençal sunshine to Dublin. Larger-than-life proprietor Philippe Misischi is a wonderfully Poirot-like character who exudes such potent Gallic hospitality and charm that would-be critics are disarmed even before orders are taken. Christophe Cassière, who has been chef de cuisine since the spring of 1994, works closely with M. Misischi in association with his friend Raymond Blanc; M. Blanc (see Le Manoir aux Quat'Saisons under Great Milton, England) has made several guest appearances in the kitchen and is actively involved with menu planning on an ongoing basis – a unique situation for an Irish restaurant and a partnership which is creating some exciting results. Based on the results of his daily visits to the market, a choice of both table d'hôte (three courses at lunch, four in the evening) and a short (but unusual) carte is offered plus there's always a selection of daily fresh fish – a wonderfully tempting selection offered at its best, with understandable leanings towards Mediterranean seafood. Typically, the daily tray could include oysters, scallops, prawns (the French variety, to be butterflied and grilled, perhaps), truly wild salmon, monkfish, red mullet and much more. These maritime treasures are balanced by some of the earthy ones also

keenly appreciated by the French: panfried medallions of loin
of pork served with Calvados sauce; supreme of grilled chicken
served with bacon and baby onions; pig's trotters, well-known
as hearty pub food in some areas, but here typically served
caramelised as a first course, the tender meat stripped from the
bone, formed into a roundel, seasoned quite sharply and dressed
with fine Provençal breadcrumbs. Some of the dishes are visually
quite stunning. Main courses are served with a choice of side salad
or the day's vegetables and, while fish is served with wonderfully
aromatic sauces (monkfish with a thyme-and rosemary-scented
petit jus de volaille), apparently simple offerings such as supreme
of grilled free-range chicken are not only unexpectedly
flavoursome but might arrive at the table spilling with bright
green broad beans, smoked bacon and the tiniest of baby onions.
Classic desserts such as a deeply dark chocolate marquise perfectly
balanced by a pale *crème anglaise* or a terrine of fresh fruits served
with orange caramel please by their unaffected simplicity and
flavour. The excellent cheeseboard is unashamedly French. Freshly
brewed coffee is served by the cup. Service is attentive throughout
and attracts an automatic surcharge of 12½%. *Seats 60. Parties 16.
Private Room 40. L 12-2.30 D 7.30-11. Set L £12.95
Set D £18.95. Closed L Sat, all Sun, Bank Holidays & 5 days
Christmas.* AMERICAN EXPRESS *Access, Diners, Visa.*

Dublin **Mitchell's Cellars**	**£35**
Tel 01 668 0367	**R**
21 Kildare Street Dublin 2	**Map 5 F2**

Here in the arched cellars under the famous Mitchell's wine
merchants and in common ownership, little seems to have
changed since this daytime restaurant first opened in the mid-70s –
but, although the *type* of food remains unchanged, it has improved
– the quiches and salads, the soups and casseroles, the homely fruit
crumbles are still there, but better than ever. Dependable home
cooking is the order of the day, with the bonus of efficient
service, and it's popular as ever, so expect to queue – but waiting
in the bar is no hardship as the wines, of course, are worth
spending some time on. *Seats 70. L only 12.15-2.30. Closed Sun
(also Sat Jun-Sep), Bank Holidays, 24-28 Dec, Easter Tuesday.
No reservations.* AMERICAN EXPRESS *Access, Diners, Visa.*

Dublin **Mont Clare Hotel** 66%	**£157**
Tel 01 661 6799 Fax 01 661 5663	**H**
Merrion Square Dublin 2	**Map 6 G3**

Sister hotel to the *Davenport* (qv) across the road and with
a similar clubby feel although a little less grand and more intimate
in style. The bar is a fine example of a traditional Dublin pub
complete with bare-board floor, enough mahogany to stock a rain
forest and lots of atmosphere. The only other sitting area is in
a small alcove off the smart marble-floored lobby. Bedrooms are
generally not large but have warm decor in stylish dark reds and
blues with darkwood furniture, air-conditioning and telephones
at both desk and bedside with a third in the good marble
bathrooms. Guests have use of the private Riverview Racquets and
Fitness Club at members' rates. Free valet parking. *Rooms 74.*
AMERICAN EXPRESS *Access, Diners, Visa.*

Dublin   National Museum Café

Tel 01 662 1269   **JaB**

Kildare Street Dublin 2   **Map 5 F2**

Before or after a stroll around the exhibits of Ireland's heritage, the
café offers a counter service selection of savoury and sweet foods.
The setting is a grand one – a fine mosaic floor, with a beautiful
crystal chandelier overhead. Tables are of pink granite and the
range of food encompasses light snacks such as scones, biscuits and
banana bread. At lunchtime, daily-changing hot specials might
include chicken and vegetable soup served with a scone and butter
(£1.65), followed by beef stroganoff and rice (£4.50) or seafood
smokies with vegetables (£5.25). Cold fare and vegetarian dishes
also, plus a good choice for the sweet-toothed. *Seats 60. Meals
10-5 (Sun 2-5). Closed Mon, 25 Dec & Good Friday.* AMERICAN EXPRESS
Access, Diners, Visa.

Dublin   No 31   £68

Tel 01 676 5011   Fax 01 676 2929   **A**

31 Leeson Close off Leeson Street Lower Dublin 2   **Map 5 F1**

In a small mews close to the city centre (and most Dublin
restaurants and nightlife), the Bennetts have opened up their
stylish home to offer charming and exclusive bed and breakfast
accommodation. You press an intercom at heavy, varnished light
oak doors set in a high perimeter wall to gain admittance. The
instant you enter, the impression is of a well-designed modern
house. It was built by the architect Sam Stephenson and was his
home for 30 years. Here he entertained celebrities of politics and
culture. Cool white, with good use of light and space, typifies the
decor. The lounge, with a mirror mosaic-lined bar in the corner,
features an eye-catching square sunken seating area, black leather
upholstery contrasting with the white. Around the walls are
numerous works of art. Upstairs, there's a large refectory table
where Mary Bennett produces excellent breakfasts between 8.30
and 10. These include vegetarian options, freshly baked scones,
home-made preserves and freshly squeezed fruit juices. Bedrooms
are bright, simply appointed and homely, one with its own patio.
Remote-control TVs, radio-alarms and hot drink facilities are
standard. Secure, locked parking is also provided, as is a laundry
service. Not suitable for children under 10. *Rooms 5. Patio, sauna.
Closed 25 Dec. Access, Visa.*

Dublin   O'Dwyer's

Tel 01 676 3574   Fax 01 676 2281   **P**

Mount Street Dublin 2   **Map 6 G2**

This large, bustling pub always has a good buzz – well supported
at lunchtime and early evening by a thriving local business and
professional community. Later, a night club attracts a younger
crowd who are especially appreciative of the renowned O'Dwyer's
pizzas. Professionally run, cheerful, central. *Open 10.30am-
11.30pm, Sun 12.30-2 & 4-11.* AMERICAN EXPRESS *Access, Diners, Visa.*

Dublin   Oisíns

£95

Tel & Fax 01 475 3433

R

31 Upper Camden Street Dublin 2

Map 5 F1

The menu at this modest little first-floor restaurant is rendered
in both Irish and English, listing a short but interesting selection
of dishes with a traditional provenance: Dublin coddle (a stew
of bacon, sausages, potatoes and onions), crubeens (pig's trotters),
Irish stew with dumplings, carrageen moss. Friendly service,
regular live music. The wine list has an Irish table wine from
Mallow. *Seats* 40. *D only 6.30-10. Closed Sun & Mon in winter,
24 Dec-end 1st week Jan.* AMERICAN EXPRESS *Access, Diners, Visa.*

Dublin   Old Dublin Restaurant

£60

Tel 01 454 2028   Fax 01 454 1406

R

90/91 Francis Street Dublin 8

Map 5 E3

An evening à la carte has increased the menu options at this
welcoming, comfortable restaurant, whose various rooms feature
marble fireplaces and good pictures. Eamonn Walsh's cooking
takes its main influences from Russia and Scandinavia: gravlax,
borsch, blinis with salted salmon, prawns, herrings or mushroom
salad, chicken Kiev. House specialities might be prawn-stuffed
turbot Odessa, oak-smoked venison and planked sirloin Hussar.
Good cheeseboard; all desserts home-made. Early bird menu (6-7)
£10. *Seats* 65. *Parties* 28. *Private Room* 16. *L 12.30-2.30
D 6-10.45. Closed L Sat, all Sun, Bank Holidays, 25 & 26 Dec.
Set L from £12.50 Set D from £19.75.* AMERICAN EXPRESS *Access,
Diners, Visa.*

Dublin   The Old Stand

Tel 01 677 7220   Fax 01 677 5849

P

37 Exchequer Street Dublin 2

Map 5 F3

A sister pub to *Davy Byrnes* (see entry), The Old Stand is a
comfortable, old-fashioned place, attractive in a strong, sensible
way with black paint outside and dark mahogany inside, good
detail behind the bar and a loyal local following. The food
is simple but good – they are famous for their sirloin steaks, both
6oz (£5.50) and 12oz (£9.95); there is a daily special (keenly
priced at only £4.25 and always the most popular dish, whatever
it is – perhaps roast beef with vegetables and potatoes), plus grills,
omelettes (£4.75), salads (£3.95-£6.75) and open sandwiches
(smoked salmon or prawn £3.95). Pheasant is popular in season.
A well-run, gimmick-free pub. *Open 10.30am-11.30pm, Sun
12.30-2 & 4-11. Bar Food 12.15-3.15 & 5-9.30, Sun 12.30-2 & 4-
8. Closed Good Friday, 25 & 26 Dec. Access, Visa.*

Dublin   101 Talbot

£32

Tel 01 874 5011

R

101 Talbot Street Dublin 1

Map 5 F4

Upstairs in a busy shopping street, close to O'Connell Street and
the Abbey and Gate Theatres, this bright, airy restaurant has
a rather arty cheap and cheerful atmosphere which harmonises
well with the wholesome Mediterranean-influenced and spicy
Eastern food. Pasta, vegetarian, fish and meat dishes all appear

on the menu: tagliatelle with pesto, baked avocado with a ginger
and green pepper glaze, Japanese-style vegetable parcels with chili
sauce, supreme of chicken with leek and pistachio nut stuffing,
cushion of lamb with juniper berry sauce, baked salmon with
Gruyère cheese and herb crust. Open all day for tea, coffee, soup,
pasta and snacks. *Seats 90. L 12-3 D 6.30-11 (light meals
10am-11pm). Closed D Mon, all Sun, Bank Holidays, 1 week
Christmas.* AMERICAN EXPRESS *Access, Diners, Visa.*

Dublin	Pasta Fresca	£30
Tel 01 679 2402		**R**
2-4 Chatham Street Dublin 2		Map 5 F2

Bustling Italian restaurant/wine bar/deli just off the smart Grafton
Street shopping area. Friendly waiting staff serve an all-day
selection of straightforward food – pasta, pizza, salads, burgers and
a few more substantial meat dishes. *Seats 85. Meals 8am-11.30pm
(Sun 12-8). Closed Good Friday, 25 & 26 Dec. Set L £4.95/£8.50
Set D £8.50. Access, Visa.*

Dublin	Patrick Guilbaud ★ ↑	£100
Tel 01 676 4192 Fax 01 660 1546		**R**
46 James Place off Lower Baggot Street Dublin 2		Map 6 G2

Approaching this purpose-built restaurant, you might wonder
if you are in the right street, so unprepossessing does the building
look from a distance. But once inside there's no mistake – a
comfortable reception lounge with several striped sofas, lots
of greenery in both the plant-filled atrium and high-ceilinged
dining room, decent art (mostly abstract paintings), and, above all,
very smartly attired and professional staff. For well over a decade
this has been *the* place in which to enjoy classical French cuisine
with a light, modern approach. The seemingly ageless Patrick is on
hand to offer advice on the menus as well as engaging customers
in conversation, whether on golf – one of his passions – or France's
chances in the Five Nations rugby championship, especially against
Ireland at Lansdowne Road! For an eponymous restaurant,
somewhat unusually Patrick is not the chef/patron – the cooking
is left to a team of French chefs, led by Guillaume Le Brun (visible
in a glass-fronted kitchen); indeed, most of the staff are French.
The ingredients, naturally, are mostly Irish, notably as in seafood
dishes, such as pan-fried king scallops served with seasonal salad
and bacon, Dublin Bay prawns in crisp pastry cases served with
mango and capers, or sea bass with wild mushroons and truffles.
Also highly recommended as starters are the carrot soup with
thyme and game torte with pepper sauce, while game dishes
in season (roast wild venison with red wine sauce or breast
of pheasant with chestnut and wild mushrooms) are eagerly
awaited by regulars. The table d'hote lunch and dinner menus
(both exclusive of a service charge of 15%, as is the à la carte) are
particularly good value, and though there's a somewhat limited
choice at dinner (four courses and coffee), lunch offers four
selections among both starters and main courses. And for a table
whose occupants cannot make up their minds, why not try the
menu surprise (£45 per person)? Desserts (a tart lemon mousse,
berry cheesecake or poached pear in red wine) and French cheeses
are quite splendid, as is the variety of breads offered, the amuse-

gueule, the coffee and petits fours. Service is impeccable. As you would expect, the wine list is predominantly French, but not exclusively so, and – for a restaurant of this class – prices are reasonable; note the old classics in the 'Specialist Cellar'. The restaurant is now air-conditioned. *Seats 60. Private Room 28. L 12.30-2.15 D 7.30-10. Closed Sun & Mon, Bank Holidays. Set L £18.50 Set D £30 & £45.* AMERICAN EXPRESS® *Access, Diners, Visa.*

Dublin   The Pembroke

Tel 01 676 2980 Fax 01 676 6579	P
31 Lower Pembroke Street Dublin 2	**Map 6 G2**

A warm, welcoming city-centre pub with a cosy, real coal fire and exceptionally fine etched mirrors behind the bar, highlighting the mainly 1920s' decor. Dark mahogany woodwork and small, snug-like seating areas confirm this impression of intimacy and it comes as a pleasant surprise to find that you do not have to leave the premises to find good bar food at a fair price, and even outside normal meal times they will run up a simple snack. The cellar Buffet Bar serves salads and a hot food buffet at lunchtimes; fancier evening fare. Traditional Irish music Thursday evenings. *Open 12-11.30. Bar Food 12-11.30. Pub closed Sun, 25 & 26 Dec, Good Friday.* AMERICAN EXPRESS® *Access, Visa.*

Dublin   Periwinkle Seafood Bar

Tel 01 679 4203	JaB
Unit 18 Powerscourt Townhouse Centre South William Street Dublin 2	**Map 5 F3**

Established over 13 years in a ground-floor corner of a colourful, bustling 'arty crafty' shopping mall, Phena O'Boyle's and Anne Green's Periwinkle has the simplest of decors – split-level quarry-tiled floors, varnished pine tables and counters with low or high stools depending on where you choose to sit. Blackboard menus proclaim the day's offerings, of which the most popular item is thick seafood chowder (£1.15/£1.75) served with freshly-baked Irish brown bread. Each day as well as the perennial seafood salads and platters there's a changing fish dish of the day, for example cod niçoise (£3.95), cheesy soufflé-topped plaice (£5.95) or crab claws in garlic butter (£6.95). Hot food becomes available at 11.30am and continues until closing time. *Seats 55. Meals 10.30-5. Closed Sun & Bank Holidays. No credit cards.*

Dublin   P Hedigan: The Brian Boru

Tel 01 830 8514	P
5 Prospect Road Glasnevin Dublin 9	**Map 3 A4**

Named after an 11th-century High King of Ireland, this smartly maintained pub is also known as *Hedigan's* after owner Peter Hedigan. Original Victorian themes – mahogany, stained glass and, especially, very fine tiling – have been carried through faithfully as alterations have been made through the years, everything is neat and clean and the eye is drawn past an abundance of strong tables and seating, to a patio/beer garden at the back, also furnished with comfortable eating in mind. It comes as no surprise that the Brian Boru has been in the same family since 1904. Bar food is best described as traditional:

lunchtime carvery £3.95-£5.25; evenings – chicken Kiev
(£5.25), sirloin steak with pepper sauce (£5.95), apple pie
(£1.50). Sunday lunch £3.95-£5.25. *Open 10.30am-11.30pm, Sun
12.30-2 & 4-11.* **Bar Food** *12-3 (to 2.30 Sun) & 3-8 (not Sun).
Garden, outdoor eating. Access, Visa.*

Dublin	**Pier 32**	£30
Tel 01 676 1494 Fax 01 676 3287		**R**
23 Upper Pembroke Street Dublin 2		Map 5 F2

Previously run as Blushes Bistro, the basement restaurant in the
Grey Door restaurant with rooms (see entry) has undergone
something of a sea change – in fact it's now been recreated as a
sort of west of Ireland pub-restaurant, with the emphasis
on Atlantic seafood and traditional music. Typical fare might
include steamed mussels with a white wine cream sauce and baked
fillet of hake with champ or Pier 32 seafood bake, tempered by a
short selection of well-tried favourites – steaks, chicken,
mushroom stroganoff – for carnivores and vegetarians. **Seats** *50.
Parties 18. L 12.30-2.15 D 6-10.45 (Fri & Sat to 11.30). Set L £10.
Set D from £10 (6-7pm). Closed L Sat, all Sun, Bank Holidays.*
 Access, Diners, Visa.

Dublin	**Pierre's**	£30
Tel 01 671 1248 Fax 01 671 1249		**R**
2 Crow Street Temple Bar Dublin 2		Map 5 F3

Simple surroundings keep costs down and allow the high quality
of food emanating from the open kitchen to take centre stage –
an unusual state of affairs in this trendy Left Bank area, where the
reverse is more often the case. Start, perhaps, with a barley and
leek soup like mother used to make, or a huge bowl of steamed
mussels with a garlic and parsley butter melting into them
to make a richly flavoured sauce, then follow on with a simple
steak (on the small side, perhaps, but delivered with panache – and
a steak knife) or supreme of chicken filled with a smoked bacon
mousse on a Cheddar and cayenne cream – simpler than it sounds
and very moreish – or an imaginative vegetarian option such
as Chinese-style wun tun with cashews and bean sprouts on fresh
egg noodles. Super vegetable selection served from a big platter
on the table. Nice cold sweets. **Seats** *60. Parties 12. L 12-3 D 6-11.
Closed 25 & 26 Dec, 1 & 2 Jan. Set L £5.90 Set D £6.90.
Access, Visa.*

Dublin	**Pigalle**	£55
Tel 01 671 9262/679 6602		**R**
14 Temple Bar Dublin 2		Map 5 F3

Edith Piaf sets the mood at Lachen Iouani's first-floor restaurant
which, although occupying a prime location in the newly
fashioned area now known as Dublin's 'Left Bank', has been
attracting a loyal clientele since 1984. The strong French
atmosphere extends to bi-lingual menus in the national colours –
and, thankfully, into the kitchen in dishes like *fruits de mer
à l'armoricaine* (assorted seafood in prawn sauce), *magret de canard
au miel et au gingembre* (thinly sliced duck breast on a well-judged,
slightly piquant honey and ginger sauce) and *rosette d'agneau*

au basilic et tomate (lean, pink lamb with a rich, well-made tomato and basil sauce) and good vegetables including a creamy garlic potato gratin. Desserts could include a faultless crème caramel and there's a magnificent cheeseboard, with Stilton and an excellent choice of French as well as Irish farmhouse cheeses, served from a marble platter, in the French style with crusty baguettes and no butter. Good strong coffee too. **Seats** *60. Parties 8. L 12.30-2.45 D 6.30-10.45 (11 Fri & Sat). Closed L Sat, all Sun, Bank Holidays, 25-28 Dec. Set £11.50 Set D from £12.50. Access, Visa.*

Dublin	**Il Primo**	**£45**
Tel 01 478 3373		**R**
16 Montague Street Dublin 2		**Map 5 F2**

Simply appointed little Italian restaurant opposite the Children's Hospital (Harcourt Street). Dishes range from hot garlic crostini with sun-dried tomatoes and basil, Roman salad with cold meats and duck liver terrine with roasted peppers to salads, pizzas and pasta. **Seats** *44. Parties 30. L 12-3 D 6-11. Closed Sun, Bank Holidays.* AMERICAN EXPRESS *Access, Diners, Visa.*

Dublin	**Raglan Lodge**	**£85**
Tel 01 660 6697 Fax 01 660 6781		**A**
10 Raglan Road Ballsbridge Dublin 4		**Map 6 H1**

Built in 1861 and epitomising the grand Victorian town-house style, the lodge stands in a select tree-lined avenue off one of the main routes to the city centre. Helen Moran has been here just over three years and has created a charming, hospitable environment. Thirteen white granite steps lead up to the main door, painted a distinctive and cheering sunshine yellow. There's a lounge on the lower ground floor, though it is little used, while on the ground floor there's a fine breakfast room wherein to enjoy the likes of slices of smoked salmon bordered by soft scrambled eggs. The seven high-ceilinged bedrooms are spotlessly maintained and feature creature comforts like sweet-smelling warm bedding, thick towels, good soaps and crystal-clear reception of all the major television channels. No dogs. **Rooms** *7. Garden. Closed 1 week Christmas.* AMERICAN EXPRESS *Access, Visa.*

Dublin	**Rajdoot**	**£48**
Tel 01 679 4274		**R**
26 Clarendon Street Westbury Centre Dublin 2		**Map 5 F3**

Part of a small UK chain (and one on the Costa del Sol) of reliable restaurants specialising in tandoori and North Indian Moghlai cooking. The latter tends to produce mild and subtly spiced dishes like chicken pasanda – the breast stuffed with flaked almonds, mint and cherries with a sauce of cashew nuts and almonds. Luxurious, somewhat exotic decor. **Seats** *92. L 12-2.30 D 6.30-11.30. Set L from £6.95 Set D from £17.50. Closed Sun, L Bank Holidays, 25 & 26 Dec, Good Friday.* AMERICAN EXPRESS *Access, Diners, Visa.*

Dublin   Roly's Bistro   ↑   £50

Tel 01 668 2611 Fax 01 660 8535	R
7 Ballsbridge Terrace Ballsbridge Dublin 4	Map 6 H1

The combination of proven individuals – restaurateur Roly Saul
and chef Colin O'Daly – makes for a successful restaurant,
deservedly popular since opening. On two floors, upstairs perhaps
has a more authentic bistro atmosphere, while the ground floor
is a little more sedate, and there's a real buzz about the place,
so much so that staff can sometimes become distracted and
unobservant, especially when you're trying to attract their
attention! First comes an excellent variety of breads, followed
by an eclectic selection of dishes from prawn bisque and warm
salad of duck breast with caramelised apple and clementine to roast
pork with apple sauce and pan-fried monkfish with almonds,
honey, dates and whisky. Good accompanying salads and
vegetables as well as the puddings (super orange crème brûlée),
coffee and inexpensive wines – many are between £10 and £15
a bottle. *Seats* 100. *Parties 10. Private room 65. L 12-2.45 D 6-10.*
Closed Good Friday, 25 & 26 Dec. Set L £9.50. AMERICAN EXPRESS
Access, Diners, Visa.

Dublin   Royal Dublin Hotel   63%   £111

Tel 01 873 3666 Fax 01 873 3120	H
40 Upper O'Connell Street Dublin 1	Map 5 F4

A modern hotel on Dublin's most famous street, with practical
overnight accommodation, an all-day brasserie and a business
centre with full facilities (maxinmum capacity 250). 24-hour
room service and secure parking for 35 cars in a basement garage.
Rooms 117. *Brasserie (7am-midnight). Closed Christmas day. Amex,
Access, Diners, Visa.*

Dublin   Ryans of Parkgate Street   £55

Tel 01 671 9352 Fax 01 671 3590	R
28 Parkgate Street Dublin 8	Map 3 A4

This professionally-run, well-appointed little restaurant over the
famous pub is popular with locals and, as it is handy for Heuston
station just across the bridge, a visit can be a treat before or after
a journey. Robert Moorehouse, chef since the restaurant first
opened in 1989, prepares interesting menus and presents them
with confidence. Typical starters from a choice of eight on the
à la carte dinner menu might include lamb's sweetbreads with
radicchio, sorrel and mustard sauce or goat's cheese wrapped
in spinach baked in filo pastry. Main courses also offer a choice
of eight, including, perhaps, feuilleté of Dublin Bay prawns and
monkfish with lemon and garlic sauce or roast rack of lamb,
thyme sauce, served with potato cutlet. Desserts include
particularly good ice creams and there's always an Irish farmhouse
cheese plate. Downstairs, one of Dublin's finest Victorian pubs has
been in the same family for three generations – the present
building is a reconstruction dating from 1896 and retains many
original features, including two snugs at the back, a magnificent
carved oak and mahogany central bar (its centrepiece a double-
faced mechanical clock), brass gas lamps and an outstanding
collection of antique mirrors. Bar fare runs from a choice of soups

and simple light snacks to traditional hot dishes, with slightly
more variety in the evening. There are also different menus
at lunchtime (fixed-price) and in the evening (à la carte). Pub
telephone: 01 677 6097. *Restaurant: **Seats** 32. L 12.30-2.30 D 7-
10 (Sat to 10.30). Closed L Sat, D Mon, all Sun, Bank Holidays. Set
L £13. Pub: **Open** 10.30am-11.30pm, Sun 12.30-2 & 4-11. **Bar
Food** 12.30-2.30 (Sat & Sun 10.30am-11.30pm, L soup and
sandwiches only), 5.30-7.30.* AMERICAN EXPRESS *Access, Visa.*

Dublin	Sachs Hotel	62%	£116
Tel 01 668 0995 Fax 01 668 6147			**H**
19-29 Morehampton Road Donnybrook Dublin 4			**Map 3 B2**

The night club at this small hotel in a Georgian terrace is a
popular attraction, and a different kind of exercise is available (free
to residents) at a leisure centre a short drive away. Bedrooms are
individually appointed in period style, and double-glazing keeps
things peaceful at the front. Conference/function facilities.
***Rooms** 20. Closed 24 & 25 Dec.* AMERICAN EXPRESS *Access, Diners, Visa.*

Dublin	Señor Sassi's	£58
Tel & Fax 01 668 4544		**R**
146 Upper Leeson Street Dublin 4		**Map 6 G1**

Busy, bustling restaurant with densely packed marble-topped
tables and currently fashionable Mediterranean/Californian style
dishes; salad of warm squid with ginger and soy, noisette of lamb
in puff pastry with mozarella and basil, fillet steak with
caramelised onions and mash, nage of fish and shellfish, bruschetta
with chargrilled vegetables. The daytime menu is in brasserie style
with dishes ranging from £1.90 (for country broth with hot
bruschetta) to £7.50 (steak with red wine jus and braised
cabbage). ***Seats** 65. Private Room 35. L 12-3 D 6-11.30 (Fri & Sat
7-12, Sun 5.30-10.30). Set L £9.50. Closed L Sat & Mon, Good
Friday, 25 & 26 Dec, 1 Jan.* AMERICAN EXPRESS *Access, Diners, Visa.*

Dublin	Shalimar	£50
Tel 01 671 0738 Fax 01 677 3478		**R**
17 South Great George's Street Dublin 2		**Map 5 F3**

Smart, comfortable restaurant opposite the Central Hotel serving
standard Indian fare in friendly fashion. ***Seats** 100. L 12-2.30
D 6-1. Closed Christmas, Good Friday. Set L £13 Set D £37.95.
Access, Diners, Visa.*

Dublin	Shelbourne Hotel	74%	£226
Tel 01 676 6471 Fax 01 661 6006			**H**
St Stephen's Green Dublin 2			**Map 5 F2**

Situated on St Stephen's Green, Europe's largest garden square, the
Shelbourne has been at the centre of Dublin life since opening its
doors early in the 19th century. The Irish Constitution was
drafted in what is now one of the many function rooms. The hotel
has retained much of its original grandeur, with a magnificent
faux-marbre entrance hall and a sumptuous lounge where morning
coffee and afternoon tea are taken. The famous Horseshoe Bar and
the newer Shelbourne Bar are among the favourite gathering
places for Dubliners, especially on a Friday night, and many

a scandal has originated from their walls. Spacious, elegantly furnished superior and de-luxe rooms and suites have traditional polished wood furniture and impressive drapes, while standard rooms in a newer wing are smaller. All rooms are well appointed, with bathrobes, mini-bars and three telephones as standard. Valet parking. 12 function rooms can cater for up to 400 for a reception. Children up to 16 stay free in parents' room. Forte Grand. **Rooms** 164. *Beauty salon, gents' hairdressing, news kiosk.* AMERICAN EXPRESS® *Access, Diners, Visa.*

Dublin   The Stag's Head

Tel 01 679 3701	P
1 Dame Court Dublin 2	Map 5 F3

Although small by comparison with the vast drinking emporiums being built today, The Stag's Head remains one of Dublin's most impressive old pubs – a lofty, spacious bar and one of the few with its original late-Victorian decor more or less untouched. Sit at the long granite bar and regret the absence of hand pumps which used to grace it, but enjoy the acres of original mahogany and admire its hand-worked detail. Some of it frames the marvellous bevelled mirrors that soar up to finish in curvaceous arches over the panelling and original fittings behind the bar. *Open usual pub hours (10.30am-11.30pm) but only 7-11pm on Sunday and Bank Holidays. Closed Good Friday, 25 Dec. No credit cards.*

Dublin   La Stampa   ↑

	£60
Tel 01 677 8611 Fax 01 677 3336	R
35 Dawson Street Dublin 2	Map 5 F2

Oh that London should have a restaurant such as this! Our 1995 Ireland Restaurant of the Year (see page 23) is big and bold, lively and fun – a place where the food really does complement the surroundings. And what a room, high-ceilinged, huge mirrors adorning the walls with shelves interspaced by candelabra, lamps, urns, plants and the odd bust at either end of the dining hall (indeed it is more hall than room). The plain wood floor emphasises the clatter and bustle, and (if you can hear it above the din) the music is often loud and uplifting. The entrance seems cosier than in the past, with comfortable banquettes, marble-topped tables and lots of art – a mixture of the old and the new.   All the staff are terrific, but why don't the lady members get to wear the same colourful waistcoats as the chaps? Kick off with decent bread (brown soda or focaccia perhaps) and scrutinise Paul Flynn's monthly-changing menu carefully. There's an eclectic mix of dishes, with lobster bisque (topped with a frothy garlic cream) sitting happily alongside Thai crab risotto and perhaps goat's cheese pizza, escalope of veal milanaise or daube of beef with cabbage, bacon, carrots and mash; one could follow with bread-and-butter pudding (served with a light, raspberry-infused custard) or a blackberry crème soufflé. Good local cheeses such as Abbey Blue, Cooleeney and Gubbeen, plus excellent coffee. The wine list is both inexpensive and cheerful. Downstairs, the bistro serves a slightly different and shorter menu, perhaps a feuilleté of mushrooms and onions, pan-fried sea trout with a citrus beurre blanc and a praline cheesecake. Three courses and coffee in the

bistro will set you back just £20. *Seats 200. Parties 14. Private
room 50. L 12.30-2.30 D 6.30-11.15 (11.45 Fri & Sat).
Closed L Sat & Sun, L Bank hols, all 25th & 26th Dec.
Set L £12.50.* AMERICAN EXPRESS *Access, Diners, Visa.*

Dublin   The Station House

Tel 01 831 3772	**P**
3-5 Station Road Raheny Dublin 5	Map 4 C4

Outside may be deceptively like any other fairly traditional
Dublin pub, but inside, the Station House has surprising Spanish-
style decor – heavy, rustic furniture upholstered in warm, 'aged'
tapestry and carpet-bagging fabrics sit comfortably around tile-
topped tables on hard wooden floors enlivened by the occasional
trompe l'oeil 'rug' strategically placed to trip the unwary.
Traditional bar food from the carvery is freshly cooked and
wholesome: roast rib of beef (£5.10), soup (£1.30), plaice and
chips (£3.95), vegetable stir-fry (£4.25), steaks (£4.50/£8.95);
also sandwiches and salads. A la carte menu (with a few children's
favourites) during the afternoons and evenings. Staff are friendly
and helpful and there's a walled garden at the back. Barbecues
most weekends (weather permitting). *Open 10.30am-11.30pm (Sun
12.30-2 & 4-11). **Bar Food & Meals** carvery 12-2.30 (Sun to 2),
à la carte 2.30-9 (Sun 4-8). Children allowed to eat in the lounge until
7.30, children's menu. Garden, outdoor eating. Closed Good Friday,
25 & 26 Dec. Access, Visa.*

Dublin   Stauntons on the Green   £88

Tel 01 478 2133 Fax 01 478 2263	**A**
83 St Stephen's Green South Dublin 2	Map 5 F2

The major programme of upgrading at Stauntons, completed this
year, has lifted it from its previous guesthouse status. The front
bedrooms overlook the beautiful St Stephen's Green while the
rear-facing rooms have almost equally attractive views over the
hotel's private gardens and Victorian Iveagh Gardens beyond.
Recently acquired, this mid-terrace Georgian property comprises
three houses of fine classical proportions. Currently there's
a traditional rear-facing sitting room while upstairs, bedrooms are
fitted with simple units and have tea/coffee facilities and remote-
control TVs. Bathrooms, all with showers, have good toiletries.
No dogs. *Rooms 33. Garden. Closed 25 & 26 Dec.* AMERICAN EXPRESS
Access, Diners, Visa.

Dublin   Stephen's Hall Hotel   65%   £143

Tel 01 661 0585 Fax 01 661 0606	**HR**
Earlsfort Centre 14/17 Lower Leeson Street Dublin 2	Map 5 F2

Situated in a thriving business and tourist area just off St Stephen's
Green and run on the same lines as *Morrison's Island* in Cork (see
entry), Stephen's Hall is an all-suite hotel. Each suite has its own
lobby and kitchenette in addition to a dining area and sitting
room. Suite types range from studios (double bed, kitchen,
bathroom) to three townhouses each with one double and two
single bedrooms, two bathrooms, sitting room, kitchen, dining
room, balcony and private entrance to the street. All are well
furnished in a pleasingly understated modern Irish style, with

thoughtfully planned bathrooms and well-designed furniture.
In addition to full room service and 24hr porter service, a special
shopping service is available for guests who wish to cook in their
suite; all meals, including breakfast, can also be taken in the
restaurant. Free, secure parking. **Rooms** *37. Garden.*
Closed 24 Dec-3 Jan. ![AMERICAN EXPRESS] *Access, Diners, Visa.*

The Bistro £50

Despite its new name and some new faces in the kitchen, there are
no obvious changes at this bright and warmly decorated semi-
basement restaurant. Menus continue to feature a well-balanced
choice of varied dishes (with an evident Oriental influence)
in starters such as tempura vegetables with sake and soy sauce
or poached chicken terrine with tomato and coriander dressing
and main courses like grilled fillet of sea trout with a light
coconut and almond sauce or marinated duck breast with a rich
plum confit; there's always just a special vegetarian option
(included on both à la carte and set menus), typically potato
gnocchi with basil, olive oil and Parmesan. Nice desserts include
good home-made ices and an Irish cheese plate. Excellent value
lunches with a choice of three or so dishes are each course.
Seats *48. Parties 8. Tables for 10 in courtyard. Private Room 3/12.
L 12.30-2.30 D 6.30-10. Closed L Sat, all Sun, Bank Holidays,
23 Dec-3 Jan. Set L £8.50/£10 Set D £15.50.*

Dublin	Ta Se Mohogani Gaspipes	£45
Tel 01 679 8138		R
17 Manor Street Stoneybatter Dublin 7		Map 3 A4

A nonsense name for a stylish little American restaurant featuring
live jazz on Friday and Saturday. Lunchtime brings pasta,
omelettes, burgers and New York strip sirloin steak, while in the
evening there's pasta plus specialities like chicken cutlet milanese
or oriental-style sautéed pork medallions. Also daily fish,
international and dessert specials ("your waitperson will inform
you"). Vegetarian dishes, too. **Seats** *47. Parties 20. L 12-3 D 7-11
(Fri & Sat to 12.30 am), Sun 1-4 (brunch menu). Closed L Sat,
D Sun, all Mon, Good Friday, 25 & 26 Dec. Access, Diners, Visa.*

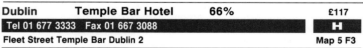

Dublin	Temple Bar Hotel	66%	£117
Tel 01 677 3333 Fax 01 667 3088			H
Fleet Street Temple Bar Dublin 2			Map 5 F3

In a cheering reversal of the usual take-over process, this well-
located hotel in Dublin's 'Left Bank' area is situated in premises
previously a bank. Everything of interest on both sides of the river
that divides the city centre is within easy walking distance and the
hotel itself has a pleasant atmosphere, starting with the spacious
reception/lounge area and adjacent cocktail bar, through the
bright and airy, all-day Terrace Café. Bedrooms (ten non-
smoking, two equipped for disabled guests) are soberly decorated
in deep shades, generally larger than average, and almost all have
a double and single bed plus TV, phone, tea/coffee-making,
hairdryer and trouser press as standard. Neat, well-lit bathrooms
have over-bath showers and marble wash basin units, all identical
except for variations in size. No private parking. **Rooms** *108.
Closed 23-28 Dec.* ![AMERICAN EXPRESS] *Access, Diners, Visa.*

Dublin   Thomas Read
| Tel 01 677 1487   Fax 01 671 2672 | **P** |

4 Parliament Street Dublin 2   Map 5 E3

Opposite the entrance to Dublin Castle and next door to the long-
established cutlers from which it gains its name, the gleaming
curved glass frontage and enticing lights within encourage the
curious to venture into this dashing example of the new breed
of café-bar – and, true to its Continental origins perhaps, this one
seems to be attracting literary types from nearby newspapers and
Trinity College. Good coffee, too. *Seats 100. L 12-4.*
Closed 25 & 26 Dec, Good Friday. AMERICAN EXPRESS *Access, Visa.*

Dublin   Toners Pub
| Tel 01 676 3090 | **P** |

139 Lower Baggot Street Dublin 2   Map 5 F2

Situated only a few hundred yards from the *Shelbourne Hotel* and
St Stephen's Green, this rare survivor of a style of pub which has
all but disappeared in Dublin is now fiercely resistant to change.
Owners, regulars and visitors alike blossom in its dimly-lit
interior, where pints are drunk in the hard-benched little snug,
or on high wooden stools at the bar with its rackety old combed-
wood divisions. Journalists from offices across the road discuss the
issues of the day, actors on location in the city come to share
the buzz and everyone enjoys the genuine charm of Toners.
Totally Irish, great crack … "you couldn't change this place".
Open 10.30am-11.30pm (Sun 12.30-2 & 4-11).
Closed Good Friday, 25 Dec. No credit cards.

Dublin   Tosca
| Tel 01 679 6744   Fax 01 677 4804 | **JaB** |

20 Suffolk Street Dublin 2   Map 5 F3

The rear of Tosca's bar, most unusually, features a significant
section of the blackened hull of a ship. Wrought out of papier
maché instead of steel, it looks authentic, however, complete with
rivets and portholes; in its centre is a gleaming brass espresso
machine. All this strikes you immediately you enter and it sets
the tone for what is a stylishly modern restaurant serving suitably
fashionable new-wave Italian food ("Southern European") plus
pizzas (calzone £6.95). Tomato crostini (£2.20), black pudding
croustade (£8.95), amaretto chicken (£9.25), a variety of pasta
dishes (from £6.75) and fresh fruit tart or tiramisu gateau (£3.50)
are typical of the imaginative and enjoyable cooking on offer here.
*Seats 80. Parties 30. Private Room 15. Meals 11am-midnight (to 1am
Thur-Sat). Closed Good Friday, 25 & 26 Dec.* AMERICAN EXPRESS
Access, Visa.

Dublin   The Westbury   79%   £189
| Tel 01 679 1122   Fax 01 679 7078 | **HR** |

Off Grafton Street Dublin 2   Map 5 F3

Part of the Doyle Hotel Group since 1985, the Westbury
is located within walking distance of many Dublin landmarks.
The major shops are also close at hand, and the hotel has its own
shopping mall. Among the day rooms are the Terrace Bar and the

Sandbank Seafood Bar. Pinks and blues are key colours in the
bedrooms, which offer a high standard of comfort and accessories;
they range from modernised singles to luxury penthouse suites.
Business gatherings and banquets (to a maximum of 200) are
accommodated in elegantly furnished boardrooms and function
suites. Here, as elsewhere, the Westbury has the atmosphere of a
top-class hotel with legions of staff providing a good level
of service. The hotel is currently undergoing a process
of refurbishment scheduled for completion in Spring 1995.
*Rooms 203. Gymnasium, spa bath, beauty & hair salon, news kiosk,
coffee shop (10am-10pm).* *Access, Diners, Visa.*

Russell Room   £85

The traditional French menu holds few surprises, though the
cooking is sound and both service and surroundings suitably
stylish. A three-course table d'hote lunch (four courses at dinner)
offers a choice of five or so dishes at each course – a typical choice
might be sauté of lamb kidneys with chipolatas and mushrooms
followed by fricassee of monkfish with mussels and gratin
of seasonal fruits with passion fruit coulis to finish. *Seats 96.
L 12.30-2.30 D 6.30-10.30. Set L £15.50 Set D £25.50.*

Dublin   Wong's   £60

Tel 01 833 4400   **R**

436 Clontarf Road Dublin 3   Map 4 C4

Black marble gleams invitingly at this well-established northside
Chinese restaurant, featuring the cuisines of Peking, Shanghai,
Szechuan and Canton, and a loyal local following continues
to appreciate the high standard of service and easy-going attitude
as much as the consistent excellence of the food. From a lively à la
carte which forms the basis of the set dinners for a given number
of diners, start perhaps with an authentic rendition of Peking duck,
or meat sung, a delicious mixture of minced pork, roast duck and
crunchy vegetables on a bed of crispy rice noodles, served
individually on fresh iceberg lettuce leaves. To follow, a typical
Cantonese speciality might be fillet steak with garlic and black
bean sauce, served of a sizzling hot plate or, from Shanghai, hot
peppery chicken, sliced and stir-fried with herbs and spices,
or Szechuan chicken, stir-fried with celery and spicy garlic sauce.
Weak desserts, but China tea makes a refreshing ending. *Seats 120.
Parties 10. Private Room 40. L 12.30-2.30 (1-23 Dec only) D 6-12
(12.30 Fri & Sat). Set L from £12 Set D from £18.50. Closed 24-
26 Dec.* *Access, Diners, Visa.*

Dublin   The Yacht

Tel 01 833 6364   Fax 01 833 3009   **P**

73 Clontarf Road Dublin 3   Map 4 C4

This old-established local is known variously as 'The Yacht' and
'Tobin's,' and is like a great white steamer looking over to the
port. Within, decorative buff 'sails' soften the height of the light,
airy bar and a mixed collection of maritime bric-a-brac – some
of it genuinely old and including artefacts from the much-loved
old back bar, the 'Tiller Room' – combine old and new to create
a lively atmosphere which goes far beyond the usual 'theme decor'.
Bar food at this friendly, well-run pub is unpretentious,

wholesome, good value – and predictably popular, and luckily there is plenty of counter and table space for a fair crowd to eat in comfort. Everything is home-made, roast beef from the carvery is good value (£4.95) and comes with two styles of potato and four other fresh vegetables; Pavlova (£1.30) is the favourite dessert. The wide pavement is popular for alfresco relaxation in summer, despite the traffic. *Open 10.30am-11.30pm (Sun 12.30-3 & 4-11). Food carvery 12.30-3. **Bar Food** 3-10 (Sun 12.30-3, 4-7.30). Children allowed in bar to eat until 6.30pm, children's menu. Patio, outdoor eating. Closed Good Friday, 25 Dec. Access, Visa.*

Dublin   Yellow House

Tel 01 493 2994	**P**
Willbrook Road Rathfarnham Dublin 14	Map 3 A1

The Yellow House is named after the unusual shade of the bricks with which it was built, and is the landmark pub of Rathfarnham. It makes a perfect rendezvous point, with no chance of confusion. It's tall and rather forbidding from the outside, the warmth of the interior comes as a pleasant surprise and repays closer examination of pictures and old decorative items of local historical interest. Daily lunchtime carvery (around £5) in the lounge bar; basket snacks and straightforward dishes like chicken drumsticks (£2.95), minute steak (£4.95), crab claws (£3.95), lasagne (£4.50) in the evening. Evening à la carte (and Sunday lunch) in the restaurant upstairs (no children after 7pm) – but our recommendation is for bar food. *Open 10.30am-11.30pm (Sun 12.30-2 & 4-11).* **Bar Food** *Mon-Fri 5-8 (Sat 12-8). Carvery Mon-Fri 12.30-2.30. Closed Good Friday, 25 & 26 Dec.* AMERICAN EXPRESS® *Access, Diners, Visa.*

Dublin   Zen   ↑

	£50
Tel 01 497 9428	**R**
89 Upper Rathmines Road Dublin 6	Map 3 B2

An unusual Chinese restaurant in many respects, not least that the south-city premises occupy what was once a Church of England meeting hall – the lofty hammer-beam roof is still evident. Purchased by the present owner in the 60s, the building started its new life as a snooker and slot machines hall, but the advent of the national lottery put a stop to that! The other reason it's unusal is because it's owned by an Irishman, Dennis O'Connor, who doesn't speak a word of Chinese, yet imports his chefs and staff directly from Beijing. They eventually arrive after many months of bureaucratic red tape. The cooking is mainly Szechuan with the particularly hot and spicy dishes asterisked on the menu, such as the hot (in both senses) appetizer of dumplings in a ginger, garlic and chili sauce, guaranteed to burn (in a tasteful manner) the roof of your mouth! For the less adventurous there are more conventional starters: sesame prawn toast, crispy spring rolls and orange-flavoured sliced beef. Main dishes include succulent and carefully prepared prawns (fried with cashew nuts or in a garlic sauce), steamed whole black sole in ginger sauce or various sizzling meats. Aromatic or smoked duckling arrive less highly seasoned, or you could give a day's notice and order crispy Beijing duck, roasted whole, its skin and meat mixed with spring onions and bean paste, then rolled in wheat pancakes. For those undecided there are several set dinners from which to choose, or else one can

ask for a cross-section of specialities. Charming service can
sometimes be a little hesitant; incidentally, the house white wine
goes extremely well with the style of cooking. *Seats 90.
L 12.30-2.45 D 6-11.30. Closed L Mon-Wed & Sat, 25 & 26 Dec,
Good Friday. Set L £8, D from £16.* AMERICAN EXPRESS *Access,
Diners, Visa.*

Dublin   Places of Interest

British Embassy Merrion Road Tel 01 269 5211
Tourist Information Tel 01 284 4768
Dublin Airport Tel 01 844 5387
Bus Eirann (Irish Bus) Booking Information Tel 01 836 6111
Automobile Association Tel 01 283 3555
Bank of Ireland College Green Tel 01 661 5933
Trinity College (Book of Kells) and Dublin Experience
   University of Dublin Tel 01 677 2941
The Curragh Co Kildare Tel 045 41205
Dublin Zoo Phoenix Park Tel 01 677 1425
Fairyhouse Racecourse Ratoath Tel 01 825 6777
Irish Whiskey Corner Bow Street Distillery Tel 01 872 5566
Gaelic Athletic Association (GAA) Tel 046 23638
Croke Park Football Ground Hurling and Gaelic Football
   Tel 01 836 3222
Irish Rugby Union Tel 01 668 4601
Lansdowne Road Rugby Ground Baub Bridge Tel 01 668 4601
   Theatres and Concert Halls
Abbey and Peacock Theatres Lower Abbey Street Tel 01 878 7222
Andrew's Lane Theatre Exchequer Street Tel 01 679 5720
Gaiety Theatre South King Street Tel 01 677 1717
Gate Theatre Cavendish Row Tel 01 874 4045
Olympia Theatre Dame Street Tel 01 677 7744
Tivoli Theatre Francis Street Tel 01 454 4472
National Concert Hall Earlsfort Terrace Tel 01 671 1888
Point Depot (Exhibitions and Concerts) North Wall Quay
   Tel 01 836 6000
Irish Film Centre Eustace Street Tel 01 679 3477
   Museums and Art Galleries
Dublinia, Christchurch Tel 01 475 8137
Chester Beatty Library and Gallery of Oriental Art Shrewsbury Road
   Tel 01 269 2386
Civic Museum South William Street Tel 01 679 4260
Dublin Writer's Museum Parnell Square North Tel 01 872 2077
Fry Model Railway Museum Malahide Castle Tel 01 845 2758
Irish Museum of Modern Art/Royal Hospital Kilmainham
   Tel 01 671 8666
Guinness Brewery James's Gate Tel 01 453 6700 ext 5155
Hugh Lane Municipal Gallery Parnell Square Tel 01 874 1903
National Gallery of Ireland Merrion Square West Tel 01 661 5133
National Museum of Ireland Kildare Street Tel 01 661 8811
National Wax Museum Granby Row, Parnell Square Tel 01 872 6340
Natural History Museum Merrion Street Tel 01 661 8811
   Historic Houses, Castles and Gardens
Ashtown Castle Phoenix Park Tel 01 661 3111
Drimnach Castle Longmile Road Tel 01 450 2530 *4 miles*
Dublin Castle Dame Street Tel 01 677 7129
Joyce Tower Sandycove Tel 01 280 9265
Kilmainham Gaol Kilmainham Tel 01 453 5984
Malahide Castle Malahide Tel 01 845 2655
Marsh's Library St Patrick Close Tel 01 454 3511
National Botanic Gardens Glasnevin Tel 01 837 7596
Newbridge House Donabate Tel 045 31301
Newman House St Stephen's Green Tel 01 475 7255

Number Twenty Nine Lower Fitzwilliam Street Tel 01 702 6165
Powerscourt Townhouse South William Street Tel 01 679 4144
Royal Hospital Kilmainham Tel 01 671 8666
  Cathedrals & Churches
Christ Church Cathedral Christ Church Place Tel 01 677 8099
St Patrick's Cathedral Patrick's Close Tel 01 475 4817
Whitefriar Street Carmelite Church Aungier Street Tel 01 475 8821
Pro Cathedral Marlborough Street Tel 01 287 4292

Dublin Airport	**Forte Crest**	**57%**	**£132**
Tel 01 844 4211 Fax 01 842 5874			**H**
Dublin Airport Co Dublin			Map 1 D3

Conference facilities for 160, 10 meeting rooms, ample car parking and 24hr room service in a modern hotel within the airport complex. Some non-smoking rooms, some of family size (children up to 16 stay free in parents' room). *Rooms 188.* *Closed 25 Dec.* AMERICAN EXPRESS *Access, Diners, Visa.*

Dugort	**Gray's Guest House**	**£36**
Tel 098 43224		**A**
Dugort Achill Island Co Mayo		Map 1 A3

Since 1979 Vi and Arthur McDowell have been running this legendary guesthouse, renowed for its relaxing properties and gentle hospitality and occupying a series of houses, each with a slightly different atmosphere especially appropriate to particular age groups, in the attractive village of Dugort. Public areas include a large, comfortably furnished sitting room with an open fire and several conservatories for quiet reading. Rooms and bathrooms vary considerably due to the age and nature of the premises, but the emphasis is on old-fashioned comfort and there are extra shared bathrooms in addition to en-suite facilities. Children are welcome (free in parents' room up to 4, under-12s 50%), cots provided at no extra charge, high-chairs, children's early evening meal (6pm). There's an indoor play room and safe outdoor play area, also pool and table tennis for older children. Small conferences (25-30 delegates). *Rooms 17 (4 family rooms).* *Closed 1 Nov-1 Mar. No credit cards.*

Dun Laoghaire	**Chestnut Lodge**	**£50**
Tel 01 280 7860 Fax 01 280 1466		**A**
2 Vesey Place Monkstown Dun Laoghaire		Map 4 D1

Built in 1844, the building is a very fine example of classical Regency architecture. From its position almost at the end of a row of similar houses on a hillside, there are glimpses of the sea visible through the chestnut trees which were planted in a small park across the road at the front. This is very much a family home with breakfast taken communally at a beautiful highly polished mahogany dining table in the drawing room. Here, after a very comfortable night's sleep in one of the spacious, warm and well-appointed bedrooms, you can enjoy freshly squeezed orange juice, a choice of fresh fruit salad, yoghurts, stewed fruits and cereals before tucking into a delicious traditional Irish cooked breakfast finished off by oven-warmed croissants and home-made preserves. Very usefully located close to the Dun Laoghaire/Holyhead ferry terminal. No dogs. *Rooms 4. Garden. Access, Visa.*

Dun Laoghaire   Restaurant na Mara   £75

Tel 01 280 0509   Fax 01 284 4649   **R**

1 Harbour Road Dun Laoghaire Co Dublin   **Map 4 D1**

Railway buffs will be fascinated by this elegant harbourside
restaurant, as it is the old Kingstown terminal building and
is owned by Irish Rail Catering Services. In 1970 a preservation
order was issued by the local authority. The interior has classical
decor throughout in soft soothing tones. French-influenced menus
are a mixture of traditional and modern styles, with a strong
emphasis on the sea in dishes like lobster bisque, crab and sole
terrine wrapped in salmon, pan-fried sea trout, steamed fillet
of sole. At dinner flambéed specialities feature and there is a short
choice of meat and vegetarian dishes. A good sprinkling of New
World wines supplements the extensive French selection; prices
are fair, champagne abundant, and there's no shortage of half
bottles. *Seats* 75. *Private Room 30. L 12.30-2.30 D 5-10.30.
Closed Sun, 1 week Christmas, Bank Holidays. Set L from £15
Set D £23.* AMERICAN EXPRESS *Access, Diners, Visa.*

Dun Laoghaire   Royal Marine Hotel   64%   £120

Tel 01 280 1911   Fax 01 280 1089   **H**

Marine Road Dun Laoghaire Co Dublin   **Map 4 D1**

Imposing Victorian hotel set in four acres of grounds overlooking
the ferry port yet just moments from the main street of town.
Grand day rooms feature faux-marble columns, high ceilings and
elaborate coving. Upstairs, it's a hotel of two halves with the best
rooms, off broad chandelier-lit corridors in the original building,
having nice lightwood furniture and smart bathrooms; eight
of the rooms here are particularly large, with four-poster beds,
antique furniture and spacious bathrooms boasting chunky
Victorian-style fittings. The remaining bedrooms are in the 1960s'
Marine Wing and offer ageing shelf-type fitted units and
a textured finish to the walls. Substantial cooked breakfast.
Complimentary secure parking. No dogs. ***Rooms** 104. Garden.*
AMERICAN EXPRESS *Access, Diners, Visa.*

Dun Laoghaire   The South Bank   £55

Tel 01 280 8788   **R**

1 Martello Terrace Dun Laoghaire Co Dublin   **Map 4 D1**

A solitary survivor on a seafront once renowned for its fine
restaurants and just around the corner from *Bistro Vino* (see entry
under Sandyeire). David and Deirdre Byrne have run The South
Bank since 1986 and are now wisely introducing their offspring
to the business, with son Garrett now in the kitchen. It's a neat,
slightly formal place in a cosy semi-basement safe from the
onshore winds which sometimes lash across the seafront here, but
a piano and photographs recording high-profile visits indicate that
any formality may melt away as the evening progresses and
a friendly waitress eases guests through quieter times. Food tends
to be fairly traditional, as in duck liver and brandy paté enlivened
by a home-made fruit chutney and freshly baked wholemeal
bread; soup might be a pleasingly smoky bacon and spinach.
There's no hint of special preferences in the wide-ranging main

courses, but although there is always a choice of fish – typically poached salmon with a light lemon and sorrel sauce – vegetarian options (and any other dietary requirements) should be arranged when booking. Good homely desserts – rhubarb tart, fruit salad – or Irish cheeseboard. Unlimited, freshly-brewed coffee. *Seats 50. L by arrangement D 6.45-10.45. Closed 23 Dec-27 Dec. Set D £11 & £17.* AMERICAN EXPRESS *Access, Diners, Visa.*

Dun Laoghaire   Places of Interest

Tourist Information Tel 01 280 6984/5/6
National Maritime Museum Haigh Terrace Tel 01 280 0969
James Joyce Tower Sandycove Tel 01 280 9265

Dundalk Ballymascanlon House Hotel	**61%**	**£75**
Tel 042 71124 Fax 042 71598		**H**
Ballymascanlon Dundalk Co Louth		**Map 1 D3**

Set in acres of parkland 2 miles on the Belfast side of Dundalk, this Victorian mansion makes a comfortable and characterful medium-sized hotel with plenty of space for guests to relax and friendly, helpful staff. Bedrooms vary considerably in size but all are en suite and, although some small singles have shower only, most have bath and over-bath shower. The leisure complex (built in the mid-70s and one of the earliest of its kind) is being refurbished and upgraded for the 1995 season, when it will have a new steam room and jacuzzi. 24hr room service. Banqueting/conferences for 250/300. Children under 4 may stay free in their parents' room; baby-sitting by arrangement; outdoor & indoor play rooms; cots, high-chairs available. *Rooms 35 (3 interconnecting family rooms). Leisure centre, tennis, table tennis, snooker. Closed 24-26 Dec.* AMERICAN EXPRESS *Access, Diners, Visa.*

Dundalk Quaglino's		**£55**
Tel 042 38567		**R**
88 Clanbrassil Street Dundalk Co Louth		**Map 1 D3**

Northern influences are much in evidence at this extensive well-appointed first-floor restaurant – both in style, which is more traditional than equivalent restaurants further south, and in quantity, which is very generous. Comfort is a high priority and also service, which, under the watchful eye of restaurant manager Pat Smyth, ensures maximum enjoyment of chef Pat Kerley's confident use of fine local produce. Oysters might be gratinated and served hot, with garlic butter, and confit of duck leg hot and crispy in contrast to its bed of mixed leaves. Well-flavoured soups come with home-baked brown bread, then there might be Cooley lamb, cooked pink and juicy then laid on a bed of imaginatively prepared vegetables, or light yet richly flavoured fillets of sole *bonne femme*. Desserts, which are read aloud, rather than written on the menu, lean towards the rich and creamy, with a special emphasis on chocolate nicely balanced by good coffee, served by the pot. *Seats 50. Parties 12. D only 6.30-11 (Sat to 11.30). Closed Sun (except Mothers Day), 3 days at Christmas. Set D £20.* AMERICAN EXPRESS *Access, Diners, Visa.*

Dundalk   Places of Interest

Tourist Information Tel 042 35484
Basement Gallery Town Hall Tel 042 32276
Dundalk Racecourse Dowdallshill Tel 042 34419
Moyry Castle
Kilnasaggart Pillar Stone

Dundrum   Dundrum House   66%   £95
Tel 062 71116   Fax 062 71366   **H**
Dundrum Co Tipperary   **Map 2 B5**

The Crowe family take great pride in their hotel, a large Georgian
house set in 150 acres through which a trout-filled river runs.
Public rooms include a lofty reception hall, a comfortable drawing
room furnished with wing chairs and, in the old chapel, a bar
with live music every night in summer. Spacious bedrooms (all
redecorated this year) are furnished with antiques. The 150-acre
County Tipperary Golf and Country Club is incorporated within
the extensive grounds. *Rooms 55. Garden, tennis, riding, golf (18),
fishing, snooker.* AMERICAN EXPRESS *Access, Diners, Visa.*

Dunkerrin   Dunkerrin Arms
Tel 0505 45377/45399   **P**
Dunkerrin Birr Co Offaly   **Map 2 C4**

Set well back from the road but clearly visible, this pristine pink-
washed pub makes a good place for a break on the Limerick-
Dublin road. Six en-suite rooms (not inspected) were just coming
on stream as we went to press, and a new conservatory-style self-
service restaurant is due to open in summer '95. *Bar Food 7.30-
10pm. Closed Good Friday, 25 Dec. Access, Visa.*

Dunkineely   Castle Murray House   69%   £48
Tel 073 37022   Fax 073 37330   **HR**
Dunkineely Co Donegal   **Map 1 B2**

Since they opened in September 1991 some hidden force has
gradually drawn the cognoscenti to Thierry and Clare Delcros'
dramatically situated small clifftop hotel a few miles west
of Donegal town. Overlooking the ruins of the castle after which
it is named, with stunning views of the rugged Donegal coastline
and crashing seas, the location is truly breathtaking – and this
sturdily built and well-run establishment lives up to it. On to the

original structure the Delcros have built well-judged additions
including a long and comfortable stone-floored semi-conservatory
along the front (imaginatively lit at night and well placed to make
the most of the view) and a second phase of spacious bedrooms,
furnished simply but to a high standard with pristine white-tiled
bathrooms to match. A cosy bar and residents' sitting room beside
the dining room opened last year. ***Rooms*** *10. Closed mid Jan-
mid Feb. Access, Visa.*

Restaurant   £55

The large, well-appointed dining room has tweed-curtained,
double-glazed windows on two sides to take full advantage of the
views and a big continental-style table-height log fire, providing
an appropriate setting for Thierry Delcros' excellent French
cooking. Menus change by the season, with a stronger emphasis on
seafood in summer, and pricing by choice of main course allows
semi à la carte flexibility of choice with set menu economy, but
their understated language does nothing to prepare the diner for
the richly imaginative treats Thierry has in store – or for his sure-
handed skill in the execution of, typically, mussels in garlic butter
finished unexpectedly with melted cheese and served fiercely hot
with a crispy seaweed garnish. In addition to a wide range
of seafood, main courses might offer an unusual combination like
kebabs of duck fillet, wrapped in bacon, tightly packed on wooden
skewers and served on a little bed of crisp cabbage. Pretty desserts,
a mixed French and Irish farmhouse cheese selection and good
coffee. ***Seats*** *45. Parties 40. L 1-2 (Sun only) D 7-9.30.
Closed Mon & Tues Nov-Easter, 24-26 Dec, 2 weeks Feb.*

Dunlavin	Rathsallagh House	72%	£110
Tel 045 53112 Fax 045 53343			**AR**
Dunlavin Co Wicklow			Map 2 C4

Joe and Kay O'Flynn's delightful, rambling country house (built
in the former stables of a Queen Anne house which burned down
in 1798) has an award-winning walled kitchen garden, 280-acre
farm and seemingly endless rolling parkland. Fishing and deer-
stalking are easily arranged (also hunting in season) and the new
18-hole golf course is a further attraction – or you can simply
catch up with your reading by the fireside in the delightfully
lived-in drawing room. Rooms are generally spacious and quite
luxurious in an understated way, with lovely country views; some
smaller, simpler rooms in the stable yard have a special cottagey
charm. Three bedrooms were added last year. There is a
completely separate private conference facility for up to 50
theatre-style (25 boardroom-style) in a courtyard conversion at the
back. Outstanding breakfasts are served in the traditional way
from a huge sideboard. No children under 12. ***Rooms*** *17. Garden,
croquet, indoor swimming pool, tennis, golf (18), snooker, helipad.
Closed 23-26 Dec.* AMERICAN EXPRESS *Access, Diners, Visa.*

Restaurant   £65

The elegant country-house atmosphere of the restaurant
is enhanced by lovely views over rolling parkland; within, there
are impressive paintings, antiques (notably the huge mahogany
sideboard where magnificent Edwardian-style breakfasts are laid
out each morning on hotplates covered with gleaming cloches),
white-clothed tables and an all-pervading sense of order. Although

Kay O'Flynn still supervises the kitchen herself, chef Owen Sherry moved here from John Moloney's kitchens at nearby *Tinakilly House* in July 1994. Under his influence the cuisine has taken on a more sophisticated aspect, in dishes such as wild salmon 'chop' (chopped salmon marinated in lime juice with chopped avocado and fresh herbs and served with a wedge of wonderfully light and herby home-made focaccia) and a delicate mousse of chicken flavoured with pine nuts and gin and served on a hot bacon and spring onion vinaigrette. The roast beef continues to be as good as ever, most recently experienced as rare fillet, perfectly cooked and presented on a little bed of colcannon with a light, thyme-flavoured gravy; Rathsallagh House wins our 1995 Irish Beef and Lamb award (see page 66) for its superb use of prime local beef and Wicklow lamb. The satisfyingly traditional dessert trolley remains utterly irresistible, offering a choice of at least eight calorific splendours as well as a good basket of half a dozen farmhouse cheeses. Coffee is served in true country-house style by the fire in the recently refurbished drawing room where a little of the inviting, lived-in feeling has perhaps been lost but elegance undoubtedly gained. *Seats 50. Private Room 15. L by arrangement for groups, not Sun. D 7.30-9. 3 days Christmas. Set D £27.*

Dunmore East   The Ship

`Tel 051 383144`   **P**

Dunmore East Co Waterford   Map 2 C5

This well-located roadside bar/restaurant is situated high up over the bay, but is more remarkable for its atmosphere than a sea view. The solidly-built house dates back to Victorian times and, since the mid-80s, has enjoyed a national reputation under the present ownership for local seafood served in pleasantly informal surroundings. The bar area near the entrance develops gradually into a dining area, with unusual, sturdy furniture made from old barrels, darkwood walls and a strongly nautical theme – the interior is dimly atmospheric in contrast to the bright roadside patio area used for casual summer meals. They no longer serve bar food, but the à la carte menu is available lunch and dinner in summer (lunch Sun only in May & Oct, dinner in winter except Sun & Mon). *Open 12-11.30 (winter from 6, Sun 12.30-2 & 4-11).* AMERICAN EXPRESS *Access, Visa.*

Durrus   Blairs Cove House Restaurant   £60

`Tel 027 61127`   **R**

Blairs Cove Durrus nr Bantry Co Cork   Map 2 A6

Converted from the characterful outbuildings of the 17th-century Blairs Cove House, in a lovely waterside location overlooking Dunmanus Bay, Sabine and Philippe de Mey's restaurant has been delighting guests with its unique style since 1981. The renowned buffet groans under an abundance of starters (local seafood, patés and salads), then a wide range of main courses that includes locally caught fish – kebab of scallops, perhaps, or John Dory with vegetables, lemon and soya dressing – and specialities like rack of lamb or steak cooked over an open wood-fired grill in the restaurant. To finish, irresistible desserts and local farmhouse cheeses are dramatically displayed on top of the grand piano. The loos are up a long flight of stairs. Well-equipped, self-catering accommodation is available on the premises and nearby. Look for

the blue entrance gate, 1½ miles outside Durrus, on the Goleen/
Barley Cove road. *Seats 70. D only 7.30-9.30. Closed Sun (also
Mon Sep-Jun), & Nov-mid March. Set D £24. Access, Diners, Visa.*

East Ferry   The Marlogue Inn

Tel 021 813390	P
East Ferry Marina Cobh Co Cork	Map 2 B6

Despite the name, which somehow conveys the impression of an
old-established hostelry, this beautifully located little waterside
pub only opened in 1992 and improvements are still ongoing,
especially in the patio/barbecue area on the river side. Bar food
covers a range from rolls, sandwiches, salads and creamy
mushrooms (£2.95) to fish pie, poached or grilled salmon
(£6.50), a daily pie (£4.75) and fruit tart (£1.40); however,
a new chef has arrived since our most recent visit. In addition,
there's a full restaurant menu. Children under 12 welcome until
7pm. Occasional entertainment in winter. *Open 12-11.30 (to 11 in
winter), Sun 12-11. Bar Food 12-8.30. Garden, outdoor eating.
Closed 25 & 26 Dec. Access, Visa.*

Ennis   Auburn Lodge   61%   £74

Tel 065 21247 Fax 065 21202	H
Galway Road Ennis Co Clare	Map 2 B4

1995 sees the continuation of a comprehensive programme
of refurbishment in the public areas of this modern low-rise hotel
on the N17 20 minutes from Shannon airport. Practical
accommodation, friendly staff and versatile conference/function
facilities for up to 650. Ample free parking. No dogs. *Rooms 100.
Garden, tennis.* AMERICAN EXPRESS® *Access, Diners, Visa.*

Ennis   The Cloister

Tel 065 29521 Fax 065 24783	P
Abbey Street Ennis Co Clare	Map 2 B4

Built right in the walls and garden of a 13th-century Franciscan
abbey, this famous pub is steeped in history and the back windows
of its cosy low-ceilinged rooms overlook the friary and its
brilliant emerald-green grass surrounds. The main restaurant
incorporates rooms from the original abbey kitchen. In winter,
fires create a sense of cheer and, in the event of fine summer
weather, an attractive patio garden provides an escape from the
unseasonable dimness of the bar. Although well supported
by locals, the reputation for good food here extends far beyond
the immediate area with a compact, well-balanced à la carte
restaurant menu and an £18, three-course table d'hote offering
a good choice – from game and foie gras roulade and Fergus
salmon with gazpacho sauce to winter's fruit pudding with brandy
butter. Lunchtime sees the likes of fish pie, scrambled eggs with
smoked salmon, lasagne, Irish stew, chicken pot pie along with
daily fish and meat specials. After 6pm the bar menu incorporates
both snacks (soup of the evening with brown bread, goat's cheese
salad with port sauce) and more substantial dishes (Dijon chicken
en croute, steamed Ballyvaughan mussels with garlic bread –
£6.50, herby rack of lamb – £10.50). *Open 12-11.30 (Sun to 11).
Bar Food 12-3 & 6-9.30 Nov-Easter. Children's menu and portions
available. Patio, outdoor eating. Closed Sun & Mon Nov-Easter.*
AMERICAN EXPRESS® *Access, Visa.*

Ennis   Old Ground Hotel   66%   £99

Tel 065 28127   Fax 065 28112   **H**

Ennis Co Clare   **Map 2 B4**

This famous old ivy-clad hotel next to Ennis cathedral is handy
for Shannon Airport and a convenient base for touring Clare.
Some of the ground-floor bedrooms are suitable for disabled
guests, and conference facilities for up to 250 (banquets 150) are
provided. Children under 12 may stay free in their parents' room;
children's menu and holiday entertainment. Forte Heritage.
Rooms *58. Closed 24-26 Dec.* AMERICAN EXPRESS *Access, Diners, Visa.*

Ennis   West County Inn   59%   £84

Tel 065 28421   Fax 065 28801   **H**

Clare Road Ennis Co Clare   **Map 2 B4**

"Hospitality is our strength" is the motto of this bright modern
hotel, and that extends to families, disabled guests (some rooms
expecially fitted out) and conference delegates. 1994 saw the
completion of a programme of refurbishment in the bedrooms;
new health and conference centres are also planned to open
in May '95 – in the meantime guests have free use of the leisure
centre at the sister hotel *Clare Inn* (Newmarket-on-Fergus).
Rooms *110. Tennis, Snooker.* AMERICAN EXPRESS *Access, Diners, Visa.*

Ennis   Places of Interest

Tourist Information Tel 065 28366
Graggaunowen Bronze Age Project Quin Tel 061 367178
Knappogue Castle Quin Tel 061 361511

Enniskerry   Curtlestown House   £50

Tel 01 282 5083   Fax 01 286 6509   **R**

Curtlestown Enniskerry Co Wicklow   **Map 2 D4**

A charming country restaurant in a little farmhouse half an hour's
drive from Dublin. Colin Pielow's traditional menus change with
the seasons, game being a winter stalwart, with fish taking centre
stage in summer. Poached salmon with watercress sauce, chicken
with wild mushrooms and Pernod sauce, braised saddle of rabbit
and peppered sirloin steak show his admirably straightforward
style. Sunday lunch is much more a family affair than the
evenings. One room is reserved for non-smokers. **Seats** *45.
Private Room 25. L (Sun only) 12.45-2 D 8-9.30. Closed Mon
& D Sun. Set Sun L £12 Set D from £18. Access.*

Enniskerry   Enniscree Lodge Hotel
& Restaurant   59%   £55

Tel 01 286 3542   Fax 01 286 6037   **HR**

Enniskerry Co Wicklow   **Map 2 D4**

Beautifully located, high up on the sunny side of Glencree, this
comfortable inn has been run by siblings Paul Johnson and Lynda
Fox to growing acclaim since 1989. Its many attractive features
include good informal meals, a cosy bar with an open log fire for
winter and a south-facing terrace for warm days. Most of the
comfortably furnished, individually decorated bedrooms have
lovely views and, although slightly dated, all have neat en-suite

bathrooms. A residents' sitting room doubles as a small function room. **Rooms** 10. *Closed Mon-Thur in Jan & Feb.* AMERICAN EXPRESS *Access, Diners, Visa.*

Restaurant   £55

Sweeping views across Glencree provide a fitting setting for chef Paul Moroney's imaginative, confident combination of traditional and contemporary cuisine. Typical offerings start with a speciality soup, based on an 18th-century recipe (and rich beef stock) then there might be a warm terrine of white fish and salmon with a compote of tomato and basil, medallions of Wicklow lamb with a home-made mint chutney and vegetarian options such as Emmental and spinach tart with a garlic mayonnaise, or a vegetarian pastry parcel of pulses and nuts with a purée of olives. Good home-made breads, luscious desserts, farmhouse cheeses and freshly brewed coffee to round it all off. *Seats 40. Parties 8. Private Room 20. L 12.30-3 D 7.30-9.30. Closed 25 Dec, Mon & Tue in Nov, Jan & Feb. Set L (Sun only) £14 Set D £18.*

Enniskerry   Places of Interest

Powerscourt Gardens and Waterfall Tel 01 286 7676
Fernhill Gardens Sandyford Tel 01 295 6000 *3 miles*

Fahan   Restaurant St John's   £55

Tel 077 60289   **R**
Fahan Innishowen Co Donegal   Map 1 C1

In a substantial period house overlooking Lough Swilly, Reg Ryan's warm welcome is underlined by a glowing open fire in the bar area and the decor throughout is comfortably unassertive, leaving the mind clear to enjoy Phil McAfee's confident cooking to the full. A two-tier system offers a five-course restricted choice £15 menu, or more choice at £20. Start perhaps with smoked chicken salad with hazelnut oil and balsamic vinegar or gravad lax with a dill sauce, followed by a home-made soup – typically carrot and tarragon or a chowder – then a tossed mixed leaf salad. Main courses might include tender crisp-skinned roast duckling, cooked on the bone but served off it, lamb with a home-made gooseberry mint jelly or a wide choice of fish – turbot, brill, John Dory – with fennel sauce. Details – delicious home-baked bread, imaginative vegetables, desserts with the emphasis on flavour rather than show, such as peaches in brandy with vanilla ice cream and wonderful choux petits fours with spun sugar served with freshly brewed coffee – all add up to a great dining experience. There's a good selection of half bottles and New World wines on the comprehensive wine list at friendly prices. *Seats 40. Private Room 10. No smoking in rear dining room. D only 7-9.30. Closed Sun-Tue, 2 days Christmas, Good Friday. Access, Diners, Visa.*

Ferrycarrig Bridge   Ferrycarrig Hotel   61%   £80

Tel 053 22999   Fax 053 41982   **HR**
Ferrycarrig Bridge nr Wexford Co Wexford   Map 2 D5

All bedrooms in this well-run modern waterside hotel overlook the Slaney estuary and there is a path leading to Ferrycarrig Castle. Comfortably furnished public rooms include the Dry Dock bar and two restaurants, all enjoying the views. Stylish bedrooms have well-equipped bathrooms with plenty of shelf space. There's conference space for up to 400, ample free parking and up-to-date leisure facilities. **Rooms** *39. Garden, gymnasium, sauna, steam room, solarium.* AMERICAN EXPRESS *Access, Diners, Visa.*

The Conservatory   £60

Renovations and extensions continue at Ferrycarrig, but the Conservatory restaurant remains a pleasant spot beside a paved garden, making good use of the waterside location. Well regarded locally and perhaps best known for Sunday lunch, the kitchen (under head chef Mairead Kennedy since 1992) is at its best when stretched on the à la carte. Local produce is highlighted in, for example, a zesty starter of crab meat enhanced with root ginger, spring onion and pimento, bound with dairy cream and served with a tossed salad; this might be followed by a choice of local beef, pork or seafood and a more unusual choice such as new season's guinea fowl, boned and wrapped in smoky bacon, roasted and served on a piquant cranberry and orange vinaigrette. Desserts range from the homely, as in warm rhubarb and ginger tart with crème anglaise, to more sophisticated offerings and there's always a farmhouse cheeseboard. Also The Boat House restaurant (à la carte D only 6.30-9.15, seats 65). **Seats** *90. L 12.30-2.15 D 7-9.15. Set Sun L £10.50 Set D £22. Closed D Sun-D Thurs Jan-Mar.* AMERICAN EXPRESS *Access, Diners, Visa.*

Fighting Cocks   Fighting Cocks

Tel 0503 48744	**P**
Fighting Cocks Co Carlow	Map 2 C4

Tim Redford's attractive, well-run crossroads pub is a real local, with open fire, snooker and darts plus traditional Irish music every Saturday and Sunday night, all year. Although visually striking, with a collection of agricultural and rural artefacts displayed to advantage around the lofty main bar area, this seems more a fair reflection of bygone ways of country life in the area than just another theme pub. Watch out for a Carlow speciality, hot brandy – just the thing to keep out the cold. Watch out also for eccentric opening hours: "some days we don't even open . . ." *Garden. Closed Good Friday and 25 Dec.*

Foulksmills   Horetown House   £50

Tel 051 63771 Fax 051 63633	**R**
Foulksmills Co Wexford	Map 2 C5

Horetown House is best known as a residential equestrian centre with a relaxed country atmosphere. Residents generally use the dining room in the main house (where a hearty farmhouse dinner is offered as an alternative to the more formal table d'hote). Alternatively, the Cellar Restaurant, which is cosy and atmospheric, with an open fire, whitewashed arches and sturdy country furniture, is open to non-residents and very popular in the area, especially for Sunday lunch (2 sittings). Proprietor Ivor Young and his head chef David Cronin can be relied on to produce meals based around quality ingredients, including local salmon, wild Wicklow venison and other game in season. Mid-week early bird (6.30-7.30) menu: £16. **Seats** *40.*

Private Room 25. L (Sun only) 12.30-2.30 D 6.30-9.30.
Set L £10.50 Set D from £19.50. Closed D Sun, all Mon, Bank
Holidays, 3 days Christmas. Access.

Furbo	**Connemara Coast Hotel**	**71%**	**£120**
Tel 091 592108 Fax 091 92065			**H**
Furbo Co Galway			**Map 2 B4**

Snuggled down into rocks between Barna and Spiddal, on the sea
side of the road, this pleasingly unobtrusive, low-rise modern hotel
has been developed with an environmentally considerate design
policy already successfully applied at the sister hotel, *Connemara
Gateway*, at Oughterard. Spacious public areas include
an impressive foyer/lounge area, large restaurant and
banqueting/conference rooms (capacity up to 450/500)
overlooking the sea and a well-equipped leisure centre. Most
bedrooms have sea views and, although not individually
decorated, are comfortably furnished with neat en-suite
bathrooms. 24hr room service. Good family facilities include six
interconnecting rooms, a playroom and crèche (ring to confirm
supervision and availablity times), high tea and a children's
entertainment programme. No dogs. ***Rooms** 112. Garden, tennis,
indoor swimming pool, children's splash pool, gym, sun beds, sauna, spa
bath, steam room, beauty salon. Closed 24 & 25 Dec.* AMERICAN EXPRESS
Access, Diners, Visa.

Galway	**Ardilaun House**	**66%**	**£104**
Tel 091 21433 Fax 091 21546			**H**
Taylors Hill Galway Co Galway			**Map 2 B4**

The original house was built in 1840 and contains handsomely
proportioned day rooms looking out over the attractive grounds.
Sympathetic extensions have been added over the past 30 years
or so, providing unpretentious, traditionally furnished bedrooms
of various sizes, and a conference facility for up to 400 delegates.
Friendly, helpful staff. No dogs. ***Rooms** 89. Garden, gymnasium,
sauna, solarium, snooker.* AMERICAN EXPRESS *Access, Diners, Visa.*

Galway	**Brennans Yard**	**64%**	**£90**
Tel 091 68166 Fax 091 68262			**H**
Lower Merchants Road Galway Co Galway			**Map 2 B4**

A new hotel created from stylishly converted old warehousing
in Galway city's 'Left Bank' area. First impressions are of an
attractive building with unexpectedly cramped entrance, but the
second phase of development will include the foyer as originally
planned. Public rooms currently in operation include a pleasantly
bright if smallish dining room (also to be extended) and, at the
back, the striking Oyster Bar for informal meals, especially local
seafood. Individually decorated bedrooms make up in style what
is lacking in space – well-planned, clean-lined rooms have old
stripped pine pieces, locally-made pottery and neat, functional
bathrooms; three rooms have both a double and single bed;
family facilities are provided. Direct-dial phones, radio and TV,
tea/coffee-making facilities, hairdryer and toiletries included
as standard. ***Rooms** 24.* AMERICAN EXPRESS *Access, Diners, Visa.*

Galway   Bridge Mills Restaurant

Tel 091 66231   **JaB**

O'Briens Bridge Galway Co Galway   Map 2 B4

Just beside O'Brien's Bridge, overlooking the turbulent Corrib
River, this informal restaurant is snugly situated in the recently
renovated old mills, now used as an educational and arts and crafts
centre. The structure of the building divides the restaurant area
up naturally into a series of 'rooms', some of which have fine
views down river, allowing convenient arrangement of non-
smoking areas. Vegetarians are well catered for as specialities
include the Bridge Mills omelette, available with a wide choice
of fillings (£4.25), as well as a vegetarian dish of the day and
a variety of salads (from £2.95). Good for morning coffee
or afternoon tea with home-made scones or cakes. *Seats 60
(+8 balcony tables). Open 12.30-5.30. Closed Christmas week.
Access, Visa.*

Galway   Casey's Westwood Restaurant   £60

Tel 091 21442/21645   **R**

Dangan Upper Newcastle Galway Co Galway   Map 2 B4

Bernie and Mary Casey have been running this popular eating
place since 1982 and the long, low building houses a number
of bars and restaurant areas to suit various occasions. An evening
in the main restaurant starts in the cocktail lounge, where orders
are taken before you settle into a comfortable carver or banquette
at a well-appointed table to enjoy son John Casey's sound cooking;
there's no doubting John's commitment or his imaginative flair
in the kitchen. His menus offer a wide choice – perhaps offering
a timbale of smoked salmon and cream cheese with mango
mayonnaise, stuffed fillet of pork with wild mushroom sauce and
feuilleté of grapes with a Kirsch sabayon at lunchtime, from
a three-course menu with three choices at each stage. Four-course
dinners see more involved dishes, from ravioli of chicken and
cheese with smoked bacon and basil sauce to half a roast pheasant
served with a purée of parsnip and chocolate and raspberry sauce,
and blackberry and blackcurrant délice with home-made fig and
port ice cream – flavours galore! Vegetables are imaginative,
desserts unusual and prettily presented and home-made petits
fours are served with coffee. Low-cholesterol and vegetarian
dishes available. *Seats 60. L 12.30-2.15 D 6.30-9.45.
Closed 5 days Christmas. Set L £10.95 Set D £22.50.*
Access, Visa.

Galway   Corrib Great Southern Hotel   68%   £117

Tel 091 755281   Fax 091 751390   **H**

Dublin Road Galway Co Galway   Map 2 B4

Overlooking Galway Bay, a large, modern hotel on the edge
of the city, offering a wide range of facilities for both business
guests and family holidays. Bedrooms vary considerably;
refurbished rooms are much improved and new, spacious
'superior' rooms are well planned with good attention to detail
and stylish bathrooms. Children under 12 stay free in parents'
room, £20 per night for over-12s, children's early supper 5-6pm.

The (smallish) swimming pool has a lifeguard at all times and, in summer only, children's entertainment and a crèche are provided. New state-of-the-art business/convention centre has facilities for groups of 8 to 850, with banqueting for up to 650. Public areas include a cosy residents' lounge and O'Malleys Pub, a big, lively bar with sea views. **Rooms** 180. *Indoor swimming pool, steam room, spa bath, snooker, helipad. Closed 24-26 Dec.* AMERICAN EXPRESS®, *Access, Diners, Visa.*

Galway	Glenlo Abbey	68%	£115
Tel 091 26666 Fax 091 27800			**H**
Bushy Park Galway Co Galway			**Map 2 B4**

An 18th-century abbey conversion whose newest rooms include six suites with whirlpool baths. All the rooms have king-size beds, personal safes and roomy, well-designed marble bathrooms. There are two bars – the Kentfield for cocktails and the convivial Oak Cellar, and a variety of function rooms. An 18-hole golf course with clubhouse and restaurant were added recently; two tennis courts, a gymnasium and sauna were promised for spring 1995. 134-acre waterfront position, with 800-metre frontage on to the river Corrib. **Rooms** *45. Garden. Closed 24-29 Dec.* AMERICAN EXPRESS® *Access, Diners, Visa.*

Galway	Great Southern	69%	£113
Tel 091 64041 Fax 091 66704			**H**
Eyre Square Galway Co Galway			**Map 2 B4**

Overlooking Eyre Square right in the heart of Galway, this historic railway hotel (built in 1845) has retained many of its original features, and old-world charm mixes easily with modern facilities. Refurbished public rooms are quite grand and include O'Flahertys Pub bar as well as a cocktail lounge. Bedrooms, also undergoing an upgrade, are generally spacious and traditionally furnished with dark mahogany units, brass light fittings and smart fabrics. Various rooms offer conference facilities for up to 300 (banquets 250). Roof-top swimming pool with magnificent views over the city. **Rooms** *116. Indoor swimming pool, sauna, steam room, hair salon.* AMERICAN EXPRESS® *Access, Diners, Visa.*

Galway	Hooker Jimmy's Steak & Seafood Bar	
Tel 091 68351		**JaB**
The Fishmarket Spanish Arch Galway Co Galway		**Map 2 B4**

John, Margaret and James Glanville run this determinedly middle-market steak and seafood bar near Jurys Inn. Decor has been transplanted from their old premises, with dark green paintwork and soft-toned upholstery, lots of divisions making private corners and, in summer, there are terrace tables overlooking the river. Good value is the keynote and, whether it's a quick steak served as you like it with baked potato and stir-fry vegetables (from £6.95), half-a-dozen oysters baked in herb and garlic butter (£4.75), or seafood chowder (£2.10/£3.25) served with dark, moist home-made bread, good value is what you will get. A family-owned trawler ensures that all the seafood from Galway Bay is as fresh as it can be. 'Diaper deck' provided for baby-

changing in the disabled toilet; high-chairs provided. *Seats 90.*
Open 11.30-11. Closed 25 & 26 Dec. ▮AMERICAN EXPRESS▮ *Access,*
Diners, Visa.

Galway   House of St James

Tel 091 65507	JaB
Castle Street Galway Co Galway	Map 2 B4

Everything is home-made on the premises at this informal daytime
gallery restaurant, situated upstairs in an interesting craft shop –
a constant supply of freshly-made foods is delivered from the
kitchen at the back to the buffet, which is well run and moves fast.
A good place for a wholesome, keenly-priced lunch from the
blackboard menu, or just a cuppa with a slice of seriously
irresistible lemon meringue pie. *Seats 110. Open 9-5.30.*
Closed 25 & 26 Dec.

Galway   Jurys Galway Inn   60%   £61

Tel 091 66444 Fax 091 68415	H
Quay Street Galway Co Galway	Map 2 B4

The emphasis at the Galway Inn is firmly on value for money;
run on the same lines as the new *Jurys Christchurch Inn* in Dublin,
this 'inn' offers a good standard of basic accommodation without
frills. Rooms, almost all with lovely views, are large (sleeping
up to four people) with everything required for basic comfort and
convenience – neat en-suite bathroom, TV, phone – but no extras.
Beds are generous, with good-quality bedding, but wardrobes are
open; tea/coffee-making facilities are provided but not room
service. Public areas include an impressive, well-designed foyer
with seating areas, a pubby bar with a good atmosphere and a self-
service informal restaurant. Obviously a good place for family
accommodation and budget-conscious travellers; booking some
way ahead is advised. *Rooms 128. Closed 24-26 Dec.* ▮AMERICAN EXPRESS▮
Access, Diners, Visa.

We welcome bona fide complaints and recommendations on
the tear-out pages at the back of the Guide for readers'
comments. They are followed up by our professional team.

Galway   Tigh Neachtain

Tel 091 66172	P
Cross Street Galway Co Galway	Map 2 B4

One of Galway's most relaxed and unspoilt pubs, Tigh Neachtain
has great charm and a friendly atmosphere. The mysterious, dark
interior reflects the medieval origins of the building, which has
been in the same family for a century now, but it's not a bit
precious. The pint is good and there's bar food (although the
evening restaurant next door is the main food association) but
perhaps the nicest thing of all is the way an impromptu traditional
music session can get going at the drop of a hat. *Open 10.30am-
11.30pm (11pm in winter, Sun 4-11). Bar Food 12.30-2 exc.*
Sat & Sun). No credit cards.

Galway   Places of Interest

Tourist Information Tel 091 63081
Bus Eirann (Irish Bus) Booking Information Tel 091 62000
Arts Festival (July) Tel 091 583800
Oyster Festival (September) Tel 091 22066
Thoor Ballylee Gort Tel 091 31436 *W B Yeats' home*
Coole Gort Tel 091 31804 *Nature Reserve*
Galway Racecourse Ballybrit Tel 091 53870
Aran Islands Tel 091 63081

Glandore   Hayes' Bar

Tel 028 33214	P
Glandore Co Cork	Map 2 B6

The beautifully situated village of Glandore boasts a surprising
number of excellent hostelries, each with its own particular
character and most with pavement tables and lovely harbour
views, but when choices have to be made Hayes' Bar has
a powerful attraction in Ada Hayes' famous bar food. Sensible
tables and chairs, the right height for comfortable consumption,
provide the first promising hint of priorities, then there's
an unusual emphasis on wine, both decorative and actual: clearly
this is not your average Irish bar. The menu is short and
inscrutable – chicken & vegetable soup, sandwiches, a few 'specials'
like paté on toast or prawn salad (the house speciality) – but the
soup reminds you of the kind your granny used to make and the
sandwiches (perhaps tuna and corn, garlic sausage, Westphalian
salami or egg and chive) are nothing short of a new culinary art
form. A 'prawn special' sandwich, for example, is made with
lovely fresh brown bread stuffed with masses of freshly cooked
prawns in home-made mayonnaise, quartered and prettily served
with thinly-sliced fruit – apple, plum, orange – and a cocktail stick
kebab of cherry tomatoes, olives and cucumber, then garnished
with a mixed-leaf salad. Everything is served on different
plates (Ada is a collector and never returns from her frequent
travels without a new batch of ware) and attention to detail
is outstanding, even for something as simple as a cup of coffee:
a little tray is laid with an individual cafetière, a large French cup
and saucer with matching tiny jug of cream and bowl of sugar,
a café noir biscuit and a neapolitan chocolate – and all for 80p!
Spiced beef, too often restricted to the role of Christmas fare,
is a speciality here and makes excellent sandwiches and the
(farmhouse) cheese and (home-made) chutney is an unusually
good vegetarian alternative. *Open 12-11.30pm Mon-Sat (to 11pm
in winter), Sun 12.30-2, 4-11pm: June-end Aug, Christmas, Easter &
all weekends.* **Bar Food** *all day. Closed weekdays Sept-June except
Christmas & Easter. No credit cards.*

Glandore   The Marine Hotel   £56

Tel 028 33366 Fax 028 33366	H
Glandore Co Cork	Map 2 B6

This friendly family hotel is right down beside the harbour, with
most of the family rooms in an attractive ivy-clad annexe in a
converted stable block alongside a courtyard car park. Rooms
in the main hotel are on the small side and simply furnished,
without phones, but all are en suite and some have harbour views.

Public areas include two bars, one recently refurbished, where bar menus, including children's early evening meals, are served.
Rooms 16. Closed 31 Oct-1 Mar (unless by arrangement).
AMERICAN EXPRESS Access, Diners, Visa.

Glandore   Pier House Bistro   £45

Tel 028 33079   Fax 028 33634   **R**

Glandore Co Cork   Map 2 B6

Tucked into a corner beside the harbour, Rachel Bendon's Pier House Bistro lives up to its promise of 'Quality You Can Afford' by offering wholesome fare ranging from a full Irish (or Continental) breakfast, through light lunches to lively, keenly priced evening fare including a full vegetarian menu. Regular evening menus offer starters like crab (or sometimes even lobster) salad, alongside houmus or home-made soup such as carrot and coriander, followed perhaps by freshly-caught cod in light-as-a-feather crispy batter, or home-made burgers served with big colourful salads. A choice of local farmhouse cheese or homely desserts – lemon cheesecake, baked bananas, pavlova – and freshly brewed coffee. **Seats** 32. D only 7-9.30. Closed mid Sep-Easter. Access, Visa.

Glandore   The Rectory   £65

Tel 028 33072   **R**

Glandore Co Cork   Map 2 B6

Situated in a lovely south-facing waterside location, this beautifully proportioned Georgian residence has been restored to its former elegance and now provides a delightful setting for a fine restaurant. Throughout the reception and dining areas, bold, deep wall colours are picked up in the soft-hued floral curtains that frame long views over Glandore Harbour towards islands of Adam and Eve, while crisp white linen, fine plain glasses, fresh flowers, comfortable balloon-back mahogany chairs and traditionally uniformed staff all set the scene for Ciarán Scully's skilful cooking. Carefully sourced ingredients – including fish caught from their own boat and landed just below the restaurant each day – feature on a well-balanced table d'hote menu that changes weekly and a carte varied every few weeks according to seasonal availability, in first courses like tender lamb's liver, pan-fried until just pink and served on a Marsala jus with piquant, naturally sweet-sour onion confit, a puffball of featherlight Yorkshire pudding, or unusual steamed skate wings with a parsley and caper sauce, the white flesh scattered jewel-like with glistening diced carrot and leek. Good home-made breads (brown soda and white sesame seed rolls) accompany good soups – a smooth, carefully balanced combination such as smoked salmon with leek, perhaps – or alternatively a crisp, colourful mixture of garden salads and fresh herbs. Strong seafood main courses – typically four of nine on the carte, including turbot, monkfish, John Dory and wild salmon – are balanced by imaginative meat and poultry including, perhaps, roast saddle of rabbit with baby vegetables, sun-dried tomatoes, Parma ham and Madeira jus, or juicy sliced breast of chicken stuffed with a mousseline of salmon and prawn encircling a crisp tri-colour spaghetti of vegetables, served on a light prawn sauce – a complex dish and a delight to the eye which could disappoint in less skilful hands, but Ciarán Scully balances colours, textures and flavours with the skill of a master juggler. Organically grown vegetables, always a selection of at least five, are served on individual gratin dishes. Tempting desserts include a baked rhubarb compote with simple country flavours in contrast to the sophistication of, say, dark, milk and white chocolate marquise with hazelnut fudge sauce and lemon andorange jelly. Farmhouse cheeses are all local and there's an unusually wide selection of speciality teas and tisanes plus good coffee to accompany imaginative petits fours. *Seats 80. Parties 12. Private Room 40. D only 7-9.30. Set D £21.50. Closed 25 Dec & various times Oct-May ring to check.* AMERICAN EXPRESS Access, Diners, Visa.

Glasson	Glasson Village Restaurant	£50
Tel 0902 85001		**R**
Glasson Athlone Co Westmeath		Map 1 C3

An attractive stone building (once a barracks) in a pretty village off the main road in Goldsmith country. The atmosphere is friendly, and the place really bustles at Sunday lunchtime. Owner-chef Michael Brooks is something of a seafood specialist – choose lobster or oyster fresh from the new tank or, from the dinner menu, perhaps goujons of lemon sole with garlic butter, hot terrine of salmon and hake with a sweet red pepper sauce, seafood soup or the fresh fish dish of the day. Other choices could include a warm salad of spicy lamb sausages, tandoori-style julienne of chicken with mint sauce and roast rack of lamb *persillé.* *Seats 50. Private Room 16. L 12.30 & 2.15 (Sun only, 2 sittings) D 7-10.15. Closed D Sun, D Mon (except Bank Holidays), 3 weeks from mid Oct, 24-26 Christmas. Set L £10 Set D £17.25. Access, Diners, Visa.*

Glasson	Grogan's	
Tel 0902 85158		**P**
Glasson nr Athlone Co Westmeath		Map 1 C3

"Established 1750", Grogan's is a delightfully quaint, family-run pub in the pretty and accessible village of Glasson, near Athlone. The cosy, low-ceilinged front bar is divided in the traditional manner, with an open fire at one end and a fair choice of chilled or 'soft' Guinness at both. Simon Grogan presides over the kitchen and supplies as wholesome a range of simple bar meals as anyone could wish for, with home-made soup and home-made bread (£1), smoked salmon (£2.55), prawn cocktail (£3.25) and oysters, fresh or grilled with garlic butter (£3.50/£3.75), as well as salads and snacks including speciality toasted sandwiches such as black pudding (£1.45). "Soup and snacks all day." There's also a larger back bar and a beer garden where summer barbecues are held. Traditional music every Wed and Sun night. *Bar Food 12.30-3.30 & 7-9 (Sun in summer only 12-2 & 4-8). Children allowed in bar to eat. Garden. Closed Good Friday, 25 Dec. No credit cards.*

Glasson   Wineport Restaurant   £40

Tel 0902 85466   Fax 0902 85466   **R**

Glasson nr Athlone Co Westmeath   Map 1 C3

In an idyllic waterside location on Lough Ree, just outside
Athlone, this relaxed, well-appointed restaurant is decorated on a
stylish nautical theme and seems to offer the best of every world,
with a cosy reception area and open fire at one end and views
over the lough from most tables. Thérèse Gilsenan's confident
cooking puts flesh on simple but imaginative seasonal menus for
different occasions – all-day food in summer, early dinners (called
the Tee-Bird Menu in honour of regulars from Glasson Golf
Club), Sunday brunch and à la carte dinner menu – in dishes like
warm duck liver, sweet and sour dressing (crisp, colourful mixed
leaves, crusted juicy pink livers, judiciously light vinaigrette) with
freshly baked brown and white breads, a traditional Sunday roast
(pink-cooked lamb, perhaps, with home-made redcurrant and
mint jelly), fresh cod fillet updated with an unusual but not
overpowering basil and pine nut sauce, delicious home-made ices
and warm fruit pies, aromatic freshly-brewed coffee. All this and
great service, a wonderful view and often a pair of visiting swans
to boot. An enterprising 'pot-luck' system of browsing through the
bottles in stock rather than consulting a list provides entertainment
and safeguards the budget, as most sell at a flat rate of £8.95, with
half of any bottle for £5.50; there's also a smaller selection
of classics at £18.95. *Seats 45. Parties 30. L Sun only 12-4
D 5.30-10 (except June-Aug Meals 12-10). Closed 25 & 26 Dec.
Set D £12.50.* AMERICAN EXPRESS *Access, Diners, Visa.*

Glen of Aherlow   Aherlow House   63%   £55

Tel 062 56153   Fax 062 56212   **H**

Glen of Aherlow nr Tipperary Co Tipperary   Map 2 B5

Standing four miles from Tipperary in the middle of a forest,
Aherlow House was originally a hunting lodge. The decorative
inspiration is Tudor, and beyond the heavy oak doors the
atmosphere is set by darkwood beams and log fires. A large terrace
outside the bar commands views of the glen. Well-appointed,
individually furnished bedrooms include two suitable for families
(under-tens free in parents' rooms). Conference/function facilities.
No dogs. *Rooms 10. Closed Mon-Thu Nov-early March.*
AMERICAN EXPRESS *Access, Diners, Visa.*

Glen of Aherlow   Place of Interest

Tipperary Racecourse Tel 062 51357

Glencullen   Fox's Pub

Tel 01 295 5647   Fax 01 295 8911   **P**

Glencullen Co Dublin   Map 2 D4

"Eat fish – live longer; eat oysters – love longer; eat mussels – last
longer; eat from the sea to see your way back to Fox's Famous
Seafood Pub!" One of the best-known pubs in the south Dublin
area, Anthony and Geraldine McMahon's pub is situated in a
hamlet in the Dublin mountains and claims (albeit along with
numerous other pubs around the country) to be the highest

licensed premises in Ireland. Purists may wince a little at the inevitable sawdust strewn on the stone floor and the somewhat contrived collection of bric-à-brac and old country furniture, but it's a friendly, entertaining place and the open fires have real warmth. Famous for traditional Irish music since the 1950s when RTE broadcast regular Sunday night sessions from here on the wireless, and, more recently, for 'Fox's Seafood Kitchen', an extensive choice of home-cooked seafood in the bar. Lobster bisque (£1.75), steamed mussels (£4.50), wild Irish oak-smoked salmon (£5.95, with prawns and salad £9.75), hot vegetable and pasta bake (£5.95), hot crab claws tossed in garlic butter (£5.50), 1lb lobster £19.95, and even Beluga caviar with blinis £95; open sandwiches (£2.60-£4.95) for the smaller pockets and appetites! A wooden inscription on the wall reads: "There are no strangers here, only friends who have never met". *Open 10.30-11.30 Mon-Sat (to 11 winter) Sun 12-2, 4-11.* **Bar Food** *12-10 (Sat to 9, Sun 4-10).* AMERICAN EXPRESS *Access, Diners, Visa.*

Glengarriff   The Blue Loo

Tel 027 63167	**P**
Main Street Glengarriff Co Cork	**Map 2 A6**

Philip Harrington's unusually named pub may well inspire a first visit out of curiosity alone, but its friendliness will ensure a return. Spick and span, with a choice of sitting indoors in a pleasant traditional country atmosphere or at roadside tables and benches out in the sun, it is a pleasingly simple place, with food (May-Oct) to match – fresh crab and fresh or smoked wild salmon are the specialities, served in open (£4) or closed sandwiches (£1-£2.50). Only simple snacks in winter. *Open 10.30am-11.30pm (Sun 12.30-2 & 4-11). Closed Good Friday, 25 Dec. No credit cards.*

Glin   Glin Castle

	£256★
Tel 068 34173 Fax 068 34364	**A**
Glin Co Limerick	**Map 2 B5**

Home for 700 years of the Fitzgerald family, hereditary Knights of Glin, Glin Castle – described by the present Knight with magnificent understatement as "basically a plain Georgian house with later castellations and many windows" – is now the home of the 29th Knight and his wife, who are continuing restoration work, which was mainly completed in the 1950s, and welcome guests. The interior is breathtakingly impressive, but mercifully devoid of the museum-like atmosphere such grandeur normally entails – in fact it has an astonishingly real, matter-of-fact feeling about it and everything is kept just the same as usual for guests. Accommodation is all in suites, some even grander than others and dinner – prepared by professional catering teacher Deirdre Brennan – is served communally in the beautiful dining room. Children may stay in their parents' suite without extra charge up to the age of 16. ★Half-board only. Both the garden and house are open to non-residents at certain times. Banqueting for 40, small conferences of up to 12. **Rooms** *6 (all suites). Garden, croquet, shooting, tennis. Access, Visa.*

Gorey	**Marlfield House**	81%	£154

Tel 055 21124   Fax 055 21572 | **HR**

Gorey Co Wexford | Map 2 D5

Built in 1820 and standing in lovely gardens and woodland, the
mansion has been owned and run by the Bowe family since 1978.
Mary Bowe is a wonderful hostess and duly wins our Ireland
1995 Host of the Year award (see page 27). There are fine beaches
and many tourist spots within walking distance or a short drive,
but it's equally pleasant to 'stay put' and relax in the sumptuous,
stylish day rooms. These include a semi-circular hall (note the
splendid 18th-century marble fireplace) and an elegant lounge.
Bedrooms are individually decorated and vary from charming
smaller rooms at the top of the house – some with four-posters
and all with good facilities and beautiful bedding including fine,
broderie anglaise-trimmed, cotton sheets – to a very grand series
of six luxurious suites on the ground floor, each different but all
with elaborate use of exclusive fabrics, carefully chosen antiques
and pictures and appropriately large, well-appointed bathrooms.
Colours throughout the house are rich and subtle and beautiful
fresh flowers abound. Dogs by arrangement. *Rooms 19. Garden,
sauna, tennis, helipad. Closed 17 Dec-1 Feb.* AMERICANEXPRESS *Access,
Diners, Visa.*

Restaurant £90

In one of the loveliest formal dining rooms of any Irish country
house, trompe l'oeil greenery leads effortlessly into a conservatory
richly hung with well-maintained plants and through to the
garden with its immaculate lawns and borders backed by mature
trees. Kevin Arundel took over as head chef in the spring of 1994
and, working closely with the owner Mary Bowe, produces
sophisticated seasonal menus firmly based on local produce, much
of it grown under Ray Bowe's supervision in a neat kitchen
garden almost within sight of the dining room window. Local
game features in season, and the area is famous for its soft fruit,
especially strawberries which take pride of place on high summer
dessert menus; there is always fresh fish straight from Courtown
harbour and also mussels from Wexford in season. A typical
dinner might start with tartare of smoked salmon with
a cucumber and lemon dressing, followed by a classic French
onion soup and pan-fried monkfish and cod on a bed of fennel,
with a chive and tomato sauce. Garden vegetables are just that,
appearing in side dishes and vegetarian alternatives like a little
quiche of mixed vegetables topped with blue cheese and a lovage
cream sauce. Sophisticated desserts like iced praline and armagnac
parfait with a blackcurrant and cassis coulis or pear and cinnamon
crème brulée compete for attention with Irish farmhouse cheeses,
including one of the longest-established and best, locally-made
St Killian from Carrighbyrne. Formal luncheon is available in the
dining room and, in addition, a library snack menu offers superior
bar food. The wine list is long on French classics (with notes
on Bordeaux and Burgundy vintages) but short on half bottles,
and there's only a modest section on the New World. *Seats 80.
L 12.30-1.45 D 7-9.30. Set L £17.50 Set D £28.*

Greencastle	Kealy's Seafood Bar	£45

Tel 077 81010 **R**

The Harbour Greencastle Co Donegal   Map 1 C1

Unexpected sophistication awaits the visitor to this rugged commercial fishing port – James and Tricia Kealy's bar is more cocktail than fisherman's and, although tables are simply laid with paper napkins and inexpensive cutlery and glasses, it is immediately obvious that the food is taken seriously. Wholesome all-day snacks give way to a good value four-course dinner menu, often including popular dishes lifted out of the ordinary by giving them a new twist – avocado may come with pesto and sun-dried tomatoes, for instance, baked brill with orange and almonds, even the ubiquitous seafood cocktail, though simply described as 'a mixture of white fish', has been known to conceal large chunks of lobster. Sirloin steak is offered as a concession to non-fish eaters, vegetables are served simply and generously on a platter and desserts range from homely and hot (apple pie, crepes suzette) to sophisticated cold (passion fruit delight); black plates are used to good effect for fish and desserts. No smoking room. *Seats 52. Parties 10. Private Room 20. L 12.30-3 D 7-9.30. Closed Mon & Tues in winter, Good Friday, 25 Dec.* AMERICAN EXPRESS *Access, Diners, Visa.*

> We endeavour to be as up-to-date as possible, but inevitably some changes to key personnel may occur at restaurants and hotels after the Guide goes to press.

Greystones	The Hungry Monk	£55

Tel 01 287 5759 **R**

Greystones Co Wicklow   Map 2 D4

On the first floor, over a building society, this characterful little restaurant is unassuming from the street and the contrast inside is remarkable – a glowing fire and candlelight – even at Sunday lunch, now sensibly extended to make a very Irish lunch, with last orders at 8pm – add to the warm welcome. Well-appointed tables with fresh flowers, delicious home-baked bread, serious wine glasses and, of course, a plethora of monk-related pictures and bric-a-brac complete the picture. Menus, changed seasonally, keep an eye on fashions and inject popular dishes with a dash of originality – as in warm salad of garlic mushrooms or roast lamb with a herb crust and minted lamb jus – but top-quality ingredients are the vital link, including game in season and daily seafood blackboard specials, from nearby Greystones harbour. Best of all, perhaps, are the prices – value for money is a priority here and the size of the bill is often a welcome surprise. A quite splendid and very fairly-priced wine list features an inexpensive house section, and a really comprehensive world-wide selection with the New World well represented, as are Italy, Spain and Portugal. *Seats 40. Parties 20. L Sun only 12.30-8 D 7-11. Closed D Sun & all Mon & Tue, 25 Dec, Good Friday. Set L Sun £10.95 Set D (not Sat) £14.95.* AMERICAN EXPRESS *Access, Diners, Visa.*

Hodson Bay   Hodson Bay Hotel   65%   £90

Tel 0902 92444   Fax 0902 92688   **H**

Hodson Bay Athlone Co Westmeath   Map 1 C3

Large, lively, lakeside hotel offering extensive conference and
leisure facilities. Golfing is available in the Athlone Golf Club,
located next to the hotel, boating and watersports on Lough Ree
and River Shannon and a wide number of pursuits in the hotel's
excellent leisure and activity centre. Practical en-suite bedrooms,
large foyer-lounge, dining room plus self-service food area,
waterside bar. Expansion plans are afoot to increase the number
of bedrooms to 100. *Rooms 46. Garden, tennis, indoor swimming
pool, gymnasium, keep-fit equipment, sauna, solarium, fishing.*
AMERICAN EXPRESS *Access, Diners, Visa.*

Hodson Bay   Place of Interest

Athlone Castle Athlone Tel 0902 92912

Howth   Abbey Tavern

Tel 01 839 0307   Fax 01 839 0284   **P**

Howth Co Dublin   Map 2 D4

Situated next door to Howth Abbey and its 12th-century Chapter
House, halfway up a hill above the picturesque harbour, the
Abbey Tavern has all the hallmarks of a cosy, convivial pub.
Blazing turf fires warm the two rooms, which are characterised
by thick stone walls, flagstone floors with converted church pews,
gas lamps and polished darkwood furniture adding flavours to a
venue that is popular with locals as well as visitors from the
Dublin area. The Irish evenings of music and song (held here most
nights) are a major attraction and booking is required. "Old-world
charm, authenticity and simplicity (no gimmicks)." Nevertheless,
group catering (for up to 200) is big business here. *Open 3pm-
11pm Mon-Fri, 1pm-11pm Sat (1pm-11.30pm in summer), 12.30pm-
11pm Sun. Closed Good Friday, 25 Dec.* AMERICAN EXPRESS *Access,
Diners, Visa.*

Howth   Adrian's   £50

Tel 01 839 1696   Fax 01 839 0231   **R**

3 Abbey Street Howth Co Dublin   Map 2 D4

Adrian Holden and his daughter (and head chef) Catriona change
menus frequently at this small restaurant offering interest, variety
and careful use of fresh produce. Crudités and a tasty dip are
on the table to welcome new arrivals and a basket of home-made
breads, warm from the oven, follows very shortly afterwards.
From the £16 dinner menu, fish sausage with a red pepper sauce
and orange Thai rice cakes make lively starters. Vegetarian tastes
are always considered on the main course options, as in three tarts
with tomato coulis, and local seafood is strong but dependent
on the weather – but Adrian is known for buying his meat well,
so pork with mango and coriander sauce should not disappoint.
Vegetables tend to be reliably simple and plentiful; desserts can
be variable: sometimes stunning, sometimes less so. Daytime
menus offer more flexibility, although there are also 2/3-course set
lunches. Children are not encouraged. *Seats 33. Parties 16.*

Private Room 15. L 12.30-6 (Fri & Sat to 2.30), D 6-9.30 (Sun to 8).
Set L £6.50/£7.90 (Sun £9.95) Set D £16. Closed 25 & 26 Dec,
Good Friday. AMERICAN EXPRESS *Access, Diners, Visa.*

Howth   Casa Pasta

Tel 01 839 3823   **JaB**

12 Harbour Road Howth Co Dublin   **Map 2 D4**

Tiny, buzzy little first-floor restaurant overlooking the harbour.
Atmosphere is the main attraction as the "new age Italian" food
can vary somewhat. Blackboard menu with the likes of grilled
fresh sardines, deep-fried Brie with spicy chutney, Caesar salad,
seafood pasta, tiramisu and banoffi pie. Live music most nights.
Booking recommended. Three high-chairs provided. Plenty
of parking on the seafront. ***Seats** 40. Open 6-12pm Mon-Sat, 1pm*
until late Sun. Closed Good Friday, 25 & 26 Dec. AMERICAN EXPRESS
Access, Visa.

Howth   Deer Park Hotel   64%   £75

Tel 01 832 2624   Fax 01 839 2405   **H**

Howth Co Dublin   **Map 2 D4**

Located high up on the Howth peninsula and surrounded by 1200
acres that includes five golf courses (18, 9 and 12-hole par 3, 18-
hole pitch and putt, plus a new 9-hole course). Deer Park also
enjoys excellent views to the north and east with Howth harbour,
Ireland's Eye and Lambay islands in one direction, Dublin in the
other. Built in 1973, it has a fairly modern appearance. There's
a bright, airy first-floor residents' lounge with a terrace for fine
weather, while on the ground floor the bar offers excellent views
to the east and Dublin. Bedrooms are of good size, offering smart
darkwood furniture. Some have their own fridge and toaster
as well as the usual tea/coffee facilities. Bread and cereals can
be provided for those with early planes to catch from Dublin
airport. Vinyl-floored bathrooms, all with showers, have enamel
baths. ***Rooms** 49. Garden, golf. Closed 24-26 Dec.* AMERICAN EXPRESS
Access, Diners, Visa.

Howth   Howth Lodge Hotel   65%   £90

Tel 01 832 1010   Fax 01 832 2268   **H**

Howth Co Dublin   **Map 2 D4**

Built 175 years ago and since considerably enlarged (but keeping
the original style), with the whole frontage painted a distinctive
black and white, Howth Lodge offers good standards
of accommodation as well as a very fine leisure centre across the
road (note that the gym is only available to fully experienced
users). On the ground floor, public areas are open-plan, featuring
a spacious lounge with bamboo furniture that leads to a cosy,
beamed bar with stripped bare floorboards at the rear. There
are 13 older bedrooms in the original building, but the majority
are in a purpose-built modern block completed last year. All
bedrooms are well equipped, double-glazed and offer at least
a partial view of the sea. The new bedrooms are excellent –
of good size and very prettily decorated. Front rooms have
traditional-style darkwood furniture, while the rear rooms have
lightwood pieces. Bathrooms are bright and clean; six have bidets.

No dogs. *Rooms 46. Garden, indoor swimming pool, plunge pool,
beauty salon, solarium, sauna, spa bath, steam room.
Closed 1 week Dec.* AMERICAN EXPRESS *Access, Diners, Visa.*

Howth	King Sitric	£70
Tel 01 832 6729 Fax 01 839 2442		**R**
East Pier Harbour Road Howth Co Dublin		**Map 2 D4**

Howth is home to one of the largest fishing fleets in Ireland,
so King Sitric, a very well-established fish restaurant, is perfectly
placed on the harbour front. Sashimi, crab and horseradish mousse,
moules marinière, fillet of brill with mustard sauce, queen scallops,
black sole meunière or Colbert, lobster taken from the tank,
grilled or poached turbot, monkfish with wild mushrooms,
oysters from Galway Bay ... these and many more classics you'll
find on Aidan MacManus's mouthwatering menus. His wonderful
'mixed fish grill' wins our Ireland 1995 Seafood Dish of the Year
award (see page 55). Lunch in the seafood bar provides great
views and excellent value for money. King Sitric is not only
an outstanding seafood restaurant but boasts one of the finest wine
lists in Ireland with excellent house recommendations, from which
one really needs to look no further; however, for those wishing to
indulge, the predominantly French list offers a good choice from
every region – particularly Chablis, Alsace and Loire. *Seats 60.
Private Room 22. L 12.30-3 Mon-Sat (May-Sept & pre-Christmas
only) D 6.30-11. Closed Sun, Bank Holidays, 1st week Jan, & Easter.
Set D £23.* AMERICAN EXPRESS *Access, Diners, Visa.*

Howth   Place of Interest

Howth Castle Gardens Tel 01 832 2624

Inishbofin Island	Day's Hotel	61%	£40
Tel 095 45809			**H**
Inishbofin Island Co Galway			**Map 1 A3**

Just beside the harbour, close to the landing place for ferries from
the mainland six miles away (boats leave Cleggan 11am, 2pm and
6pm daily, weather permitting), this unpretentious hotel has been
in the Day family since 1918 and still offers the same warm
welcome and genuine hospitality today. Families thrive on the
away-from-it-all atmosphere and Mary Day's good home cooking
– and visitors out for the day can organise a lobster lunch
by phoning the night before. Three family rooms. Children's early
evening meal. *Rooms 14 (8 en-suite). Patio. Closed 1 Oct-31 Mar.*
AMERICAN EXPRESS *Access, Visa.*

Inishbofin Island	Day's Bar	
Tel 095 45829		**P**
Inishbofin Island Co Galway		**Map 1 A3**

Conveniently situated close to the ferry, a very pleasant family-
friendly bar run by John and Olive Day, with Olive's good home
cooking on offer seven days a week from the beginning of June
to mid-September. After that it's a matter of pot luck but winter
visitors only have to ask: 'Nobody need go hungry', says John.
Given the location, seafood is unsurprisingly popular, typically

in scallops mornay, garlic prawns or scampi, but steaks are also
in great demand and Olive often does roasts of lamb, pork or beef.
Vegetarians can choose from a selection of omelettes or a special
salad and there's a short children's menu as well as half portions.
No special facilities for children but they're happy playing on the
beach in front of the bar. *Open 10.30am-11.30pm Mon-Sat (to 11
in winter), Sun 12.30-2, 4-11. **Bar Food** 12-5, 7-10. Closed 25 Dec,
Good Friday.* AMERICAN EXPRESS *Access, Visa.*

Inistioge	The Motte	£60
Tel 056 58655		R
Inistioge Co Kilkenny		Map 2 C5

Set in one of Ireland's prettiest villages, everything about Tom
Reade-Duncan and Alan Walton's intimate, characterful little
restaurant is just right – the antiques, artistic candle-lit table
settings and warm, welcoming atmosphere. The menu, which
is changed with the seasons according to availability of produce
and sensibly limited to a choice of about six on each course,
is interesting and chef Alan Walton follows through with style.
Start, perhaps, with avocado and tomato with Roquefort sauce,
duck liver mousse with Cumberland sauce, feta cheese with
rosemary pepper honey, followed by crisp-skinned pink-fleshed
Barbary duck with a wild mushroom and pine nut sauce or pan
fried halibut in tarragon and mustard sauce. Details are excellent:
three kinds of olives to nibble over aperitifs and three kinds
of bread, served with nice little chunks of butter in a pottery
bowl, good choice of imaginatively presented vegetables,
farmhouse cheese selection, delicious gimmick-free desserts, lovely
aromatic coffee. *Seats 24. Parties 20. D only 7-10. Set D £18.50.
Closed Sun & Mon, Christmas week.* AMERICAN EXPRESS *Access, Visa.*

Innishannon	Innishannon House Hotel 63%	£95
Tel 021 775121 Fax 021 775609		H
Innishannon Co Cork		Map 2 B6

Built in 1720 for a wealthy farmer, Innishannon House enjoys
a romantic setting in gardens and parkland on the Bandon River
(fishing available here and on the Brinny). Bedrooms, all en suite,
are individual in their size, shape and furnishings; some overlook
the river, others the gardens. A newly created, airy suite features
a period bathroom. There's a cosy residents' bar (snacks served all
day), a restaurant, sitting room and conservatory. Popular
afternoon teas. *Rooms 14. Garden, fishing, boating.* AMERICAN EXPRESS
Access, Diners, Visa.

Innishannon	Place of Interest

Timoleague Castle Gardens Tel 023 46116 *10 miles*

Kanturk	Alley Bar	
Tel 029 50171		P
Strand Street Kanturk Co Cork		Map 2 B5

A little gem of a drinking pub, run by the same family for several
decades (daughter Alice took over from mother Mary). It's
opposite the creamery and tucked away behind a modest grocery
which is stocked with some items not held by many more

glamorous shops. Look out for 'The Ballad of Ned Jones's Toyota', a true story in verse. *Open 10.30am-11.30pm (Sun 12.30-2.30 & 4-11). No credit cards.*

Kanturk	**Assolas Country House**	**72%**	**£110**

Tel 029 50015   Fax 029 50795   **AR**

Kanturk Co Cork   **Map 2 B5**

Only an hour from Cork city, Assolas is well situated as a base for visiting West Cork and Kerry. The charming creeper-clad house goes back to the 17th century and is currently home to three generations of Bourkes, including the manager, Joe, and his wife Hazel, a very talented chef. An exceptional welcome is backed up by open log fires, elegant furnishings and antiques, excellent housekeeping and a high level of comfort throughout. Of the nine bedrooms, three in the main house are designated 'Superior' and are large, with the finest views; three are in a restored old stone building in the courtyard. Despite its undeniable elegance, Assolas has all the warmth and hospitality of a family home – best summed up, perhaps, by the collection of wellington boots in the hall for anyone who feels like seeking out the otters along the riverbank. No dogs in the house. ***Rooms** 9. Garden, croquet, tennis, fishing. Closed Nov-mid March.* AMERICAN EXPRESS *Access, Diners, Visa.*

Restaurant   ★   **£65**

They do things properly at Assolas and the deep red walls, polished antique furniture and neatly uniformed staff provide a fitting background for Hazel Bourke's wonderful food, much of it produce from their own beautifully maintained walled kitchen garden (in which herbs, vegetables and soft fruit grow) or from trusted local suppliers – allowing maximum variety for residents. Start, perhaps, with Union Hall prawns with lemon mousseline, typically followed by a pink grapefruit sorbet or dressed Assolas greens. Local lamb, served with anchovies and scallops, might tempt from a choice of five main courses, which always includes an imaginative vegetarian option. Simplest desserts are sometimes the best – superb blackcurrant ice cream or a shimmering jewel-like compote of garden fruits – and the local farmhouse cheeseboard is kept in immaculate condition – winner of our 1995 Irish Cheeseboard of the Year award (see page 73 for a full description). Coffee and petits fours are served beside the fire in the drawing room. There are no New World wines on an otherwise decent wine list that features many top growers. No children under 7. ***Seats** 26. Private Room 28. D only 7-8.30. Set D £28. Closed Nov-mid March.*

Kanturk	**The Vintage**	

Tel 029 50549   **P**

O'Brien Street Kanturk Co Cork   **Map 2 B5**

Stephen Bowles has owned this pleasant, well-run riverside pub since 1985 and it is well worth a visit, whether for a quiet pint or a bite to eat. The interior is pleasingly traditional and comfortably furnished. The pub can provide a quick snack or a complete meal; choose from traditional dishes like bacon and cabbage or Irish stew, T-bone steak or a traditional roast on Sundays. Daily-changing blackboard specials always include a vegetarian main dish. *Open 10.30am-11.30pm Mon-Sat, 12.30-2 & 4-11 Sun.* **Bar Food** *12.30-9.30 Mon-Sat, 12.30-2 & 6-9.30 Sun. Access, Visa.*

Keel   The Beehive

Tel 098 43134	**JaB**
Keel Achill Island Co Mayo	**Map 1 A3**

Husband-and-wife team Patricia and Michael Joyce opened this attractive craft shop and informal restaurant in 1991 and it has now become a regular stop for visitors to the island, whether for a light bite (soup of the day with home-baked brown bread £1.30, tea/coffee 55p/65p, freshly baked scones with home-made jam and cream 60p) or a full meal (salmon salad £6.50, rhubarb pie and cream £1.90). *Open 10am-6.30pm. Closed 1 Nov-Easter. Access, Visa.*

Kenmare   d'Arcy's   £70

Tel 064 41589 Fax 064 41589	**R**
Main Street Kenmare Co Kerry	**Map 2 A6**

Matthew d'Arcy moved across the road from the *Park Hotel* in 1992 to set up in this converted bank and his wife Aileen provides a warm welcome. There's a real fire glowing where the main banking hall used to be and the vault at the back is opened up on busy nights. Staff are informal and friendly and the menu longish and ambitious. Poached pear filled with Stilton mousse or leek and chicken timbale with tomato and onion sauce could start your meal, with noisette of monkfish tail seved with a chutney of three peppers and lemon butter sauce or beef in pastry with mushroom stuffing to follow. Desserts include an excellent orange and Cointreau soufflé. Previously known as *The Old Bank House.* Five neat, comfortably furnished rooms are individually decorated in homely style. Smallish bathrooms (some with shower only, just two en suite) have plenty of thick towels and toiletries supplied. Sitting room with TV. *Seats 35. Private Room 25. D 6-10.30. Set D £16.50. Closed Mon, Tues & Wed in winter, 24-27 Dec & 24 Jan-13 Feb.* AMERICAN EXPRESS *Access, Visa.*

Kenmare   Dromquinna Manor Hotel   60%   £79

Tel 064 41657   Fax 064 41791   **H**

Blackwater Bridge nr Kenmare Co Kerry   **Map 2 A6**

About three miles out of town and beautifully situated
in extensive grounds leading down to the private foreshore and
a little quay and newly built marina (the setting for their informal
summer Old Boathouse Bistro restaurant), this Victorian manor
boasts a unique tree-house apartment as well as many more
orthodox attractions, including a Great Hall with original oak
panelling. Generously proportioned bedrooms are individually
decorated, all en suite, some with four-poster or brass beds.
A generally relaxed atmosphere pervades the hotel. *Rooms 28.
Garden, keep-fit equipment, games room, tennis, mooring, fishing.*
AMERICAN EXPRESS® *Access, Diners, Visa.*

Kenmare   The Horseshoe   £35

Tel 064 41553   **R**

3 Main Street Kenmare Co Kerry   **Map 2 A6**

Behind its unassuming exterior The Horseshoe hides a pleasantly
rustic old-fashioned bar. Behind this again, there's a cosy, informal
restaurant with open fire, oil-clothed tables, (real) cattle stall
divisions and an unpretentious menu backed up by owner-chef
Irma Weland's simple, wholesome food. Old favourites like
seafood cocktail take on a new lease of life in Irma's hands, and,
while steaks and fish are reliable, a vegetarian main course such
as vegetable stir-fry can be memorable. A daily specials board
makes good use of the freshest ingredients. Good desserts may
include a moreish caramelised apple and pear flan. Tables outside
in summer. *Seats 28. Parties 8. Meals midday-11.30pm. Closed Mon
Nov-May, all Feb and March, Good Friday, 25 Dec. No credit cards.*

Kenmare   The Lime Tree   £50

Tel 064 41225   Fax 064 41402   **R**

Shelbourne Street Kenmare Co Kerry   **Map 2 A6**

This attractive stone building next to the Park Hotel was taken
over by Tony and Alex Daly in 1994 and given a face lift – the
predominant colour is now a cheering Mediterranean yellow,
with big mirrors, modern paintings and dashingly artistic still life
arrangements adding a touch of class – to provide an appropriate,
informal setting for chef Michael Casey's zesty food. Menus reflect
Cal-Ital influences, with more than a passing nod to traditional
Irish fare along the way: oven-cooked smokies come with an Irish
potato pancake, local smoked salmon is served on buckwheat
blinis with sour cream, Kerry lamb's liver is sautéed with bacon,
shallots and sherry vinegar – all served with 'sweet and sassy café
veg & potatoes' (a stir-fry of seasonal vegetables and steamed
potatoes). Delicious desserts might include a 17th-century queen
of puddings alongside an excellent strawberry crème brulée, with
a selection of teas and coffees to finish. *Seats 75. Parties 10. Private
Room 30. D only 6.30-9.30. Closed Mon-Wed 1 Nov-Easter.
Access, Visa.*

Kenmare	Packie's	£45
Tel 064 41508		**R**
Henry Street Kenmare Co Kerry		**Map 2 A6**

Owner-chef Maura O'Connell Foley packs in the crowds with cooking that's short on pretension and long on flavour. The sunny influences of California and the Med combine with domestic traditions on a menu typified by fillet of salmon with Hollandaise or chili sauce, pan-fried scallops with olive oil and pesto, traditional Irish stew with fresh herbs and breast of chicken with tomato and basil or fruity curry sauce with lemon grass. Among the desserts you might find chocolate pots, tiramisu or baked bananas with butterscotch sauce. *Seats 35. D only 5.30-10. Closed Sun, Nov-Easter. Access, Visa.*

When telephoning establishments in the Republic from *outside* the Republic, dial 00-353 then the number we print less the initial zero: eg The Strawberry Tree in Killarney is 00-353 64 32688.

Kenmare	Park Hotel Kenmare	87%	£272
Tel 064 41200 Fax 064 41402			**HR**
Kenmare Co Kerry			**Map 2 A6**

In late Victorian times the gentry travelled from various parts of the country by train, stopping at Kenmare, and the hotel was built in 1897 by the Great Southern and Western Railway Company for passengers to stay overnight, before continuing their journey the next day. The company sold the hotel in the late 70s, and since then, under the direction of Francis Brennan, it has enjoyed an enviable reputation – indeed, it was our Hotel of the Year in 1988. Set in eleven acres of unspoilt gardens on the shores of Kenmare Bay, and yet only a short walk from town, the hotel is particularly renowned for its fine antiques, stained-glass windows, marvellous paintings, attention to detail (an expert Dutch gilder spends the entire off-season painstakingly restoring every crevice in the ornate plasterwork and cornices), comfortable and elegant day rooms, and beautiful flower arrangements. On a cold day one can relax in front of a crackling log fire, or in summer and autumn take a stroll in the grounds and admire the changing colours. Guests sleep both soundly and in supreme comfort – the nine suites and most of the rooms are very spacious indeed with wonderful views, and offer every conceivable luxury, from bathrobes, slippers and exquisite toiletries in the marble bathrooms to fresh fruit, mineral water and books. Quality bed linen, good furniture, fine fabrics and excellent towels, backed up by superb housekeeping, complete the picture. Breakfast is a quite wonderful experience, including a 'healthy' alternative prepared in accordance with the recommendations of the world's heart associations. Special 'programmes' for Christmas and New Year – ask for their brochure. Banqueting for 80, conference facilities for 60. No dogs. *Rooms 50. Garden, croquet, tennis, golf (18), games room. Closed mid Nov-22 Dec, 4 Jan-Easter.* AMERICAN EXPRESS *Access, Diners, Visa.*

Restaurant ★ £90

The Park's warm welcome and special magic continue right from the ever-burning fire in the hall through to the beautifully appointed, yet surprisingly relaxed, high-ceilinged dining room with its wonderful views. Formal touches such as antiques are amusingly offset by quirks of personal taste – no designer co-ordinations here. Enjoy an aperitif in the bar, where the door opens to give a view of the mountains beyond, framed by palm trees stirring in the wind. If you're lucky enough to sit at a window table the view broadens to include the upper reaches of the estuary and hotel lawn. Both daily-changing tables d'hote (3-course at lunch, 4-course at dinner) and carte are available, the former offering a choice of three dishes at each stage, the latter tempting with dishes described in refreshingly plain English on a menu that uses a watercolour of Kenmare's rich scenery as a backdrop. Chef Brian Cleere works with obvious confidence and verve in his recently revamped kitchen, often presenting breathtakingly beautiful dishes, and also understanding when to let the natural flavours and textures speak for themselves. Typically, a table d'hote lunch doesn't stint on the involved nature of dishes, starting with gratinated goat's cheese on toasted brioche, followed by pithvier of Aylesbury duck with a Morel sauce, with trio of chocolate with a raspberry coulis to finish. The carte might offer roast salad of quail with parma ham, oyster mushrooms and a truffle vinaigrette, seafood (including lobster) from Kenmare Bay, grilled fillet of beef studded with truffles fricassee of wild mushrooms and a shallot sauce and half a dozen or so tempting desserts. A selection of Irish cheeses is served with home-made walnut bread and a glass of port – a very civilised way to end an enjoyable meal in a delightful setting. Service under Jim McCarthy mirrors the balance shown in the kitchen – superbly professional complemented by the right amount of friendliness. The exceptional wine list offers several French classics of different vintages, as well as a comprehensive Californian section of over 30 bins; the Australian, Italian and Spanish sections present perhaps the best value. *Seats* 90. *Private Room* 30. *L* 1-1.45 *D* 7-8.45. *Set L* £18.50 *Set D* £37.

Kenmare   The Purple Heather

Tel 064 41016	**P**
Henry Street Kenmare Co Kerry	Map 2 A6

One of those delightful Kerry establishments which begins as a bar near the door and goes on to declare its real interest in food with tables and chairs properly set up for comfortable eating towards the back, the Purple Heather began serving good, simple food long before it was fashionable in these parts, in 1975. Gutsy home-made soups served with home-made, crusty brown bread (£1.70), wild smoked salmon with salad (£6.95), home-made chicken liver terrine with Cumberland sauce (£3.95), omelettes (from £4) and a wide range of sandwiches (from £1.35) – regular, open and toasted – are typical savoury offerings, followed by irresistible desserts like wholemeal apple crumble or hazelnut meringue. *Open 10.45am-7pm.* **Bar Food** *noon-6pm. Closed Sun. No credit cards.*

Kenmare	**Sallyport House**	**£45**
Tel 064 42066		**A**
Kenmare Co Kerry		Map 2 A6

Exceptionally well-appointed accommodation in a recently renovated country house on the edge of Kenmare town, in a quiet and convenient location overlooking the harbour and with views over an orchard towards mountains at the back. A large entrance hall with welcoming fire sets the tone: spacious rooms are individually furnished with a mixture of antique and good reproduction furniture, orthopaedic beds, well-placed lights and mirrors, TV and phone. Practical, well-lit, fully-tiled bathrooms have good over-bath showers and built-in hairdryers. Delicious breakfasts are served in a sunny dining room overlooking the garden. Ample parking. No dogs. Not suitable for children under 10. **Rooms** 5. *Garden. Closed 1 Nov-Easter. No credit cards.*

Kenmare	**Sheen Falls Lodge**	**87%**	**£257**
Tel 064 41600 Fax 064 41386			**HR**
Kenmare Co Kerry			Map 2 A6

There are several remarkable aspects of this hotel, not the least being that only a small part – the original 17th-century house – is not new, though you wouldn't know it from looking at the rest of the buildings. So cleverly has it been designed, and so beautifully does it blend into its surroundings – on one side the cascading waters from the Sheen River, on the other woodland and gardens overlooking Kenmare Bay – that it's really not apparent that the hotel has only been open for four years. On the site of a country estate dating back to the 1600s, including a long stretch of the river (private salmon fishing arranged), there are over 300 acres of grounds featuring lawns, semi-tropical gardens and tranquil woodland walks. Inside, the spacious foyer features marbled columns and a welcoming fire; there's also a mahogany-panelled library with deep green leather sofas, relaxing lounges, and a snooker room with arguably the finest views you'll ever cue in! Really spacious bedrooms, featuring natural wood and fine fabrics, include a self-contained apartment and eight suites (one suitable for disabled guests); all have equally spectacular views and feature amenities such as three telephones, personal safe, remote-control satellite TV and video recorder, iron and trouser press, mineral water and a bowl of fresh fruit daily. Naturally, there's a nightly turn-down service, and in the marble bathrooms with his and hers washbasins you'll find bathrobes, slippers, hairdryer, excellent toiletries and decent-sized towels. The state-of-the-art William Petty Conference Centre, named after the original landowner, can accommodate up to 140 delegates and lies in the basement, almost undetected and unnoticed by other guests, alongside the superbly equipped leisure facilities. **Rooms** 40. *Garden, croquet, gymnasium, sauna, spa bath, steam room, solarium, tennis, riding, bicycles, clay-pigeon shooting, coarse & game fishing, games room, boutique, golf. Closed 5 Dec-23 Dec, Jan-mid Feb.* AMERICAN EXPRESS® *Access, Diners, Visa.*

See over

La Cascade Restaurant ★ £90

Chef Fergus Moore's sophisticated menus are as attractive as the
glorious views of the falls, which are floodlit at night. Both
a daily, four-course table d'hote dinner and an extravagant à la
carte are offered and should please even the most discerning diner.
Typical starters might include coriander-scented lasagne of prawns
with buttered juices, oven-roasted quail on a tatin of glazed apple,
and slivers of fresh lobster with a concassé of tomato and red
onion and a sea urchin rouille; main courses continue the involved
theme with dishes like lightly wood-smoked fillet of beef on a
fumet of Hermitage and shallots, fillets of black sole with sesame
prawns and a red wine butter sauce, plus a vegetarian choice
of agnolotti of wild mushrooms on a bed of steamed couscous
finished with white butter and chervil. Local wild Atlantic salmon
is cured and smoked on the premises, served with a sour cream
and fresh herb dressing to start or (fresh) chargrilled and served
with a purée of new potatoes with saffron and truffle oil dressing.
Finish, perhaps, with chocolate marjolane, baked kumquat and
orange pekoe tart with a mascarpone cream or compote of cherries
with a brulée of sweet rice. Irish farmhouse cheeses are served
with Parmesan biscuits. Excellent service is now led by Frances
Hayden. Weekday food is waitress-served in the lounge from
11am-11pm (oysters, open sandwiches, fish casserole, stir-fried
chicken, tasting plate of desserts), and afternoon tea (£8.50) from
3-5pm. The impressive wine list is notable for its good selection
of half bottles; yes, it's quite expensive, but not too outrageous for
a hotel of this class. Visit the marvellous cellars, which are also
used for private parties, tastings and after-dinner imbibing!
*Seats 140. Parties 16. Private Room 24. L Sun only 1-2 D 7.30-9.30.
Set Sun L £17.50 Set D £37.50.*

Kilcolgan   Moran's Oyster Cottage
Tel 091 96113   Fax 091 96503   P

The Weir Kilcolgan Co Galway   Map 2 B4

Willie Moran, champion oyster-opener, is the sixth generation
of Morans to run this immaculate thatched cottage pub, whose
bar looks out on to the pier. Gigas oysters (£7.50 a dozen) are
available all year round, others from September to April.
Alternatives include crab and smoked salmon (platters
or sandwiches), mussels, seafood chowder, seafood cocktail and egg
mayonnaise. All dishes are served with home-made brown bread.
Open 10.30am-10.45pm (Sun 12-3 & 4-11). **Bar Food** *served all
day. Garden, outdoor eating. Closed Good Friday, 24 & 25 Dec.*
AMERICAN EXPRESS *Access.*

Kilkee   Halpin's Hotel   63%   £66
Tel 065 56032   Fax 065 56317   H

Erin Street Kilkee Co Clare   Map 2 A5

In common ownership with *Aberdeen Lodge*, Dublin and operated
with the same attention to personal supervision, this Victorian
hotel has been in the Halpin family since the '70s and was
completely renovated in 1993. Architectural limitations mean that
the bedrooms which now have bathrooms tend to be rather small;
however, they are neat and comfortable, with phone, TV and
hairdryer. Rooms at the top have windows in their sloping

ceilings to give sea views; four rooms are for non-smokers. Public
areas include a popular basement bar with open fire, where the
many visiting golfers get together at night. 24hr room service.
Parking (6 spaces). *Rooms 12. Garden. Closed 4 Jan-15 Mar.*
Access, Diners, Visa.

Kilkenny   An Caisléan Uí Cuain

Tel 056 65406   **P**

2 High Street Kilkenny Co Kilkenny   **Map 2 C5**

Eccentric, perhaps, but popular nonetheless, this tall, narrow pub
on three floors is situated on a prominent corner in the city centre
and is striking, both inside and out. The interior is a mix of simple
modern and traditional, with lots of aged wood and a good
scattering of original posters. It has a relaxed, friendly and
comfortable atmosphere and attracts a youngish, cosmopolitan
crowd; writers, artists and musicians tend to congregate here due
to the bar's reputation for lively discussion in Irish and for their
live music. Officially, all year round, Monday night is traditional
Irish music night but, in practice, an impromptu session can take
off without warning at any time, to the great delight of all.
Food varies according to seasonal demand and, in addition
to conventional bar fare (soup £1.30, starters £2.75, main courses
£3.95, desserts £1.50) there's now an à la carte restaurant at the
top of the pub. *Open 11am-11.30pm (Sun 12-11). Bar Meals
12.30-3, 5.30-8.30, no food Sun eve in summer. Children allowed
in bar to eat. No credit cards.*

Kilkenny   Kilkenny Kitchen   £20

Tel 056 22118   Fax 056 65905   **R**

Kilkenny Design Centre Castle Yard Kilkenny Co Kilkenny   **Map 2 C5**

Situated in the Design Centre, a collection of craft shops and
studios in the beautifully built outbuildings opposite the Castle,
the Kilkenny Kitchen offers good home cooking on the premises
and, in the shape of crusty home-made breads and delicious cakes,
also to take away. Both hot and cold meals are much admired for
their variety and general wholesomeness. Typical dishes on
the daily menu are salmon terrine, vegetarian quiche, chicken
Wellington and braised steak. Among the desserts (all home-
made) are Irish whiskey gateau and apple Bakewell tart.
Afternoon tea is delicious. *Seats 165. Light meals 9-5.*
Closed Good Friday, Christmas. *Access, Diners, Visa.*

Kilkenny	**Lacken House**	£60

Tel 056 61085   Fax 056 62435 **RR**

Dublin Road Kilkenny Co Kilkenny Map 2 C5

One of Kilkenny's leading restaurants (and guesthouses) is run
by highly respected chef Eugene McSweeney and his wife Breda;
they have built up their reputation over the last ten years. Situated
on the edge of the town in a Victorian house with a pleasant, well-
proportioned drawing room/bar, the basement restaurant has
rather small tables, but the quality of the food is more than
adequate compensation. Eugene's dinner menu is in a progressive
Irish mode and changes frequently, offering a well-balanced choice
based on the classics but with concesssion to current trends; typical
dishes might include terrine of goose with Cumberland sauce,
baked salmon in pastry with leek cream, breast of chicken
chausseur and medallion of wild boar with apple and cream sauce;
Lacken House 'dessert plate' to finish. The choice is small, but
only the freshest of local produce is used, much of it organic,
particularly the vegetables. A varied Irish farmhouse cheese plate
includes local specialities, notably Blue Abbey and Croghan goat's
cheese. **Seats** *35. D only 7-10. Closed Sun & Mon, 1 week
Christmas. Set D £22.* *Access, Diners, Visa.*

Rooms £60

Eight bedrooms, all with shower or bath, provide simple
accommodation; children up to 4 stay free in parents' room;
under-12s sharing parents' room, £10 B&B. Breakfast is excellent
and is served either in the dining room or via room service.
Garden.

Kilkenny	**Langton's**	

Tel 056 65133   Fax 056 63693 **P**

69 John Street Kilkenny Co Kilkenny Map 2 C5

One of the best-known (and most praised) pubs in the country,
run by Edward Langton since 1978 when he took over from
his father. Edward has made a point of adding an extension
or opening up a new area every year, so the huge premises are
now a series of bars, each with its own individual style but all
furnished to the highest standards in durable materials. Open fires
with attractive basket grates are generously distributed through
the various seating areas, all equally comfortable but with
different attractions – one low-ceilinged area has a clubby
atmosphere with buttoned leather wing chairs and banquette
seating, while the next features an atrium, with walls of hanging
plants and a genteel 'afternoon hotel tea' sort of atmosphere. Well-
trained staff in black-and-white uniforms are helpful and efficient
and bar menus offer food appropriate to the time of day –
lunchtime sees a long list of sensibly-priced dishes (from chicken,
honey and almond salad or fresh soup to smoked cod with egg
and caper sauce, oyster-cut bacon and cabbage), through to a
greater choice of dishes (like egg and Kilkenny ham mayonnaise,
brunch, mussels farci, chicken curry and a daily special) in the
afternoon and evening. Leave room for the likes of strawberry
millefeuille and pear and chocolate trifle (£1.75). Both fixed-price
(£15 & £18.50) and à la carte menus are offered in the restaurant.
Dancing Tue & Sat eves. *Open 10am-11pm (Sun 12-11).* **Bar Food**

all day. **Restaurant Meals** *12-3 & 5.30-10.30. Children allowed in bar to eat, children's menu. Garden. Garden, outdoor eating. Closed Good Friday, 25 Dec.* AMERICAN EXPRESS *Access, Diners, Visa.*

Kilkenny   Newpark Hotel   58%   £95

| Tel 056 22122   Fax 056 61111 | **H** |

Castlecomer Road Kilkenny Co Kilkenny — Map 2 C5

The leisure centre and the banqueting/conference facilities supplement acceptable overnight accommodation at a 60s' hotel on the N77. All-day snack service in the lobby. No dogs.
Rooms *84. Garden, indoor swimming pool, children's pool, keep-fit equipment, sauna, spa bath, steam room, solarium, tennis, table tennis, outdoor children's play area.* AMERICAN EXPRESS *Access, Diners, Visa.*

Kilkenny   Shem's

| Tel 056 21543 | **P** |

61 John Street Kilkenny Co Kilkenny — Map 2 C5

Pleasantly unfussy, clean-lined premises run along the lines of the simple old country pubs by Shem and Julie Lawlor. Lots of wood and, in winter, generosity with the heating, make this a warm and welcoming place and its relative simplicity and small size will please those who find larger premises somewhat overpowering. Julie looks after the cooking herself and takes pride in preparing simple food well – home-made daily soups (seafood chowder, Chinese chicken, Irish potato, all £1.20), main courses (all £3.95-£4.95) such as fisherman's pie, brown beef stew, daily pasta dishes, plus the likes of bread-and-butter pudding, fresh fruit pavlova and gateau Diane to finish (all puddings £1.25). Sandwiches (open, closed, toasted) also on an all-day bar snack menu. Children's menu of favourites (3 courses £3.50). *Open 10.30am-11.30pm (Sun 12.30-2 & 4-11).* **Bar Food** *12-9.30, bar snacks 3-6. Children allowed in bar to eat, children's menu. Closed Good Friday, 25 & 26 Dec. Access, Visa.*

Kilkenny   Tynan's Bridge House Bar

| Tel 056 61828 | **P** |

Bridge House 2 Johns Bridge Kilkenny Co Kilkenny — Map 2 C5

One of the most genuine and interesting of Kilkenny's old pubs, Tynan's has had the same landlord for over 50 years – Michael Tynan, and his father was here before him. The spotless little bar features a marble counter, lots of mahogany and a charming tapestry on a wall. No children after 8pm. *Open 10.30am-11.30pm (Sun 12.30-2 & 4-11). Closed 25 Dec, Good Friday. No credit cards.*

Killaloe   Goosers

| Tel 061 376792 | **P** |

Killaloe Ballina Co Tipperary — Map 2 B4

This delightful pub, in a quiet situation just across the road from the lake, has built up a formidable reputation for its double act of good food and characterful ambience. Settle into your choice of several intimate bar areas, each with its own fireplace and simply but comfortably furnished with country furniture and a finely-judged selection of decorative rustic bric-a-brac, and enjoy anything from a quick snack to a three-course meal from the blackboard menu. Seafood from West Clare is the star among the bar food, including crab, mussels (£4.50) and scallops. Sandwiches and salads provide satisfying snacks, and larger appetites will be allayed by bacon and cabbage (£5), Irish stew or a steak. *Open (& **Bar Food** served) 10.30-10, Sun 12.30-2 & 4-10. Children's menu and portions available. Closed 25 Dec. Access, Visa.*

Our inspectors **never** book in the name of Egon Ronay's Guides. They disclose their identity only if they are considering an establishment for inclusion in the next edition of the Guide.

Killarney   Aghadoe Heights Hotel   70%   £190

Tel 064 31766   Fax 064 31345   HR

Aghadoe Killarney Co Kerry   Map 2 A5

Low-rise concrete and glass hotel of 1960s' origin refurbished in varying styles but to a generally high standard in public areas and the views over Lake Killarney and the mountains beyond are wonderful, especially from the elegantly appointed dining room. Leisure facilities, although conspicuous from the road, do not intrude. Bedrooms and bathrooms are neat, although not large. Conference/banqueting facilities for 70/100. Sister hotel to *Fredrick's* in Maidenhead, England. ***Rooms** 60. Garden, indoor swimming pool, gymnasium, sauna, spa bath, steam room, solarium, tennis, fishing.* AMERICAN EXPRESS *Access, Diners, Visa.*

Fredrick's Restaurant   ↑   £100

In this luxuriously appointed first-floor dining room with dramatic (probably unrivalled) views over the Lakes of Killarney, chef Robin Suter is running a very fine kitchen with dinner menus changing daily and lunch menus every week. The style is formal, imaginative, distinctly French and based on superb quality produce – everything positively zings with freshness and portions are unexpectedly generous. Try, perhaps, braised ox tongue and chicken livers with mustard sauce followed by panache of Kerry coast seafood in Champagne. An exceptional selection of freshly baked breads, handed separately, will undoubtedly prove irresistible. Typical main courses on the lunch menu might include supreme of chicken and langustines on red pepper sauce or roast rack of lamb with wild mushrooms. An imaginative vegetable selection might typically include new potatoes, pommes almondines, braised fennel, batons of carrot, very light crisp onion rings and crisply cooked broccoli. Fritters are a favourite dessert, mixed fruit perhaps, very light and crisp, followed by fragrant cafetière coffee and delicious home-made petits fours. Lively Sunday lunch with a buffet and a jazz band. An interesting wine list includes some selected for exceptional value, from £13-£19.50, a collection of 'Wild Geese' wines from Irish-connected families, and a good selection of half bottles. Winner of our Ireland 1995 Best Table Presentation award (see page 39 for further details). *Seats 130. Private Room 70. L 12.15-2 D 7-9.30. Set L £17.50 D £29.50.*

Killarney   Cahernane Hotel   66%   £110

Tel 064 31895   Fax 064 34340   **HR**

Muckross Road Killarney Co Kerry   **Map 2 A5**

Killarney's lakes and mountains create a majestic backdrop for
a fine hotel that was once the residence of the Earls of Pembroke.
Inside, Conor O'Connell and his staff create a warm, friendly
atmosphere, and standards of service, comfort and housekeeping
are high. There is a choice between traditional master bedrooms
in the main house and simpler but spacious and well-appointed
rooms in a sympathetic modern wing. Children under 12 may
stay free in parents' room. *Rooms 48. Garden, hairdressing, tennis,
pitch & putt, game fishing, boutique. Closed 1 Nov-1 Apr.*
AMERICAN EXPRESS *Access, Diners, Visa.*

The Herbert Room Restaurant   £65

In the smartly refurbished Herbert Room Eddie Hayes offers
a choice of menus for dinner – four courses plus coffee and petits
fours on the table d'hote, or a wide-ranging à la carte. The former
is slightly more traditional, with dishes such as garlic mussels, beef
consommé, escalope of salmon with sorrel cream and entrecote
steak with mushrooms. Other choices – mignons of beef fillet
with forest mushrooms and Guinness sauce, braised monkfish with
celeriac and mustard sauce – move into the slightly more
adventurous realms of the carte, where you could find snails
cooked in port, served on black pasta with a sauce of gorgonzola,
cream and wild mushrooms, or a vegetarian Buddhist stew.
On this menu, too, are classics like sole véronique and steak Diane.
Light lunches are served in the lounge. Something for everyone
on the well-rounded wine list, though a bottle of mineral water
will set you back £4 and champagne £40! *Seats 90.
Private Room 14. D 7-9.30. Set D £25.*

Killarney   Dingles Restaurant   £45

Tel 064 31079   **R**

40 New Street Killarney Co Kerry   **Map 2 A5**

Genuine hospitality and congenial surroundings are the keynotes
at Gerry and Marion Cunningham's relaxed restaurant and it is
obviously a favourite rendezvous for locals who appreciate Gerry's
easy welcome as much as Marion's excellent uncomplicated food,
which is based on the best ingredients and delivered with
admirable simplicity. Open fires, ecclesiastical furniture and old
plates on the walls create a characterful ambience in which
to enjoy anything from a home-made burger with freshly-cut
chips cooked in olive oil to a 4-course dinner. *Seats 45. D only
6-10. Closed Sun (except holiday w/ends). Nov-1 Mar.* AMERICAN EXPRESS
Access, Diners, Visa.

Killarney   Hotel Europe   72%   £96

Tel 064 31900   Fax 064 32118   **H**

Killorglin Road Fossa Killarney Co Kerry   **Map 2 A5**

A large modern hotel next to Killarney Golf and Fishing Club,
catering equally well for private guests and conference delegates
(up to 500 theatre style). The mountain and lake views are quite
a feature, and most of the spacious bedrooms have balconies

to make the most of the setting. Day rooms include a lounge with a pine ceiling copied from an English castle. There's an excellent health and fitness centre. *Rooms 205. Garden, indoor swimming pool, gymnasium, solarium, sauna, spa bath, beauty salon, hair salon, fishing, tennis, riding, games room, snooker room, news kiosk, boutique, helipad. Closed Nov-Mar.* AMERICAN EXPRESS *Access, Diners, Visa.*

Killarney	Foley's Town House	£80
Tel 064 31217 Fax 064 34683		**RR**
23 High Street Killarney Co Kerry		Map 2 A5

A Killarney landmark since the late 40s, Foley's is another example of the winning Kerry format – a front-of-house bar which gradually develops into a fully-fledged restaurant further back – in this case a cosy bar with an open fire, furnished to encourage lingering, backed by rather business-like rows of tables indicating clearly the level of turnover which might be expected in high season. With Denis and Carol Harnett here since 1967, the well-established feel of Foley's is reassuringly disregarding of fashion and, although emanating from modern, well-equipped and scrupulously clean kitchens, Carol Harnett's menus reflect this in style and content, in dishes like soup of the day (mushroom, perhaps – a thick country purée), sole on the bone and scallops in potato-piped shells, both served surprisingly with roast potato and mixed side salads reminiscent of the 60s. On such an outstanding and comprehensive wine list it's a shame that half bottles are in such short supply. House wines, however, are well chosen and very fairly priced, while the classics feature many of the great houses. Families are made welcome with good facilities for tots and their parents. *Seats 86. Private Room 25. L (bar food) 12.30-3 D 5-11. Closed 3 weeks Feb/Mar.* AMERICAN EXPRESS *Access, Visa.*

Rooms   £77

Foley's Town House is the culmination of Carol Harnett's long-held ambition to provide top-class accommodation at the restaurant – twelve rooms are individually decorated to a high standard and much thought has gone into planning each room to maximise use of space and comfort, including double-glazing to reduce traffic/late-night noises; special care was taken with the bathrooms, which are all exceptionally well appointed with unusual colour schemes, quality tubs and washbasins, special tiles and all the touches more usually found in leading hotels. Guests use a separate entrance and public areas include a residents' lounge and a private dining room. Banqueting/conference facilities for up to 95/20. No dogs. *Closed 1 Nov-1 Mar.*

Killarney	Gaby's Seafood Restaurant	£60
Tel 064 32519 Fax 064 32747		**R**
27 High Street Killarney Co Kerry		Map 2 A5

Although only in the present purpose-built premises since 1992, chef Geert Maes has been indispensable to the Killarney dining scene since 1976. The new restaurant is larger and has a bar area near the door, with a little garden at the back. Within, the space is cleverly broken into several levels, creating an unexpectedly intimate atmosphere that is enhanced by plants and good lighting.

Whether for an informal lunch (home-made soups, open
sandwiches, seafood platter) or a leisurely dinner (cassolette
of prawns and monkfish, grilled lobster), this is a place where
respect for fresh local produce can be depended upon – seafood
is the speciality, but it is reassuringly dependent on availability.
A most fairly priced wine list offers an outstanding worldwide
selection and, unusually for a seafood restaurant (though it does
serve steaks and lamb), includes a super repertoire of red wines
as well. *Seats* 70. L 12.30-2.30 D 6-10. *Closed all Sun & L Mon,
Christmas week & Feb.* AMERICAN EXPRESS *Access, Diners, Visa.*

Killarney   Great Southern   69%   £132
Tel 064 31262   Fax 064 31642   H
Killarney Co Kerry   Map 2 A5

Situated close to the town centre (3 minutes' walk), this former
railway hotel is a substantial building set in 36 acres of gardens
that curve around the main building and bedroom extensions.
The entrance hall is impressive, with Ionic columns, chandeliers
and a large seating area. Bedrooms vary considerably in size and
style; many have been recently refurbished (as have the main
public areas). Leisure facilities are good and the hotel offers
a variety of function facilities, taking conferences of up to 1400
theatre-style and banquets up to 650. Business centre (Fax 064
35300). The Punch Bowl cocktail bar overlooks the hotel gardens.
Supervised children's events. *Rooms* 180. *Garden, indoor swimming
pool, sauna, spa bath, gymnasium, tennis, hairdressing, indoor children's
playroom. Closed Jan/Feb.* AMERICAN EXPRESS *Access, Diners, Visa.*

Killarney   Kathleen's Country House   £60
Tel 064 32810   Fax 064 32340   A
Tralee Road Killarney Co Kerry   Map 2 A5

Just a mile from the centre of Killarney, this family-run
establishment is peacefully set in well-maintained gardens and
equally well-known for the warmth of Kathleen O'Regan-
Sheppard's welcome and her scrupulous attention to detail. Public
areas are spacious and individually decorated bedrooms with
views exceptionally well appointed, all with fully-tiled bath and
shower en suite, direct-dial phone, trouser press, tea/coffee
facilities, individually controlled central heating, radio alarm
clock, orthopaedic beds, TV and hairdryer. Good breakfasts are
cooked to order and served in an attractive dining room
overlooking the garden and unspoilt countryside. All rooms
non-smoking. No children under 7. *Rooms* 17. *Garden, croquet.
Closed Dec-17 Mar. Access.*

Killarney   Killarney Park Hotel   73%   £150
Tel 064 35555   Fax 064 35266   H
Kenmare Place Killarney Co Kerry   Map 2 A5

This newish hotel with classical lines enjoys a central setting
in attractive gardens set with mature trees. First impressions are
carried through to the smart foyer, which is spacious, with fires,
plenty of comfortable seating and, in common with most of the
other public areas, notably the bar, a pleasingly bold colour
scheme with fabrics mixed to good effect. The restaurant is more

restrained and has a cosy area especially appropriate for winter dining. Although not individually furnished, bedrooms are planned in groups to have variety in shape and size as well as colour schemes; all are spacious, several very large and especially suitable for families, and marbled bathrooms are well appointed. Banqueting/conference facilities for 140/60. The leisure centre "Club at the Park" opens out on to its own furnished patio. No dogs. *Rooms 66. Patio, indoor swimming pool, mini-gymnasium, steam room, keep-fit equipment. Closed 24-26 Dec.* AMERICAN EXPRESS *Access, Diners, Visa.*

Killarney	Killarney Towers Hotel	57%	£130
Tel 064 31038 Fax 064 31755			**H**
College Square Killarney Co Kerry			Map 2 A5

Very centrally located, this new hotel has quite spacious, identical, but comfortably furnished bedrooms with tea-making facilities, multi-channel TV and neat en-suite bathrooms. Children under 3 share parents' room free; 3- to 12-year-olds half price. Two bars include a residents' lounge and the lively Scruffy's pub. Lock-up car park. *Rooms 157.* AMERICAN EXPRESS *Access, Diners, Visa.*

Killarney	Randles Court Hotel	£120
Tel 064 35333 Fax 064 35206		**H**
Muckross Road Killarney Co Kerry		Map 2 A5

Well situated – it is convenient for Muckross House and Killarney National Park but also within walking distance of the town centre – this attractive Edwardian house underwent extensive refurbishment before opening as an owner-run hotel in 1992. Period features including fireplaces and stained glass windows have been retained however and comfortably furnished public areas include a small bar, spacious drawing room with log fire, murals and antiques and an elegant restaurant opening on to a sheltered patio. Bedrooms have direct-dial telephones, satellite television, radio, hairdryer and well-appointed bathrooms; children under 5 may stay free in their parents' room. *Rooms 37. Patio. Closed 6 Jan-17 Mar.* AMERICAN EXPRESS *Access, Visa.*

Killarney	The Strawberry Tree	£65
Tel & Fax 064 32688		**R**
24 Plunkett Street Killarney Co Kerry		Map 2 A5

Owner-chef Evan Doyle and restaurant manager Denis Heffernan have been running this first-floor restaurant to growing acclaim since 1983 and now, as the first Irish restaurant to make an absolute commitment to using wild, free-range and organic produce in 1993, a new standard has been set. The ambience is comfortably cottagey but sophisticated, with open stone and whitewashed walls, open fires and low ceilings with elegantly appointed tables and thoughtfully written menus which give a hint of serious goings-on in the kitchen. Wild salmon is home-smoked over oak and apple wood, producing a pale, unusually subtle smoke, real (that is, organic) vegetable soups come with wonderful warm breads and corned beef and cabbage is served, unusually, as a starter – and, more unusually still, they can tell you exactly where the beef came from. A sorbet might be made of gorse and wild mint, a duet of wild foods could be pan-fried breast of wood-pigeon with home-made rabbit sausages. Desserts include a good bread-and-butter pudding and home-made ices, such as lemon balm and honey. Fragrant coffees or herbal teas come with irresistible petits fours. The excellent house wine selection is made democratically each year by friends and regulars. **Seats** 30. *L by arrangement, D 6.30-9.30. Set Early Bird menu (6.30-8) £14.95. Closed Jan/Feb, Mon & Tues except high season, Good Friday.* AMERICAN EXPRESS *Access, Diners, Visa.*

Killarney	Torc Great Southern	63%	£94
Tel 064 31611 Fax 064 31824			**H**
Park Road Killarney Co Kerry			**Map 2 A5**

30 rooms have been completely refurbished this year at this modern, low-rise hotel half a mile from the town centre on the main Cork road. Well-run, with views of the Kerry mountains, it makes a good base for a holiday in the area. **Rooms** 94. *Garden, sauna, table tennis, creche, indoor play room. Closed Oct-end Mar.* AMERICAN EXPRESS *Access, Diners, Visa.*

Killarney	West End House	£50
Tel 064 32271 Fax 064 35979		**R**
New Street Killarney Co Kerry		**Map 2 A5**

Situated opposite St Mary's church, this pleasant restaurant has a somewhat Tyrolean atmosphere and features an unusual open fire, built high into the wall of the bar end of the restaurant to cast warmth right across the room. Table settings are perhaps inappropriate for an otherwise up-market restaurant: paper mats and foil-wrapped butter even at dinner. A starter such as pink grapefruit segments gratinated with brown sugar, a dash of rum and little balls of rum sorbet could equally well end a meal; presentation is attractive without ostentation and cooking of hearty dishes like soups (onion with port or leek and potato with country bacon) with home-made brown bread and rack of Kerry lamb is sound. Accommodation also available: three rooms, at around £40 per night. **Seats** 60. *Parties 20. Private Room 25. L 12-2 D 6-10. Closed Mon. Set D £16.50. Access, Visa.*

Killarney	Yer Man's Pub	
Tel & Fax 064 32688		**P**
24 Plunkett Street Killarney Co Kerry		**Map 2 A5**

Underneath *The Strawberry Tree* restaurant and in common ownership, a characterful, old-fashioned pub is to be found. The modern accoutrements nowadays essential to a well-run bar have been skilfully disguised, while the comforts of yesteryear are much in evidence – the long, narrow bar has two open turf fires, each with its own collection of mismatched but comfortable seating, including an old leather-upholstered car seat and the top half of an Edwardian armchair, easily set on a box. Plenty of shelf-height hooks for outerwear and a small back bar with original black range add to the appeal. Wholesome soups (perhaps chowder £1.95 or vegetable £1.75), sandwiches, pie, quiche, mussels and oysters from *The Strawberry Tree* kitchen are offered on a short

bar menu. Also home-made ice cream (£2.45). Live music
most nights in high season. *Open 12.30pm-1am, Sun 12.30-2 &
4-12.* **Bar Food** *12-3 (no food Sun). Closed Good Friday, 25 Dec.*
AMERICAN EXPRESS® *Access, Diners, Visa.*

See the 'Listing in County Order' section (highlighted by
colour pages) at the back of the Guide for instant comparison
of establishments in a particular area.

Killeagh   Ballymakeigh House   £40

Tel 024 95184   Fax 024 95370   **A**

Killeagh Co Cork   **Map 2 B6**

Set in the lush countryside of east Cork at the heart of a working
dairy farm, this attractive old house is immaculately maintained
and run by Margaret Browne, who provides an exceptional
standard of comfort and hospitality in one of the most outstanding
establishments of its type in Ireland. Guests have comfort and
space, both in the various public rooms – including a lovely
conservatory – and in all the individually decorated, thoughtfully
furnished, en-suite bedrooms. **Rooms** *5. Garden, terrace, patio,
tennis. Closed Christmas week. Access, Visa.*

Killiney   Court Hotel   68%   £92

Tel 01 285 1622   Fax 01 285 2085   **H**

Killiney Bay Killiney Co Dublin   **Map 2 D4**

Half an hour from the city centre by car or DART railway, this
extended Victorian mansion looks over landscaped gardens
to Killiney Bay. The most recent additions include a new cocktail
bar and conservatory and the reception area has also been enlarged
and modernised. Bedrooms, most with sea views, are spacious and
pleasantly decorated with darkwood furniture and co-ordinated
fabrics; under-12s stay free in parents' room. The largest room
in the international conference centre can accomodate up to 300
delegates. No dogs. **Rooms** *86. Garden.* AMERICAN EXPRESS® *Access,
Diners, Visa.*

Killiney   Fitzpatrick's Castle   68%   £162

Tel 01 284 0700   Fax 01 285 0207   **H**

Killiney Co Dublin   **Map 2 D4**

Dating back to 1741 and converted by the present owners
in 1974, this imposing castle hotel is half an hour's drive from
Dublin city centre and, despite its size and style, has a surprisingly
lived-in atmosphere. Extensive facilities include two large lounges,
two restaurants, a basement disco and a conference suite for up to
560 delegates. Roomy bedrooms, including some mini-suites, have
darkwood furniture and draped curtains. Children's programme
of events, children's menu, supervised play area. **Rooms** *90.
Garden, indoor swimming pool, gymnasium, squash, sauna, steam
room, hair & beauty salon, tennis, table tennis, children's play area.*
AMERICAN EXPRESS® *Access, Diners, Visa.*

Killiney   Place of Interest

Ayesha Castle Tel 01 285 2323

Killorglin   Nick's Restaurant   £65

Tel 066 61219   Fax 066 61233   **R**

Lower Bridge Street Killorglin Co Kerry   **Map 2 A5**

Nick and Anne Foley's popular seafood restaurant always has
a good buzz and Nick's cooking, which relies entirely on daily
catches for its seafood and local suppliers for lamb, beef and
organically grown vegetables, is mainly traditional French. From
a wide seafood selection, boosted by daily specials, could come
oysters, lobster, plaice, sole and salmon, plus grilled fillets of brill,
turbot and John Dory with lemon butter sauce. Elsewhere on the
menu you might find asparagus with hollandaise, ballotine of duck
with cherry relish, chicken Cordon Bleu, pork or lamb cutlets and
various steaks. France is comprehensively covered on the excellent
wine list, but not to the exclusion of the rest of Europe and the
New World; well-chosen throughout – bravo! *Seats 70.
Private Room 35. D only 6.30-10. Set D £23/£25. Closed Nov,
Mon & Tue Dec-March, 3 days Christmas.* AMERICAN EXPRESS® *Access,
Diners, Visa.*

Kilmoon   The Snail Box

Tel 01 835 4277   **P**

Kilmoon Ashbourne Co Meath   **Map 1 D3**

Four miles north of Ashbourne on the N2, this pleasant local has
a pool table bang in the middle of the friendly public bar and
a comfortable lounge in rustic style, both with open fireplaces. But
its curious name and the story of its origins are unique, going back
to the early 1800s when the site was common land and a hedge
schoolmaster settled there for a while. Taking exception to this
intrusion, the local landlord took him to court to get him evicted
– but the justice of the day ruled that 'the snail and his box can
settle where he chooses'. No food. *Open 4-11.30 (Fri & Sat from
12.30, Sun 12.30-2 & 4-11). Garden, outdoor tables.
Closed Good Friday, 25 Dec. No credit cards.*

Kilmuckridge   Boggan's

Tel 053 30181   **P**

Kilmuckridge Co Wexford   **Map 2 D5**

In the family for 180 years and currently in the capable hands
of Mary Boggan, who has instigated many sensitively handled
improvements over the last few years, this attractive pub consists
of a series of bars, each with its own special atmosphere but all
equally welcoming. Thick stone walls, original flagstones and
open fires have traditional appeal, especially in cold weather,
whereas the two large courtyards provide seating for up to 200
when the 'sunny south-east' lives up to its name. Bar food
specialities include farmhouse cheeses – including dishes such
as local goat's cheese with basil and plum tomatoes – and
an unusual range of home-baked breads. There are blackboards
and chalk for children to play with and even a children's theatre
organised one evening a week in July and August. Toilet accessible

for the disabled. No children in the bar after 9pm (but allowed
in courtyard). **Bar Meals** *1-5pm (to 3pm in winter).*
Closed Good Friday, 25 Dec. AMERICAN EXPRESS *Access, Visa.*

Kingstown	Kille House	£50
Tel & Fax 098 21849		**A**
Kingstown Clifden Co Galway		Map 1 A3

In a magnificently isolated location north of Clifden, this restored
Victorian manor house provides a comfortable base to return
to after a day walking the unspoilt Connemara hills or lonely
beaches nearby. The spacious reception rooms have open fires and
are elegantly furnished with antiques as are the pretty bedrooms,
which have lovely views. Children are welcome and under-8s stay
free in parents' rooms, some en-suite and all large enough
to accommodate extra beds (by arrangement) and cots (free
of charge). There's also a high-chair available and children's teas
can be served in the kitchen. Self-catering cottage for four also
available by March '95. Small conferences/private parties (12).
Rooms *4. Garden. Closed 1 Nov-1 Mar. Access, Visa.*

Kinnegad	The Cottage	
Tel 044 75284		**JaB**
Kinnegad Co Westmeath		Map 1 C3

Baking is a speciality at this neat, homely cottage restaurant,
so afternoon tea is a good time to drop in for scones, cakes and
preserves. Sandwiches, salads and omelettes are popular orders for
light meals, while at the luxury end of the menu are fresh and
smoked salmon. **Seats** *40. Private Room 26. Meals 8am-7pm.*
Closed D Sat, all Sun, 10 days Christmas. No credit cards.

Kinsale	Actons Hotel	60%	£100
Tel 021 772135 Fax 021 772231			**H**
Pier Road Kinsale Co Cork			Map 2 B6

Overlooking the harbour, this attractive quayside hotel was
created from several substantial period houses. Conference/
banqueting facilities for up to 300. Children up to 14 stay free
in parents' room. Forte Heritage. **Rooms** *57. Indoor swimming pool,
gymnasium, sauna, solarium.* AMERICAN EXPRESS *Access, Diners, Visa.*

Kinsale   Blue Haven Hotel   £96

Tel 021 772209   Fax 021 774268   **HR**

3 Pearse Street Kinsale Co Cork   Map 2 B6

Serious fishermen and trenchermen alike should head for the cosy
Blue Haven hotel near the quay, where not only is there a 36′
ocean-going angling boat for hire, but also good food and
comfortable accommodation after a hard day's sport. Bedrooms
are all in a new wing, and all are neat with smart white furniture
and pictures by local artists. All have en-suite facilities, some with
baths, some with just showers. The bar serves a wide choice
of imaginative food – from a choice of soups to sandwiches and
good seafood – and is very attractive, with wood panelling,
natural stone and a log fire, and has many snug corners. It opens
on to a cane-furnished conservatory which, in turn, leads on to
a patio. The entrance has been upgraded and a new wine
shop/delicatessen opened just off the lobby. No dogs. *Rooms 18.
Bar & conservatory (10.30am-9.30pm), teas & light snacks (3-5pm),
sea fishing. Closed 25 Dec.* AMERICAN EXPRESS® *Access, Diners, Visa.*

Restaurant   £60

The diner is left with no doubt as to the specialities of the
characterful restaurant, which has a strong maritime theme and
overlooks an attractive courtyard garden. Chef Stanley Matthews
kicks off with starters of seafood chowder, garlic mussels or baked
Rossmore oysters, followed by Oriental seafood Kashmiri, brill
and scallop bake or scallops on a skewer with bacon and
mushrooms. Seafood is balanced by dishes like Stanley's chicken
liver paté, warm goat's cheese salad, Mitchelstown venison
or prime fillet steaks. Good local farmhouse cheeses, including
Carrigaline. A very fairly priced and comprehensive wine list
with many 'Wild Geese' Bordeaux; perhaps light in half bottles,
compensated by the New World offerings. *Seats 80. Parties 40.
L 12.30-3, D 6.30-10.30. Closed 25 Dec.*

Kinsale   The Bulman Bar

Tel 021 772131   **P**

Summer Cove Kinsale Co Cork   Map 2 B6

About a mile along the harbour in the Charles Fort direction, this
traditional little waterside bar enjoys a tremendous setting looking
over the harbour towards Kinsale. The bar is sometimes quiet and
cosy, at other times very busy, and the large car park is liable
to turn into "the biggest lounge bar in Ireland". *Open 10.30am-
11.30pm, Sun 11-2 & 4-11. outdoor tables. Closed Good Friday,
25 Dec. No credit cards.*

Kinsale   Chez Jean-Marc   ↑   £55

Tel 021 774625   Fax 021 774680   **R**

Lower O'Connell Street Kinsale Co Cork   Map 2 B6

A cheerful yellow outside, beamed and country-cosy within, this
is a warm, welcoming place offering excellent food and efficient
service. Jean-Marc Tsai's cooking is traditional French with
Oriental accents (Sun night Chinese menu). From the classic
repertoire come French onion soup, garlicky baked mussels, duck
à la bigarade and roast pheasant with shallots and brandy sauce

and *pommes darphin.* Striking a more exotic note are warm salad paysanne, Thai stir-fry and millefeuille of salmon and lobster ravioli. Desserts are simple and delicious. During the summer the special Chinese night on Sundays is very popular with the locals. The wine list includes a good choice of house bottles. Upstairs from the restaurant Jean-Marc has now opened *Time Out,* a 60-seater piano bar/brasserie serving bistro-style fare – dishes range from black tiger prawn cocktail, beef and trotters salad and Vietnamese barbecue pork to pizza, steak and fish and chips. *Seats 60. D only 7-10. Closed all Mon Sept to June, 5 Feb-5 Mar.* AMERICAN EXPRESS *Access, Diners, Visa.*

Kinsale   The Dock Bar

Tel 021 772522	**P**
Castle Park Kinsale Co Cork	Map 2 B6

Well situated between the small marina at Castle Park and one of the few south-facing sandy beaches in the area (a few hundred yards across the peninsula), this traditional black-and-white pub looks over towards Kinsale and, although the town is very near, it feels like a world apart. The patio, where tables have a choice of sun or leafy shade, has a slightly Continental atmosphere and the interior is comfortable in the modern Irish idiom – quarry tiles, varnished tables, upholstered benches and photographs of some of landlord Michael Vance's winning horses to remind him of his years as a trainer. *Open 10.30am-11.30pm, Sun 12.30-2 & 4-11. Garden, outdoor eating area. No credit cards.*

Kinsale   Man Friday

Tel 021 772260	£55
	R
Scilly Kinsale Co Cork	Map 2 B6

A popular and convivial restaurant housed in a series of little rooms high above the harbour. Seafood is the natural speciality, with oysters cold or poached, crab au gratin, sweet and sour scampi, black sole (grilled or Colbert) and monkfish with a prawn sauce among the wide choice. That choice extends outside the fishy realms to the likes of Robinson Crusoe's warm salad (mixed leaves, croutons and bacon), deep-fried Brie with a plum and port sauce, Swiss-style veal escalope and roast rack of lamb with rosemary and a red wine sauce. Strawberry crème brulée, chocolate terrine, grape pudding or home-made ice creams round things off. Consistency is a keynote here, and it's owner-chef Philip Horgan (in charge since 1978) who maintains it. *Seats 80. Private Room 40. D only 6.30-10.30. Closed Good Friday, 24-26 Dec.* AMERICAN EXPRESS *Access, Visa.*

Kinsale   Max's Wine Bar

Tel 021 772443	£40
	R
Main Street Kinsale Co Cork	Map 2 B6

Wendy Tisdall is celebrating 20 years at her charming little restaurant, where highly varnished tabletops reflect fresh flowers and plants. Menus are always light and tempting – seafood chowder, half a dozen oysters or spinach pasta with fresh salmon could start a meal, or there are some speciality salads eg. roasted vegetable and baked goat's cheese. Next might come the day's fish

catch, breast of chicken with mushroom sauce, beefburgers or rack
of lamb, with home-made ice cream, lemon pancakes or chocolate
rum mousse to finish in style. The early bird menu offers
particularly good value for money (6.30-8pm £12). No smoking
in the conservatory (10 seats). *Seats 40. L 12.30-3 D 6.30-10.30.
Closed Nov-Feb. Set L & D £12. Access.*

Kinsale	The Moorings	£70
Tel 021 772376 Fax 021 772675		**A**
Scilly Kinsale Co Cork		Map 2 B6

Overlooking the marina in a unique waterside location, Pat and
Irene Jones' thoughtfully designed guesthouse was purpose-built
to maximise views across the harbour from a large conservatory
(used for breakfast if guests prefer not to take it in their rooms,
as well as for lounging) and most bedrooms. Spacious rooms have
well-appointed bathrooms, TV, phone and tea/coffee facilities and
are comfortably furnished to a high standard, including balconies
with seating in some cases. There is a bedroom equipped for
disabled guests. *Rooms 8. Garden. Access, Visa.*

We do not accept free meals or hospitality – our inspectors
pay their own bills.

Kinsale	The Old Bank House	£80
Tel 021 774075 Fax 021 774296		**A**
11 Pearse Street Kinsale Co Cork		Map 2 B6

A Georgian building of some character, formerly a branch of the
Munster and Leinster Bank. Individually furnished bedrooms are
spacious, elegant and comfortable, with good antiques and well-
appointed bathrooms. Public areas, including breakfast room
and sitting room, are non-smoking. Babies are accommodated,
but 2 to 7-year-olds are not encouraged. *Rooms 9.
Closed 4 days Christmas.* AMERICAN EXPRESS *Access, Visa.*

Kinsale	Old Presbytery	£48
Tel 021 772027		**A**
Cork Street Kinsale Co Cork		Map 2 B6

Victorian antiques, many of rural interest, are a feature of Ken and
Cathleen Buggy's peaceful, comfortable home. The six bedrooms
are decorated in traditional style, with big beds and Irish linen,
and there's a comfortable sitting room with an open fire. Breakfast
is a splendid spread, with a choice of 52 items including freshly
baked bread, home-made preserves and yoghurts, apricots and figs
in cider, pickled herrings and cheese. "Children and dogs are not
turned away if at the door, but are not really encouraged." The
old kitchen has been turned into a small restaurant, where Ken
produces short, daily-changing dinner menus with old-fashioned
unusual soups, Continental salads and freshly-caught fish among
the specialities. Restaurant only open to residents (dinner only,
set menu £18, closed Sun & Mon & Oct-Jan). *Rooms 6. Garden.
Closed 1 week Christmas. Access, Visa.*

Kinsale   Scilly House   65%   £86
Tel 021 772413   Fax 021 774629   A
Scilly Kinsale Co Cork   Map 2 B6

An old house of great charm and character overlooking the
harbour and Kinsale Bay. The style is American country, with old
pine furniture, antiques, traditional American quilts, floral prints
and folk art. Public rooms include a bar/library with grand piano,
a cosy sitting room and a dining room with views over the
garden down to the sea. There are views, too, from most of the
individually appointed bedrooms, which include one suite.
No children under 12. *Rooms* 7. *Garden, solarium.*
Closed 1 Nov-10 Apr. AMERICAN EXPRESS *Access, Visa.*

Kinsale   1601
Tel 021 772529   P
Pearse Street Kinsale Co Cork   Map 2 B6

Named after the year of the Battle of Kinsale, details of which
form an interesting and decorative presentation in the front
lounge, this centrally located pub has earned a reputation for good
bar food and is popular with locals and visitors alike. Their well-
priced, freshly home-made food is worth waiting for; the menu
changes daily. There's always a choice of chowder (£2.75) and
another soup of the day (£1.60) and a short, well-balanced menu
offers starters/light main courses such as a warm salad of goat's
cheese (£4.25), crab cocktail (£4.25), several local seafood dishes,
traditional Irish fare like boiled bacon and cabbage with parsley
sauce (£5), Irish stew (£4.95) and the house special, '1601 Battle
Burger' (£4.95), a home-made burger served with chips, salad and
a choice of piquant dipping sauces such as chili, ketchup and
chutney. The rear of the Lounge Bar is the Art Gallery restaurant,
where food is served all day when it's busy. Food also served all
day in summer. Live traditional Irish music on Monday nights.
*Open 10.30am-11.30pm, Sun 12.30-11. **Bar Food** 12.30-3 & 6.30-9
(to 7 Sun). Children allowed in the bar to eat. Closed Good Friday, 25
Dec.* AMERICAN EXPRESS *Access, Visa.*

Kinsale   The Spaniard Inn
Tel 021 772436   P
Scilly Kinsale Co Cork   Map 2 B6

High above the harbour near the *Man Friday* restaurant, The
Spaniard dispenses good cheer, good food and good music. Mary
O'Toole's bar food is plain and simple, running from salads, soups
and open sandwiches (try one with smoked Kinsale wild salmon
£3.75) to old favourites like Irish stew or bacon and cabbage
(£4.75); also cheese platter with home-made relish and soda bread
(£3.75), home-made apple pie (£1.75) and ice cream (£1.75).
Lunch can be taken on the terrace when the sun shines. Music
sessions include light jazz, rock and blues (winter) and Irish
traditional. The inn comprises several low-beamed rooms with
stone floors, country furniture and assorted items of local interest
– notably a 35lb salmon caught in 1912 at Little Island,
Ardfinnan. *Open 10.30am-11.30pm Mon-Sat (to 11 in winter,*

Sun 12-2.30 & 4-11). **Bar Food** *12.30-3 May-Sept, snacks only
in evenings and all day Sun. Patio, outdoor eating.
Closed Good Friday, 25 Dec. No credit cards.*

Kinsale	The White Lady Inn	£50
Tel 021 772737		**H**
Lower O'Connell Street Kinsale Co Cork		**Map 2 B6**

All rooms at this unpretentious family-run hotel in a back street
near the marina have recently been refurbished with co-ordinated
furnishing schemes, TV and phone, while neatly tiled well-
planned en-suite bathrooms have efficient, user-friendly showers.
Public areas include a bar used by locals and a franchised informal
restaurant, where breakfast is served. There is a night club at the
back, but thoughtful staff ensure that rooms which might
be affected by noise are only let to guests attending the function.
Rooms *10.* AMERICAN EXPRESS *Access, Visa.*

Kinsale	Place of Interest

Gourmet Festival (October) Tel 021 774026
Charles Fort Tel 021 772263

Kinvara	Sayre's	£40
Tel 091 87417		**R**
Kinvara Co Galway		**Map 2 B4**

This stylish little bright and airy first-floor restaurant is in
an interesting old building a little way up the hill from the
picturesque harbour. PVC cloths, classical music and a fascinating
appliqué wallhanging provide a pleasing background while
waiting for the likes of fat local mussels in white wine, with
home-made brown bread, followed, perhaps, by fish of the day
from the blackboard choice, rounded off by home-made ice
cream. No bookings. **Seats** *26. Meals 12-10pm. Closed Mon,
end Sep-mid April.* AMERICAN EXPRESS *Access, Visa.*

When telephoning establishments in the Republic from *outside*
the Republic, dial 00-353 then the number we print less the
initial zero: eg The Strawberry Tree in Killarney is
00-353 64 32688.

Kinvara	Tully's
Tel 091 37146		**P**
Kinvara Co Galway		**Map 2 B4**

A real local pub in the old tradition, with a little grocery shop
at the front and stone-floored bar at the back, Tully's has a small
enclosed garden with a few parasoled tables for fine weather but,
better still, a fine old stove in the bar for cosy winter sessions. Not
a food place – although sandwiches and tea or coffee are always
available – but, as the old photographs and newspaper cuttings
around the walls proclaim, definitely a spot for traditional music.
*Open 10.30am-11.30pm Mon-Sat (till 11 in winter), Sun 12.30-2,
4-11. Closed 25 Dec, Good Fri. No credit cards.*

Kylemore Abbey   Kylemore Abbey Restaurant

Tel 095 41146

JaB

Kylemore-in-Connemara Co Galway

Map 1 A3

A neatly self-contained modern building in the grounds
of Kylemore Abbey, run by the Benedictine nuns in conjunction
with an excellent craft shop, everything at this daytime self-service
restaurant is made on the premises and the range of wholesome
offerings encompasses a good selection of hot and cold savoury
dishes, including several vegetarian options, typically black-eye
bean casserole or vegetarian lasagne; home baking is a special
strength and big bowls of the nuns' renowned home-made jams
for the freshly baked bread and scones stand beside the till, for
visitors to help themselves. Reinforcing the appeal while the mood
is on you, the next thing to catch your eye is a big display
of neatly labelled jars, so the chances are you will buy some to take
home too. The abbey itself, a neo-Gothic crenellated mansion now
used as a convent school, is dramatically situated on the lake shore
near the restaurant car park and a short walk further along the
wooded shore leads to the beautiful Gothic church (built in 1868),
a miniature replica of Norwich Cathedral – due to reopen after
restoration in spring 1995. Baby-changing facilities are provided.
Car parking for 150. *Seats 240. Open 9.30-5.30 (to 5pm off-season).
Closed Nov-end Mar.* AMERICAN EXPRESS *Access, Visa.*

Set menu prices may not always include service or wine.
Our quoted price for two does.

Laragh   Mitchell's of Laragh

£45

Tel & Fax 0404 45302

R

The Old Schoolhouse Laragh Co Wicklow

Map 2 D4

Jerry and Margaret Mitchell's lovingly restored old cut-granite
schoolhouse, with leaded window panes, open fires and country
pine furniture, provides adults with a tranquil haven from the
crowds which nearby Glendalough tends to attract – and very
good home cooking to boot. Menus, changed with the seasons,
might include sautéed lamb's kidneys, piquant with whiskey and
orange, or crisp hot button mushrooms on toast, fragrant in lemon
and garlic, followed by tender, juicy roast lamb with ginger sauce
or smoked salmon and trout salad. "All types of food are served all
day to our visitors from all around the world", says Margaret,
so one can eat quiche for breakfast or a fry-up for dinner if it takes
one's fancy. Margaret's home baking is a great strength and, not
surprisingly perhaps, afternoon tea is a speciality. Not suitable for
children. Accommodation is offered in five neat en-suite twin
rooms with pleasant rural outlook. Two more rooms and a guest
sitting room were added in summer '94. No dogs in the rooms.
*Seats 30. Private Room 20. Meals 9am-9.30pm (Sun 9pm). Set Sun
L £10.95 Set D £15.95. Closed from D Sun to D Tues in winter,
4 weeks in winter, 2 days at Christmas, Good Friday.* AMERICAN EXPRESS
Access, Visa.

Lecanvey   Staunton's

Tel 098 64850

P

Lecanvey Westport Co Mayo   Map 1 A3

In the same family ownership for about two hundred years, the
current landlord of this roadside pub (it is on a shallow bed and
hard to miss when driving from Louisburgh to Westport) is a
charming young lady, Thérèse Staunton. It's a 'real' pub,
traditional but not hide-bound by age and custom, with a good,
comfortable atmosphere and is popular with locals and visitors
alike. Therese currently offers just soup and sandwiches but
is hoping to widen the scope in the summer of 1995 (when a new
kitchen might be added). *Pub open 10.30am-11.30pm, Sun 12.30-2,
4-11 (to 10 in winter). Closed Good Friday, 25 Dec. No credit cards.*

Leenane   Delphi Lodge

£70

Tel 095 42211   Fax 095 42296

A

Leenane Co Galway   Map 1 A3

Set in a spectacular, unspoilt valley and surrounded by Connacht's
highest mountains, this early 19th-century sporting lodge was
built by the Marquis of Sligo in one of the most beautiful (and
wettest) parts of Ireland. The current owners, Peter and Jane
Mantle, have restored and sensitively extended the house which
now has eleven guest bedrooms. They vary considerably in size
and layout in keeping with the age of the house, but all are
en suite, with lovely views over the lake or woodlands and
mountains. A comfortable family atmosphere prevails and,
although it's quite grandly furnished with antiques, sporting
paraphernalia and abundant reading matter everywhere ensure the
relaxed comfort of guests. Dinner, for residents only, is served at a
long mahogany table, presided over by the captor of the day's
biggest salmon. Just across the road, four restored cottages offer
self-catering accommodation. ***Rooms** 11. Garden, fishing, snooker.
Closed 1 Nov-31 Jan. Access, Visa.*

Leenane   Killary Lodge   59%

£56

Tel 095 42276   Fax 095 42314

A

Leenane Co Galway   Map 1 A3

Superbly located in woodland with beautiful views through
to Killary Harbour, this unusual hotel is owned by Jamie and
Mary Young, who also run the renowned Little Killary
Adventure Centre nearby, and provides the best of both worlds
for people attracted to the idea of a healthy outdoor activity
holiday but also willing to pay for the comfort of a hotel rather
than returning to a bleak hostel at the end of a long day in the
fresh air. Rooms, mostly twin but also some singles and doubles,
all with shower or bath en suite, are comfortably furnished and
have phones but no television (as a matter of policy). Children
up to 14 stay free in parents' room. Activities such as horse riding,
canoeing, orienteering, archery, sailing and tennis are available;
no experience is necessary, as trained guides will ease guests into
new activities to suit their individual pace. Relaxation is the aim.
***Rooms** 18. Garden, tennis, games room, shop. Closed Dec & Jan.
Access, Visa.*

Leenane   Portfinn Lodge   £55

Tel 095 42265   Fax 095 42315   **RR**

Leenane Co Galway   Map 1 A3

Rory and Maeve Daly have been running this seafood restaurant
at the head of Killary Harbour since 1988 and the dining area
is shared between a room of the main house and an adjoining
conservatory, both with western window tables (on a good
evening) offering views of the sun sinking behind the mountains.
Very good moist brown soda bread with sunflower seeds is on the
table to welcome guests; thereafter seafood takes pride of place
although the menu actually offers quite a wide choice, including
a number of Oriental dishes. A typical meal might start with
a roulade of stuffed smoked salmon, or a seafood bisque followed,
perhaps, by monkfish and scallops with a tomato, garlic, basil and
brandy sauce or roast duck with Grand Marnier sauce. Finish with
something like 'Dad's gooey meringue pudding', or stay safe with
an Irish cheeseboard. *Seats 36. Parties 10. Private Room 40. D only
5.30-9 (flexible). Closed 1 Nov-Easter. Set D £16.50. Access, Visa.*

Rooms   £35

Eight neat, purpose-built en-suite rooms, all sleeping three and one
with four beds; accessible (but not specially equipped) for disabled
guests.

Leighlinbridge   The Lord Bagenal Inn   £45

Tel 0503 21668   **R**

Leighlinbridge Co Carlow   Map 2 C4

Food, wine and hospitality are all dispensed in good measure
at this renowned old inn just off the main M9 Waterford-Carlow
road. The style of cooking is always evolving, and more modern
dishes are joining old favourites like the oysters and mussels, the
crabs and the scallops, the home-made patés, the steaks and the fine
fresh fish. The whole family is made very welcome and there's
a special children's menu. Booking is advised for Sunday lunch.
Also a new tourist menu and plenty of vegetarian dishes.
Farmhouse cheeses. There are surprisingly few half bottles on an
otherwise enterprising, outstanding and fairly-priced wine list that
provides helpful notes. *Seats 90. Parties 25. Private Room 40.
L 12.30-2.30 D 6-10.30 (bar food 12.30-10.30). Closed 25 Dec,
Good Friday. Set L £9.50 Set D £11.50/£16.95. Access,
Diners, Visa.*

Leighlinbridge   Place of Interest

Altamont by Tullow Tel 0503 59128

Letterfrack   Rosleague Manor   72%   £110

Tel 095 41101   Fax 095 41168   **HR**

Letterfrack Connemara Co Galway   Map 1 A3

Owned and managed by the welcoming Foyle family, the
Georgian manor stands in 30 acres of gardens overlooking
Ballinakill Bay. Character and comfort are in generous supply, the
former including carefully chosen antiques and paintings, the latter
assisted by central heating and peat fires. Bedrooms are nearly all
of a very good size (with separate seating areas or mini-suites) and

all have good bathrooms. There are two drawing rooms and
a conservatory bar. **Rooms** 20. *Garden, sauna, tennis, billiards,
fishing. Closed Nov-Easter.* *Access, Visa.*

Restaurant

Nigel Rush's four-course dinner menus are served at round antique
tables under chandeliers in a delightfully civilised room. Local
produce (some of it home-grown) is put to excellent use in dishes
that range from fresh prawn mayonnaise, duck liver paté and
marinated mushrooms in red wine, honey and herbs among the
starters to potato and walnut soup as a second course, then grilled
wild salmon with scallion butter, guinea fowl with brandy and
raisins, and medallions of pork in cider sauce. Only cold dishes
at lunchtime. Home-made ice creams feature among the sweets.
Teas and coffees are served in the drawing rooms. No smoking
in the dining room. **Seats** 65. *Parties 20. L 12.30 D 8-9.30 (Sun
to 9). Set D from £25.*

Letterfrack   Place of Interest

Kylemore Abbey (*see entry*) Connemara Tel 095 41146

Letterkenny   Carolina House Restaurant   £65

Tel 074 22480	**R**
Loughnagin Letterkenny Co Donegal	Map 1 C1

Despite its somewhat domestic atmosphere, this modern bungalow
on the outskirts of Letterkenny was purpose-built as a restaurant
in 1990 by Charles and (Ballymaloe-trained) Mary Prendergast,
who named it after the field on which it stands. Aperitifs and
orders are taken in a cosy sitting room (with an open fire for
chilly evenings) and the spacious, hexagonal dining room
is elegantly appointed in soft tones of pink and white, with fresh
flowers, crisp linen, fine glasses and a basket of freshly-baked bread
setting the scene for Mary's confident cooking. A well-balanced
à la carte menu offers plenty of choice starting perhaps with 'salad'
of home-smoked beef with mango, papaya and apricot chutney
and then a simple but unusual dish of prawns and mussel kebabs
with sun-dried tomatoes and basil butter. Main courses offer
a choice of ten including a vegetarian option; fillet of ling might
come with a nutty crust on a spicy cream sauce or tender, juicy
fillet of beef in a deliciously rich stout and dried mushroom sauce,
all served with local vegetables. Temptations on a traditional
dessert trolley could include plums in mulled wine and home-
made ices (changed nightly) served from a big ice bowl,
Ballymaloe-style. Finish with freshly brewed coffee by the cup and
a piece of home-made fudge. **Seats** 50. *Parties 14. D only 6.30-9.30.
Closed Sun, Mon, also 2 weeks early autumn, 4 days Christmas.*
 Access, Diners, Visa.

Letterkenny   Castle Grove Country House   £90

Tel 074 51118 Fax 074 51384	**A**
Letterkenny Co Donegal	Map 1 C1

Well-tended gardens and parkland, ample parking and a striking
entrance hall ensure good first impressions at this fine 17th-
century house overlooking Lough Swilly. Well-proportioned
reception rooms are appropriately furnished and have welcoming

fires and, although bedrooms (three non-smoking) vary in size and outlook, all have en-suite bath or shower, direct-dial phones and hairdryers; there's a trouser press on the landing. Friendly, helpful staff and good management by Mary Sweeney, who also personally supervise the kitchen – excellent breakfasts include delicious freshly-baked bread, home-made preserves and a good selection of fish. **Rooms** 8. *Garden, croquet, tennis, shooting, fishing (dogs and ghillies supplied). Closed 9 Jan-14 Feb, 24-27 Dec.* AMERICAN EXPRESS *Access, Diners, Visa.*

Letterkenny   Place of Interest
Tourist Information Tel 074 21160

Limerick   Castletroy Park Hotel   74%   £131
Tel 061 335566 Fax 061 331117	**HR**

Dublin Road Limerick Co Limerick   Map 2 B5

Located on the Dublin road on the outskirts of town, this well-designed red-brick hotel meets every business need and is a worthy winner of our Ireland 1995 Business Hotel of the Year award (see page 85 for further details). The new university concert hall and foundation building, just three minutes' walk away, will greatly enhance Limerick's growing reputation as a major conference centre, and with its own state-of-the-art conference and leisure facilities the hotel is ideally situated to benefit. A welcoming atmosphere warms the wood-floored entrance hall and conservatory, while the Merry Pedlar 'pub', which also serves bistro-style food, offers traditional and authentic Irish hospitality and a decent pint. Bedrooms are large with plenty of writing space, good lighting and up-to-date features – satellite TV, fax and computer points, two phones, minibar and trouser press; bathrooms are on the small side. Executive rooms offer more extras including king-size bed, bathrobe and turn-down service plus several other complimentary items. Whether your needs require facilities for a conference (up to 300) or a private boardroom, the hotel can cater for both and also provides a fully-equipped business centre. Note the amenities available in the superbly equipped leisure centre. Good buffet breakfast served in the restaurant. 24hr room service. No dogs. **Rooms** 107. *Garden, terrace, indoor swimming pool, children's splash pool, gymnasium, keep-fit equipment, solarium, sauna, spa bath, steam room, beauty salon.* AMERICAN EXPRESS *Access, Diners, Visa.*

McLaughlin's Restaurant   £65

Widely regarded as one of the leading restaurants in the area, McLaughlin's tries hard to be cosy, with candle light and shelves of old books to soften the surroundings – although the atmosphere is still inclined to be impersonal, with a rather businesslike approach by staff ('Smoking or non-smoking, madam?'), a reminder that the restaurant is located in a large hotel. On the four-course dinner menu Pat O'Sullivan, head chef since late 1992, presents reliable *cuisine moderne* starting, perhaps, with a tasty *amuse-bouche* such as a miniature barbecued kebab, followed by prawns with herb dumplings or hot fricassee of wild mussels and clams, then a choice of soups or citrus sorbet. Main-course choices tend to lean towards fish or, perhaps, noisettes of lamb with white bean and tomato sauce. Informal lunch and evening

meals are available from an international bar menu at the hotel's
Merry Pedlar 'pub'. *Seats* 76. *Parties* 14. *L* 12.30-2 *D* 7-9.30.
*Set L £14.50 Set D £24. Closed L Sat, D Sun, L Bank Holidays,
Dec 24-4 Jan.*

Limerick	Greenhills Hotel	62%	£107
Tel 061 453033 Fax 061 453307			**H**
Ennis Road Limerick Co Limerick			**Map 2 B5**

Continual improvement is the aim at this family-run hotel and,
although older rooms (due for refurbishment this year) seem quite
dated they have a pleasant outlook over garden or tennis court and
are all well equipped, with telephone, tea/coffee-making facilities,
trouser press and television. Newer rooms are larger and more
comfortable, with well-finished, fully-tiled bathrooms. Public
areas include a leisure centre, spacious lobby and a pleasant bar.
A new restaurant – *The Bayleaf* – was opened last year. No dogs.
Rooms *60. Garden, indoor swimming pool, children's pool, gymnasium,
sauna, steam room, solarium, beauty salon, tennis. Closed 25 Dec.*
AMERICAN EXPRESS *Access, Diners, Visa.*

Limerick	Jurys Hotel	68%	£120
Tel & Fax 061 327777			**H**
Ennis Road Limerick Co Limerick			**Map 2 B5**

Centrally situated just across the bridge from Limerick's main
shopping and business area, Jurys prides itself on hospitality and
service as well as convenience. A good impression is created in the
spacious lobby area and carried through the public areas, including
the pleasant Limericks Bar (which features the history of the
famous rhyming verse), two restaurants and extensive leisure
facilities, while a continuous programme of refurbishment has
ensured that standards are maintained. Service is a priority,
friendly staff provide 24 hour room service. Newer bedrooms are
larger and more stylishly decorated with smarter bathrooms but
older rooms are equally well equipped (including trouser press
and multi-channel TV; tea/coffee-making facilities available
on request) and kept up to date with ongoing refurbishment.
Rooms *96. Garden, indoor swimming pool, children's splash pool, gym,
sauna, steam room, spa bath, tennis, coffee shop (7am-10.30pm).
Closed 24-26 Dec.* AMERICAN EXPRESS *Access, Diners, Visa.*

Limerick	Limerick Inn Hotel	68%	£118
Tel 061 326666 Fax 061 326281			**H**
Ennis Road Limerick Co Limerick			**Map 2 B5**

The helipad in front of this low-rise modern hotel attracts
considerable attention from passing traffic and there is usually a bit
of a buzz around the large, airy reception area and public rooms.
Good-sized rooms at the back of the hotel have a pleasant outlook
over countryside, have well-designed bathrooms and are equipped
to a high standard, including trouser press complete with iron and
ironing board in addition to hairdryer, phone, tea/coffee-making
facilities and multi-channel TV while superior rooms and suites
also have mini-bars. Conference and business facilities for up to
600 delegates include secretarial services. Good health and leisure
facilities; resident hair stylist and beautician. **Rooms** *153. Garden,*

indoor swimming pool, gymnasium, sauna, solarium, steam room, whirlpool bath, tennis, putting, snooker, coffee shop (7.30-2.30 & 6-10.30). Closed 25 Dec. **AMERICAN EXPRESS** *Access, Diners, Visa.*

Limerick	Quenelle's Restaurant	£55
Tel 061 411111		**R**
Corner of Mallow & Henry Street Limerick Co Limerick		**Map 2 B5**

Kieran and Sindy Pollard burst on to the Limerick dining scene in the summer of 1993 and their interesting little three-level city-centre restaurant overlooking the river is already making its mark. Although especially popular at lunchtime, when a bargain three-course menu draws the crowds, a calmer evening visit is required to do justice to Kieran's confident, adventurous cooking and a more elegant table presentation. A typical five-course menu might include parcels of wild boar (in season), a choice of soups and also an unusual, amusingly presented sorbet and a full range of local produce in the main-course choices, including excellent steak given a new twist with a nutty bacon crust, perhaps an interesting vegetarian option such as vegetables crepes with a cheese and basil sauce and, of course, a selection of local seafood. Imaginative desserts might include an excellent classic crème caramel delicately decorated with fresh fruit fans and there's a good selection of farmhouse cheeses. Attention to detail is outstanding throughout, from the presentation of little amuse-bouche on arrival, through garnishing side vegetables with a dainty filo moneybag parcel filled with a julienne of vegetables, to the minted truffles served with coffee. *Seats 35. L 12-2.15 D 7-10. Closed L Sat, all Sun & Mon, 24-26 Dec, Good Friday. Set L £5.20 Set D £19.75. Access, Visa.*

Hotel sporting facilities are highlighted in the Quick Reference
lists for easy comparison.

Limerick	Restaurant de La Fontaine	£60
Tel 061 414461 Fax 061 411337		**R**
12 Upper Gerald Griffin Street Limerick Co Limerick		**Map 2 B5**

Appropriately named after the great writer of fables, Alain Bras' first-floor restaurant has an other-worldliness which strikes the first-time visitor immediately on climbing wide carpeted stairs – distinctly reminiscent of the approach to 1950s' picture houses – to the reception area. Once inside, it could be provincial France, a feeling strongly reinforced by chef Bernard Brousse's evocative *cuisine grand'mère* in dishes such as venison terrine, accompanied by delicious little Puy lentils, and excellent robust country main courses like rabbit with cabbage. An exceptional French wine list (for other countries you must ask). The entrance has recently been converted into a 30-seat wine bar, where lunches and apéritifs are served. *Seats 40. L 12.30-2.30 D 7-10. Set L £10 Set D £21.50. Closed L Sat, all Sun, Bank Holidays & Christmas.* **AMERICAN EXPRESS** *Access, Diners, Visa.*

Limerick   Two Mile Inn Hotel   63%   £78

Tel 061 326255   Fax 061 453783   **H**

Ennis Road Limerick Co Limerick   **Map 2 B5**

Actually just three miles from the centre of Limerick, this striking
modern hotel features an enormous lobby with a large seating
area, rather like an airport lounge, but the hotel as a whole
is imaginatively laid out and other areas are surprisingly intimate.
Bedrooms are attractively arranged around garden areas which
afford a feeling of quietness and privacy and are furnished with
deck chairs and sunshades in summer. Conference centre, with
banqueting for up to 300. Good children's menu and daily
children's entertainment in the summer. No dogs. *Rooms 123.
Garden, shop.* AMERICAN EXPRESS *Access, Diners, Visa.*

Limerick   Places of Interest

Tourist Information Tel 061 317522
Bus Eirann (Irish Bus) Booking Information Tel 061 313333
City Gallery of Art Upper Mallow Street Tel 061 310663
City Museum John Square Tel 061 417826
King John's Castle Tel 061 411201
St John's Cathedral Tel 061 414624
St Mary's Cathedral Tel 061 310293
Limerick Racecourse Tel 061 29377
Cratloe Woods House Cratloe Tel 061 327028 *5 miles*
Lough Gur Interpretative Centre Lough Gur Tel 061 85186 *6 miles*

Lisdoonvarna   Sheedy's Spa Hotel   66%   £50

Tel 065 74026   Fax 065 74555   **H**

Lisdoonvarna Co Clare   **Map 2 B4**

In family ownership for generations, the Spa is now an attractively
furnished and immaculately maintained small hotel under the
management of the current owners, Frank and Patsy Sheedy. The
well-tended approach and warm ambience of the sunny foyer
with its warm wooden floor, open fire and soft country colours
creates a good first impression, which is carried through all the
public areas (note the cosy night-time bar just off the foyer)
to bedrooms which vary in size, but are all en suite, neatly
decorated in a pretty, not too overpowering style and well
equipped, with phone, hairdryer and tea/coffee-making facilities.
Four ground-floor rooms are accessible for disabled guests. Fax
and photcopying facilities are available at reception on request.
Ample free parking. *Rooms 11. Tennis. Closed 1 Oct-1 Apr.*
AMERICAN EXPRESS *Access, Diners, Visa.*

Maddoxtown   Blanchville House   £55

Tel 056 27197   **A**

Dunbell Maddoxtown Co Kilkenny   **Map 2 C5**

Easily recognised by the folly in its grounds, this elegant Georgian
house is on a working farm and, while conveniently close to the
crafts and culture of Kilkenny city, has all the advantages of peace
and restfulness associated with the country – and similarly Tim
and Monica Phelan aim to provide guests with 20th-century
comfort to balance 19th-century style. The house has a lovely,
airy atmosphere, with matching, well-proportioned dining and

drawing rooms on either side of the hall and pleasant, comfortably furnished bedrooms (most en-suite, two with private bathrooms) overlooking lovely countryside. Dinner is available to residents by arrangement and, like the next morning's excellent breakfast, is taken at the communal mahogany dining table. **Rooms** 6. *Garden. Closed 1 Nov-1 Mar. Access, Visa.*

Malahide	**Bon Appétit**	**£80**
Tel & Fax 01 845 0314		**R**
9 St James Terrace Malahide Co Dublin		**Map 1 D3**

An elegant Georgian terrace house, overlooking the estuary, has been the setting for both the home and business of Catherine and Patsy McGuirk since 1989. Aperitifs are served in the ground-floor drawing room/bar, notable for its pleasing local watercolours, while the cosy restaurant, decorated in warm tones of red and dark green, is in the basement. Chef Patsy serves classical French food based on top-quality fresh ingredients (Dingle Bay scallops, Carlingford lobster, Kilmore crab, east coast mussels), with a handful of daily specials added for variety. Thus, snails in garlic butter and fillets of brill Cardinal sit happily alongside roast mallard, monkfish Thermidor and medallions of venison vin rouge. The super wine list has many fine French classics, most of which are accompanied by tasting notes; the best value is outside these, with lots of good drinking under £20. **Seats 55.** *Private Room 20. L 12.30-2 D 7-10 (10.30 weekends). Closed L Sat, all Sun, Bank Holidays, 1 week Christmas. Set L £10 Set D £22.* AMERICAN EXPRESS® *Access, Diners, Visa.*

Malahide	**Eastern Tandoori**	**£40**
Tel 01 845 4154/5 Fax 01 677 9232		**R**
1 New Street Malahide Co Dublin		**Map 1 D3**

Although it's on the first floor, overlooking the new Malahide marina development, the atmosphere at this out-of-town branch of the well-known city centre restaurant is distinctly other-worldly, with an all-Indian staff, authentic furnishings and sound effects. Choose from four set menus at varying prices, or from the à la carte: between them they offer a wide, well-balanced choice of dishes ranging from gently aromatic to fiery hot, suiting the novice without offending old hands. Old favourites are there in mild onion bhajee, served with a small salad, various tandoori dishes – chicken tikka, mackerel, even quail and crab claws – and several jalfrezi dishes such as beef, lamb or chicken, hot with chili, fresh ginger and coriander. Chef's recommendations are more interesting, some desserts garnished with the classic silver leaf, and side dishes like tarka dal (lentils with fresh coriander) and aloo jeera (dry potatoes with cumin seed) are good. Wine is pricy, but Cobra Indian beer suits the food better anyway. Branches also in central Dublin (34-35 South William Street Tel 01 671 0428 open 7 days, closed Sun L), Deans Grange in Blackrock (Tel 01 289 2856) and Cork (Emmet Place Tel 021 272 020). **Seats 64.** *Parties 20. L 1-4 (Sun only) D 6-11.30.* AMERICAN EXPRESS® *Access, Diners, Visa.*

Malahide   Giovanni's

Tel 01 845 1733	**JaB**
Townyard Lane Malahide Co Dublin	Map 1 D3

This buzzy little pizza place and family restaurant in a lane near
the new marina complex is run by two friendly, unflappable
North Africans and is so popular that it has had to double in size
since they opened in 1991. The menu reads much like many other
pizza places, with some pasta, a few chicken dishes and even some
steaks, but everything is unpretentiously nice and wholesome and
fresh, including the grated parmesan on the table – which must
be the secret of their success. They still keep the flasks of chianti
hanging from the ceiling as part of the decor – corny, but kids
love it. Swift service. *Seats 80. Open 12.30pm-12am (Sun from
3pm). Closed Good Friday, 3 days Christmas, 1 Jan.*

Malahide   Grand Hotel   66%   £108

Tel 01 845 0000 Fax 01 845 0987	**H**
Malahide Co Dublin	Map 1 D3

Polished double doors in the splendid cream-painted frontage lead
into a pillared entrance hall resplendent with fine crystal
chandeliers, marble fireplace, comfortable, well-spaced settees and
winged armchairs. At the rear of the ground floor is Matt Ryan's
bar, a split-level room decorated in a distinctive 20s' Mackintosh
style, while to the left of the entrance is the Griffin bar, open
evenings only and due for refurbishment. Newer bedrooms
contrast markedly with the older ones (although almost all have
now been refurbished) in having smart pickled pine furniture and
a host of amenities as well as being double-glazed and possessing
bright, well-equipped bathrooms. *Rooms 100. Garden.*
Closed 25 & 26 Dec. AMERICAN EXPRESS *Access, Diners, Visa.*

Malahide   Malahide Castle   £40

Tel 01 846 3027 Fax 01 846 2537	**R**
Malahide Co Dublin	Map 1 D3

While the castle and grounds are owned and run by Dublin
County Council, the restaurants at Malahide Castle have been
operated under franchise by Mary O'Callaghan since 1989. Both
restaurants are in the basement of the castle – atmospheric with
tall narrow windows, whitewashed walls and pikes and other
deadly weapons of bygone ages as decoration. The cafeteria, which
is open every day from 10am to 6pm, has a blackboard menu
of wholesome (if rather expensive) snacks and hot dishes made
on the premises, ranging from tea or coffee with freshly baked
scones, through homely soups with brown bread or more
substantial quiches or salads, to cakes and biscuits for afternoon tea.
The formal restaurant, known as The Talbot Room, operates
a £12.50 table d'hote lunch menu daily and has a little bar area (at
the base of a turret, therefore round) and waitress service; during
the week The Talbot Room is popular with local business people
– it can't open for dinner as the castle is closed. Typical menus
offer a choice of six in each course, typically garlic mushrooms
or chicken liver paté to start, an emphasis on fish in the main
courses (maybe three out of six including, perhaps, a platter

of smoked salmon and Dublin Bay prawns), followed
by traditional desserts from a trolley or an Irish cheese selection.
Seats 50. Meals 10-6 (cafeteria), 12.30-3 (restaurant).
Closed Good Friday, 25 & 26 Dec. Set L £12.50. AMERICAN EXPRESS
Access, Diners, Visa.

Malahide   Roches Bistro   £55
Tel 01 845 2777.   **R**
12 New Street Malahide Co Dublin   Map 1 D3

Sisters Orla Roche and Niamh Boylan continue to charm diners
at their cosy, informal restaurant, with its cheerful blue-and-white
checked cloths and reassuring bias towards French country
cooking. Wide-ranging menus are changed daily, with local
produce, especially seafood, featuring strongly and everything
cooked in a meticulously maintained open kitchen, watched with
interest by guests having a drink or coffee at the dividing bar.
Delicious home-baked breads and crudités set the tone for a meal
which might start with a warm terrine of seafood, simply zinging
with freshness and tasting of the sea, or piquant venison sausage,
thinly sliced and served with spiced pear chutney. Main-course
fish of the day could be a big, pure-white fillet of hake with a little
scattering of finely chopped red pepper and a subtle horseradish
cream, and there might be mignons of pork, luscious, nicely
browned but tender, juicy and full of flavour with a delicious rich,
creamy thyme sauce with sherry or Madeira. Vegetarians are well
looked after in dishes like oven-baked wild mushroom risotto and
there are plated farmhouse cheeses or lovely homely desserts,
notably apple and frangipane tart, and freshly brewed coffee
to finish off. *Seats 30. Parties 7. L 12.30-2.30 D 6-10.30. Closed
D Tue & Wed, all Sun & Mon, Bank Holidays, 24 Dec-12 Jan.
Set L £10.95 Set D from £13.95 (6-7.30).* AMERICAN EXPRESS *Access,
Diners, Visa.*

When telephoning establishments in the Republic from *outside*
the Republic, dial 00-353 then the number we print less the
initial zero: eg The Strawberry Tree in Killarney is
00-353 64 32688.

Malahide   Siam Thai Restaurant   £45
Tel 01 845 4698/845 4489   Fax 01 478 4798   **R**
Gas Lane Malahide Co Dublin   Map 1 D3

Authentic Thai food is rare in Dublin, which is probably one
reason for the immediate success of this attractive new venture
near the marina complex in Malahide. Head chef Kong Keaw
Srakhunthod came to Ireland via the Oriental Hotel in Bangkok
and brings confidence and freshness to his cooking – the lengthy
à la carte menu may be daunting to first-time diners here, but
the set dinner menus for a given number provide a reliable
introduction to both the subtle flavours and hot spicing of
Thai cuisine. *Seats 74. Parties 12. L 12-3 (Sun only) D 6-12.
Closed 25 & 26 Dec. Set L from £7.50 Set D from £13.50.*
AMERICAN EXPRESS *Access, Diners, Visa.*

Malahide   Silks Restaurant   £45

Tel 01 845 3331   **R**
5 The Mall Malahide Co Dublin   Map 1 D3

This well-established Chinese restaurant moved into smart new
premises (complete with floodlit miniature garden, with stream
and bridge) two years ago and weekend bookings have been
in even greater demand since then. Menus, including the special
menus for given numbers in a group, give little away although
one or two of the chef's specials look more than usually promising
– but it's the sheer quality of the cooking, teamed with seamless
service from charming staff, that explain this restaurant's great
succcess. Taking an ordinary set menu, chicken or crab and
sweetcorn soup, barbecued ribs, chicken satay, Cantonese spring
rolls with barbecue sauce all sound quite ordinary, yet chef Derek
Sung breathes new life into these familiar dishes, a reminder of the
reasons they are now so well known. Garlic prawns, duck
Cantonese, beef with green pepper all tell the same story and,
although certainly not Chinese, even the desserts are above
average. **Seats** 90. Private Room 20. D only 6-12.30 (Sun 5-11).
Closed Good Friday, 25-27 Dec. Set D from £15. Facilities for
disabled. AMERICAN EXPRESS Access, Diners, Visa.

Malahide   Place of Interest

Malahide Castle (see entry) Tel 01 845 2655

Mallow   Longueville House   72%   £116

Tel 022 47156   Fax 022 47459   **HR**
Mallow Co Cork   Map 2 B5

Three miles west of Mallow on the N72 Killarney Road, this
handsome Georgian house built in 1720 has been run as a hotel
since 1969 by the O'Callaghan family, descendants of the original
occupants. While grandly proportioned, the gracious house has
an easy informality which makes it seem natural to be surrounded
by gilt-framed mirrors, family portraits and impressive fireplaces
with log fires burning. Bedrooms are stylishly furnished with
antiques, good fabrics and thoughtfully equipped modern
bathrooms. Breakfast offers a fine choice, both hot and cold,
including home-made bread. No dogs. **Rooms** 20. Garden,
game & coarse fishing, games room, snooker, table tennis. Closed
18 Dec-mid March. AMERICAN EXPRESS Access, Diners, Visa.

Presidents' Restaurant   ↑   £65

William O'Callaghan's creative, imaginative cooking is surveyed
by previous Presidents of Ireland, who look down from the walls
of an elegant, lofty room. Produce from their private fishing
on the Blackwater and his father's farm and gardens supplies most
of his needs in the kitchen. Specialities on the short, well-chosen
menus (fixed-price or à la carte) include home-smoked salmon
timbale, ravioli of Castletownbere prawns and noisettes
of Longueville lamb filled with tarragon mousse. Garden
vegetables, served in little bouquets, are what they claim to be and
have great depth of flavour. Desserts often come from the garden
too, as in summer fruit soup. A highly unusual and very tempting
alternative is caramelised pear on a slice of brioche with beer ice

cream. The surprise menu (£35) is available from 7-9 and only to an entire party. Irish farmhouse cheeses are excellent and home-made chocolates and petits fours come with the coffee. *Seats 50. Parties 8. Private Room 14. L 12.30-1.45 D 7-9. Set L £16 Set D £27. Closed 25/26 Dec, 31 Jan.*

Mallow   Places of Interest

Annes Grove Gardens Castletownroche Tel 022 26145
Mallow Racecourse Mount Ruby Tel 022 21565

If we recommend meals in a hotel or inn a **separate** entry is made for its restaurant.

Maynooth	Moyglare Manor	75%	£135
Tel 01 628 6351 Fax 01 628 5405			**HR**
Moyglare Maynooth Co Kildare			Map 2 C4

Traffic-wise, Maynooth can be something of a bottleneck, but Moyglare itself is a couple of miles down the road past the church. A long tree-lined avenue leads to the fine Georgian house, which has a lovely garden and overlooks peaceful parkland and mountains beyond. Owned by Norah Devlin and managed by Shay Curran, the hotel is stuffed full of antiques, objets d'art, paintings and all manner of lamps. The public rooms are a veritable Aladdin's Cave of memorabilia and comfortable furnishings – a tranquil doze in front of the marble fireplace in the lounge is to be recommended. Period-style bedrooms, several with four-posters or half-testers, are individually furnished, but if you want a TV to interrupt or spoil your surroundings you must ask – they are available on request. A ground-floor garden suite is particularly grand. Bathrooms have been modernised and provide generously-sized towels and decent toiletries. Look out for the freshly-baked scones and bread which accompany excellent cafetière coffee at breakfast. No children under 12. No dogs. *Rooms 17. Garden, tennis. Closed 3 days Christmas.* AMERICAN EXPRESS *Access, Diners, Visa.*

Restaurant   £75

The setting is romantic, with candles or Victorian lamps on the tables, and the menu features many fish dishes. Try a smoked trout and herring salad, crab claws in garlic butter or poached fillets of brill served with a shrimp sauce. Hormone-free sirloin steak comes grilled with a green peppercorn sauce, while pork is done with cream and Dijon mustard sauce. Lunch menus offer less choice. Sample the home-made bread and there's a good cheeseboard and a choice of sweets (white chocolate terrine perhaps), followed by either tea or coffee accompanied by home-made petits fours. A very fine wine list, extensive and Catholic as far as France is concerned, though quite sparse elsewhere, with only Spain well represented. The inexpensive list of wines for the month is a good idea, but only listing four bottles (2 red, 2 white) hardly provides the customer with any choice at all. No smoking. *Seats 85. Parties 40. Private Room 36. L 12.15-2.15 (Sun 12-2.30) D 7-9.30. Closed 3 days Christmas. Set L £11.95 Set D £22.*

Maynooth   Place of Interest
Castletown House Celbridge Tel 01 628 8252

Midleton   Bailick Cottage
£50
Tel 021 631244   **A**
Midleton Co Cork   Map 2 B6

Charming, unusual accommodation in a riverside location just ten minutes walk from the town (as timed to Farmgate restaurant). All rooms have private bath or shower and there's a lovely elegant drawing room for guests' use. The garden is important and throughout the house there's a restful sense of being 'in' it. Breakfasts include cheese on toast and farmhouse cheeses as specialities. Children welcome – under-10s may stay free in their parents' room; cots, high-chairs, early evening meal available by arrangement; indoor playroom. No dogs. *Rooms 6. Garden, croquet. Closed 25 Dec. No credit cards.*

Midleton   Farmgate
£45
Tel 021 632771   **R**
The Coolbawn Midleton Co Cork   Map 2 B6

Maróg O'Brien and Kay Harte have been delighting visitors to their lovely food shop and restaurant since 1984 – good things (and especially produced good things) are the order of the day, whether in the delicious home-baked breads, cakes and biscuits served with morning coffee and afternoon tea, more substantial snacks and main dishes on the lunch menu – open crab sandwich, perhaps, a traditional bowl of tripe or vegetarian salad – or the more sophisticated offerings on weekend dinner menus, which might kick off with Farmgate tapénades, followed by pan-fried slices of beef fillet served with a Jameson sauce (from the distillery down the road), then a wedge of tart lemon tart. At the time of going to press Kay Harte was just about to open their new venture, Farmgate Café (Tel 021 278134), a 94-seater restaurant over the English market in Cork city, open 8.30am-5.30pm Mon-Sat, L 12-4 with live music on piano, 12.30-3. Food at the café is based on produce from the market below, notably fresh fish and traditional dishes like tripe and drisheen. *Seats 60 (+20 outside). Meals 9am-5.30pm. L 12-4 D 7.30-9.30 (Fri & Sat only). Closed Sun, Bank Holidays, 25 Dec & Good Friday. Access, Visa.*

Midleton   Jameson Heritage Centre
Tel 021 613594   **JaB**
Midleton Co Cork   Map 2 B6

A pleasant little restaurant area in the Jameson Heritage Centre offers a sensibly restricted choice of simple home-made food – typically a freshly-made sandwich of Irish Cheddar and home-made chutney or baked ham and wholegrain mustard (£1.20), perhaps a ploughman's lunch (£3.95) or quiche and salad (£2.95). Tempting home-made cakes are all £1.10, scones and jam with tea/coffee £1.30. *Seats 25. Private Room 200. Food served 9am-5.30pm. Closed 21 Nov-1 Mar except for private parties. No credit cards.*

Midleton   Midleton Park Hotel   68%   £75

Tel 021 631767   Fax 021 631760   **H**

Midleton Co Cork   **Map 2 B6**

This low-rise modern hotel close to the Jameson Heritage Centre
has spacious public areas and good facilities for exhibitions,
conferences and functions of all kinds. Bedrooms are all en suite,
with TV, video, phone, hairdryer and trouser press, and include
a 'presidential suite' for VIP guests; two rooms reserved
for non-smokers and one equipped for disabled guests.
Banqueting/conferences 300. Coffee shop 10am-12pm. Ample free
parking. Children welcome – under-8s stay free in parents' room
(four family rooms); cots, extra beds, baby-listening/sitting, high-
chairs, early evening meal available by arrangement. Dogs
allowed. **Rooms** 40. Closed 25 Dec. AMERICAN EXPRESS Access,
Diners, Visa.

Monkstown   The Bosun

Tel 021 842172   **P**

Monkstown Co Cork   **Map 2 B6**

Nicky Moynihan recently completely renovated and refurbished
his waterside pub, which is just beside the Cobh car ferry and
unofficial clubhouse to the local sailing fraternity after racing.
It's a very pleasant place now – light and bright, with a good
buzz and a chef available to cook fresh bar food at any time.
Seafood is a speciality – anything from chowder (£2.20)
to crab claws or Dingle Bay scampi (£11.25) and also steaks.
Bar Food 10.30am-9pm, L 12-2.30. Closed 25 Dec & Good Friday.
AMERICAN EXPRESS Access, Diners, Visa.

> Please note there are two places named **Monkstown**,
> one in Co Cork (see Map 2 B6), the other in Co Dublin
> (see Map 4 D1/2 D4).

Monkstown   Coopers Restaurant   £40

Tel 01 284 2037   **R**

8a The Crescent Monkstown Co Dublin   **Map 4 D1**

Well-established restaurant (owned by Fitzers) in a characterful
old building with eating areas spread between an upstairs room,
downstairs wine bar and new, no-smoking rear conservatory.
Mussels in garlic, cream and white wine, lasagne with spinach and
roasted vegetables, salsa and avocado home-made burger, roast
duck with citrus sauce and steak with pepper sauce show the style.
Pasta and warm salad dishes feature on the longer evening menu.
Also a handful of bar snacks: steak sandwich (£5.50), vegetarian
lasagne (£5.95). Daily-changing specials are displayed on a
blackboard. Branches at Leeson Street (Tel 01 676 8615),
in Kilternan (Tel 01 295 9349) and in Greystones (Tel 01 287
3914). **Seats** 120. Open 12-11.45 (Sat from 5.30, Sun 12.30-10).
Closed L Sat, Good Friday, 25 & 26 Dec. AMERICAN EXPRESS Access, Visa.

Monkstown   FXB's

Tel 01 284 6187	JaB
3 The Crescent Monkstown Co Dublin	Map 4 D1

This large, middle-market restaurant is owned by F.X. Buckley, the highly regarded Dublin butchers, so red meat is the thing here, especially steaks (from £8.95). The rather long printed menu is shared with a second restaurant in Pembroke Street (in the centre of Dublin), which is slightly smaller but run on the same lines and under a common executive chef. Take time to look through it carefully – fish, poultry and even vegetarian options are there if you want them; you can tuck into a one-pound T-bone steak (£10.95) or even larger steaks 'available on request'! If that's too much try the excellent wok-charred strips of sirloin with Szechuan peppers, oyster sauce, ginger and red onion. Interestingly, FXB also offer a 'low-cal menu'. *Seats 150. Open 5.30-11.30 (Sun 12-9.30). Closed L Mon-Sat (except by arrangement), 25 & 26 Dec.*
Also at:
Pembroke Street Dublin 2 Tel 01 676 4606 100 seats   Map 6 G2

> Changes in data sometimes occur in establishments
> after the Guide goes to press. Prices should be taken
> as indications rather than firm quotes.

Monkstown   Purty Kitchen

Tel 01 284 3576 Fax 01 284 5106	P
Old Dunleary Road Monkstown Co Dublin	Map 4 D1

Passers-by might be forgiven for thinking that this is the kind of pub that looks too good to be true. It was established in 1728, which makes it the second oldest pub in Dublin (after *The Brazen Head*) and the oldest in Dun Laoghaire. However, changes have been made under the current ownership: amazingly, the whole ground floor has been lowered, and it is well worth a visit just to work out how it was done. The result is generally deemed to be honourable – meaning that the new arrangement (which looks old to a first-time visitor) is not a travesty of the original pub. Soothingly cool and dark, it has plenty of tables dotted around for the comfortable consumption of food from a tempting bar menu that ranges from the usual soups and nibbles – chowder (£2.95, half bowl £1.95), 'crab toes' in garlic butter (£4.50) – to deep-fried goat's cheese with plum sauce (£4.50), open seafood sandwiches served on home-made brown bread (£3.95.£5.50), steak and even duck sandwiches (on home-made white bread £5.95) to full main courses such as fillet steak with pebble mustard and Jameson sauce (£12.95), or even hot buttered lobster (£22). Also seafood specialities like baked cocotte – a combination of fresh and smoked cod in a mushroom cream sauce topped with breadcrumbs. Desserts range from perennial favourites like apple crumble or tangy, light lemon tart to seasonal specialities such as a very moreish chocolate roulade with fresh strawberries and cream. *Open 10.30am-11.30pm Mon-Sat (Sun 12-2, 4-11).* **Bar Food** *12-7. Closed Good Friday, 25 Dec.* *Access, Diners, Visa.*

Moone   Moone High Cross Inn

`Tel 0507 24112`   **P**

Bolton Hill Moone Co Kildare   Map 2 C4

The Clynch family are the most welcoming of hosts, and their
rambling 18th-century pub is up among the front-runners in the
hospitality and home cooking stakes. Morning coffee, lunch,
afternoon tea and evening meals are all available, and the bar
menus are based on the best of ingredients, generously served. The
lounge service menu (lunch every day) announces that Jacob sheep
roam freely in the 16 acres around the inn – at their peril, perhaps,
because they also appear inside as roasts; other favourites on the
various menus include brown bread sandwiches with home-
cooked meats or local Cheddar, vegetable soup, traditional bacon
and cabbage, Irish stew and the grandmother of apple pies. Steaks
feature on the evening à la carte; Sunday lunch is a particularly
popular occasion. There is a proper dining room (but it is the bar
food that has our recommendation here), but many visitors opt
for a seat by the fire in the back bar, or a spot in the new beer
garden. Children are very welcome "if supervised." *Open 11am-
11.30pm (Sun 12-2 & 4-11). Bar Meals 11-10. Children allowed
in bar to eat. Garden, outdoor eating. Closed 25 Dec & Good Friday.
Access, Visa.*

Mountrath   Roundwood House   58%   £64

`Tel 0502 32120   Fax 0502 32711`   **HR**

Mountrath Co Laois   Map 2 C4

A "love it or loathe it" kind of place, with some visitors objecting
to the very air of eccentricity which makes the majority of guests
love Frank and Rosemarie Kennan's small, early Georgian
Palladian villa enough to keep coming back for more. Don't
expect curtains at your bedroom windows, but the big wooden
shutters (correct for a house of this period) will be snugly closed
while you communally enjoy Rosemarie's unpretentious good
home cooking around a large polished mahogany table in their
lovely dining room. Old-fashioned bathrooms have all that
is needed, including towels that are mismatched but plentiful and,
like the rest of the house, lovely and warm; there will also be a
water bottle tucked into your bed when you finally make it there.
Frank is the host, dispensing pre-dinner drinks in front of the huge
drawing room fire and letting guests in on the local scene. In the
morning, guests wake to a chorus of birdsong from the
surrounding woods and children, especially, will enjoy visiting the
yard to see if there are any chicks or kittens around, or perhaps
to collect a warm egg for breakfast. Tariff reductions for stays
of two nights or more; children under 2 stay free whilst under-12s
pay 50% of tariff when sharing with their parents. Stabling
available. *Rooms 6. Garden, croquet, fishing, table tennis, indoor
children's playroom. Closed 25 Dec.*

Restaurant   £60

Non-residents can book for Sunday lunch (when separate tables
are laid), or dinner if there is room. Rosemarie's food continues to
make friends – lovely home cooking, cooked on the Aga, is the
norm. Roasts with fresh herbs, simple, lightly cooked vegetables,
gratins of potato (with more than a generous hint of garlic),

farmhouse cheeses with home-made biscuits, a choice of wickedly gooey or wholesome desserts. Finish with coffee by the fireside. ***Seats*** *24. Parties 24. D 8.30pm. Set L (Sun only) £12 Set D £20. Amex, Access, Diners, Visa.*

Mountrath Place of Interest

Damer House Roscrea Heritage Centre Tel 0505 21850 *16 miles*

Moyard Rose Cottage

£30

Tel 095 41082

A

Rockfield Moyard Co Galway

Map 1 A3

Situated on a working farm in a scenic location surrounded by the Twelve Bens mountains, this neat, cottage-style farmhouse is a pleasing blend of the old and the new and very much a family affair. Expect a warm welcome from Mary Shanley O'Toole or one of her family, simple but comfortable accommodation and good home cooking (especially baking) and you won't be disappointed. There's a sitting room with an open turf fire and television, a dining room for guests (separate tables) and six modest bedrooms, all with showers en suite, tea/coffee-making trays and hairdryers. Nearby attractions include sandy beaches, scenic walks, fishing, island trips, traditional Irish music, horse riding and golf. ***Rooms*** *6. Closed 1st Oct-30 Apr.* AMERICAN EXPRESS *Access, Diners, Visa.*

Moycullen Cloonnabinnia House Hotel 63%

£55

Tel 091 85555 Fax 091 85640

HR

Ross Lake Moycullen Co Galway

Map 2 B4

Although the building is typical of the 1960s, landscaping has helped soften its hard edges and the views over Ross Lake are magical – and it's the warmth and genuine hospitality of the Kavanagh family that make a visit to this unpretentious hotel a memorable experience. The bar is Tommie's domain, equally appealing to locals and guests for its relaxing chat about fishing or, perhaps, a quiet game of draughts, while Norah Anne presides over other public areas comfortably furnished with a homely mixture of new and old, modest en-suite bedrroms (with lovely views) and the kitchen. Function rooms (conferences 200/banquets 250) are downstairs, well away from residents and with a separate entrance. Children are made very welcome, with 3 family rooms, cots available at no extra charge, baby-sitting by arrangement, under-9s allowed to stay free in their parents' room and a children's menu/early evening meal. Angling is the main attraction, however, and Tommie runs a purpose-built Angling Centre on site, providing everything from bait and boat hire to maps and freezing facilities. Three self-catering cottages are also available, with full access to hotel facilities. ***Rooms*** *14. Garden. Fishing. Closed 1 Nov-17 Mar. Access, Diners, Visa.*

The Ross Restaurant

£45

Cathal Kavanagh ably manages the restaurant with its wonderful sunset views over the lake, while his mother Norah Anne, previously a fish cookery demonstrator with BIM (Irish Fisheries Board), makes good use of local produce, including home-grown herbs and wild watercress and hedgerow fruits in unpretentious,

wholesome meals. Start, perhaps, with pan-fried Atlantic prawns
served with a colourful seasonal salad and home-made breads,
followed by roast rack of local Connemara lamb with a red wine
and rosemary sauce and maybe a stir-fry of local vegetables, all
rounded off with one of Fidelma Keady or Ruth Kavanagh's
luscious desserts – a frozen chocolate terrine perhaps, or light, crisp
fresh fruit tartlet or some farmhouse cheeses. *Seats 50. Parties 20.
D only 7-9.30.*

Moycullen	Drimcong House Restaurant	★	£65
Tel 091 85115			**R**
Moycullen Co Galway			Map 2 B4

Gerry Galvin, and his wife Marie have been running their
renowned restaurant just west of Moycullen on the Galway-
Clifden road since 1984, and it is still one of the most remarkable
establishments in the country. Gerry's classical skills are put to the
test nightly in inventive cooking based firmly on the best local
ingredients, with both 3/5-course dinner menus and the à la carte
changing regularly to make best use of produce at its peak. The
choice is remarkable for a small restaurant, including a 5-course
vegetarian menu (£16.50) and, unusually for any leading
restaurant (but typical of a chef who has a special reputation for
encouraging the young), children who are old enough to cope are
made particularly welcome with a special 3-course menu 'for pre-
teenage people' (£9.50). There is ample time to inwardly digest
the menus in the comfortable, book-strewn bar before moving
through to the oak-polished formality of the dining room that
overlooks gardens on two sides. A typical evening's offerings
might include grilled goat's cheese with a zinging mixed leaf salad,
followed by a choice of soup or sorbet, while main courses usually
include local Connemara lamb – roast, perhaps, with wild garlic –
and fish of the day, typically baked hake in a chervil cream sauce,
giving an ever-so-subtle flavour of anise to complement the fresh-
from-the-boat fish. A la carte options might extend to baked
oysters with crab and grapefruit or warm sweetbread and cabagge
roulade in pistachio sauce to start, with main courses like confit
of duck with ginger and passion fruit sauce or roast baby chicken
and pigeon with grapes and shallots to follow. Tempting desserts
tend to be classical – frozen amaretto soufflé in raspberry sauce,
grape and almond tart – although a dessert 'pizza' shows signs
of reinventing the wheel! Always an excellent Irish farmhouse
cheeseboard, served with home-baked biscuits. The modest wine
list offers wines in two sections: under and over £14. *Seats 50.
Private Room 32. D only 7-10.30. Closed Sun, Mon & Jan & Feb.
Set D £16.95/£19.95.* AMERICAN EXPRESS *Access, Diners.*

Moycullen	Moycullen House	£55
Tel & Fax 091 85566		**A**
Moycullen Co Galway		Map 2 B4

Originally a sporting lodge – built in the arts and crafts style at the
beginning of the century and still featuring the original iron locks
and latches on solid oak doors – Moycullen House is above the
village (on the Moycullen-Spiddal road), overlooking Lough
Corrib and set peacefully in 30 acres of rhododendrons and azaleas,

with its own supply of pure spring water. Spacious rooms
furnished with antiques all have private baths and the residents'
sitting room and dining room have period fireplaces with
cheering log fires. Children welcome; cot/extra bed available;
baby-sitting by arrangement. **Rooms** 5 (*3 large, suitable for families*).
/Garden. Closed 1 Nov-1 Mar. AMERICAN EXPRESS *Access, Visa.*

Moycullen   White Gables Restaurant   £50

Tel & Fax 091 85744   **R**

Moycullen Village Co Galway   Map 2 B4

Right on the main street of Moycullen, chef Kevin Dunne and his
wife Anne have attracted a growing following since opening their
cottagey restaurant in 1991. Well-appointed, with thick walls
providing cosy insulation from traffic noise as well as inclement
weather, the open stonework, low lighting, candlelight (even
at lunchtime) and a soothing away-from-it-all atmosphere create
a fitting setting for Kevin's well-balanced menus. Start, perhaps,
with a smoked venison salad or, in season, fresh asparagus
hollandaise, both served with excellent home-made brown bread
and scones. Connemara lamb is *de rigueur* on menus in these parts
– roast rack with a rosemary gravy, maybe, or roast baron with
mint jelly, with freshly dug potatoes as part of a generous,
imaginative vegetable selection. Good ices, soft fruit in season,
aromatic coffee. **Seats** 45. Parties 10. L (*Sun only*) 12.30-2.30 D 7-
10. *Closed Mon in winter, 24 Dec-13 Feb.* AMERICAN EXPRESS *Access,
Diners, Visa.*

Moydow   The Vintage   £45

Tel 043 22122   **R**

Moydow Co Longford   Map 1 C3

Former cookery teacher Regina Houlihan has developed The
Vintage bar into quite a catering enterprise, looking after both
local functions and serving dinner three nights a week (plus
Sunday lunch). The four-course Sunday lunch menu may be a
terrine of country paté followed by home-made soup, then roast
rib of beef, and a pudding to follow. The evening dinner menu
offers a reasonable choice, possibly including woodland salad,
pheasant and pigeon terrine with pear purée, lightly braised
noisettes of pork with Calvados and fillet of chicken Indian style.
A la carte dishes are also available. Open Thurs-Sun only but open
all week in December and possibly during the summer season in
'95. Children's menu and portions of any meal available. **Seats** 40.
Parties 10. L 1-5 (*Sun only*) D 7-10.30. Set Sun L £8 95 Set
D £15.95. Garden, outdoor eating. Closed Mon-Weds Jan-Nov (*see
above*). AMERICAN EXPRESS *Access, Visa.*

Mullingar   Crookedwood House   £55

Tel 044 72165   Fax 044 72166   **R**

Crookedwood Mullingar Co Westmeath   Map 1 C3

Noel and Julie Kenny have plans to add accommodation (opening
May '95) to the excellent restaurant at their 200-year-old former
rectory overlooking Lough Derravaragh. Noel's menus change
with the seasons and feature the best of local produce. From
a winter selection come game terrine with a red wine and damson

coulis, cream of carrot and orange soup, millefeuille of smoked
salmon with horseradish and yoghurt sauce, and a trio of pheasant,
partridge and venison with a wild mushroom and juniper berry
sauce. Good simple desserts, Irish farmhouse cheeses. *Seats 35.*
Parties 14. Private Room 25. L (Sun only) 12.30-2 D 6.30-10.
Closed D Sun & Mon, 2 weeks Nov. Set L £12 Set D £18.50.
 Access, Diners, Visa.

Mullingar   Place of Interest

Tourist Information Tel 044 48761
Tullynally Castle and Gardens Castlepollard Tel 044 61159 *16 miles*

Mulraney   Rosturk Woods   £40

Tel & Fax 098 36264	A
Rosturk Mulraney Co Mayo	**Map 1 A3**

It is only on close examination that the first-time visitor realises
that this attractive, traditional house in a lovely shoreside location
between Westport and Achill is recently built, so well does it fit
into its snug wooded setting and so convincingly do the recycled
building materials deceive. The result in this comfortable and
welcoming family home is an ideal combination of new and old,
an unusually successful marriage of convenience and style which
pervades reception rooms and thoughtfully planned, imaginatively
decorated bedrooms and en-suite bathrooms alike. Children are
welcome (free up to 4 in parents' room), there's a cot provided
at no extra charge, baby-sitting by arrangement, high-chairs and
children's early evening meal in the kitchen from 5-7pm. *Rooms 4*
(1 suitable for a family). Closed 1 Nov-mid Mar (except for private
parties). Access, Visa.

Naas   Fletcher's

Tel 045 97328	P
Commercial House Naas Co Kildare	**Map 2 C4**

A characterful pub that's well worth a visit just for the interest
of being there. It's a very old-fashioned place, a long, narrow hall,
broken up into sections in the traditional way with a mahogany
divider complete with stained-glass panels. Having escaped the
scourge of modernisation, Fletcher's remains somewhat austere and
masculine: the plain wooden floor and very long mahogany bar
with its full complement of built-in drawers and shelves behind
is softened by the occasional aspidistra in an old cachepot and
a collection of magnificent meat plates displayed high on the end
wall. Masculine – and adult, too: they prefer no children in the
bar. *Open 10.30am-11.30pm (Sunday 12.30-2 & 4-11). Closed Good*
Friday, 25 Dec. No credit cards.

Naas   The Manor Inn

Tel 045 97471	P
Main Street Naas Co Kildare	**Map 2 C4**

The Manor Inn offers warmth, hospitality and good food
in refreshingly 'undesigned' surroundings. Local interest is reflected
in pictures and mementos connected with horses and the army
base at the nearby Curragh, car racing at Mondello (note the clock
in a racing helmet) and a clutter of notices giving due warning

of upcoming local events. The menu offers a wide variety
of familiar pub fare, from sandwiches, salads and omelettes
to pasta, burgers, pies, grills, steaks and four choices 'from the
smoke house'. High-chairs and a menu of children's favourites
are provided. *Bar Food 12-10.30 (Sun 12.30-2.30 & 5-10.30).
Children allowed in bar to eat. Closed Good Friday & 25 Dec.*
AMERICAN EXPRESS *Access, Diners, Visa.*

Naas   Places of Interest

Punchestown Racecourse Naas Tel 045 97704
Naas Racecourse Tel 045 97391

Navan   Ardboyne Hotel   60%   £75

| Tel 046 23119 Fax 046 22355 | **HR** |

Dublin Road Navan Co Meath   Map 1 C3

A friendly, well-run modern hotel standing in its own grounds
on the outskirts of town. Bedrooms, all with compact tiled
bathrooms, are simple and practical, with fitted furniture and
good desk/dressing table space. There's a bright, comfortable
lounge and a warm, convivial bar. All-day snacks are available
in the bar/foyer area. Children are more than welcome, and
under-12s can stay free in their parents' room. *Rooms 27. Garden,
disco (Fri & Sat).* AMERICAN EXPRESS *Access, Diners, Visa.*

Terrace Restaurant   £55

Simple, straightforward dishes are available on several menus,
including à la carte, tourist, luncheon, table d'hote and early bird.
'Chef Recommends' on the carte include prawns provençale,
wiener schnitzel, shish kebab and sirloin steak. Sweets from the
buffet. *Seats 97. Private Room 50. L 12.30-3 D 6.30-10.30 (Sun till
9). Set L £10.50 Set D £11.35/£17.95.*

Navan   Places of Interest

Hill of Tara Tel 046 25903
Navan Racecourse Tel 046 21350
Butterstream Garden Trim Tel 046 36017

New Quay   Linnane's Bar

| Tel 065 78120 | **P** |

New Quay Burrin Co Clare   Map 2 B4

This unassuming country pub has sliding doors at the back, which
open virtually on to the rocks in summer and bring the
magnificent seascape beyond right inside. In winter, it is inward-
looking, as visitors (who may have had difficulty finding it if,
as sometimes happens, gales have blown down local road signs)
cluster round the peat fire. It has rightly attracted attention for the
quality of its seafood: in addition to luxury lobster there's plenty
of good but less expensive fare at Linnane's, with the best choice
in summer: a steaming bowl of chowder, perhaps, served with
brown bread; scallops New Quay, cooked in a wine sauce and
served in a gratin dish, layered with rice to mop up the aromatic
juices; or a huge crab salad, the plate burgeoning with the white
meat of at least a pair of crabs. Simply delicious. *Open 12-11.30*   *See over*

(Sun to 11, Nov-Mar 5-11 and usual hours weekends).
Bar Food *12-9 (no food Nov-Mar except by arrangement). Children's
portions. No credit cards.*

Newbawn	Cedar Lodge	62%	£75
Tel 051 28386 Fax 051 28222			**H**
Carrigbyrne Newbawn Co Wexford			**Map 2 C5**

14 miles from Wexford on the main Rosslare-Waterford road,
this family-run hotel stands in lush countryside beneath the slopes
of Carrigbyrne Forest. Redbrick walls, wooden ceilings and open
fires create a warm and welcoming atmosphere in the public
rooms and paintings and frescos by local artists provide interesting
focal points. Bedrooms are practical and neatly appointed.
Conference/function suite for up to 70 in adjoining low-rise
wings. **Rooms** *18. Garden. Closed 25 & 26 Dec, mid Dec-1 Feb.
Access, Visa.*

Newbawn	Place of Interest

John F Kennedy Arboretum Tel 051 88171

Newbay	Newbay Country House	£58
Tel 053 42779 Fax 053 46318		**A**
Newbay nr Wexford Co Wexford		**Map 2 D5**

A comfortable family-run country house dating from 1822 but
incorporating earlier outbuildings. The outside impression is a
touch stern, but the real atmosphere is very warm and relaxed.
Day rooms are of imposing proportions, with interesting antiques,
amply sized country furniture and displays of dried flowers
arranged by Mientje (Min) Drum. Bedrooms are spacious,
comfortable and individually furnished with four-poster beds but
without TVs or phones. Paul Drum's food (for residents only),
offers no choice and is served at one large table. The house
is situated 2 miles from Wexford and not far from the ferry port
of Rosslare. No dogs. **Rooms** *6. Garden. Closed Christmas day.
Access, Visa.*

> Our inspectors **never** book in the name of Egon Ronay's
> Guides. They disclose their identity only if they are
> considering an establishment for inclusion in the next
> edition of the Guide.

Newbridge	Hotel Keadeen	68%	£85
Tel 045 31666 Fax 045 34402			**H**
Ballymany Newbridge Co Kildare			**Map 2 C4**

Leave the M7 at exit 10 and head back towards Newbridge
to find 'the inn on the Curragh', a well-kept hotel in a garden
setting near the famous racetrack. Conferences and functions (up
to 800) are big business, but private guests are well catered for
in good-sized bedrooms furnished in a variety of styles. No dogs.
Rooms *37. Garden. Closed 25-27 Dec.* AMERICAN EXPRESS® *Access,
Diners, Visa.*

Newbridge   The Red House Inn   £55

Tel 045 31516/31657 Fax 045 31934	R

| Newbridge Co Kildare | Map 2 C4 |

Despite its location just off the Naas dual carriageway, this cosy inn has a surprisingly away-from-it-all atmosphere, notably in the very pleasant old-world bar area and the conservatory and garden at the back. Long-serving staff include restaurant manager Tom Tinsley and chef Willie Ryan, who have been practising their teamwork here since 1980 in presenting traditional food appropriate to the well-appointed dining room. From a well-balanced menu, a typical meal might begin with an arrangement of salads with smoked salmon or breaded brie with Oxford sauce, followed perhaps by baked salmon in puff pastry with lemon butter, or fillet of beef Madeira. Vegetarian options are always given, freshly baked scones are on the table, simple vegetables are crisp and colourful and popular desserts include good home-made ices. *Seats 70. Outside seating 20 (garden off conservatory). Parties 14. Private Room 40. L 12.30-2.30 (Sun only) D 6.30-10.15. Closed D Sun, all Mon, 1st 2 weeks Jan. Set L £10.95 Set D from £19.* AMERICAN EXPRESS *Access, Diners, Visa.*

Newbridge   Places of Interest

Japanese Gardens Tully Tel 045 21251 *5 miles*
Irish National Stud Tully Tel 045 21617 *5 miles*
Emo Court and Gardens Emo Tel 0502 26110 *10 miles*

We endeavour to be as up-to-date as possible, but inevitably some changes to key personnel may occur at restaurants and hotels after the Guide goes to press.

Newmarket-on-Fergus   Clare Inn Hotel   64%   £99

Tel 061 368161 Fax 061 368622	H

| Dromoland Newmarket-on-Fergus Co Clare | Map 2 B4 |

Outstanding leisure facilities are provided at the modern, low-rise Clare Hotel, which stands in the middle of Dromoland's 18-hole golf course (£17 green fee). The leisure centre (free to guests; children under 16 must be accompanied, no children after 6pm) includes a fully-equipped gymnasium, and deep-sea fishing can be arranged from the hotel's catamaran, the *Liscannor Star*. The Castlefergus Bar, with weekend entertainment, is a good place to unwind, and there are residents' lounges, two restaurants and a children's playroom. Bedrooms are of a decent size, most of them suitable for family occupation. Children up to 4 are accommodated free (5-10s £13, 11-16s £16) which includes B&B and high tea. Conference facilities for up to 400. Nine miles from Shannon Airport on the main Limerick/Galway road. *Rooms 121. Garden, indoor swimming pool, gymnasium, sauna, steam room, spa bath, solarium, tennis, pitch & putt, crazy golf, croquet, lawn bowling, outdoor draughts, indoor children's playroom, coffee shop (12.30-10pm). Closed Nov, Jan & Feb.* AMERICAN EXPRESS *Access, Diners, Visa.*

Newmarket-on-Fergus   Dromoland Castle   79%   £269

Tel 061 368144   Fax 061 363355   **HR**

Newmarket-on-Fergus Co Clare   Map 2 B4

The castle's history can be traced back to the 16th century when
the estate belonged to the O'Brien clan, direct descendants of Brian
Boru, High King of Ireland; hence the name of the magnificent
and newly built conference venue, comprising a great hall, gallery,
boardrooms and business centre catering for up to 450 delegates.
Close to Shannon airport, the hotel is set among 370 acres
of woods and parkland (a stroll through the walled garden is also
a must) that include a championship golf course, the eighth green
of which is overlooked by the library bar. If the outside
is imposing, the public rooms inside are surprisingly intimate and
relaxed with roaring log fires, elegant and comfortable seating,
many period antiques and a huge collection of family portraits, not
to mention the fine fabrics, glittering chandeliers, intricate
plasterwork and high ceilings. There is a variety of bedrooms,
some necessitating long walks down corridors; many of the rooms
have recently been refurbished and the best are extremely spacious
with lovely views of either the lake or the grounds. Each
is beautifully appointed with high-quality fabrics, excellent bed
linen and impressive furniture, and all the usual extras that you
would expect from a hotel of this class: flowers, fresh fruit and
mineral water on arrival, together with bathrobes, slippers,
toiletries and decent towels in the good bathrooms (some of which
are on the small side). Standards of service, under the direction
of General Manager Mark Nolan, are high and housekeeping
is exemplary (a nightly turn-down of beds can be expected,
of course). Children up to 12 stay free in their parents' rooms.
No dogs. Sister hotel to *Ashford Castle*, Cong (see entry).
Rooms *73. Garden, golf, riding, fishing, clay-pigeon shooting, hair
salon, shooting, archery, tennis, snooker, bicycles, gym, indoor
swimming pool, sauna, spa bath.* AMERICAN EXPRESS *Access, Diners, Visa.*

The Earl of Thomond Room   ↑   £115

The elegance of the castle is perhaps best illustrated by the
grandness of the dining rooms: high ceilings, chandeliers and
splendid drapes matched by fine china, gleaming crystal and linen
cloths. In the evenings you'll be further seduced by a traditional
Irish harpist and maybe even a fiddler, together with the dishes
of long-serving executive head chef Jean-Baptiste Molinari.
He presents a variety of menus: a four-course table d'hote, say pan-
fried scallops 'niçoise' style, beef consommé, supreme of chicken
roasted with a confit of shallots in a thyme-scented jus and a choice
of dessert; a £45 6-course Taste of Ireland (also written in Gaelic)
featuring such dishes as mixed seasonal salad with pan-fried
chicken livers, clear seafood consommé, a platter of salmon and
sole with nettle cream sauce and rhubarb sorbet; or à la carte – a
home-made ravioli, braised fillet of turbot with potato leaves on a
tomato jus, ending with an iced chocolate and coffee souflée.
Much work goes into the composition of the menus, reflected
by the high standard of execution, and it's a real pleasure
to encounter such professional, courteous and knowledgeable staff.
The good-quality bread, coffee and petits fours complete the
satisfaction one will experience here. Prices on the the good wine

list are not modest – you will have to hunt carefully for bargains!
Seats 100. *Parties* 25. *Private Rooms* 24 & 60. L 12.30-2
D 7.30-9.30. Set L £18 Set D £33.

Newport	Newport House	67%	£124
Tel 098 41222 Fax 098 41613			**HR**
Newport Co Mayo			Map 1 A3

A creeper-clad Georgian house stands in large gardens adjoining
the town and overlooking the Newport river and quay – an
unusual location for one of the most attractive and hospitable
country houses in Ireland, run by Kieran and Thelma Thompson.
Fishing is the major attraction, with salmon and sea trout fishing
on the river and nearby loughs. Golf, riding and pony trekking
are also available locally, but the appeal of the house itself with its
beautiful central hall and sweeping staircase (now clad in a hand-
woven McMurray carpet from Connemara) and gracious drawing
room is enough to draw guests without sporting interests.
Bedrooms, like the rest of the house, are furnished in style with
antiques and fine paintings and bathrooms which can be eccentric
but work well; most of the rooms are in the main house, a few
in the courtyard. The day's catch is weighed and displayed in the
hall and a cosy fisherman's bar provides the perfect venue for
a reconstruction of the day's sport. *Rooms 19. Garden, sea & game
fishing, snooker. Closed 6 Oct-18 Mar.* AMERICAN EXPRESS *Access,
Diners, Visa.*

Restaurant £70

A high-ceilinged dining room overlooking the gardens and
decorated in restrained period style provides an elegant setting for
John Gavin's confident cooking, based on the best of local produce,
much of it coming from the organically-worked walled kitchen
garden. Home-smoked salmon makes a perfect starter on a 6-
course dinner menu, followed by soup (cream of vegetable
or carrot and coriander) and, perhaps, pan-fried quail with
mousseline of chicken and a tarragon sauce or roast salmon with
lemon and chive cream sauce. Oysters (either *au naturel* or baked
Rockefeller) are usually offered as an additional course. Vegetables
and salads are as fresh as it is possible to be and there's a choice
of farmhouse cheese or a fine dessert menu (Baileys soufflé with
chocolate sauce, rhubarb tartlet with fruit coulis and vanilla sauce)
to finish. Though Italian wines are sandwiched between Jura and
Provence, the predominantly French wine list is otherwise clearly
laid out and easy to use; however, there are no tasting notes, not
much from the New World and nothing from California.
No smoking in the dining room. *Seats 38. Parties 12.
Private Room 35. D only 7.30-9.30. Set D £28.*

Oughterard	Connemara Gateway Hotel	66%	£108
Tel 091 82328 Fax 091 82332			**H**
Oughterard Co Galway			Map 1 B3

Originally a typical 60s' motel, the Connemara Gateway has been
cleverly extended and developed to make the discreetly stylish
modern building it is today. Warmth, comfort and a relaxed
atmosphere are the keynotes and, although the decor is generally
low-key, the work of local artists, including impressive

wallhangings on Celtic themes in the reception area, create a nice feeling of continuity – an idea successfuly developed in the cosy bar, which is based on a rural agricultural theme and has a welcoming turf fire – definitely a cut above the average modern hotel bar. Rooms vary considerably in age and appointments, but local tweed is used to advantage in most and the emphasis is on homely comforts, such as properly organised tea and coffee facilities; similarly, bathrooms, although variable, have nice touches like hanging space for guests' hand laundry. Family facilities include an indoor swimming pool, children's entertainment in high season and high teas (5.30pm) and videos (7pm) every evening. Bicycle hire nearby. Banqueting/conference facilities for up to 260/320. No dogs. *Rooms 62. Garden, croquet, indoor swimming pool, sauna, solarium, tennis, children's outdoor playground. Closed end Dec-Jan (open New Year). Access, Diners, Visa.*

Oughterard	**Currarevagh House**	**65%**	**£92**
Tel 091 82313 Fax 091 82731			**AR**
Oughterard Co Galway			Map 1 B3

Harry and June Hodgson, fifth generation and here for nearly 30 years, practise the art of old-fashioned hospitality in their Victorian manor house set in parkland, woods and gardens by Lough Corrib. Day rooms are homely and traditional, and the drawing room is the perfect setting for afternoon tea. Bedrooms are peaceful, with no phones or TV. The hotel has sporting rights over 5000 acres and fishing facilities that include boats and ghillies. *Rooms 15. Garden, tennis, fishing, mooring, hotel boats. Closed Nov-Mar. No credit cards.*

Restaurant £50

A succulent meat dish is the centrepiece of no-choice five-course dinners prepared by June Hodgson from the pick of local produce. That dish might be roulade of pork in Calvados sauce, rack of lamb with honey and Guinness or roast beef with Yorkshire pudding. Preceding it could be prawns in garlic butter or twice baked cheese soufflé, with a dessert, Irish cheeses and coffee to complete a really satisfying meal. No smoking. Snack lunches. *Seats 28. D only at 8. Set D £18.*

Oughterard	**Powers**		
Tel 091 82712			**P**
The Square Oughterard Co Galway			Map 1 B3

Despite its picturesque exterior, unchanged for 180 years, this little thatched pub in the middle of Oughterard is a genuine local and all the better for that. The previous owners had it in the family for a century and a half and, when the current owner Frank O'Meara took over in 1990 after it had been disused for a decade, he was determined that the oldest pub in the town should retain its character. There's a big open fire in the original front bar in winter and, although no food is currently available, there are plans to provide bar meals for the summer season in 1995. Children are welcome if supervised. *Pub open 10.30-11.30 (to 11 in winter, Sun 12.30-2, 4-11 all year). Closed 25 Dec, Good Fri. No credit cards.*

Oughterard   Sweeney's Oughterard House   59%   £94

Tel 091 82207   Fax 091 82161   H

Oughterard Co Galway   Map 1 B3

Unobtrusive newer extensions do not detract from the old-
fashioned charm of this 200-year-old hotel just across the road
from a particularly pretty stretch of the Owenriff River. The
cottagey impression extends to cosy public rooms, furnished with
antiques, and well manicured lawns provide a perfect setting for
tea on a sunny afternoon. Bedrooms, where under-12s may stay
free with their parents, vary considerably in size and
appointments. *Rooms 20. Garden. Closed 22 Dec-15 Jan.*
AMERICAN EXPRESS *Access, Diners, Visa.*

Oughterard   Place of Interest

Aughnanure Castle Tel 091 82214

Oysterhaven   Finders Inn   £70

Tel 021 770737   R

Nohoval Oysterhaven Co Cork   Map 2 B6

Situated snugly in a row of converted stone cottages, this attractive
family-run restaurant has an easy charm with its quirkily
decorated bar and series of antique-filled dining rooms –
an ambience many would find irresistible without a pick of food.
But food there is, in plenty – chef Rory McDonnell offers
generous, traditional menus, made special through the quality
of ingredients. Wild salmon might be served with watercress
picked by him that morning, and vegetables are organically
grown. Local seafood takes pride of place in dishes like scallops
beurre blanc, for example, or refreshingly simple sole on the bone,
but carnivores take consolation in tender fillet steak, or succulent
roast Fermoy duckling, cooked on the bone and served crisp-
skinned and partially boned with an orange sage sauce. Finish with
a plate of local farmhouse cheeses, or a simply presented dessert
(home-made ices are good) and an aromatic cup of coffee. *Seats
140. Private Room 70. D only 7-10. Access, Visa.*

Oysterhaven   The Oystercatcher   £65

Tel 021 770822   R

Oysterhaven Begooly Co Cork   Map 2 B6

Bill and Sylvia Patterson, both originally from Scotland, run
a most attractive, cottagey restaurant known for its charming
atmosphere and consistently excellent food. Oysters naturally
make appearances on the dinner menu – simmered in garlic butter
with almonds, in sausages on a saffron sauce and in angels
on horseback. Wild mushrooms in a brioche is another speciality
dish, and you might also find clams steamed with wine and herbs,
gateau of foie gras with apples, pig's trotter stuffed with veal
sweetbreads and venison in pepper sauce. With advance warning
a vegetarian menu can also be made available. Fine fresh cheeses,
and a selection of savoury alternatives to "the sweet things in life".
There's a good all-round wine list with plenty of excellent
drinking under £20. *Seats 30. Parties 20. Private Room 20.
D 7.30-9.30 (bookings only in winter). Closed for a month in winter –
phone for details. Set D £23.95.* AMERICAN EXPRESS *Access, Visa.*

Parknasilla Great Southern 72% £163

Tel 064 45122 Fax 064 45323 **H**

Parknasilla Sneem Co Kerry Map 2 A6

Overlooking Kenmare Bay (on which the hotel's own *Parknasilla Princess* offers pleasure cruises) and set in 200 acres of sub-tropical parkland, this late-Victorian building blends well with its exotic surroundings. An air of tranquillity is immediately conveyed by a sense of space, antiques and fresh flowers in the foyer and the tone of restful luxury is continued through all the public areas to elegantly decorated bedrooms. Good indoor leisure facilities are matched by a wide range of outdoor attractions, including a series of scenic walks through the estate. Banqueting for 70. *Rooms 84. Garden, indoor swimming pool, outdoor Canadian hot-tub, sauna, spa bath, steam room, tennis, golf (9), riding, games room, snooker, sea-fishing, water sports, bicycles, clay-pigeon shooting, archery. Closed Jan-Mar.* AMERICAN EXPRESS *Access, Diners, Visa.*

Parknasilla Place of Interest

Derrynane National Historic Park Caherdaniel Tel 066 75113

Pontoon Healy's Hotel 60% £55

Tel 094 56443 **HR**

Pontoon Co Mayo Map 1 B3

A creeper-clad hotel overlooking Lough Cullen. Healy's has provided a home-from-home to generations of fisherfolk who prefer things not to change too much, so expect traditional comforts without undue concern for fashion – though not smart, the piano and dancing area in the bar suggest many a good night had by all, for instance. Bedrooms, while not large, are individually decorated overlooking the lake, with direct-dial phone, en-suite facilities and television available on request. Children are welcome – and may stay free in their parents' room up to the age of 12; cots, extra beds and baby-sitting by arrangement. Children's menu, high-chairs, early evening meal. *Rooms 10. Conferences/banqueting 60/70. Garden. Closed 1 Nov-early April. Access, Visa.*

The Lough Cullen Room Restaurant £50

Attractively-appointed, comfortable restaurant providing wholesome food, nicely cooked without frills. Good home cooking is the aim, fresh fish from nearby lakes and seafood from Clew Bay the specialities. Local girls provide friendly service and family connections with Australia are reflected in the wine list. *Seats 54. L Sun only 1-3 D 7-9.45. Set D £16.95. Bar food available in lounge 1-3pm and 5.30-8pm.*

When telephoning establishments in the Republic from *outside* the Republic, dial 00-353 then the number we print less the initial zero: eg The Strawberry Tree in Killarney is 00-353 64 32688.

Portmagee   Fisherman's Bar

Tel 066 77103 | **P**

Portmagee Co Kerry | **Map 2 A6**

Just beside the bridge over to Valentia Island, this comfortable,
well-run pub has tables on a sunny site overlooking the water for
fine days and a good choice on the all-day bar menu. Local seafood
is a natural choice – chowder £2.50, perhaps, or hot crab claws
with garlic butter £6, both with home-made brown bread. More
substantial dishes include a wide range of seafood platters, from
smoked mackerel at £4.50 to Portmagee lobster at £12 per lb.
Irish stew £4 or a range of grills and hot snacks – from steaks
to pizzas. *Open 10.30-11.30 (to 11 in winter), Sun 10.30-2, 4-11.*
Bar Food *served throughout opening times Easter-end Sept only. No
food in winter. Closed Good Friday & 25 Dec. No credit cards.*

Ramelton   The Manse   £40

Tel 074 51047 | **A**

Ramelton Co Donegal | **Map 1 C1**

Expect little in the way of modern conveniences at Mrs Scott's
remarkable house, as she has made few changes since setting
up home as a bride in 1930. In compensation for the lack of en-
suite facilities, however, there is the pleasure of using a genuinely
old bathroom (complete with canopy shower and original
fittings), sharing the family library, sleeping in a room untouched
by fashion and enjoying Mrs Scott's inimitable company.
No room service, but all are welcome to help themselves to tea
and coffee from the kitchen; breakfast is served at 9 o'clock,
when a bell is rung. Not suitable for children (because of the
large number of breakable treasures on display), but do
make a point of seeing the 'children's room'. ***Rooms*** *3. Garden.
Closed mid Sep-Easter, unless by arrangement. No credit cards.*

Rathcoole   An Poitín Still

Tel 01 458 9205 | **P**

Rathcoole (off Naas Road dual carriageway) Co Dublin | **Map 2 C4**

Established in 1643, this famous thatched inn has grown
considerably in recent years. It is divided into a number of bars,
each with its own individual character and there's a surprising
degree of intimacy. Note the fine old copper still, from which the
pub takes its name, and a lot of original 'Arkle' memorabilia – it's
very much a sporting house and frequently packed with punters
from the nearby racecourses, often including a good sprinkling
of famous faces. Although it's best known for the carvery, which
offers a wide range of hot food through a four-hour lunchtime
period every day (with a selection of about ten main courses,
including a vegetarian choice, all £4.95), there's a limited bar food
menu available throughout normal opening hours. Traditional
music is another big draw five nights a week (Wed-Sun). ***Bar
Food*** *10.30am-11.30pm (11pm in winter). Carvery 11.45-3.45.
Closed Good Fri, 25 Dec.* AMERICAN EXPRESS® *Access, Diners, Visa.*

Rathmullan   Rathmullan House   62%   £104

Tel 074 58188   Fax 074 58200   **HR**

Rathmullan nr Letterkenny Co Donegal   Map 1 C1

For more than 30 years Bob and Robin Wheeler have run their extended Georgian mansion, which stands in lovely tranquil gardens running down to the shore of Lough Swilly. Open fires warm the antique-furnished day rooms, which include a period drawing room, library and cellar bar. Not the least of the distinctive features here is the unique pool complex with Egyptian Baths. Accommodation ranges from well-appointed master suites to family rooms and budget rooms without bathrooms. Outstanding breakfasts. **Rooms** *23. Garden, indoor swimming pool, steam room, tennis. Closed Nov-mid Mar.* AMERICAN EXPRESS® *Access, Diners, Visa.*

The Pavilion   £60

The famous tented Pavilion restaurant makes a delightful setting for one of the best hors d'oeuvre buffet displays in the country (a speciality on Sundays) although the temptation is to try too many things from a selection of fishy starters including eels, smoked salmon and various terrines (both sliced to order), lots of salads and vegetarian options. Main-course choices also take vegetarians seriously and are understandably strong on seafood; good soups, interesting sauces and accompaniments. Desserts usually include carrageen pudding, which also appears with a choice of fruits on the breakfast buffet, and coffee is served with petits fours in the drawing room. Booking essential for both lunch and dinner. **Seats** *60. L (Sun only) 1-2. D 7.30-8.45. Set Sun L £12.50 Set D £22.50. Closed Nov-mid Mar.*

Rathmullan   Places of Interest

Glebe House and Gallery Church Hill Letterkenny Tel 074 37071
Glenveagh National Park Tel 074 37088

Rathnew   Hunter's Hotel   60%   £85

Tel 0404 40106   Fax 0404 40338   **HR**

Newrath Bridge Rathnew Co Wicklow   Map 2 D4

The Gelletlie family and their forebears have been running this delightfully old-fashioned coaching inn since 1820, so it is not surprising that it should encompass a mixture of styles, including some interesting antiques. The current owner, Maureen Gelletlie, adds just the right element of eccentricity to the very real charm of the place. Rooms vary considerably; co-ordinated schemes are not to be expected, but all rooms were being upgraded to include en-suite facilities as we went to press. More important is the meticulously maintained garden leading down to a river at the back, with its wonderful herbaceous borders – the perfect place for their famous afternoon tea, an aperitif or coffee after a meal. Inclement weather is also anticipated, with a welcoming open fire in the cosy bar. Friendly, informal service is excellent. **Rooms** *16. Garden. Closed 25-28 Dec.* AMERICAN EXPRESS® *Access, Diners, Visa.*

Restaurant   £55

Several steps back in time, the restaurant overlooks the garden and everything about it, including the service, is refreshingly old-

fashioned. Long-standing chef John Sutton offers daily-changing
3- and 4-course set menus; try oak-smoked fresh trout fillets, roast
Wicklow lamb with fresh herbs, vegetables from the garden and
nursery puddings such as apple and rhubarb tart or lemon
meringue pie. Prices are fair on a cosmopolitan wine list. *Seats 54.
Parties 12. L 1-3 D 7.30-9. Set L £13.50 Set D £20.*

> If we recommend meals in a hotel or inn a **separate**
> entry is made for its restaurant.

Rathnew   Tinakilly House   76%   £116

Tel 0404 69274   Fax 0404 67806   **HR**
Rathnew Wicklow Co Wicklow   Map 2 D4

A substantial Victorian mansion built in the 1870s for Captain
Robert Halpin, Commander of the *Great Eastern*, which laid the
first telegraph cable linking Europe and America. It's set in seven
acres of gardens overlooking a bird sanctuary and sweeping down
to the Irish Sea. The building has been extensively renovated both
inside and out, with the addition of a period-style wing
comprising fifteen suites and half suites, and run as a hotel
by William and Bee Power since 1983. Furnished to a high
standard with antiques, good pictures and an interesting collection
of Halpin memorabilia, the interior is a model of good taste with
a deal of old world charm – a fine mix of Victorian style and
modern comforts. Comfortably furnished period bedrooms vary;
the best are large, with four-posters and lovely sea views; ground-
floor rooms have direct access to the garden. Children are
welcome, with cots, high-chairs and baby-sitting provided
by arrangement. Apart from the bedrooms the new wing houses
the restaurant and conference and banqueting facilities for up to
150. Friendly, professional service. Very good breakfasts; all-day
snacks, including afternoon tea, served in the residents' lounge.
No dogs. *Rooms 29. Garden, tennis, putting green, croquet.*
AMERICAN EXPRESS *Access, Diners, Visa.*

Restaurant   £75

"Splendid fresh food in elegant Victorian surroundings" rings true
– the best of old and new combine in John Moloney's cooking.
His creative seasonal menus are based on the best of local produce,
especially seafood; fresh fruit and vegetables are grown on the
premises. For a light lunch, try a smoked salmon salad and cheeses
with some of Bee's renowned brown bread; alternatively, the set
lunch menu might offer a warm salad of duck livers followed
by loin of Wicklow lamb with thyme fresh from their own
garden; a chocolate and orange terrine on a mango coulis to finish.
The four-course table d'hote dinner changes daily, offering the
likes of open ravioli with wild mushrooms, a freshly made soup
(perhaps tomato and orange or courgette and rosemary), pan-fried
fillet of beef with red wine and chanterelles, with iced passion
fruit cake to finish. A French and Irish (when available)
cheeseboard is also offered. The wine list covers a diverse
range and there's a good selection of half bottles. *Seats 70.
Private Room 20. L 12.30-2 D 7.30-9. Set L £17.50 Set D £28.50.
Residents only 24-27 Dec.*

Rathpeacon   Country Squire Inn

Tel 021 301812   **P**

Mallow Road Rathpeacon Co Cork   **Map 2 B6**

A couple of miles out of Cork on the N20 towards Mallow, Pat
McSweeney's immaculate roadside pub is very much geared up to
eating. The small bar has not only old 'sewing machine' tables but
also some of the original cast-iron 'Singer' stools, now comfortably
upholstered to match the banquette seating. Bar lunches are
a blackboard affair (minimum charge of a main course) with the
likes of vegetable soup or chicken broth (£1.50), grilled garlic-
stuffed mussels (£4.75/£8), crusty-topped shepherd's pie (£5) and
noisettes of pork with a rich port and orange sauce (£10). The
home-cooked food is generously portioned, so bring a healthy
appetite. In the evenings (only), a cosy, 28-seat candle-lit restaurant
offers similar fare with meals from around £19 – priced
according to one's choice of main course – perhaps sirloin steak
with garlic butter or pepper sauce, salmon with prawns, a daily
fish dish or escalope of turkey with a rich cream sherry sauce.
No children under 12. *Open 12.30-2.30 (not Sun) & 5-11.*
Bar Food *12.30-2.30 (not Sun) & 6.30-9.30 (not Sun or Mon).*
Restaurant *7.30-10 Tue-Sat. Closed L Sun & 1 week Jan.*
Access, Visa.

Recess   Lough Inagh Lodge   68%   £104

Tel 095 34706   Fax 095 34708   **H**

Inagh Valley Recess Co Galway   **Map 1 A3**

Once a sporting lodge in common ownership with *Ballynahinch
Castle*, this small hotel is set in spectacular scenery on the shores
of Lough Inagh, 42 miles from Galway. Completely refurbished
by the present owners and opened as a hotel in 1990, it combines
the advantages of the old and the new – in large, well-
proportioned rooms, interesting period detail and lovely fireplaces
with welcoming log fires, balanced by modern comfort and
practicality. Public areas include two drawing rooms, each with
an open fire, a lovely dining room with deep-green walls and
graceful spoonback Victorian mahogany chairs and a very
appealing bar, with a big turf fire and its own back door and tiled
floor for dripping fisherfolk. Bedrooms, some with four-posters,
are all well appointed and unusually spacious with views of lake
and countryside and walk-in dressing rooms leading to well-
planned bathrooms. While it has special appeal to sportsmen,
Lough Inagh is a good base for touring Connemara and there
is golf and pony trekking nearby. Children up to 12 stay free
in parents' room. ***Rooms*** *12. Garden, fishing. Closed Oct-Apr.*
AMERICAN EXPRESS *Access, Diners, Visa.*

Renvyle   Renvyle House   63%   £118

Tel 095 43511   Fax 095 43515   **H**

Renvyle Co Galway   **Map 1 A3**

Once owned by Oliver St Gregory, this famous Lutyens-esque
house is approached by a stunning scenic drive along a mountain
road with views down into a blue-green sea of unparalleled
clarity. However, once reached, the hotel itself seems to be

snuggling down for shelter and has only limited views. Public areas celebrate the house's glorious past, when it was visited by the rich and famous, including Sir Winston Churchill; the bar, which is the scene of many a late-night revel, has a particularly poignant atmosphere and also a memory-laden back corridor, lined with photographs and press cuttings. There's a pleasant lounge/sun room leading on to a sunny verandah near the swimming pool and an interesting, well-appointed dining room (Lutyens-style furniture still casts its spell over much of the house), but bedrooms are very variable and although there are two pleasant suites with little balconies overlooking the pool, and a number of other good-sized rooms of character, many would disappoint guests attracted by the illustrious history of the place. Some refurbishment is planned for 1995. Beyond protective boulders on the sea side, there is little sign of the storm damage suffered several years ago, although the golf course has been upgraded since. Conference facilities for up to 120, banqueting for 150. *Rooms 65. Garden, croquet, outdoor swimming pool, tennis, golf (9), putting, bowling green, riding, fishing, snooker, bicycles, indoor children's playground. Closed 1 Jan-1 Mar.* AMERICAN EXPRESS *Access, Diners, Visa.*

Riverstown	Coopershill House	69%	£90
Tel 071 65108 Fax 071 65466			**AR**
Coopershill Riverstown Co Sligo			Map 1 B3

Standing at the centre of a 500-acre estate, this immaculate Georgian mansion has been home to seven generations of the O'Hara family since it was built in 1774 and now successfully combines the spaciousness and elegance of the past with modern amenities and the warmest of welcomes. The rooms retain their original regal dimensions and are furnished in period style with family portraits and antiques. Spacious bedrooms all have en-suite bathrooms and most have four-poster or canopy beds; no smoking in the bedrooms. Peace and tranquillity sum up the atmosphere: no TVs or radios, but books and personal touches like fresh flowers and mineral water. A splendid breakfast starts the day at this most hospitable of country hotels. No dogs in the house. *Rooms 7. Garden, croquet, outdoor tennis, coarse and game fishing, boating. Closed 1 Oct-mid Mar.* AMERICAN EXPRESS *Access, Diners, Visa.*

Restaurant	£50

Antique polished tables, silver candelabra and a log fire in the white marble fireplace provide a fitting setting for Lindy O'Hara's good home cooking. A no-choice 5-course menu might include cheese parcels, a traditional soup, roast duck with cranberry sauce, a good choice of farmhouse cheeses and, perhaps, lemon mousse. No smoking. *Seats 28. Parties 20. D only 7.30-8.30. Set D £21.*

Rosses Point	Austie's	
Tel 071 77111		**P**
Rosses Point Co Sligo		Map 1 B2

Named after the previous owner, Austie Gillen, and close to the house where Yeats and his brother used to stay on summer holidays (now neglected and in disrepair), this 200-year-old pub overlooking Sligo Bay is a nautical place – not a 'theme' pub but one that has always been associated with a seafaring family and is crammed full of nautical paraphernalia which is both decorative and fascinating to anyone with an interest in maritime history. The simple bar menu is strong on local seafood – chowder, garlic mussels, open sandwiches or salads with crab, prawns and salmon. *Open 12-11.30, to 11 in winter (Sun 12.30-2 & 4-11).* **Bar Food** *12-10, winter from 5. Pub closed until 4pm in winter. Waterside terrace. Closed Good Friday, 25 Dec. Access, Visa.*

Rosses Point	The Moorings	£45
Tel 071 77112		**R**
Rosses Point Co Sligo		**Map 1 B2**

With an almost waterside location (there's a road between it and the sea), views over Sligo Bay and a cosy dining room with open beams and traditional furniture, The Moorings makes an attractive venue and, not surprisingly, Sunday lunch is a speciality. Local seafood predominates in old favourites – moules à la crème, pan-fried brill with Chablis sauce, poached turbot mousseline, monkfish in garlic butter. Popular food, freshly cooked at reasonable price. **Seats** *75. Parties 40. L (Sun only) 12.30-2.30 D 5.30-9.30. Set L £8. Closed Mon low season, variable closures in winter-ring for details. Access, Visa.*

Rosslare	Great Southern	62%	£99
Tel 053 33233 Fax 053 33543			**H**
Rosslare Co Wexford			**Map 2 D5**

Its position overlooking Rosslare harbour makes this modern hotel a useful stopover for ferry-users and there's plenty to keep children happy with a creche, playground and their own restaurant. Public rooms, many refurbished this year, are light and spacious, with ample seating; many of the simply furnished bedrooms are suitable for family occupation. Up to 225 conference delegates can be accommodated theatre-style, 200 for a banquet. Ask for their helpful golfer's guide to local courses. No dogs. **Rooms** *99. Terrace, indoor swimming pool, keep-fit equipment, tennis, sauna, steam room, snooker, hairdressing, indoor and outdoor children's play area. Closed Nov-Mar.* *Access, Diners, Visa.*

Rosslare	Kelly's Resort Hotel	76%	£99
Tel 053 32114 Fax 053 32222			**HR**
Rosslare Co Wexford			**Map 2 D5**

Total relaxation is the aim at Kelly's, family-run for four generations and often referred to as "the hotelier's hotel" because so many in the business find its professionalism and hospitality offers the perfect switch-off. In its centenary year, Kelly's is a very worthy recipient of our Ireland 1995 Hotel of the Year award (see page 19 for further details). Constant renovation and refurbishment have ensured a very high standard of comfort throughout, from the many seating areas and two bars through elegant, spacious and thoughtfully furnished bedrooms – all with excellent bathrooms and some with balconies or direct access to garden or patio – to exceptional leisure facilities (including two new swimming pools) and a wide range of health and beauty treatments such as aromatherapy and underwater massage.

Children welcome (14 family rooms); indoor playroom, outdoor play area, children's entertainment, high-chairs, early evening meal. One room is equipped for disabled guests. No dogs. *Rooms 99. Garden, terrace, patio, croquet, leisure centre, indoor swimming pool, sauna, spa bath, steam room, gym, squash, tennis, games room, snooker, beauty & hair salon. Closed 4 Dec-20 Feb.* [AMERICAN EXPRESS]® *Access, Diners, Visa.*

Restaurant   £55

In an L-shaped room cleverly designed to retain a surprisingly intimate atmoshphere for its size, the restaurant is elegantly appointed and smoothly run, with some striking examples of the hotel's well-known art collection providing a special background for confident cooking under the direction of Jim Aherne, *chef de cuisine* since 1973. Menus reflect respect for local ingredients – Helvic mussels, Rosslare lamb, St Helen's crab and lobster, Wexford strawberries, game in season, farmhouse cheeses – mainly in traditional dishes with a contemporary twist: venison and forest mushroom pie may come with buttered noodles, baked pork steak in won ton pastry, cold lobster with garlic-dressed tomato salad. Sunday lunch is always a sell-out and dinner ends with a sing-song at the piano in the aptly-named Carmen Bar. On the wine list you'll find lots from France, but not much else; the New World is represented only by Australia. No children under 10 in the restaurant after 7.30. *Seats 220. Parties 12. Private Room 35. Meals served from 8.30am. L 1-2.15 D 7.30-9. Set L £11 Set D £19.95.*

Rosslare   Places of Interest

Ferry Terminal Tourist Information Tel 053 33622
Windsurfing Centre Tel 053 32101

Many hotels offer reduced rates for weekend or out-of-season bookings. Always ask about special deals.

Rossnowlagh   Sand House Hotel   69%   £98

Tel 072 51777   Fax 072 52100   **H**
Rossnowlagh Co Donegal   Map 1 B2

Improvements continue at the crenellated Sand House Hotel, which sits right by a large sandy beach overlooking immense Donegal Bay and the Atlantic Ocean. The Atlantic conservatory lounge takes full advantage of views that are also enjoyed by many of the bedrooms (those with the very best views attract a small supplement). Mary and Brian Britton, together with their son and staff, extend a warm welcome, reinforced by a fire in the Victorian-style lobby. Bedrooms, immaculate like the rest of the hotel, are individually decorated with expensive, stylish fabrics; furniture varies from antiques to fairly modest fitted units, and superior rooms have chaises longues. A delightful, peaceful hotel, as the many regular guests will testify. Banqueting/conference facilities for 60. Good golf and riding facilities nearby. *Rooms 40. Garden, tennis, mini-golf, croquet, surfing, canoeing, board sailing, sea, game & coarse fishing, games room, snooker, table tennis. Closed late Oct-Easter.* [AMERICAN EXPRESS]® *Access, Diners, Visa.*

Rossnowlagh   Smugglers Creek Inn   £40

Tel 072 52366   **IR**

Rossnowlagh Co Donegal   **Map 1 B2**

Conor Britton's imaginatively restored pub and restaurant
is perched high on the cliffs overlooking the wonderful golden
strand at Rossnowlagh. Visitors have the endless fascination
of watching the powerful Atlantic rollers come in from afar
to spend themselves on the beach far below – and all this while
sitting in considerable comfort, with open fires and delicious bar
food. Accommodation is offered in five rooms, all en suite,
interestingly decorated and with sea views. Rooms vary
considerably and most are on the small side – one corner room,
with windows in two walls, is slightly larger than average and has
even better views. Children are well catered for. **Rooms** 5. *Garden.
Closed Good Friday (bar only), 24 & 25 Dec, Mon & Tue in winter.
Access, Visa.*

Restaurant   £40

Across the corridor from the bar, the rustic/nautical atmosphere
is continued in the stone-floored restaurant, furnished with
pleasing informality using stripped-pine dressers and old country
kitchen furniture to advantage and lots of plants. Tables near the
window have splendid sea views, while those at the back are in a
cosy non-smoking area. All share cheerful service and a wide
menu that works the smugglers' theme to death. There's
a predictable emphasis on seafood in dishes like deep-fried squid
(crispy rings with provençale sauce), Smugglers sea casserole
(scallops, salmon and prawns mornay) or classic pan-fried sole
on the bone. Simple meat dishes cater for carnivorous tastes and
there are always vegetarian options. No children after 9pm.
Seats 50. Parties 10. Private Room 24. *L (Restaurant Sun only, bar
snacks daily from 1-6pm) 12.30-2.30 D 6.30-9.30. Set L £8.75 (Sun
only). Access, Visa.*

Roundstone   O'Dowd's Seafood Bar
and Restaurant

Tel 095 35809   **P**

Roundstone Co Galway   **Map 2 A4**

A reassuringly unchanging traditional pub and seafood bar
overlooking the harbour. It's an oasis of calm where regular
summer visitors – notably Dublin lawyers and doctors, plus the
odd politician – return to recharge their batteries. The simple, old-
fashioned bar is a relaxing place to renew old friendships over
a pint and a bite from the reasonably-priced bar menu, which
includes a good range of seafood choices – chowder (a speciality),
Mannin Bay oysters, crab claws in garlic, stuffed mussels, crab
salad, smoked salmon pasta and an unusually named salmon
burger with spicy tomato sauce – plus old favourites like
shepherd's pie and sirloin steak for carnivores and vegetarian
specialities such as bean burgers. Salmon is smoked or cured locally
for gravlax; herbs and lettuce come from their own garden.
Lobster, grilled oysters, game (mallard, quail, venison and
pheasant) and blackberry and apple pie are always popular in the
restaurant; a roast goose is a traditional offering on New Year's
Eve. *Open 11am-11.30pm (Sun 11-2 & 4-11).* **Bar Food** *12.30-9.30*

(Sun 12.30-2 & 4-10). **Restaurant Meals** *12.30-9.30. Restaurant closed mid Oct-Christmas & 2nd week Jan-Easter, 25 Dec.* AMERICAN EXPRESS® *Access, Visa.*

Roundwood	Roundwood Inn	£60
Tel 01 281 8107		R
Roundwood Co Wicklow		Map 2 D4

Set amid spectacular scenery in the highest village in the Wicklow Hills, Jürgen and Áine Schwalm's 17th-century inn is furnished in traditional style with wooden floors, darkwood furniture and huge log fires throughout. Chef Paul Taube's restaurant menu leans towards dishes like rack of Wicklow lamb, roast wild Wicklow venison (a speciality) and other game in season. German influences are evident in long-established specialities like wiener schnitzel, triple liqueur parfait and a feather-light fresh cream gateau which is not to be missed. Booking is advisable for Sunday lunch (three-courses £13.95), when roast suckling pig is a long-standing attraction. A mainly European wine list, strongest in France and Germany, starts at under £10 for the house selection and ascends to 40 times that for a 1967 Pauillac. No children after 7.30pm.

The Roundwood Inn also has a unique reputation for excellent, varied **Bar Food**, which is served swiftly and efficiently by friendly staff at big sturdy tables in front of the ever-burning log fire. Specialities on the bar menu range from nourishing home-made soups and enormous bowls of Irish stew (a comparatively recent arrival but now an established favourite, especially with hill-walkers) through goulash and hearty venison casseroles served with red cabbage and potatoes boiled in their jackets to the refinement of local smoked Wicklow trout and lobster salads, served with home-baked brown bread. Blackboard specials broaden the range and, with one or two desserts added from the restaurant menu, a wonderful value, balanced 3-course meal can be enjoyed informally (but in considerable comfort) in the bar throughout the day and evening. Winner of our Ireland 1995 Bar Food of the Year award. **Seats** *Restaurant 45. Parties 35. Private Room 32. L 1-2.30 D 7.30-9.30 (Sat to 10). Bar open 10.30-11.30, (Sun 12-2, 4-11). Bar food served 12 noon-10 pm (Sun 12-2, 4-10). Restaurant closed D Sun, all Mon. Closed 25 Dec, Good Friday. Access, Visa.*

Sandycove	Bistro Vino	£40
Tel 01 280 6097		R
56 Glastmile Road Sandycove Co Dublin		Map 2 D4

A buzzy little first floor restaurant near the seafront at Sandycove (only a stone's throw from the old Mirabeau) and clearly a big hit with the locals who appreciate the moderate prices, unpretentiously good, lively food and informal atmosphere. A not over-ambitious (and all the better for it) à la carte menu is offered, plus an early evening set menu. Typically, a warm salad of marinated wood pigeon comprises a delicious combination of slivered pigeon breast, mixed leaves, sun-dried tomatoes and toasted pine kernels with a zesty olive oil dressing and crusty garlic bread. Seafood is strong, as in a dish of mixed shellfish in a tomato, cream and black pepper sauce, served with angel hair pasta. Nice tarts and homely puds on the blackboard dessert menu. Beware the steep stairs as you leave. No children under 12. *Seats* 45. *Parties 35. D only 5-11.30. Closed 25 Dec, Good Friday. Set D £9.95 (Early Bird 5-7pm). Access, Visa.*

Sandycove	**Morels Bistro**	**£55**
Tel 01 230 0068		**R**
Glasthule Road Sandycove Co Dublin		**Map 2 D4**

Alan O'Reilly, owner-chef of *Clarets* (see entry under Blackrock) opened this stylish new restaurant at the end of last year. Up a flight of stairs over the Eagle House pub, it's decorated in zinging Mediterranean colours – summer blues, bright yellows and hot reds – with blue-striped blinds and large modern paintings by American artist Emer Diamond and Irish artist Killian O'Connell. Curvaceous metal and rattan chairs contrast with tables simply but formally appointed with white linen and fresh flowers. Paul O'Reilly's menus are very much in tune with the times: start, perhaps, with a gutsy Tuscan vegetable soup with pesto, or crostini of wood pigeon and wild mushrooms followed, typically, with tempura sole with sesame and lobster aïoli or pot-roasted rabbit with mustard and pappardelle. Vegetables (which are charged extra) might include five-spiced greens and stuffed potato skins; tempting desserts range from homely bread-and-butter pudding to a good crisp crème caramel (perhaps with blackberries). Freshly-baked breads, aromatic coffee. *Seats 72. Parties 10. L 12.30-2.45 (Sun only) D 6.30-10.30. Set L £9.95 (Sun). Closed 1 week Christmas. Access, Visa.*

Schull	**Adèle's**	**£40**
Tel 028 28459		**R**
Main Street Schull Co Cork		**Map 2 A6**

From early in the day, the aroma of Adèle Connor's yeast bread wafting through from the bakery at the back sets the tone at this popular little café-restaurant and the display of home-made foods at the counter is well-nigh irresistible at any time of day. Evening menus bring a shift of emphasis, when the first-floor dining room comes to life and Simon Connor takes to the kitchen to produce lively informal meals with the emphasis on pasta dishes and zesty salads. *Seats 40. Parties 8. Meals 9.30-6.30 D 7-10 (Sun to 9.30). Closed D Tues (low season), 1 Nov-mid Dec, 9 Jan-Easter. No credit cards.*

Schull	**Bunratty Inn**	
Tel 028 28341 Fax 028 28702		**P**
Schull Co Cork		**Map 2 A6**

Since taking over in 1986, Val and Vera Duffy have built up a well-deserved reputation for the bar food in this comfortably appointed pub – and apart from providing an interesting menu overall, they are justifiably proud of several specialities. When roast pork is offered, for example, it is no ordinary meat – kitchen waste from Bunratty Inn goes to feed pigs on a farm in Gubbeen, which eventually supplies the bar with free-range pork: hence their unique 'recycled pork'. Such curiosities aside, Vera's brown bread is renowned and ingredients are locally sourced wherever possible. There's a good choice of local seafood – Union Hall smoked salmon, Rossmore oysters and smoked mackerel, crab claws – farmyard duck from Ballydehob and of course all those lovely West Cork cheeses in, for example, a ploughman's selection plate of several including Milleens and Durrus or in speciality open toasted sandwiches made with smoked salmon and Gubbeen or Cashel Blue. Don't forget to leave room for desserts like home-made ice creams, fresh strawberry cheesecake or individual pavlovas with chocolate sauce. *Open 10.30am-11.30pm Mon-Sat (to 11pm in winter), Sun 12.30-2, 4-11. **Bar Food** 12-5 (Sun to 2) Apr-Oct, 12-4 Nov-Mar weekdays only. Closed 25 Dec, Good Fri. Garden, patio, outdoor eating. Access, Visa.*

Schull	La Coquille	£55
Tel 028 28642		**R**
Schull Co Cork		Map 2 A6

Jean-Michel Cahier's chic little restaurant is situated in the main street and convenient to the harbour but, in contrast to the majority of restaurants in the area, sets seafood in context on a wide-ranging menu including typically Gallic offerings such as frogs' legs as well as red meat and poultry. Competently handled classics are the main feature in starters like smoked salmon and crab mayonnaise, well-made soups and main courses like quail with brandy and raisins, fillet steak in pepper sauce and sole on the bone and, while desserts include an excellent tarte tatin, M Cahier's cheeseboard concedes the quality of local produce. Professional service by French staff. *Seats 25. L (Jul & Aug only) 12.30-2.30 D 7-9.30. Closed Sun (except Bank Holiday weekends), Feb. Set L £12 Set D £16/£20. Access, Visa.*

> We endeavour to be as up-to-date as possible, but inevitably some changes to key personnel may occur at restaurants and hotels after the Guide goes to press.

Schull	Corthna Lodge	£40
Tel & Fax 028 28517		**A**
Schull Co Cork		Map 2 A6

Set in large well-designed gardens overlooking the islands of Roaring Water Bay, this spacious modern house has a suntrap patio with sweeping sea views where residents may relax on fine days and a cosy sitting room with an open fire for cooler weather. Good-sized, individually decorated bedrooms are comfortably furnished, all with en-suite showers but no phones or TV – the aim is to provide a peaceful retreat (although there is a small television in the sitting room). Excellent standard of housekeeping. Breakfast options include the local Gubbeen cheese, plain or smoked, served with freshly-baked brown bread. Children welcome. Parking (10 spaces). Two rooms are non-smoking. No dogs. *Rooms 6. Garden. Closed 1 Nov-1 Apr. No credit cards.*

Schull   East End Hotel   60%   £45

Tel 028 28101   **H**

Schull Co Cork   **Map 2 A6**

Ongoing improvements and renovations at Derry and Dorothy
Roche's friendly family hotel – smartly painted in yellow and
navy blue – reflect the steady interest of the owners. Bedrooms are
modest but some have harbour views, others overlook the garden
and hills behind – and most are now en suite, although there are
plenty of extra bathrooms (also available to non-residents when
required by bedraggled sailing folk). Family-friendliness is central
to the hotel, expressed in a generally relaxed attitude: most rooms
can sleep at least 3, children under 4 may stay free in their parents'
room, there are cots, extra beds, baby-sitting by arrangement and
lots of high-chairs. Public areas include a streetside bar/lounge
and rather cramped reception area, but the dining room will
be extended and refurbished for the 1995 season. Banqueting for
120. No private parking, but ample free public parking nearby.
Rooms 17. Garden. Closed 1 week at Christmas. Access, Visa.

Schull   Restaurant in Blue   £50

Tel 028 28305   **R**

Crookhaven Road Schull Co Cork   **Map 2 A6**

Since they opened in 1992, Burvill Evans and Christine Crabtree
have been building up a loyal following at their charming little
restaurant near Schull. A dingly-dell garden, thick walls, small
windows and homely antique furnishings create a relaxed and
charmingly cottagey atmosphere in which to enjoy Burvill's
splendid food from the blackboard menu. Start, perhaps with
locally farmed snails, or a thick creamy stew of mussels with
warm home-baked yeast breads, typically followed by an
imaginative fish dish like steamed sea bass fillets with ginger,
served on a crunchy bed of finely shredded spring cabbage,
or breast of local free-range chicken (bought whole and boned out
by Burvill) rolled and stuffed with spring onions and oyster
mushrooms, served with delicious organic vegetables. Finish with
local cheeses or a quartet of desserts – small servings of four daily
desserts, served in ramekins on a large plate – and lovely aromatic
cafetière coffee. *Seats 30. Parties 6. D only 7.30-9.30, unless
by arrangement. Closed Sun-Wed off season, unless by arrangement;
early Jan-14 Feb. Set D £18.50, also à la carte.* AMERICAN EXPRESS *Access,
Diners, Visa.*

Schull   T J Newman's

Tel 028 28223   **P**

Corner House Main Street Schull Co Cork   **Map 2 A6**

Situated close to the harbour, where the main street joins the road
down to the quay, this characterful little bar is especially popular
with sailing people, but its unchanging charm is in inverse
proportion to its size and the attraction is genuine. Visitors calling
at a quiet time may enjoy its old-fashioned decor (including the
turquoise paint which never changes), but on summer evenings,
when the crowd spills out on to the street, there is little time

to notice such unnecessary diversions from the main task in hand (literally). *Open 10.30am-11.30pm (Sun 12.30-2 & 4-11). Garden. No credit cards.*

Scotshouse — Hilton Park

Scotshouse	**Hilton Park**		**£111**
Tel 047 56007 Fax 047 56033			**A**
Scotshouse nr Clones Co Monaghan			Map 1 C3

Magnificent woodlands and gardens make a lovely, peaceful setting for 18th-century Hilton Park. The mansion has been in the Madden family for over 250 years and Johnny and Lucy are the eighth generation to live here. They run it very much as a family home which takes in guests, and it's full of interest, with heirlooms, family portraits and four-poster beds. Large bedrooms, some with dressing rooms and characterful bathrooms, afford wonderful views. Lucy cooks an excellent no-choice five-course dinner in traditional country house style, with most of the raw materials produced in their own grounds or locally. The estate covers 600 acres, including three lakes where swimming, boating and fishing keep visitors occupied. A fine breakfast starts the day, served in the bright, charming Green Room. Enter the estate by the main entrance on the Clones-Scotshouse road and look out for a black gate with silver falcons. Children between eighteen months and six years of age are not encouraged. No dogs.
***Rooms** 5. Garden, golf (9), coarse & game fishing, boating. Closed Oct-end Mar except for parties by arrangement. Access, Visa.*

Scotshouse — Place of Interest

Castle Leslie Glasloughby Monaghan Tel 047 88109

Shanagarry — Ballymaloe House

Shanagarry	**Ballymaloe House**	**66%**	**£120**
Tel 021 652531 Fax 021 652021			**A R**
Shanagarry Co Cork			Map 2 B6

Part of an old castle that became a farmhouse, modernised through the centuries, but with the 14th-century keep remaining in its original form. The hotel is situated in the middle of a 400-acre farm, both owned and run by Ivan and Myrtle Allen, and part of a group of family enterprises that includes a cookery school, craft shop and the *Crawford Gallery Café* in Cork (see entry). Two miles from the coast, near the small fishing village of Ballycotton, the main house provides the day rooms, a large drawing room with an open fire and a TV room, complete with video recorder. Throughout, there's an interesting collection of modern Irish paintings with works by Jack B Yeats in the dining room. Thirteen bedrooms in the main building are traditionally furnished, and a further five modern, garden rooms open on to a lawn. Another eleven rooms, more cottagey in character, surround the old coachyard, with some at ground level suitable for wheelchairs. Teenagers especially will appreciate the self-contained 16th-century Gatehouse, which has its own small entrance hall and a twin-bedded room with its bathroom up a steep wooden staircase. Ballymaloe is a warm and comfortable family home, especially welcoming to children of all ages (high tea is served at 5.30pm), who can rely on the Allen (grand)children to relay the latest news from the farm or share the sandpit and pool. For the delightful breakfasts, all the ingredients are local or home-made, with even the oatmeal used for porridge ground in an old stone mill down the road. *Rooms 29. Garden, croquet, outdoor swimming pool, tennis, golf (5), children's outdoor play area. Closed 24-26 Dec.* AMERICAN EXPRESS *Access, Diners, Visa.*

Restaurant ★ £80

Perhaps more than anyone else in the country, Myrtle Allen has nurtured, encouraged and cajoled chefs from her kitchen to spread their wings further afield after first achieving high standards here. Wherever you go in Ireland, you're likely to come across an individual who at some time has cooked alongside this doyenne of Irish chefs. There are several smallish interconnecting dining rooms, any of which can be used privately, all furnished with antiques, and a conservatory with a black-and-white tiled floor, Lloyd Loom furniture and lots of greenery. With the bread home-baked, the fish caught locally (sometimes the menu is deliberately late to see what the fishing boats have brought in), and the salads and vegetables picked that day, you can certainly rely on the ingredients being fresh and wholesome – indeed, much produce comes from their own farm. With Irish and French as the main influences, the cooking is simple, enhancing the quality of the raw materials. Typically, nightly-changing menus might feature Ballycotton fish soup, hot buttered oysters on toast, baked plaice with hollandaise sauce, a selection of patés, hot buttered lobster, cod *à la dieppoise*, grilled chicken with two sauces or fillet of pork en croute with apple and celery sauce. Try some Irish cheeses before the dessert (perhaps an apricot tart or praline gateau) and linger awhile over some excellent cafetière coffee. Ivan Allen has built up a fine wine cellar over many years; it's strong in France but light elsewhere and there are few half bottles; the spelling on the handwritten wine list, however, is eccentric! *Seats 40. Private Room 45. L 12.30-2 D 7-9.30 (Sun buffet at 7.30). Set Sun L £16/£20. Set D £30.*

Our inspectors **never** book in the name of Egon Ronay's Guides. They disclose their identity only if they are considering an establishment for inclusion in the next edition of the Guide.

Shannon	Oakwood Arms Hotel	63%	£101
Tel 061 361500 Fax 061 361414			**H**
Shannon Co Clare			Map 2 B4

A family-owned, redbrick hotel (opened in 1991) that creates a good first impression with its neatly laid-out flower beds. If the mock-Tudor style of the hotel is somewhat surprising in this setting, its aviation theme is less so: the lounge bar and function room both honour the memory of the pioneer female pilot Sophie Pearse, who came from the area, and the restaurant is named after Howard Hughes's famous flying boat, *The Spruce Goose*. Public areas are quite spacious and comfortably furnished and, although not individually decorated, bedrooms have all the necessary comforts and are double-glazed. *Rooms 46. Patio. Closed 25 Dec.* AMERICAN EXPRESS *Access, Diners, Visa.*

Shannon   Place of Interest

Airport Tourist Information Tel 061 61664/61565

Shannon Airport	Great Southern	64%	£124
Tel 061 471122 Fax 061 471982			**H**
Shannon Airport Shannon Co Clare			Map 2 B4

Situated directly opposite the main terminal building, a modern airport hotel, totally refurbished four years ago. Soundproofed bedrooms include 11 Executive rooms and three suites. Fourteen rooms are designated non-smoking. Conference facilities for up to 200, banqueting for 150. *Rooms 115. Garden.* AMERICAN EXPRESS *Access, Diners, Visa.*

Skerries	Red Bank Restaurant	£60
Tel 01 849 1005		**R**
7 Church Street Skerries Co Dublin		Map 1 D3

Winner of our Ireland 1995 Seafood Restaurant of the Year (see page 51 for further details). The original safe is still in use as a wine cellar at Terry and Margaret McCoy's converted bank, which is well appointed in a pleasingly restrained style – a comfortable bar/reception for aperitifs, well-spaced tables, fresh flowers and generous wine glasses – and its close proximity to the other Red Bank (well known to the local fishing fleet) is reflected on Terry's colourful, imaginative menus. He gathers nettles and watercress in the morning for the day's soup, to be served with delicious home-baked bread (made with locally milled flour) and his menus range from seafood won ton dumpling salad or haddock Louisiana (Creole-style) through classics like sole on the bone and a carefully balanced short choice (steak, stuffed chicken breast local smoked pork) for carnivores and a thoughtfully conceived system of symbols to assist vegetarian choices. Follow with farmhouse chesses or tempting desserts from the trolley that include perennial favourites such as profiteroles and extend to favour chocolate in house specialities like baked chocolate cheesecake or a seriously wicked chocolate mocha gateau, plus a choice of coffees. *Seats 45. Parties 10. Private Room 10. L (Sun only) 12.30-2.15 D 7-10. Closed D Sun, all Mon, all Nov, Christmas week. Set L £13.75 Set D £17.95. Not suitable for children under 8.* AMERICAN EXPRESS *Access, Diners, Visa.*

Skerries   Place of Interest

Ardgillan Castle Balbriggan Tel 01 849 2212

Skibbereen	Liss Ard Lake Lodge	77%	£200
Tel 028 22365 Fax 028 22839			**AR**
Skibbereen Co Cork			Map 2 B6

Set in extensive gardens (open to the public), overlooking Lough Abisdealy, this imaginatively renovated and extended Victorian lodge opened in 1994 as a small luxury hotel, furnished and decorated with the emphasis on design, in a minimalist, Oriental style carefully judged to distract as little as possible from the garden and water views framed by every window. Black and white are dominant throughout, with lacquer red accents in some

places, softer shades in others, but the overall feeling is of great
tranquillity and other-worldliness. Rooms – all suites except
a double – are designed to maximise views and combine clean-
lined simplicity with luxury: mini-bars, TV units with video and
hi-fi and equally unusual bathrooms finished to a very high
standard. Helpful staff. 24hr room service. Well-behaved children
welcome. Also available is a six-bedroomed Georgian house
(complete with library, conference room and fitness centre) for
complete parties. Suitable for small conferences of up to 20.
No dogs. **Rooms** *10. Garden. Closed 2 weeks Nov, 2 weeks Jan.*
AMERICAN EXPRESS *Access, Diners, Visa.*

Restaurant   £80

An open fire and slightly gentler lines create a warm tone in the
restaurant, where elegantly appointed tables provide a fitting
setting for Claudia Meister's imaginative (non-dairy) limited
choice six-course menus. Freshly-baked breads are served with
little bowls of seasoned olive oil to accompany, perhaps, a clear,
bright red beetroot broth with sliced wild mushrooms suspended
in it. The next course might include leek and pine kernel
cannelloni – a play on words as the tubes in this vegetarian dish
are actually leeks, followed by a real pasta, such as spaghettini with
an olive and tomato coulis. Typical main courses might be turbot
en papillote – another surprise as rice paper replaces the expected
filo parcel – or lacquered duck, coated in a spicy mixture made
to a secret formula. Accompanying vegetables will not disappoint
and it is hard to believe that desserts such as a rich, creamy
chocolate mille-feuille are made without dairy products. Good
choice of teas and coffee; excellent breakfast (when butter
is allowed). **Seats** *25. Parties 8. D only (except for residents) 7.30-
9.30. Closed Tue (except for residents). Set D £29.*

Skryne   O'Connell's

Tel 046 25122   **P**

Skryne nr Tara Co Meath   Map 1 C3

The old castle on top of the hill is your marker for this
delightfully unspoilt old country pub, whose main attraction is a
good pint pulled by charming landlady Mary O'Connell (the pub
has been in her husband's family for three generations). The two
simple bars contain friendly locals, records of sporting endeavours
and a history of the nearby monastery. The pub was up for sale
as we went to press. *Open 10.30-11.30 (Sun 12.30-2.30, 4-11.30).
Closed Good Friday, 25 Dec. No credit cards.*

Sligo   Bistro Bianconi

Tel 071 41744   **JaB**

44 O'Connell Street Sligo Co Sligo   Map 1 B2

Decor at this attractive middle-market restaurant is in the
currently popular Roman revival style, with frescos and whatnot
in terracottas and soft sandy tones all gently lit with cleverly
designed wall lights and brought to life with large, leafy plants.
The food is unpretentious and simple – a wide range of pizzas
(from £4.70) and some good pasta, all based on fresh, lively
ingredients and cooked to order. Vegetarians are well catered for
and 'healthy options' (low in calories, fat and cholesterol) are

highlighted on the menu; daily lunch specials are especially good value. **Seats** 85. *Parties 25. L 12.30-2.30 D 6-12 (till 2am Fri & Sat). Closed Good Friday, 25 & 26 Dec. Ames, Access, Diners, Visa.*

Sligo   Hargadon's

Tel 071 70933   **P**

O'Connell Street Sligo Co Sligo   **Map 1 B2**

Hargadon's is one of the great legendary pubs of Ireland: bought by a British MP in 1868, it passed into the hands of the Hargadon family in 1908 and has been maintained by them, unspoilt, ever since. Bar food includes soup and sandwiches served all day plus one or two hot dishes like hearty Irish stew (£3.75) or home-made maetballs at lunchtime; dinner is served in a room at the back where it will not interfere with the real business of running a bar. Otherwise it is as it was – the snugs, the pot-belly stove, the wooden benches and the shelves which used to hold groceries. Children allowed in the bar during the daytime only. Go and enjoy. Beer garden. *Open 10.30am-11.30pm (Sun 12-2, 4-11).* **Bar Food** *10.30-7 (no food Sun). Closed Good Friday, 25 Dec. Garden, outdoor eating. No credit cards.*

Sligo   McGettigan's (An Cruiscín Lán/ Cruskeen Lawn)

Tel 071 62857   **P**

Connolly Street Sligo Co Sligo   **Map 1 B2**

Liam and Geraldine McGettigan's comfortable, unselfconscious pub is well supported by locals and visitors alike. Its reputation is based on serving good, plain food at a very fair price; the emphasis throughout is on old-fashioned courtesy and service rather than on quaintness of decor or tradition. Expect simply presented, middle-of-the-road food in generous portions, with value for money firmly in mind. Good-value lunches offer the likes of Irish stew, home-made lasagne and roast stuffed chicken and bacon; bar snacks, including children's favourites, are served all day every day. Leave room for sherry trifle and custard or home-made apple tart and cream (both £1.20). Accommodation is also offered in 11 modest rooms (B&B £27 for two – not en suite and inspected). *Open 10.30am-11.30pm (Sun 12.30-2 & 4-11), closed 3-5 in winter months.* **Bar Meals** *12-2.15 (no food Sat & Sun except in high season). Children allowed in bar to eat, children's menu, high-chair provided. Closed Good Friday, 25 Dec. No credit cards.*

Sligo   Sligo Park   58%   £99

Tel 071 60291   Fax 071 69556   **H**

Pearse Road Sligo Co Sligo   **Map 1 B2**

In the absence of any real competition, this modern hotel set in seven acres of parkland on the southern edge of town attracts a high proportion of the area's business. Bedrooms are adequate and children up to 4 may stay free in their parents' room; 4s-under 12s are charged 50% when sharing; 17 rooms were recently refurbished – insist on one when booking. The hotel's main strengths are its conference and banqueting facilities, which can cater for up to 500 (theatre-style conferences), and a particularly

good leisure centre. **Rooms** 89. *Garden, indoor swimming pool &*
children's splash pool, gym, solarium, sauna, spa bath, steam room,
tennis, snooker. 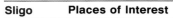 *Access, Diners, Visa.*

Sligo	Truffles Restaurant	£25
Tel 071 44226		**R**
The Mall Sligo Co Sligo		Map 1 B2

Bernadette O'Shea's 'new age pizza' restaurant is unusual, to say the
least: a delightfully wacky dining room with amusing trompe
l'oeil decorations and a peat fire setting the tone. Thoroughly
original treatments for the humble pizza (served in 8″ and 10″
sizes) include a variety of eclectic ingredients – the Californian
Classic will include sun-dried tomatoes and roasted garlic, the
Mexicano, spicy sausage and fresh hot chili peppers and so on, but
the best of all is the Irish Cheese Board, a surprisingly light taste
experience adding melting goat's cheese, Cashel blue, smoked Brie,
cream cheese, cottage cheese, Irish mozzarella and fresh herbs to a
crisp base and fresh tomato sauce. Home-made soups, garlic bread,
filled stromboli bread, wonderful main-course salads – including
Italian, Roquefort and Greek – based on locally grown organic
produce, and a choice of fresh pasta (made with free-range eggs)
are other attractions. It's a small, eccentric place ("service charge
not included, but anticipated"), now deservedly popular, so book
ahead. The wine bar upstairs is open from 7pm (Sun 5-10pm).
Seats 34. *Parties 8. D only 5-10.30. Closed Sun & Mon, 2 weeks*
Nov, Bank Holidays. No credit cards.

Sligo	Places of Interest

Tourist Information Tel 071 61201
Lissadell House Drumcliffe Tel 071 63150
Parkes Castle Tel 071 64149
Sligo Racecourse Cleveragh Tel 071 62484/60094

Spiddal	Boluisce Seafood Bar	
Tel 091 83286 Fax 091 83285		**JaB**
Spiddal Connemara Co Galway		Map 2 B4

Kevin and Monica MacGabhaun have kept more or less to the
formula operated so successfully by the Glanville family for 20
years. Seafood features in both the first-floor restaurant and the
downstairs bar. Also steaks and stir-fries in the bar; children's
portions. **Seats** 60. *Parties 10. Meals 12-10 (Sun 12.30-10).*
Closed Good Friday, 24-26 Dec. *Access, Visa.*

Spiddal	Bridge House Hotel	59%	£65
Tel 091 83118			**H**
Spiddal Connemara Co Galway			Map 2 B4

The relaxed atmosphere of this comfortable, unpretentious family-
run hotel has been attracting a loyal clientele since 1959 and,
despite renovation of the hotel frontage and redecoration of the
foyer this year, this seems unlikely to change. En-suite bedrooms
are neat and homely. French windows open on to the back

garden from the bar and dining room. The Stirrup Room grill
is open all day for informal food. No dogs. ***Rooms 16. Garden.***
Closed Christmas-mid Feb. AMERICAN EXPRESS *Access, Visa.*

Stillorgan	**Beaufield Mews**	**£55**

Tel 01 288 0375 Fax 01 288 6945	**R**
Woodlands Avenue Stillorgan Co Dublin	**Map 4 C1**

Located in a romantically rural oasis just off the Stillorgan dual
carriageway, this rustic black-and-white beamed property set in a
real country garden cleverly combines the attractions of antiques
and food – aperitifs served upstairs in the beamed coach house take
on an extra dimension while scrutinising the price labels
on surrounding furnishings (what may be gone after dinner in the
adjacent hay loft restaurant?) Predictably, perhaps, the food plays
second fiddle to atmosphere and, bearing the strength of old-
fashioned charm in mind, traditional specialities – chicken liver
paté with finger toasts, tournedos Rossini, roast duckling with sage
and onion stuffing and apple sauce, game in season – are the wisest
choices, although an excellent gazpacho, for instance, may surprise.
Good home-made bread. Helpful, charming staff. ***Seats 120.***
Parties 20. Private Rooms 40/60. D only 6.30-10.15.
Closed Sun & Mon, Bank Holidays, 25-27 Dec. Set D £16.95.
AMERICAN EXPRESS *Access, Diners, Visa.*

Stillorgan	**China-Sichuan Restaurant**	**£50**

Tel 01 288 4817 Fax 01 288 0882	**R**
4 Lower Kilmacud Road Stillorgan Co Dublin	**Map 4 C1**

The China Sichuan Food Authority sponsors this smart, civilised
restaurant five miles south of Dublin city centre, and many of the
dishes are hot with spices and chili. Among these (denoted on the
menu by an asterisk) are orange-flavoured sliced cold beef, fried
prawns in garlic sauce and fried lamb shreds in aromatic sauce. For
its unusual use of pork, China-Sichuan wins our 1995 Irish Pork
Award (see page 67 for full details). Wines include Great Wall
white and red from China. ***Seats 46. L 12.30-2.30 D 6-10.45.***
Closed 25-27 Dec, Good Friday. Set L from £8 Set D £16.50.
AMERICAN EXPRESS *Access, Visa.*

Stillorgan	**The Millhouse**	

Tel 01 288 8672 Fax 01 283 6353	**P**
Lower Kilmacud Road Stillorgan Co Dublin	**Map 2 D4**

The Mill House is hard to miss with its coat of bright pink and
shiny gold paintwork. Inside, once past the rather off-putting
porch/hall area, the interior is surprisingly calm and peaceful,
broken up into a number of small semi-snug areas with plenty
of gas coal-effect fires. The large, irregular mahogany bar
is pleasingly solid and there's a lot of dark wood in the traditional
style, successfully offset by plenty of mirrors, pictures and plants
in old china cachepots. Daily carvery in the Lounge (12.30-2.30
Mon-Fri); standard bar food menu (steak sandwiches, chicken
Kiev and so on) from 2.30pm. Pepper Cannister Restaurant open
Mon-Sat from 6pm, Sun 12.30-9pm (£9.25); also open for lunch   *See over*

before Christmas. *Open 10.30am-11.30pm (Sun 12-2 & 4-11).*
Bar Food *12.30-9.30 (Sun 12.30-2 & 4-9.30). Patio.*
AMERICAN EXPRESS® *Access, Diners, Visa.*

Stillorgan   The Stillorgan Orchard

Tel 01 288 8470	P
The Hill Stillorgan Co Dublin	Map 2 D4

Despite its slightly incongruous situation close to a large suburban
shopping centre, the Orchard's main claim to fame is 'the largest
thatched roof in Ireland'. Inside, there's a surprisingly genuine
country cottage atmosphere with low ceilings, small windows, lots
of tapestry-style and chintzy seating in snugs and alcoves and all
the traditional clutter of brass, copper and old plates on the walls.
Bar food is now provided by the restaurant operation (which
is not specifically recommended here). *Open 10.30am-11pm (Sun
12.30-2 & 4-11).* **Bar Food** *12.30-9 (no food Sun eve). Children
allowed to eat in bar until 4pm (Sun to 7pm). Garden. Closed
Good Friday, 25 Dec.* AMERICAN EXPRESS® *Access, Diners, Visa.*

Straffan   Barberstown Castle   70%   £110

Tel 01 628 8157 Fax 01 627 7027	HR
Straffan Co Kildare	Map 2 C4

Next door to the Kildare Hotel & Country Club (with whom
they share golf and leisure facilities), Barberstown Castle is a
historically fascinating place – parts of it go back to the early
13th century (with many later additions) – and it can lay claim
to continuous occupation for over 40 years. Under the present
ownership since 1987, the castle has been thoroughly renovated
and refurbished in keeping with its age and style and now offers
very comfortable accommodation in ten well-appointed,
individually decorated en-suite rooms – some in the oldest part,
the Castle Keep, others in the 'new' Victorian wing. Public areas,
including two drawing rooms and an elegant bar, have been
renovated with the same care and there are big log fires
everywhere. A separate function room in converted stables
has banqueting facilities for 160, conferences 200. **Rooms** *10.
Closed 24-26 Dec.* AMERICAN EXPRESS® *Access, Visa.*

Castle Restaurant   £65

A series of whitewashed rooms in the semi-basement of the old
Castle Keep, with a great atmosphere heightened by fires, candles

in alcoves and on tables, and wall lighting; the table style
is appropriately simple: plain white cloths and ladderback oak
chairs. Head chef Tom Rowe has established quite a reputation for
the restaurant since his arrival in 1991, turning out tasty starters
like sautéed lamb's kidneys with bacon and red wine or warm
black and white pudding salad – an imaginative alternative
to several fashionable dishes – and an unusually richly flavoured
mushroom soup, all served with excellent dark, moist wholemeal
soda bread. Main courses might include a big plate of mixed
seafood with a tomato and dill sauce, or pork steak enlivened with
a piquant mixture of honey, ginger and spring onions. A good
selection of simply prepared vegetables is left on the table for
guests to help themselves. Desserts range from a very rich
chocolate truffle cake to a refreshing fruit salad plate with sabayon,
served with a tuile and a ball of creamy Bailey's ice cream;
farmhouse cheeses are served with home-made biscuits and big,
juicy grapes. Lovely cafetière coffee to finish. In addition to the
dinner and à la carte menus, a special tasting menu is available
to complete parties. Bar meals at weekday lunchtimes. Smoking
discouraged. **Seats** 55. *Parties 15. Private Room 35. L 1-2.30 (Sun
only) D 7.30-9.30 (Sun 7-8.30). Closed 3 day Christmas.
Set L £15.50 (£11.50 children) Set D £22.50 & £25.*

Straffan	Kildare Hotel	87%	£250
Tel 01 627 3333 Fax 01 627 3312			**HR**
Straffan Co Kildare			Map 2 C4

Already affectionately known as the K Club (attached to the hotel
is the country club which is centred around the golf course
designed by Arnold Palmer), the hotel is best reached from Dublin
(17 miles) via the N7, taking a right at Kill to Straffan. Reputedly,
previous owners of the original (Straffan) house were dogged
by bad luck, but those myths have now been discarded with the
creation of this magnificent complex, surrounded by beautifully
landscaped gardens (ask for the garden walk leaflet), with the
River Liffey running through the grounds. The new buildings
blend in tastefully with the old house (indeed it's hard to see the
'join') and inside there's much opulence, highlighted by sumptuous
furnishings, fine antiques and an outstanding collection
of paintings, including several by Jack B Yeats, who has a room
devoted to his works. Each of the spacious bedrooms has been
individually designed – note the different *trompe l'oeil*, also
apparent in the bar – and no two of the marble bathrooms
(luxury toiletries, bathrobes, slippers and huge towels) are the
same. All rooms are lavishly and handsomely furnished;
on arrival, guests are treated to a bowl of fruit, hand-made
chocolates and mineral water; satellite TV, video recorder, mini-
bar and personal safe are standard amenites, along with handily-
placed telephones. Such luxury, of course, requires levels of service,
housekeeping and maintenance to match, a task that general
manager Ray Carroll and his motivated team of staff achieve
admirably. There are two meeting rooms in the main house, one
an imposing boardroom, and up to 600 can be accommodated
in the indoor tennis arena, part of the sports centre, which is easily
transformed to suit the occasion. Also available, adjoining the
hotel, are self-contained, two-bedroomed courtyard apartments

and a three-bedroomed lodge. A function room extension to the
clubhouse is scheduled for completion in June '95. *Rooms 45.
Garden, indoor swimming pool, gymnasium, squash, sauna, solarium,
hair & beauty salon, golf (18), tennis, snooker, bicycles, coarse and
game fishing, clay-pigeon shooting.* AMERICAN EXPRESS *Access, Diners, Visa.*

The Byerley Turk   £100

The restaurant's name, perhaps unfamiliar to those who do not
follow horse-racing, comes from one of the three Arab stallions
in the male line of every thoroughbred horse in the world;
impressively draped tall windows, marble columns and rich decor
in tones of deep terracotta, cream and green harmonise perfectly
with the style of the original house. The room is cleverly shaped
to create semi-private areas and make the most of window tables,
laid with crested china, monogrammed white linen, gleaming
modern crystal and silver. Chef Michel Flamme's leanings towards
classical French cuisine are tempered by traditional Irish influences
and, with his kitchen garden now in full production, by local and
home-grown seasonal produce, as in cream of tomato soup or pavé
of salmon with artichoke and red wine sauce. An additional
Seasonal Fayre Menu offers sophisticated dishes and the three-
course table d'hote dinner menu might include nage of seafood
with champagne sabayon, followed by roast rack of lamb with
pulses and morel jus and finishing, perhaps, with a plate of caramel
desserts or a selection of Irish and French cheeses. Modest (but not
modestly priced) wine list. The Legend Restaurant in the golf club
offers a buffet lunch in summer and table d'hote in winter; à la
carte in the evenings. *Seats 65. Parties 30. Private Room 44. L 1-2
D 7-10. Set Sun L £22 Set D £39.*

Straffan   Places of Interest

Steam Museum Tel 01 627 3155
Castletown House Celbridge Tel 01 628 8252
Irish National Stud Tully Tel 045 21617 *15 miles*
Japanese Gardens Tully Tel 045 21251 *15 miles*

Swords   Forte Travelodge   £45
Tel 01 840 9233   L
N1 Dublin/Belfast Road Swords bypass nr Dublin Co Dublin   Map 1 D3

On the southbound carriageway of the Swords bypass at Swords
roundabout, 1½ miles north of Dublin airport, 16 miles north
of Dublin city centre. The room rate of £31.95 (without
breakfast) could include up to 3 adults, a child under 12 and
a baby in a cot. *Rooms 40.* AMERICAN EXPRESS *Access, Diners, Visa.*

Swords   The Old Schoolhouse   £50
Tel 01 840 4160   Fax 01 840 5060   R
Coolbanagher Swords Co Dublin   Map 1 D3

Set in a quiet backwater away from the main road, this old stone
building has been sympathetically restored and converted to make
a delightful restaurant. There are always daily specials on the
blackboard: warm scallop and bacon salad, baked crab with
brandy and cream, Galway oysters and particularly good fish from
nearby harbours Skerries and Howth. Other typical à la carte
dishes might be venison tartlets glazed with grain mustard, Greek

salad, a choice of up to four home-made soups, beef stroganoff, roast half Barbary duckling with orange and black cherry sauce and a couple of vegetarian options. Steaks of 6, 8 or 10 ounces are served with a choice of sauces. Interesting desserts like apple pie, strawberry mousse in dark chocolate cups, profiteroles with caramel sauce and sunken chocolate soufflé with Amaretto prunes. *Seats* 70. *Private Rooms 10/20. L 12.30-2.30 D 6.30-10.30. Closed L Mon, all Sun, 1 week Christmas. Set L £10.95/£12.95 Set D £19.50.* *Access, Diners, Visa.*

Swords   Place of Interest

Newbridge House Donabate Tel 01 843 6534 *4 miles*

Tahilla Long Lake	£350
Tel 064 45100 Fax 064 45147	A
Tahilla Sneem Co Kerry	Map 2 A6

Described variously as 'an extravagant sanctuary' and a 'luxurious cruise liner on dry land', no expense was spared when building this beautifully located house – objets d'art from around the world, a library of travertine, fine rugs on heated marble floors, and a finely cut onyx window are all typical of this extraordinary pocket of luxury. It's very much an architect's house – and a Continental one at that: clean lines contrast with rare and beautiful materials to create a unique work of art built to maximise on sunshine and views and set in lovely gardens which gradually blend into the natural beauty of their surroundings. Bedrooms are equally luxurious in the Continental style, with cool colours (a lot of white), high-tech beds and direct access to balcony or garden. The dining room (which non-residents may visit to attend musical evenings with John O'Conor – usually first Saturday in the month during summer, when dinner is an option at £20 + concert admission £10) is formally appointed, with wonderful sea and mountain views. Most suitable for parties of 6 to 8 people. The top-floor apartment has a huge living room and magnificent views. Three-bedroom self-catering chalet in grounds also available. ***Rooms** 4. Garden, sauna, spa bath, steam room, massage, games room, power boat and helicopter available.* *Access, Diners, Visa.*

Termonfeckin Triple House Restaurant	£55
Tel & Fax 041 22616	R
Termonfeckin Co Louth	Map 1 D3

On cold evenings a welcoming log fire in the reception area (an alternative to the conservatory used for aperitifs in the summer) sets the tone at Pat Fox's attractive restaurant in the pretty village of Termonfeckin, the better to consider his hearty "Celebration Dinner Menu" and blackboard seafood extras from nearby Clogherhead. Typical first courses might include an unusual warm salad of smoked halibut or spinach-filled pancakes, a house speciality with a colourful light tomato sauce and cheese topping. A choice of soup or well-dressed salad follows, with freshly baked bread accompanying, then a wide choice of main courses with the emphasis on fish, but plenty else beside, including an imaginative vegetarian option and red meats such as slivers of fillet steak "Nostrovia", a light, creamy mixture with mushrooms, peppers

and spices. Finish, perhaps, with a speciality dessert, a dacquoise
that varies with the season's fruits, or a plated selection
of farmhouse cheeses. *Seats 40. Parties 12. L 1-2 (Sun only) D 7-10.
Closed Sun & Mon, Oct-Mar & 3 days Christmas. Set L £9.95
Set D £14.95. Access, Visa.*

Thomastown	Mount Juliet	84%	£195
Tel 056 24455 Fax 056 24522			**HR**
Thomastown Co Kilkenny			Map 2 C5

Some 75 miles south of Dublin and signposted from the main
N9 Waterford road, Mount Juliet is in fact an estate of around
1500 acres of parkland and formal gardens through which flow
the Rivers Kings and Nore. It is also home to the Ballylinch stud,
where the four-bedroomed house complete with personal
housekeeper can be rented, the David Leadbetter Golf Academy,
the Jack Nicklaus-designed golf course, and the Iris Kellett
Equestrian Centre. Add to these facilities a self-contained spa and
leisure centre, tennis, archery, hunting, fishing and shooting and
you have the complete sporting estate. It's a long and picturesque
drive to reach the main house, built in the 18th century, where
you'll encounter elegant and handsome public rooms with fine
fireplaces, historical pictures, all commanding splendid views
of the river and estate. The walls of the club-like Tetrarch Bar list
home winners of major horse races through the years. Most (32)
of the spacious bedrooms are in the main house, each individually
and charmingly designed with good furniture and seating, and
fine bathrooms to match. On arrival you will be welcomed by a
box of chocolates, a bowl of apples and a bottle of wine, and
among the host of extras, you will find a safe concealed in the
writing desk, a decent hairdryer and luxurious bathrobes.
Housekeeping is exemplary and there's a full turn-down service
at night, typical of the high standards from all the staff. A nice
touch is a printed weather forecast delivered with your morning
newspaper. More rustic accommodation is available in the
Courtyard rooms and Rose Garden suites at the Hunters Yard,
converted from the old stableyard. A short club away from the
1st tee, this is also the site of the golf shop, spa, bars and the Loft
restaurant. Children under 12 stay free in their parents' room.
Banqueting for up to 50, theatre-style conferences 80. *Rooms 54.
Garden, croquet, indoor swimming pool, spa bath, sauna, steam room,
exercise room, beauty salon, tennis, snooker, game fishing, golf (18),
archery, clay-target shooting, riding, bicycles.* *Access,
Diners, Visa.*

Lady Helen McCalmont Dining Room   £80

An elegant room decorated in Wedgwood style, with all the
trappings of luxury from crisp Irish linen and fine crystal
to gleaming silver and the ceremonious lifting of cloches. New
chef Tina Walsh cooks in a sound and enterprising manner, using
prime ingredients, though sometimes dishes don't always come off,
for instance a 'middle' course of papaya and lime sorbet, and the
ill-conceived accompaniment of a side plate of ordinary vegetables
and potatoes with an otherwise excellent steamed escalope
of salmon Chinese-style with ginger, spring onion and soya sauce
finished with sesame seed oil. A stir-fry of Chinese vegetables
would have been much more appropriate. On the other hand

a warm ballotine of guinea fowl on a bed of creamed potato with a hint of nutmeg served with a game jus was exemplary, contrasting with a crème brulée not properly set. However, staff are really professional and correct in every manner. Pity the wine list is littered with spelling mistakes and has few half bottles, though there are some good bin ends. The Loft Restaurant, open from 7 to 10pm (12-7pm Nov-Feb), serves more traditional and hearty dishes (grilled black pudding, Irish stew, apple strudel) as well as a Sunday brunch, suitable for families. *Seats 48. Parties 12. Private Room 30. D only 7-10 Set D £33.*

Timoleague   Dillon's

Tel 023 46390   **P**

Mill Street Timoleague Co Cork   **Map 2 B6**

That one can see in through the plant-filled clear shop window immediately distinguishes Dillon's from the usual Irish town bar; their description of themselves as a café-styled bar is very apt. There's a conventional bar counter down one side of the single room, a mixture of furniture that includes a few Lloyd Loom chairs around eating-height tables and arty black-and-white photos of the likes of James Dean and Billie Holliday on the walls. It's run by two French sisters, Isabelle (Dillon) and Anne (Boulineau) who provide good bar food like seafood chowder (£2.60), shepherd's pie (£2.90), Goan fish curry (£7.50), beef bourguignon (£5.50), lasagne (£3.95), pizzas (£4.50) and tarte tatin (£1.95) or cheesecake (£1.95). There's also usually a couple of vegetarian options. The same menu is available throughout the opening hours. Good cafetière coffee and pots of tea are served alongside the pints of stout. The nearby Franciscan Friary in Timoleague Abbey is of great historical interest and dates back to 1230 AD. *Open 12-11.30 (Sun 12.30-2 & 4-11).* **Bar Food** *all day (mid March-Oct & Christmas). No credit cards.*

Timoleague   Lettercollum House   £40

Tel 023 46251   **R**

Timoleague Co Cork   **Map 2 B6**

In a period house which was once a convent and now operates as an independent hostel, organic produce grown on the premises in a walled kitchen garden forms the basis for some unexpectedly sophisticated fare served in a well-proportioned, high-ceilinged dining room with tall windows overlooking the garden and some striking modern paintings. 'Innovative country cooking' is a fair description of the style in dishes like garden salad composé (a mixture of leaves and fresh herbs with, for example, Jerusalem artichoke and a tangy rouille-style dressing), flavoursome, simply presented side vegetables and strong vegetarian options, such as red bean houmus with crudités followed by a hazelnut roast with tomato butter sauce or spinach roulade. Local seafood might feature in a filo parcel with *fines herbes* sauce, roast lamb comes with an unusual tarragon cream and delicious desserts include a range of home-made ices and sorbets, served with dramatic simplicity in a tall iced goblet. *Seats 40. L (Sun only) 1-3 D 7.30-9.30 (to 9 in winter). Closed 1st week Jan-mid Mar. Set Sun L £10 Set D £13.50. Access, Visa.*

Tralee	**Ballyseede Castle Hotel**	60%	£100

Tel 066 25799   Fax 066 25287   **H**

Tralee Co Kerry   Map 2 A5

Just off the Killarney road, this 15th-century castle was once the chief garrison of the Fitzgeralds, Earls of Desmond. Granite pillars and wrought-iron gates stand at the entrance and impressive public rooms include a lobby with Doric columns, two drawing rooms with fine plasterwork and a dining room overlooking ancient oaks. Bedrooms are spacious and comfortable; bathrooms vary considerably. Conference/banqueting for 170. Golf, fishing, riding and shooting available nearby. Children up to the age of 6 stay free in their parents' room. No dogs. *Rooms 14. Garden. Access, Visa.*

Tralee	**Brandon Hotel**	61%	£90

Tel 066 23333   Fax 066 25019   **H**

Princes Street Tralee Co Kerry   Map 23 A5

This pleasantly situated modern hotel is in the heart of medieval Tralee, overlooking a park and the famous Siamsa Tire folk theatre. Recently refurbished throughout, public areas are impressively roomy and, while some bedrooms are on the small side, all are comfortably furnished and have neat, fully-tiled bathrooms with plenty of shelf space and thermostatically-controlled bath taps. The well-equipped leisure centre includes a beauty salon and there are conference and banqueting facilities for 1100/550. Parking for 500 cars. No dogs. The Brandon has recently built a new 49-room budget hotel 100 yards away; not inspected in time for this year's Guide. *Rooms 162. Indoor swimming pool, gym, solarium, sauna, steam room, beauty salon, nightclub.* AMERICAN EXPRESS *Access, Diners, Visa.*

Tralee   Places of Interest

Tourist Information Tel 066 21288
Kerry The Kingdom Tel 066 27777
Tralee Racecourse Tel 066 26188
Listowel Racecourse Tel 068 21144

Tuam	**Cré na Cille**		£50

Tel 093 28232   **R**

High Street Tuam Co Galway   Map 1 B3

Venetian blinds, darkwood tables with place mats, simple cutlery and paper napkins create quite a businesslike lunchtime atmosphere that is enhanced by the crush of people coming in from the street – perhaps more Toulouse than Tuam. Evenings are more formal and the setting softer, but the common link is chef Cathal Reynolds's confident use of local ingredients in generously served food at remarkably keen prices. Typical dishes include black pudding with apple and onion or pan-fried Irish brie in a vermouth sauce followed by black sole meunière or a vegetarian dish of the day. Good baked desserts, typically in classic tarts – apple, strawberry – given a modern twist. *Seats 45. Private Room 30. L 12.45-2.30 D 6-10. Closed L Sat, all Sun, 24-27 Dec, Bank Holidays.* AMERICAN EXPRESS *Access, Diners, Visa.*

Tubbercurry   Killoran's Traditional Restaurant & Lounge

Tel 071 85679   Fax 071 85111

Main Street Tubbercurry Co Sligo   Map 1 B3

"The welcome doesn't die on the doormat" is the motto at Tommy and Anne Killoran's whale of a place; no-nonsense, reliably priced food and authentic entertainment are the draws. On Thursday nights from June to September its 60-seater bar/restaurant/lounge (call it what you will) is crammed to the gunwales, with all and sundry tucking into boxty, potato cakes, crubeens and cali – a local name for hot potato, spring onion and melted butter, better known as champ – to help along the traditional music and Irish dancing. Visitors can even try their hand at butter-churning in the middle of it all. Organic vegetables, local goat's cheese (cheese plate £3) and home-made brown bread are regulars on the menu, alongside more everyday fare. In season, the salmon comes from the river right on the doorstep. There's nowhere else quite like it in Ireland – Killoran's is an original. Not elegant, not folksy, but definitely different. "Children are welcome at any time." *Open 10.30am-11.30pm (Sun from 12.30).* **Bar Food 9-9** *(bar snacks only winter eves). Garden. Closed Good Friday & 25 Dec.* AMERICAN EXPRESS *Access, Diners, Visa.*

Waterford   Dwyer's Restaurant   £55

Tel 051 77478

R

8 Mary Street Waterford Co Waterford   Map 2 C5

In a back street near the bridge Martin Dwyer's comfortable, low-key converted barracks provides an undemonstrative background for his quietly confident cooking. A limited-choice three-course early evening menu is extremely good value, or there's a more flexible table d'hote with a wider choice, plus a good à la carte menu. The Dwyer style is original without being gimmicky, with careful attention to flavour and texture contrasts/combinations. Typical dishes on a winter evening included artichoke soup, melon and cardamom sorbet, Italian-style breast of turkey, roast cod with mussels and fillet of pork with thyme stuffing. Desserts such as marquise of three chocolates or home-made ice cream are equally irresistible. *Seats 30. Parties 20. D only 6-10. Closed Sun, 1 week Christmas, 2 weeks July. Set D £18.50.* AMERICAN EXPRESS *Access, Diners, Visa.*

Waterford   Foxmount Farm   £36

Tel 051 74308   Fax 051 54906

A

Passage East Road Waterford Co Waterford   Map 2 C5

At the heart of a working farm just outside Waterford, this lovely 17th-century house is run by Margaret Kent with a well-judged balance of warmth and professionalism that cossets guests yet leaves them free to come and go – suiting families and lone travellers equally well. Furnished traditionally with grace and style throughout and meticulously maintained, Foxmount offers a rare degree of comfort in reception rooms and bedrooms that vary in size and outlook but are all – including one exceptionally large family room – thoughtfully furnished, with views over well-tended gardens and farmland. Children welcome – cots, baby-sitting, high-chair and early evening meal by arrangement. *Rooms 6 (4 en suite). Garden, tennis, table tennis, snooker. Closed early Nov–early Mar. No credit cards.*

Waterford	Granville Hotel	69%	£83

Tel 051 55111   Fax 051 70307

1 Meagher Quay Waterford Co Waterford   Map 2 C5

On the quay by the River Suir, the Granville is kept in tip-top condition by owners Liam and Ann Cusack and their staff. The style throughout the day rooms is traditional, and there are many reminders of the hotel's history: the Thomas Francis Meagher bar honours an early owner, the Bianconi restaurant salutes another owner (the man who started Ireland's first formal transport system) and the Parnell meeting room remembers where Charles Stewart Parnell made many famous speeches. Stylishly decorated bedrooms of various sizes all have good bathrooms. Children under 12 stay free in parents' room. No dogs. **Rooms 74.** *Closed 25 & 26 Dec.* AMERICAN EXPRESS *Access, Diners, Visa.*

Waterford	Henry Downes		

Tel 051 74118

10 Thomas Street Waterford Co Waterford   Map 2 C5

It is easy to miss this legendary pub so modestly unpubby is the exterior yet, once visited, it will not be forgotten. In the same family for five generations and one of the few remaining houses to bottle their own whiskey, this place is a one-off. Large, dark and cavernous, it incorporates a series of bars of various temperaments each with its own particular following, effortlessly achieving what modern pubs are spending fortunes to copy. The friendly bar staff enjoy filling customers in on the pub's proud history – and will sell you a bottle of Henry Downes' No 9 to take away. *No food. Closed Good Friday, 25 Dec. No credit cards.*

Waterford	Jack Meade's Bar		

Tel 051 73187

Cheekpoint Road Halfway House Waterford Co Waterford   Map 2 C5

This delightful early 18th-century pub has been in the Hartley family for nearly 150 years and owners Carmel and Willie continue to retain its essential character and remarkable charm. The building, which is well kept and cottagey, has not been altered or extended and they make the most of its sun-trap position, with flower tubs at the door and climbing plants up the walls contrasting with the cool, dark, low-ceilinged interior with its two small traditional bars complete with pictures and photographs of local interest and open fires for cold weather; in summer there's traditional music in the open and barbecues at weekends. An agricultural museum of farm machinery and (across the bridge) an old limekiln (for making fertiliser) and ice house (for preserving fish) are among the things to look at. Plans are afoot for an outdoor toilet with facilities for the disabled and mothers with babies. The northern end of the car park is a reeded area and has recently been declared a bird sanctuary. Only

in Ireland? *Open 10am-11.30pm (Sun 12-2.30 & 4-11).* **Bar Food**
*12-8 (Easter-end Oct). Children's playground with slide, swing and
basketball. No credit cards.*

Waterford	Jurys Hotel	61%	£111
Tel 051 32111 Fax 051 32863			**H**
Ferrybank Waterford Co Waterford			**Map 2 C5**

Large modern hotel dominating a hillside on the opposite side
of the River Suir to Waterford town. The spacious lobby/lounge
features a long white marble reception desk, a pair of fine
Waterford crystal chandeliers and a comfortable sitting area.
Of the five floors of bedrooms, all of which share the same fine
view over the city, only the top floor (which is very dated) has
yet to benefit from refurbishment with darkwood furniture,
matching floral curtains, polycotton duvets and smart new
bathrooms with white marble vanity units providing good shelf
space. Up to two children under 14 stay free in parents' room;
20 rooms have both a double and single bed. 24hr room service.
Activity club and video room for children (Mon-Fri) during
school summer holidays. 38 acres of garden. Banqueting for 600,
conference facilities for 700. No dogs. **Rooms** *98. Garden, indoor
swimming pool, plunge pool, gym, solarium, sauna, spa bath, steam
room, hair salon, tennis, children's outdoor play area.
Closed 24-26 Dec.* AMERICAN EXPRESS *Access, Diners, Visa.*

Waterford	Prendiville's Restaurant & Guesthouse	£60
Tel 051 78851 Fax 051 74062		**RR**
Cork Road Waterford Co Waterford		**Map 2 C5**

Peter and Paula Prendiville serve imaginative food at reasonable
prices and with professionalism at their converted gate lodge,
which is just out of the centre and a short drive from the crystal
factory. Paula plans her menus around the best of fresh local
ingredients, and her dishes show a deal of controlled creativity:
spinach pancake filled with smoked salmon; duck liver paté with
Cumberland sauce; roulade of stuffed guinea fowl with bacon,
honey and armagnac; fresh fish of the day. Irish farmhouse
cheeses; tempting desserts. **Seats** *50. Private Room 15. L 12.15-2.15
D 6.30-9.45. Closed Sun, Good Friday, 23-30 Dec. Set L £11.50
Set D (till 8pm) £13.25.* AMERICAN EXPRESS *Access, Diners, Visa.*

Rooms   **£49**

Eight recently redecorated, simply furnished rooms are available,
seven with en-suite facilities and all with phones. Some have
crochet bedspreads and seven rooms have TVs.

Waterford	Tower Hotel	59%	£114
Tel 051 75801 Fax 051 70129			**H**
The Mall Waterford Co Waterford			**Map 2 C5**

Opposite, and taking its name from, an ancient Viking tower,
the hotel has recently been extended and refurbished. The now
spacious lobby copes well with tour groups and a large plush
bar overlooks the River Suir. Apart from a couple of singles,
bedrooms are of a good size and similarly decorated and furnished
with plain walls and simple darkwood furniture whether in the

old or new part of the building. All have good easy chairs and modern bathrooms. 24hr room service. Banqueting for 400, conference facilities for 600. *Rooms 141. Indoor swimming pool, children's splash pool, gymnasium, solarium, sauna, spa bath, steam room. Closed 25-28 Dec.* AMERICAN EXPRESS *Access, Diners, Visa.*

Waterford	Waterford Castle	74%	£220
Tel 051 78203 Fax 051 79316			**HR**
The Island Ballinakill Waterford Co Waterford			Map 2 C5

From the town centre, head for Dunmore East and follow the signs to the hotel, which is situated on its own island. A small chain car ferry transports you across the water to the imposing 18th-century castle with its carved granite arch entrance and studded oak doors. The great hall has a roped-off coat of arms hand-woven into the carpet, a cavernous fireplace, again with the Fitzgerald coat of arms on the chimney breast, old panelling, a fine ribbon plaster ceiling and antique leather chairs, as well as many portraits on the walls. The stylish drawing room has several comfortable sofas and genuine antiques, which also feature in some bedrooms, notably the suites. Others are a combination of the old and the new, but nearly all command fine views of the surrounding parkland and water. Bathrooms, offering good toiletries and bathrobes, have freestanding Victorian bath tubs with gold fittings (but no protective shower curtains), painted washbasins and loos with wooden seats and overhead cisterns and chains! First-rate breakfast includes fresh orange juice and leaf tea. Two conference rooms can accommodate up to 80. The indoor swimming pool is housed separately, a few hundred yards from the hotel. Dogs in kennels only. *Rooms 19. Garden, indoor swimming pool, tennis, golf (18), bicycles.* AMERICAN EXPRESS *Access, Diners, Visa.*

Restaurant £80

Chef Paul McCluskey has been cooking here for several years, and the spectacular dining-room setting – old oak panelling, plaster ceiling, oil paintings and Regency-striped chairs – presents the perfect backdrop for his sound cooking. Both lunch and dinner menus change daily; the latter is twice the price, with only a soup or sorbet in addition. A typical offering might consist of asparagus with a herb mayonnaise, courgette cream soup, fillet of sea bass with bay leaves and white wine, finishing with a chocolate cup on a coffee bean sauce. Service is pleasant enough, the bread good and the coffee strong. The wine list is safe without being particularly outstanding. *Seats 64. Private Room 24. L 12.30-2 D 7-10 (Sun to 9). Set L £16 Set D £33.*

Waterford	The Wine Vault		£40
Tel & Fax 051 53444			**R**
High Street Waterford Co Waterford			Map 2 C5

Wine man David Dennison opened this busy, buzzy bistro in the oldest part of the town in 1993 and the ground-floor restaurant (situated in the remains of an Elizabethan townhouse) has proved the perfect partner for his wine shop in the vaults below, where customers are free to browse and wine tastings and courses are held. Food, under head chef Dara Costello, is informal, bistro-style

with an emphasis on seafood – shellfish spring roll is a typical
starter, the assorted shellfish tossed in garlic, onion and vegetables
and wrapped in a thin pastry (not filo) roll, a juicy, interesting
dish of contrasting textures and flavours, served with a small salad
– and strong vegetarian options, such as savoury courgette – the
vegetable split and stuffed with a delicious mixture of garlicky
vegetables, topped with melted cheese and served with crunchy
garlic bread and a well-dressed salad. Steak and chicken feature
strongly – also game in season, notably venison. Finish with some
plated farmhouse cheeses, with water biscuits and fat black grapes
or a dessert such as a whole poached pear with crunchy almond
ice cream. Diverse, unusual wine list with an exceptional choice
by the glass. **Seats** 40. Parties 10. Meals 10.30am–midnight. L 12.30–
2.30 D 5–11. Closed Sun, Good Friday, 25 Dec. Set L £6.95
Set D from £10.95 (5.30–7.30). Access, Diners, Visa.

Waterford   Places of Interest

Tourist Information Tel 051 75788
Bus Eirann (Irish Bus) Booking Information Tel 051 79000
Waterford Cathedral Tel 051 74757
Waterford Crystal Glass Factory Kilbarry Tel 051 73311
Waterford Racecourse Tramore Tel 051 81425

Waterville	Butler Arms Hotel	68%	£100
Tel 066 74144 Fax 066 74520			**H**
Waterville Co Kerry			Map 2 A6

Once one of Charlie Chaplin's favourite haunts, this landmark
hotel dominates the seafront and much has remained unchanged –
notably a reputation for hospitality and service – although many
improvements have been made in recent years. Public areas,
including two sitting rooms, a sun lounge and a cocktail bar, are
spacious and comfortably furnished for relaxation and peace, while
the characterful beamed Fishermen's Bar (which also has a separate
entrance from the street) offers contrasting buzz. Bedrooms vary
from distinctly non-standard rooms in the old part of the hotel
(which many regular guests prefer) to smartly decorated, spacious
rooms with neat en-suite bathrooms and uninterrupted sea views
in a reconstructed wing opened in 1992, but the standard
of comfort is high throughout. Under-12s may stay free in their
parents' room. 24hr room service. Conference facilites for up to
25. **Rooms** 31. Garden, fishing, tennis, games room, snooker.
Closed mid Oct–mid Apr (private shooting parties Dec & Jan).
 Access, Diners, Visa.

Waterville	The Huntsman	
Tel 066 74124		**P**
Waterville Co Kerry		Map 2 A6

Owner-chef Raymond Hunt has been serving up specialities like
lobster (from the tank), Dublin Bay prawns and local salmon
in this well-established bar and restaurant since 1978 – and red
is the predominant colour in the decor too, so the cool blues and
greys of the sea and sky make a welcome contrast. The snack
menu offers a wide choice of sensibly priced dishes ranging from
a choice of soups, including fresh crab bisque with home-made
bread, through grilled or natural oysters, mussels marinière,

smoked Waterville salmon salad and deep-fried sole with French fries to a popular selection including hamburgers, spaghetti bolognese, omelettes and curries … and Irish stew. There's also a full restaurant menu (not recommended here). The wine list is serious, with France particularly well represented, though the New World gets a look in as well. Accommodation is available – B&B or half-board (not inspected, call ahead during winter months). *Open 10.30-11.30 (Sun 12.30-11).* **Bar Food** *8am-9.30pm.* AMERICAN EXPRESS® *Access, Diners, Visa.*

Waterville   The Smugglers Inn   £33

| Tel 066 74330   Fax 066 74422 | A |

Waterville Co Kerry   Map 2 A6

Pleasantly decorated, quite spacious rooms are available over Harry and Lucille Hunt's famous clifftop pub. All are en suite – the less expensive rooms are shower-only – and there's a comfortable residents' sitting room upstairs, beside the accommodation, with sofas and armchairs, books and television. For the 1995 season the Hunts plan to move the sitting room to a larger room at the front, with magnificent sea views. **Rooms** *12 (1 suitable for disabled). Garden, golf.* AMERICAN EXPRESS® *Access, Diners, Visa.*

Westport   The Asgard Tavern

| Tel 098 25319   Fax 098 26523 | P |

The Quay Westport Co Mayo   Map 1 A3

Named after the sail training ship *Coiste Asgard* (a well-loved visitor to the port), Michael and Mary Cadden's famous quayside bar is appriately decorated with nautical artefacts. The bar menu, served daily in the lounge and Captain's Deck from noon until 9pm, also underlines links with the sea in a varied fish selection including favourites such as seafood chowder (£1.50), Clew Bay oysters (£4.50 half dozen) and main dishes like fisherman's platter (£9) and prawn salad (£7); carnivores are well catered for, too: traditional Irish lamb stew (£5), lasagne (£4.20) or burger (£4.50). The Asgard restaurant upstairs (not specifically recommended here) offers more formal meals in the evening. Music nightly. *Open 10.30-11.30 Mon-Sat (to 11 in winter), Sun 12.30-2, 4-11.* **Bar Food** *12-9. Garden. Closed Mon, Good Friday, 24-26 Dec.* AMERICAN EXPRESS® *Access, Visa.*

Westport   Matt Molloy's Bar

| Tel 098 26655 | P |

Bridge Street Westport Co Mayo   Map 1 A3

Owned by *the* Matt Molloy, of The Chieftains, this is a pleasingly dark, atmospheric pub which feels much smaller than its real extent and has some admirable features, such as a no-TV policy and no children after 9pm. Unsurprisingly, there's a lot of musical memorabilia, including plenty on The Chieftains themselves, but groceries of yesteryear, displayed on high shelves, also pay tribute to the place;s earlier role as a traditional grocer-pub. Traditional music is a big draw here – either in the back room or out at the back in fine weather. *No credit cards.*

Westport — The Olde Railway Hotel — 63% — £60

Tel 098 25166

H

The Mall Westport Co Mayo

Map 1 A3

Beautifully situated along the tree-lined Carrowbeg River on the
Mall in the centre of Westport, the Olde Railway Hotel is the real
McCoy. Once described by William Thackeray as 'one of the
prettiest, comfortablist hotels in Ireland', it was built in 1780 as a
coaching inn for guests of Lord Sligo. Now, in the hands of Mr
and Mrs Rosenkranz (who have owned it since 1984), it retains
considerable character and is well known for its antique furniture
and a pleasing atmosphere of slight eccentricity, although
concessions to the present generation of traveller have been made
in the form of en-suite bathrooms, satellite television and private
car parking, also a secretarial service including use of fax machine
and computer. 'Superior' rooms attract a tariff of £72 (£61
in low season) including service; there are three suites. Public areas
include a conservatory dining room quietly situated at the back
of the hotel and a rather splendid function room with original
stone walls. The large bar is the public face of an essentially
private hotel and the main entrance is from the mall. Children
up to 12 stay free in parents' room; extra bed or cot provided;
three family bedrooms; high-chairs provided. ***Rooms** 24. Garden.
Closed 23-27 Dec.* AMERICAN EXPRESS *Access, Visa.*

Westport — Quay Cottage Restaurant — £50

Tel 098 26412

R

The Harbour Westport Co Mayo

Map 1 A3

A strong maritime theme pervades this cosy, informal, stone-built
waterside cottage and there is much of interest to observe once
tucked into a scrubbed pine table and contemplating the meal
ahead. Not surprisingly, seafood predominates on the menu too –
although other tastes are catered for with lamb chops and steaks,
plus imaginative vegetarian options. Typically, start with whole
fresh langoustines – Dublin Bay prawns by their other name,
a dramatic dish complete with claws and fresh orange garnish, but
less to eat than in a crab salad cocktail, a winner of a dish with lots
of fresh white crab meat, a judicious amount of well-judged
cocktail sauce and a pretty salad garnish as well as plenty of lovely
home-baked brown soda bread. Main courses might include
lobster from the tank, or black (Dover) sole on the bone, or the
unexpected pleasure of monkfish with tagliatelle. Nice homely
desserts – flambéed bananas with rum, perhaps – and freshly-
brewed coffee by the cup. ***Seats** 40. Parties 8. Private Room 10.
L Sun only 1pm D 6-10pm. Closed 24 & 25 Dec, all Jan.*
AMERICAN EXPRESS *Access, Visa.*

Westport — Towers Bar

Tel 098 26534   Fax 098 27017

P

The Harbour The Quay Westport Co Mayo

Map 1 A3

A pair of ancient towers (now preserved buildings) inspired the
name of this characterful, family-friendly pub. Bar food is offered
daily from 12 noon. In addition to a range of seafood – typically
crab or prawn cocktail (£3.75), fish pie (£4.25), baked stuffed

mussels (£4.25), mixed seafood salad (crab, mussels, pranws and smoked fish £7.25) – there's simple fare like ploughman's lunch (£3), home-made burger (£1.30), filled baked potatoes with salad (£3.60) and a vegetarian salad (£2.95) option. Although on the harbour side of the road, there is a walled garden with a safe play area for children that includes a tree house and a sand pit. *Pub open 10.30am-11.30pm Mon-Sat (till 11 in winter), Sun 12.30-2, 4-11. Bar Food 12-9 (except 2-4 Sun). Garden, outdoor eating. Pub closed Good Friday, 25 Dec. Access, Visa.*

Westport   The West Bar

Tel 098 25886   **P**

Lower Bridge Street Westport Co Mayo   **Map 1 A3**

Just across the bridge from the Olde Railway Hotel on a good corner site beside the river, the West Bar is a well-run pub of some character and, being divided up into several sections, intimacy too. There's a restaurant operating separately in the evenings, but bar food is available at lunchtime. *Bar Food 12.30-2.30 Mon-Sat. No credit cards.*

Westport   Westport Woods Hotel   62%   £88

Tel 098 25811   Fax 098 26212   **H**

Louisburgh Road Westport Co Mayo   **Map 1 A3**

A low-rise 1970s building set in trees and within walking distance of Westport House and the harbour pubs and restaurants. First impressions of Westport Woods are mildly positive and, although the interior has dated (a problem particularly noticeable in the foyer/lounge, bar and corridor areas), the friendliness and courtesy of the staff quickly win over new arrivals. Medium-sized rooms also have dated decor but are comfortable, with good amenities including a double and a single bed, TV, direct-dial phone, hairdryer and trouser press, well-placed lights and mirrors and bathrooms which, although small and in need of refurbishing, have all that is necessary, including ample shelf space. Children are exceptionally well catered for: family rooms, cots, extra beds, baby-sitting, indoor/outdoor play areas, supervised activities organised by age group in school holidays, high-chairs and booster seats, early evening meal are all provided. Off-season the focus moves to an older age group and equally well-designed activities for 4-5 day Golden Holidays. *Rooms 57. Banqueting/conferences 120/150. Tennis. Closed 3 weeks Jan.* *Access, Diners, Visa.*

Westport   Place of Interest

Tourist Information Tel 098 25711

Wexford   Archer's

Tel 053 22356   Fax 053 22087   **P**

Redmond Square Wexford Co Wexford   **Map 2 D5**

Just around the corner from *The Granary* restaurant, this very pleasant pub is warm and cosy with a comfortably semi-rustic atmosphere. There's an eating area with proper tables (and a high-chair) just off the main bar for consumption of appealing bar meals – ranging from mussels in garlic butter with home-baked

brown bread to serious main courses such as black sole on the
bone or a 10oz sirloin steak – or tempting sandwiches to have
at the bar. **Bar Food** *5-9pm Mon-Sat. Closed Good Friday, 25 Dec.
Access, Diners, Visa.*

Wexford	**Clonard House**	£32
Tel & Fax 053 43141		**A**
Clonard Great Wexford Co Wexford		Map 2 D5

John and Kathleen Hayes offer a warm welcome at their large
Georgian farmhouse on a dairy farm overlooking Wexford town
and harbour – an Irish coffee at the drawing room fireside before
bed is de rigueur and ensures guests get to know each other.
Rooms vary somewhat but all have TV and en-suite shower and
three have (modern) four-posters. Children welcome (under-3s
stay free in parents' room, 50% under 12); cots, high-chairs,
playroom, outdoor play area. Limited room service. Ample
parking. No dogs. **Rooms** *9. Garden, games room. Closed 12 Nov-
Easter. No credit cards.*

Wexford	**The Granary**	£55
Tel 053 23935		**R**
Westgate Wexford Co Wexford		Map 2 D5

Cosy, with some tables in private booths, this well-established
restaurant has fascinating pictures relating to local history on the
walls and offers a choice of seasonal menus, including special value
on the 4-course dinner menu for early diners. Local produce stars
in starters such as Wexford mussels, baked with tomato, garlic,
tarragon and olive oil or Kilmore crab claws in garlic butter and
Cashel Blue cheese, melted on home-made treacle bread. Main
courses follow suit with seafood like big Kilmore scallops poached
in white wine and prime local meats – steaks with Irish whiskey
sauce or crushed pepper, crispy roast duckling and game, such
as wild duck or venison, in season. Round off with a choice
of farmhouse and local cheeses, served from a big basket,
or a simple dessert such as a compote of autumn fruits, or lemon
tart. **Seats** *45. Parties 6. Private Room 20. D only 6-10. Closed Sun
(except during Opera Festival), 3 days Christmas. Set D from £15.95.*
AMERICAN EXPRESS *Access, Diners, Visa.*

Wexford	**White's Hotel**	69%	£76
Tel 053 22311 Fax 053 45000			**H**
George Street Wexford Co Wexford			Map 2 D5

Although recent improvements mean it now appears to be
modern, much of the original interior of this famous old hotel
has been retained and skilfully integrated to provide maximum
comfort and a wide range of services without undue loss
of character. Public rooms furnished to a high standard include
a popular bar (heart of the Opera Festival social scene, late
Oct/early Nov), choice of sitting rooms, an elegantly appointed
dining room and cosy informality at the red-and-white check-
clothed Country Kitchen grill, which has direct access from the
street. Comfortable bedrooms vary considerably according to age
and situation, but all have recently been refubished with neat
en-suite bathrooms, phone, tea/coffee facilities and satellite TV.
Attractive function rooms include an atmospheric converted barn

– lofty, with exposed stonework and a huge fireplace – and Mr White's, complete with balconied walls. Leisure facilities are in the basement where a singularly sybaritic health and fitness club has been installed – and there's even an imaginative night club, The Cairo club, next door. Banqueting/conferences (600). Parking (35 spaces + 100 nearby). Children welcome (two family rooms): under-5s stay free in their parents' room; cots £2 and high-chairs. No dogs. *Rooms 82. Gym, jacuzzi, steam room, sauna, solarium, beauty salon. Closed 25 Dec.* AMERICAN EXPRESS *Access, Diners, Visa.*

Wexford Places of Interest

Tourist Information Tel 053 23111
Opera Festival (mid Oct-early Nov) Tel 053 22144
Westgate Heritage Centre Tel 053 42611
Johnstown Castle Demesne and Agricultural Museum Tel 053 42888
Irish National Heritage Park Ferry Carrig Tel 053 41733
Wexford Racecourse Tel 053 23102

> When telephoning establishments in the Republic from *outside* the Republic, dial 00-353 then the number we print less the initial zero: eg The Strawberry Tree in Killarney is 00-353 64 32688.

Wicklow Old Rectory 59% £90

Tel 0404 67048 Fax 0404 69181 **AR**

Wicklow Co Wicklow Map 2 D4

Since 1977 Paul and Linda Saunders have been welcoming hosts at their delightful early-Victorian rectory on the edge of town, near the famous Mount Usher gardens (2 miles away). It's decorated with great individuality throughout; the cosy sitting room has a white marble fireplace and traditional furnishings are brought to life by some unusual collections, notably ex-fireman Paul's display of helmets and related paraphernalia. Colourfully decorated bedrooms are all en suite and have many homely extras including fresh flowers. There's an outstanding choice at breakfast (Irish, Scottish or Swiss menus). *Rooms 5. Garden. Closed Nov-end Mar.* AMERICAN EXPRESS *Access, Diners, Visa.*

Restaurant £60

Linda Saunders presents a blend of Victorian and modern, French and Irish in the Orangery dining room area. Most guests choose the special gourmet menu, a no-choice meal which might typically comprise salmon trout quenelles, melon sorbet, pheasant en croute with damson sauce and chocolate and Cointreau mousse in a little chocolate pot accompanied by candied oranges. A particularly unusual and imaginative feature is a floral dinner menu (served only during the Co Wicklow Garden Festival, May-Jun) containing such delights as salmon with marigold sauce, floral pancakes filled with steamed vegetables, or croquembouche with frosted rose petals. No smoking. *Seats 16. Parties 8. D only at 8. Set D £26. Sun-Thu 7.30-9 Fri & Sat.*

Wicklow   Places of Interest

Tourist Information Tel 0404 69117
Mount Usher Gardens Ashford Tel 0404 40116
Arts Festival (June) Tel 045 51347

Youghal   Aherne's Seafood Restaurant   £60

Tel 024 92424   Fax 024 93633   **RR**

163 North Main Street Youghal Co Cork   Map 2 C6

The current owners are the third generation of the FitzGibbon
family to run this renowned restaurant and bar on the N25. Local
seafood is very much the star of the show, appearing famously
in chowder, moules marinière, a hot seafood selection with two
sauces and Youghal Bay lobster served thermidor or hot and
buttered. If your budget doesn't stretch to lobster, try the pasta
with smoked salmon and cream, grilled black sole on the bone
or pan-fried monkfish. The all-day bar menu offers snackier items
as in open fishy sandwiches on home-made brown bread, salads
and even a house pizza. Lovely desserts might include chocolate
roulade, lemon cheesecake or sherry trifle. The wine list, perhaps
surprisingly, has almost as many reds as whites. Prices are fair,
with several bottles under £15. *Seats 60. Private Room 20.
L 12.30-2.15 D 6.30-9.30 Bar food 10.30-10.30. Closed 6 days
Christmas. Set L £15 Set D £25.* AMERICAN EXPRESS *Access,
Diners, Visa.*

Rooms   £100

Aherne's ten stylish en-suite bedrooms are individually decorated
to a very high standard and furnished with antiques.

Youghal   Places of Interest

Myrtle Grove Tel 024 92274
Lismore Castle Gardens Lismore Tel 058 54424 *17 miles*

JAMESON

IRISH WHISKEY

Northern Ireland

Aghadowey   Greenhill House   £42

Tel 01265 868241	**H**
24 Greenhill Road Aghadowey Coleraine Co Londonderry BT51 4EU	Map 1 C1

The Hegartys bought their pleasant Georgian farmhouse in 1969
because they wanted the land and, although graciously framed
by mature trees and lovely countryside views, it is still very much
the centre of a working farm. Elizabeth Hegarty greets arrivals
at her guest house with an afternoon tea in the drawing room that
includes such an array of home-made tea breads, cakes and biscuits
that dinner plans may well waver. Rooms, including two large
family rooms, are unostentatious but individually decorated with
colour co-ordinated towels and linen; good planning makes them
exceptionally comfortable and there are many thoughtful touches
– fresh flowers, fruit basket, chocolate mints, tea/coffee-making
facilities, hairdryer, bathrobe, proper clothes hangers, even a torch.
A 5-course set dinner is available (by arrangement) to residents
(£26 for two) at 6.30pm, except on Sundays; no wines are
provided. *Rooms 6. Garden. Closed Nov-Feb. Access, Visa.*

Annalong   Glassdrumman Lodge   69%   £85

Tel 0139 67 68451 Fax 0139 67 67041	**HR**
85 Mill Road Annalong Co Down BT34 4RH	Map 1 D2

Situated just off the A2 coast road, with lovely views over the sea
or back into the Mournes, this former farmhouse now has
luxurious bedrooms with fresh flowers, fruit, mineral water and
exceptionally well-appointed bathrooms. Service is a high priority,
including 24hr room service, overnight laundry and a secretarial
service, and breakfast a speciality – you can even go and choose
your own newly-laid egg if you like. Beaches, walking, climbing,
and fishing available locally. No tariff reductions for children.
Rooms 10. Garden, tennis, riding. AMERICAN EXPRESS® *Access, Diners, Visa.*

Restaurant   £60

In the French-style restaurant good use is made of organically
grown vegetables and naturally reared beef and pork from the
hotel farm and seafood from local ports. Individual wines by the
glass are chosen to go with each course of the daily-changing
menu (£12-£14 per person extra). No smoking in the dining
room. *Seats 40. Private Room 20. L by reservation only to residents.
D at 8. Set D £25.*

Ballycastle   House of McDonnell

Tel 012657 62975	**P**
71 Castle Street Ballycastle Co Antrim BT64 6AS	Map 1 D1

Unusually, even for a characterful old pub, McDonnell's is a listed
building and as such no changes are allowed inside or out. Not
that change is much on the cards anyway, as it has been in the
family since the 18th century and is clearly much loved – as
visitors soon discover from the colourful chatelaine Eileen O'Neill,
affectionately known as 'the Tipperary Tinker'. She enjoys nothing
better than sharing the history of the long, narrow, mahogany-
countered bar which was once a traditional grocery-bar. Alas,
no food is now offered, but The Open Door, a good traditional
Northern Ireland bakery across the road, has hot snacks and

a wide range of fresh sandwiches to order. Inside the pub is a fine collection of original etched mirrors. Traditional Irish music on Friday nights and folk music on Saturday nights throughout the year. "In every sense, a real, traditional Irish pub."
Open 11.30-11 (Sun 12.30-2.30 & 7-10). No credit cards.

Ballymena	Galgorm Manor	71%	£105
Tel 01266 881001 Fax 01266 880080			**HR**
136 Fenaghy Road Ballymena Co Antrim BT42 1EA			Map 1 D1

Next to a natural weir on the River Maine, which runs through the 85 acres of grounds, this Georgian manor has recently been acquired by new owners who have made a good job of refurbishing the public areas with rich fabrics, warm colour schemes and a scattering of antiques to create an unashamedly luxurious atmosphere. The 'designer-rustic' Gillies Bar in a converted outbuilding offers a change of mood. A couple of Executive bedrooms are stylishly decorated and furnished with antiques but the remainder, although spacious, comfortable and well equipped, do not quite manage to match the style of the public areas; there are five suites. Bathrooms all have separate shower cubicles in addition to the tub. There are also six self-catering cottages in the grounds. An equestrian centre to the rear of the house includes a show-jumping course, eventing cross-country practice area, specially constructed gallops and numerous rides through the estate. The splendid Great Hall conference (for up to 500) and banqueting (up to 450) centre (quite separate from the hotel) is most impressive, with huge Waterford crystal chandeliers and quality decor to match. Considerably reduced tariff at weekends (Fri-Sun). Located to the West of town half-way between Galgorm and Cullybackey. *Rooms 23. Garden, riding, fishing.* AMERICAN EXPRESS *Access, Diners, Visa.*

Restaurant

£70

A fine room with glittering chandeliers, elaborately draped curtains and Arcadian murals depicting the four seasons. New chef Charles O'Neill arrived towards the end of last year but the style of the dinner menu (priced by the choice of main course) remains the same. Starters might be game terrine, three styles of salmon and chicken and lobster sausage and main courses include a good choice of meat (some may be offered from a chargrill) and game as well as a few fish dishes. The cheese trolley is a popular alternative to the half a dozen desserts. Shorter, fixed-price lunch menu. *Seats 73. Parties 24. Private Room 14/60. L 12-2.30 D 7-9.30 (Sun 6-9). Set L £12.90/£16 (Sun £14.50).*

Bangor	Back Street Café	£45
Tel 01247 453990		**R**
14 Queen's Parade Bangor Co Down		Map 1 D2

A dark green, windowless, single-storey building with no name, down an alleyway called The Vennel off the marina waterfront. Don't be put off by the location, though, because inside it's friendly and appealing. Paintings by friends of young chef-patron Paul Arthers adorn the rough orange- and yellow-painted walls, while bentwood chairs sit around white-clothed tables on a quarry-tiled floor. The short menu, priced for two or three

courses, offers generous portions of starters like confit of duck
with black bean sauce, spiced venison meatballs with sautéed
cabbage, thick soy sauce and poppy seeds or wild mushroom
risotto to start, followed by rack of lamb with root vegetable
purée and thyme jus, char-grilled loin of pork with salad and salsa
verde, and beef sirloin on rösti potatoes with béarnaise sauce. Fish
dishes are always a good bet with the day's selection – dependent
on the market – written up on a blackboard. Just a few puds are
offered like bread-and-butter pudding with butterscotch sauce and
an excellent lemon tart or try the plated selection of four Irish
cheeses. Good espresso coffee. Unlicensed (no corkage charge).
*Seats 45. L by arrangement D 6.30-10. Set D £15.95/£17.95.
Closed Sun & Mon, 26 Dec. Access, Visa.*

Bangor	Clandeboye Lodge Hotel	61%	£87
Tel 01247 852500 Fax 01247 852772			**H**
10 Estate Road Clandeboye Bangor Co Down BT19 1UR			Map 1 D2

Just out of town to the west, this brand-new redbrick hotel joins
a pre-existing conference (for up to 350) and banqueting (to 320)
complex near the Blackwood Golf Centre, for which guests enjoy
reduced green fees and priority booking. A few sofas in the rug-
strewn, slate-floored lobby and a small cocktail bar area constitute
the public areas. Good-sized bedrooms are both comfortable and
practical with second phone point for fax or modem and good
lightwood furniture offering plenty of desk space. Bathrooms,
which come with huge bathsheets, all have showers over bathtubs.
Room service operates in the evening and overnight until
breakfast but not during the day. Electric room heaters are
individually controllable, subject to an overriding time control
at reception; best ask for it to be left on if it looks like being a cold
night. Children under 12 stay free in parents' room. Significantly
reduced tariff at weekends for one- or two-night stays. A country-
style pub is in a Victorian schoolhouse building in the hotel
grounds. ***Rooms** 43. Golf, bikes, riding, sea fishing, scuba diving.
Closed 3 days Christmas.* AMERICAN EXPRESS *Access, Diners, Visa.*

Bangor	Shanks	↑	£60
Tel 01247 853313			**R**
Blackwood Golf Centre 150 Crawfordsburn Road Bangor Co Down			Map 1 D2

One of Ulster's newest restaurants, Shanks shares a building with
the brand-new, pay-as-you-play Blackwood Golf Centre just
outside town. The centre itself is part of the Clandeboye Estate
which provides venison, game and even their own Angus beef for
chef Robbie Millar's shortish fixed-price dinner menus. Dishes
such as rare beef salad with rocket, fried polenta and Roquefort,
fresh prawn and cod chowder with truffle oil and chives, crispy
duck confit with fresh foie gras, celeriac purée and wild
mushroom butter, seared 'Whitehead scallops' with salsify,
coriander butter and chinese five spice, and estate venison with
rösti potatoes and a port and peppercorn jus show Robbie's secure
grasp of the modern idiom. The results on the plate demonstrate
sound skills in the kitchen; these are exemplified by the selection
of first-rate home-made breads that arrive with tapénade and
houmus to keep you going while you look at the menu. Front
of house, Robbie's wife Shirley marshalls a smart, keen team who

offer friendly, professional service. Clean-cut, modern decor features a strip-wood floor, contemporary prints on yellow walls, Conran-designed furniture and a window into the kitchen. From the short, wide-ranging wine list that offers plenty of choice at less than £20 a bottle, some half a dozen or so bottles are opened each evening and offered by the glass. The restaurant is open only for dinner but an upstairs bar offers a short snack menu at both lunch and dinner (closed D Sun & D Mon) plus sandwiches and soup all day. Toilets equipped for the disabled. Winner of our Ireland 1995 Newcomer of the Year Award (see page 93). *Seats 60. Parties 16. Private Room 36. L 12.30-2.30 D 7-10. Set D £18.95. Closed all Sun & Mon, 25 & 26 Dec, 1 Jan. Access, Diners.*

Belfast	**Antica Roma**	**£65**
Tel 01232 311121 Fax 01232 310787		° **R**
67 Botanic Avenue Belfast Co Antrim BT7 1JL		Map 1 D2

Impressive decor based on ancient Rome – mosaic floor, classical murals, columns, distressed stucco – combines with more sophisticated Italian cooking at this fashionable restaurant in the university district. The evening à la carte includes the likes of wild mushrooms with crushed chili peppers, garlic and olive oil on toasted bread; gratinated oak-smoked crab claws in a light bisque sauce; boneless quails in Frascati, sage and ground pistachio and *piccata* of veal coated in egg and herbs. *Marengo al miele* (almond meringue filled with sweet mascarpone cheese and honey cream) and *banane* (hot bananas in pastry garnished with a white chocolate mousse and coconut) are typical desserts. Two good-value set menus each provide a choice of four main dishes. Particularly good Italian section on the wine list with some recherché offerings. *Seats 170. Private Room 70. L 12-3 D 6-11.30. Set L £9.95/£12.95. Closed L Sat & all Sun 25 & 26 Dec.* ᴀᴍᴇʀɪᴄᴀɴ ᴇxᴘʀᴇss® *Access, Visa.*

Belfast	**Bengal Brasserie**	**£35**
Tel 01232 640099		**R**
339 Ormeau Road Belfast Co Antrim BT7 3GL		Map 1 D2

About a mile south of the city centre, this recently refurbished Indian restaurant is situated in a modern shopping arcade. Sound Bengali cooking includes a list of daily blackboard specials such as scampi masala, tandoori duck and Indian river fish as well as a wide choice on the main menu with lamb and chicken dishes jostling for space beside prawns, lobster, crayfish and 'European dishes' (steaks with sauces, omelettes, chicken Kiev). Friendly, helpful staff. *Seats 46. L 12-1.45 D 5.30-11.15 (Sun to 10.15). Closed 25 Dec. Access, Diners, Visa.*

Belfast	**Crown Liquor Salon**	
Tel 01232 325368		**P**
44 Great Victoria Street Belfast Co Antrim BT2 7BA		Map 1 D2

Belfast's most famous and best-preserved bar, High Victorian and wonderful in its exuberant opulence. The building belongs to the National Trust and is run by the donors, Bass Taverns, who acquired it in 1979. Upstairs, The Britannic Lounge, with an Edwardian feel, is fitted out with original timbers from the *SS Britannic,* sister ship to the *Titanic. Open 11.30-11.30 Sun 12-2 & 7-10. No credit cards.*

Belfast   Dukes Hotel   67%   £98

Tel 01232 236666   Fax 01232 237177   **H**

65 University Street Belfast Co Antrim BT7 1HL   Map 1 D2

A Victorian facade covers a bright modern hotel in a residential area close to Queen's University and the Botanical Gardens. Black leather and chrome feature in the foyer seating. There are function facilities for up to 140 and a health club. Pastel decor and impressionist prints set the tone in the bedrooms, all double-glazed and some designated non-smoking. This year has seen comprehensive refurbishment of the bar, restaurant and function rooms. Children up to 16 stay free in parents' room. Much reduced weekend rates. ***Rooms** 21. Keep-fit equipment, sauna.* AMERICAN EXPRESS *Access, Diners, Visa.*

> We do not accept free meals or hospitality – our inspectors pay their own bills.

Belfast   Europa Hotel   71%   £130

Tel 01232 327000   Fax 01232 327800   **H**

Great Victoria Street Belfast Co Antrim BT2 7AP   Map 1 D2

A 70s'-built high-rise, Belfast's best-known hotel has gained an impressive new facade as part of a total refurbishment following its acquisition by Hastings Hotels, the province's largest hotel group. Smart public areas cater for all moods, from an all-day brasserie and lively public bar on the ground floor (off the large lobby) to a more relaxed and comfortable split-level cocktail bar-cum-lounge on the first floor where a pianist plays nightly. For the really energetic a disco/night club operates four or five nights a week. Double-glazed bedrooms feature darkwood furniture and matching bedcovers and curtains in stylish floral fabrics. 24hr room service. There is concessionary parking at a nearby multi-storey for which friendly, efficient porters also offer a valet parking service (ask before checking out if you want the cost added to your hotel account). Extensive conference and function facilities (for up to 1200) include a new air-conditioned Eurobusiness centre with its own reception area and full secretarial services. Substantial weekend tariff reductions. ***Rooms** 184. Brasserie (6am-1.30am). Closed 25 & 26 Dec.* AMERICAN EXPRESS *Access, Diners, Visa.*

Belfast   Kelly's Cellars

Tel 01232 324835   **P**

30/32 Bank Street Belfast Co Antrim BT1 1HL   Map 1 D2

A protected building, this characterful bar boasts the oldest cellars in Ireland, dating back to 1720. Food is served in the upstairs bar at lunchtime. Friday and Saturday bring live traditional Irish music. *Open 11.30-11 (till 1am Thur-Sat). Closed Sun & some Bank Holidays. Access, Visa.*

Belfast   Manor House Cantonese Cuisine

£40

R

Tel 01232 238755

43-47 Donegall Pass Belfast Co Antrim BT7 1DQ

Map 1 D2

The main menu at this family-run Cantonese restaurant runs
to more than 300 items, and there are others on the vegetarian and
Peking-style set menus (book 3 days ahead for the vegetarian party
menu). Sound cooking over the whole range, which adds fish
head and duck's web to all the familiar favourites. *Seats 80.
Private Room 50. Meals 12-11.30. Closed 25 & 26 Dec, 12 Jul.
Set L from £5.50 Set D from £14.50. Access, Diners, Visa.*

Belfast   Plaza Hotel   64%

£82

H

Tel 01232 333555   Fax 01232 232999

15 Brunswick Street Belfast Co Antrim BT2 7GE

Map 1 D2

Ultra-modern city-centre business hotel with well-equipped
bedrooms, all with satellite TV, hairdryer and trouser press
as standard, and five conference suites (capacity 70 theatre-style,
100 restaurant-style). There are 14 rooms reserved for non-
smokers. Children up to 10 stay free in parents' room; four rooms
have extra beds. No dogs. *Rooms 76.* AMERICAN EXPRESS *Access,
Diners, Visa.*

Belfast   Roscoff   ★

£75

R

Tel 01232 331532   Fax 01232 312093

Lesley House Shaftesbury Square Belfast Co Antrim BT2 7DB

Map 1 D2

Still *the* Belfast restaurant at which to see and be seen, new sunny
yellow walls and the recent removal of a room divider (originally
intended to make a more private dining area – but it seems that
nobody wanted to be behind it) have brightened and opened
up its modern interior. Given the cachet of a famous chef (Paul
Rankin has two TV series and several books to his credit), slick
service and quality cooking, the £21.50 fixed-price menu (three
courses, coffee and petits fours) offers excellent value for money.
With seven choices at each stage, the modern, weekly-changing
menu offers something to suit most tastes: from the
straightforward and familiar like warm salad of duck confit, sliced
potatoes and green beans, rack of lamb with garlic and parsley
crust, fillet of beef with leeks, shallots and red wine, dark
chocolate truffle cake and tarte tatin to more adventures options
such as tagliatelle with sweetbreads, pancetta and fresh rosemary,
roast haunch of venison with salsify and wild mushrooms,
peppered monkfish with soy glaze and fresh coriander cream, and
coconut creme brulée with fresh mango purée. As an alternative
to the puds there's a good British/Irish cheese trolley. A bowl
of olives and a selection of good home-baked breads give one
something to nibble while looking at the menu. The shorter lunch
menu is in similar style. New World wines are well represented
on an interesting list that also offers half a dozen or so wines
by the glass. *Seats 70. L 12.15-2.15 D 6.30-10.30. Set L £14.50
Set D £21.50. Closed L Sat, all Sun, 11 & 13 July, 25 & 26 Dec,
1 Jan.* AMERICAN EXPRESS *Access, Diners, Visa.*

Belfast   Speranza   £40
Tel 01232 230213   Fax 01232 236752   R
16 Shaftesbury Square Belfast Co Antrim BT2 7DB   Map 1 D2

Large, bustling pizzeria/restaurant on two floors with red check
tablecloths and rustic chalet-style decor. The menu offers a range
of huge crisp-based pizzas and about a dozen pasta dishes (all
at around a fiver) plus a few chicken and other meat dishes
between £6.95 and £10.95 (for the fillet steak). Attentive
service from boys and girls smartly kitted out in bright red
cummerbunds with matching bow ties. For children there are
high-chairs and a special menu written on colouring mats (crayons
supplied) that are entered each week into a prize draw for a toy.
In the same ownership as *Antica Roma* and *Villa Italia* (qv).
Seats *170. D only 5-11.30. Closed Sun, 3 days at Christmas & 11,
12 Jul. Access, Visa.*

Belfast   Stormont Hotel   69%   £137
Tel 01232 658621   Fax 01232 480240   H
587 Upper Newtownards Road Stormont Belfast Co Antrim BT4LP   Map 1 D2

Way out of town on the Newtownards Road, opposite Stormont
Castle, this modern hotel is always busy and bustling, having
various function rooms in addition to the Confex Centre with its
10 purpose-built trade and exhibition rooms. Public areas centre
around a sunken lounge (sometimes used as a conference 'break-
out' area) off which is a cosy cocktail bar. A mezzanine lounge has
huge glass windows overlooking the castle grounds. The majority
of bedrooms have been completely refurbished in recent times and
are spacious, comfortable and practical with good, well-lit work
space and modern easy chairs. Good bathrooms feature marble
tiling. A few rooms are more dated and await refurbishment but
are equally well equipped with satellite TV etc. Smart, helpful
staff offer attentive lounge service and there's a 24hr room-service
menu. Good breakfasts are served in the informal all-day brasserie.
Rooms *106.* AMERICAN EXPRESS *Access, Diners, Visa.*

Any person using our name to obtain free hospitality is
a fraud. Proprietors, please inform the police and us.

Belfast   Strand Restaurant   £35
Tel 01232 682266   Fax 01232 663189   R
12 Stranmillis Road Belfast Co Antrim BT9 5AA   Map 1 D2

Anne Turkington's popular restaurant/wine bar has been
refurbished with Charles Rennie Mackintosh inspiration, and the
eating area has been opened out somewhat. Food is served
throughout the day, and one-plate meals at a bargain £3.95 are
served from noon till 11pm (cod and chips, French onion flan,
chili con carne, liver and bacon hot pot). Sunday lunch (£6.95)
features roast beef. A la carte, the selection runs from soup, oyster
fritters and devilled kidneys to burgers, fillets of pink trout, pork
gorgonzola and aubergine parmigiana. **Seats** *68. Parties 20.
Private Room 30. Open 12-11. Closed 25 & 26 Dec, 12 & 13 July.*
AMERICAN EXPRESS *Access, Diners, Visa.*

Belfast   Villa Italia   £45

Tel 01232 328356   Fax 01232 234978   **R**
39 University Road Belfast Co Antrim BT7 1ND   Map 1 D2

Sister restaurant to *Speranza* (see above) but with a little less
emphasis on pizzas and more on pasta and other Italian dishes.
A shade more upmarket too, although still informal in style, with
quieter background music and less rustic decor. Service is equally
friendly and efficient. **Seats** *180. D only 5-11.30. Closed 24-26
& 31 Dec, 12 July & Easter Sun & Mon. Access, Visa.*

Belfast   The Warehouse   £45

Tel 01232 439690   Fax 01232 230514   **R**
35-39 Hill Street Belfast Co Antrim BT1 2LB   Map 1 D2

A popular and lively "bar with wine and restaurant", whose
menus cover a fair range of tasty, straightforward dishes. From the
evening table d'hote (available on both floors) could come leek
and potato soup, beef and mixed pepper casserole, marinated
herrings with Madeira, hot bread-and-butter pudding, chocolate
biscuit cake and home-made ice creams. Similar à la carte selection
in the restaurant at lunchtime, plus informal lunchtime menu and
evening snack menu in the wine bar. Live music Fri and Sat
nights. **Seats** *90. Private Room 45. Wine bar open for drinks
11.30-11. L 12-3 D 6-9. Closed D Mon, L Sat, all Sun, Bank
Holidays. Set D £13.95/£16.95. Closed 25-27 Dec, Easter Mon, 12
& 13 July.* AMERICAN EXPRESS *Access, Diners, Visa.*

Belfast   Welcome Restaurant   £40

Tel 01232 381359   Fax 01232 664607   **R**
22 Stranmillis Road Belfast Co Antrim BT9 5AA   Map 1 D2

The entrance is topped by a pagoda roof, and inside dragons,
screens and lanterns establish that this is indeed a Chinese
restaurant. The menu runs to over 100 items, mainly familiar,
popular dishes, and there are special menus for individuals and
small parties. **Seats** *60. Parties 20. Private Room 30. L 12-1.45
D 5-10.30. Set L £5. Closed 24-26 Dec, Set L £5, Set D from £12.*
AMERICAN EXPRESS *Access, Diners, Visa.*

Belfast   Wellington Park   59%   £90

Tel 01232 381111   Fax 01232 665410   **H**
21 Malone Road Belfast Co Antrim BT9 6RU   Map 1 D2

Redesigned foyer, amalgamated bar and restaurant areas and
bedroom upgrades have kept the Wellington Park up to date. The
locality and a thriving conference business (capacity 160 theatre-
style) ensure a lively atmosphere, but one of the three bars is kept
exclusively for residents. Children up to 12 stay free in parents'
room. Residents have free use of Queens University's sports centre,
5 minutes from the hotel. No dogs. **Rooms** *50. Closed 25 Dec.*
AMERICAN EXPRESS *Access, Diners, Visa.*

Belfast   Places of Interest

Tourist Information Tel 01232 246609
Mount Stewart House and Gardens (NT) Greyabbey Tel 012477 88387
   17 miles
Ulster Museum and Botanic Gardens Tel 01232 381251
Belfast Zoo Tel 01232 776277 *5 miles North*
Malone House Art Gallery and Gardens Upper Malone Rd Tel 01232
   681246
Dixon Park Upper Malone Rd Tel 01232 320202
Ulster Folk & Transport Museum Tel 01232 451519
Down Royal Racecourse Lisburn Tel 01846 621256 *6 miles*
   Theatres and Concert Halls
Grand Opera House Great Victoria St Tel 01232 241919
Lyric Theatre Ridgeway St Tel 01232 381081
Ulster Hall Bedford St Tel 01232 323900
Group Theatre Bradford St Tel 01232 229685

Belfast Airport   Aldergrove Airport Hotel   62%   £80

Tel 01849 422033   Fax 01849 423500   **H**

Belfast Airport Co Antrim BT29 4AB   **Map 1 D2**

The only hotel actually at the international airport, which is about
17 miles to the south of the city centre. Built two years ago as a
Novotel it is now under local management but continues to offer
good practical accommodation. All rooms have plenty of work
space and, with families in mind, a sofa bed with additional
truckle bed underneath; three rooms are equipped for disabled
guests. Two children under 10 may stay free in their parents'
room. Multi-channel TV includes flight information. 24hr room
service. Banqueting/conference facilities for 180/250. Tariff
redcutions at weekends. Formerly a *Novotel*. **Room** *108. Keep-fit
equipment, sauna, outdoor children's play area.* AMERICAN EXPRESS *Access,
Diners, Visa.*

If we recommend meals in a hotel or inn a **separate**
entry is made for its restaurant.

Bushmills   Bushmills Inn   58%   £78

Tel 012657 32339   Fax 012657 32048   **H**

25 Main Street Bushmills Co Antrim BT57 8QA   **Map 1 C1**

After the Giant's Causeway, the world's oldest distillery
at Bushmills is the biggest attraction in the area (and well worth
a visit; mid-week is most interesting); the Bushmills Inn also
attracts year-round local support. The exterior, including a neat
garden at the relocated (back) main entrance, creates a welcoming
impression that extends into the hall, with its open fire and
country antiques, and other public areas that encompass several
bars and a large dining room. Bedrooms are quite modest,
individually decorated and comfortably furnished; some family
rooms are remarkable for their ingenious use of space. A beamed
loft provides a splendid setting for private functions (up to 85
people) and the 'secret library', a unique venue for special
occasions. **Rooms** *11. Garden, fishing. Access, Visa.*

Bushmills   Places of Interest

Giant's Causeway Tourist Information Tel 012657 31855/31582
Dunluce Castle
The Old Bushmills Distillery Tel 012657 31521

Carnlough   Londonderry Arms

Tel 01574 885255   Fax 01574 885263   **P**

20 Harbour Road Carnlough Glens of Antrim Co Antrim BT44 0EU   **Map 1 D1**

In the same family for nearly half a century, this hotel-and-bar
makes a good stop at a most attractive little harbour on the famous
scenic coastal route and it's well known for 'good, plain food'. The
same snacks are available in both bars (hotel and public): soup
with home-baked wheaten bread, scones, open prawn sandwich,
paté, chef's lunchtime roast. *Open 11.30-11.30 (Sun 12-11)*. ***Bar
Food** 10am-8pm (only sandwiches after 6pm). Garden.* AMERICAN EXPRESS
Access, Diners, Visa.

Carnlough   The Waterfall

No Telephone   **P**

High Street Carnlough Co Antrim BT44 0EP   **Map 1 D1**

Not as old as it may first appear to be, the little public bar
is nevertheless full of charm, with red-tiled floor and low
beamed ceiling. Both the fireplace and bar are made of reclaimed
bricks from an old mill across the road and there's a clatter
of memorabilia hanging from the ceiling; the walls are used
to show off a collection of horse tackle and old posters. Behind,
there's a cosy lounge bar with stained-glass window (from the
owner's previous pub), decorative plates and another brick
fireplace, where bar meals are served. A welcoming place
with a lovely friendly atmosphere. *No credit cards.*

Carrickfergus   The Wind-Rose Bar   £57

Tel 019603 64192   Fax 019603 51164   **JaB**

The Marina Carrickfergus Co Antrim BT38 8BE   **Map 1 D2**

Overlooking the marina, a well-appointed, formal restaurant
on the upper floor is approached by an exterior spiral staircase and
has clear views across Belfast Lough (booking essential). A typical
meal might be terrine of monkfish followed by cutlets of lamb
and spinach soufflé with the house speciality crepes Suzette
to finish. The ground-floor wine bar below has a pubby
atmosphere with a strongly nautical theme and provides simple
bar food. ***Seats** 46. Open 12-12. Bar Food L 12-2.30 snacks 2.30-5
D 7-9. Closed Sun & Mon, 25 & 26 Dec.* AMERICAN EXPRESS *Access, Visa.*

Comber   La Mon House   59%   £85

Tel 01232 448631   Fax 01232 448026   **H**

The Mills 41 Gransha Road Comber Co Down BT23 5RF   **Map 1 D2**

Public areas in this low-rise modern hotel include a bar featuring
copper-topped tables, a small residents' lounge (which may be
in private use), carvery restaurant and a fun bar with lots
of entertainments including a Friday night disco. Practical
bedrooms have simple fitted furniture; nine large rooms have
balconies and there are eight small singles with shower only.

Families will enjoy the country health club and outdoor areas. Banqueting facilities for 450, conference up to 1100 theatre-style. Regular Saturday night dinner dances. In the countryside, 5 miles from Belfast city centre. No dogs. **Rooms** 38. *Garden, indoor swimming pool, gymnasium, sauna, solarium, whirlpool bath, games room.*  *Access, Visa.*

Hotel sporting facilities are highlighted in the Quick Reference lists for easy comparison.

Comber   Places of Interest

Down Country Museum Downpatrick Tel 01396 615218
Mount Stewart Newtownards Tel 0124774 387
Wildfowl and Wetlands Centre Castle Espie Tel 01242 874146 *3 miles*
Nendrum Monastery Mahee Island
Rowallane Garden Tel 01238 510131
Downpatrick Racecourse Downpatrick Tel 01396 612054
Newtownards Priory *3 miles*
Ballycopeland Windmill *8 miles*
Northern Ireland Aquarium Portaferry Tel 012477 28062 *26 miles*
Grey Abbey *10 miles*

Crawfordsburn	Old Inn	£85
Tel 01247 853255 Fax 01247 852775		∎
15 Main Street Crawfordsburn Co Down BT19 1JH		Map 1 D2

Located off the main Belfast to Bangor road, this 16th-century inn is in a pretty village setting and is said to be the oldest in continuous use in all Ireland. Its location is conveniently close to Belfast and its City Airport. Oak beams, antiques and gas lighting emphasise the natural character of the building, an attractive venue for business people (conference facilities and banqueting for 90) and private guests alike. Individually decorated bedrooms vary in size and style, most have antiques, some four-posters and a few have private sitting rooms; all are non-smoking. Romantics and newly-weds should head for the recently refurbished honeymoon cottage. Free private car parking for overnight guests. No dogs. **Rooms** *33. Garden. Closed 24-26 Dec.*  *Access, Diners, Visa.*

Cushendall   P J McCollam

No Telephone   **P**

23 Mill Street Cushendall Co Antrim BT4 0RR   Map 1 D1

In the family for 300 years and under the current ownership
of Joe McCollam for the last 73 years, this magical place has a tiny
front bar complete with a patchwork of photographs of local
characters, many of them sheep farmers (and great fiddle players)
who come down from the glens at weekends. The range in the
old family kitchen behind the bar is lit on cold evenings and
a converted 'cottage' barn across the yard makes a perfect
setting for the famous traditional music sessions. Hospitable
and full of character. *Open 11.30-11 (Sun 7-10pm only).*
Closed Sunday lunchtime. No credit cards.

Dunadry   Dunadry Inn   64%   £100

Tel 01849 432474   Fax 01849 433389   **H**

2 Islandreagh Drive Dunadry Co Antrim BT41 2HA   Map 1 D2

Originally a paper mill, founded early in the 18th century, later
a linen mill, now a well-known riverside hotel 15 minutes from
Belfast city centre and 10 from the airport. Best bedrooms are
on the ground floor, with access to the gardens. Executive rooms
feature computer points and fax machines. The Copper Bar under
the main staircase is a popular spot for a drink and the lunchtime
buffet. Extensive conference facilities. Children up to 5 stay free
in parents' room. No dogs. **Rooms** 67. *Garden, croquet, crazy golf,
game fishing, bicycles, indoor swimming pool, keep-fit equipment, spa
bath, sauna, steam room, solarium. Closed 24-27 Dec.* AMERICAN EXPRESS
Access, Diners, Visa.

Dunadry   Place of Interest

Antrim Round Tower

Dundrum   Buck's Head Inn

Tel 013967 51868   Fax 013967 51898   **P**

77 Main Street Dundrum nr Newcastle Co Down BT33 0LU   Map 1 D2

Situated on the main Belfast-Newcastle road, this attractive,
welcoming family-run pub offers fairly traditional bar food from
a blackboard menu which changes daily. Although recently
renovated, the decor within the pub is traditional in a comfortably
understated way, creating a warm, relaxed atmosphere. The
restaurant is in a new conservatory area added to the back of the
pub, looking out on to a walled garden where tables are set up in
summer. Light, bright and pleasantly furnished with cane chairs
and well-appointed tables, the menu includes variations on old
favourites like deep-fried Brie on a bed of crispy salad with hot
garlic butter or roast duckling with orange and ginger sauce, but
also less predictable offerings such as grilled sardines with fresh
tomato sauce. Three-course Sunday lunch £10.90 includes
tea/coffee. Local produce is put to good use in both bar and
restaurant meals. *Open 11.30-11, Sun 12-2.30, 5.30-10.* **Bar Food**
all day. **Restaurant Meals** *12-2.30, 5.30-9.30 (not Sun eve). High
tea 5.30-8.30. Children allowed in bar to eat. Garden, outdoor eating.
Closed 25 Dec. Access, Visa.*

Dunmurry	**Forte Posthouse Belfast**	67%	£86

Tel 01232 612101   Fax 01232 626546

300 Kingsway Dunmurry Co Antrim BT17 9ES

H

Map 1 D2

This business-oriented hotel is a short drive from Belfast city
centre and airport, and was until recently a *Forte Crest*.
Accommodation includes Lady Crest rooms, non-smoking rooms
and rooms designated as family-size. Children up to 16 stay free
in parents' room. 24hr room service. Conference/meeting facilities
for up to 450. Free parking for 200 cars. ***Rooms** 82. Keep-fit
equipment, squash.* *Access, Diners, Visa.*

Enniskillen	**Blakes of the Hollow**		

Tel 01365 322143

6 Church Street Enniskillen Co Fermanagh BT74 3EJ

P

Map 1 C2

Named after the natural dip at the centre of the town where it is
located, Blakes has been in the same family since 1929. Although
its age and agelessness (it was restored in 1887) are the main
attractions, body and soul can be kept together on the premises
by the consumption of sandwiches and soup (the latter
at lunchtime only). *Open 11.30-11 (Sun 7-10). Closed Sunday
lunchtime. No credit cards.*

Fivemiletown	**Blessingbourne**		£90

Tel 01365 521221

Fivemiletown Co Tyrone

H

Map 1 C2

Built in 1874 in the Elizabethan style and immaculately
maintained by its hospitable owners, Robert and Angela Lowry,
Blessingbourne is a delightful fairytale house of great character
with mullioned windows, beautiful grounds including a private
lake – and lovely views across the estate to the mountains beyond.
Furnished in style and comfort with family antiques, the reception
rooms are elegant yet relaxed and the four bedrooms (one with
a four-poster bed) are very comfortably furnished and, in true
country house tradition, share two bathrooms. An unusual
attraction is the Blessingbourne carriage and household museum,
a collection, which guests are free to browse around, open to the
public by arrangement (admission £1.50). Woodland walks are
an added attraction. ***Rooms** 4. Garden, terrace, swimming pool,
tennis, rowing, fishing. Closed Christmas week. No credit cards.*

Garvagh	**MacDuff's Restaurant, Blackheath House**		£50

Tel & Fax 0265 868433

112 Killeague Road Garvagh nr Coleraine Co Londonderry BT51 4HH

RR

Map 1 C1

A basement restaurant under a fine, immaculately kept Georgian
house, MacDuff's is characterful, comfortable and convivial.
There's a small reception area run by staff who cope well under
the busiest of circumstances. The generally relaxed atmosphere
is carried through to a comforting ring of familiarity on Margaret
Erwin's menu in starters like Stilton puffs with hot, sweet and sour
sauce and twice-baked soufflé with summer salad – popular
perennials kept on the menu by requests from regulars. Spicing is a
feature, but traditional main courses like grilled wild local salmon

with hollandaise are also given a further lift, as in a garnish
of crispy dulse; local catches feature in a classic seafood symphony
with halibut, fat prawns and mussels in a light wine sauce. Good
desserts might include hazelnut meringue with raspberries
(including a generous 'wee dram' of Drambuie in the cream)
or simple Jamaican banana, split and grilled with rum and sugar.
No children under 12. No smoking. On the A29 four miles north
of Garvagh. *Seats 36. Parties 20. Private Room 14. D only 7-9.30.
Closed Sun & Mon. Closed 3 days at Christmas. Access, Visa.*

Rooms   £60

Accommodation is available in five large, comfortably furnished
en-suite rooms with lovely views over the gardens and
surrounding countryside. No children under 12.

Garvagh   Place of Interest

Leslie Hill Farm Park by Ballymoney Tel 01265 666803

Helen's Bay   Deanes on the Square   ↑   £60
Tel 0247 852841   **R**
7 Station Square Helen's Bay Co Down BT19 1TN   Map 1 D2

When the railways arrived in the 1860s the first Marquis
of Dufferin and Ava built his own station – in Scottish baronial
style. Still a functioning railway station, the building is now
a novel restaurant and home to some exciting cooking by Michael
Deane. Dishes like smoked salmon sausage with basil pesto,
marinated duck with tandoori sausage and soya, and tender slices
of venison on rösti potato surrounded by strips of pheasant and
chicken in a mustard sauce are full of flavour and if you think
whiting is a dull fish try Michael's creamed whiting with baby
capers as a starter. Portions are generous and presentation attractive
yet unfussy. No à la carte but a couple of fixed-price menus, both
with choices, or try the multi-course tasting menu – most fun
when you allow each dish to be a surprise when it arrives. From
part of the restaurant you can see into the kitchen and some
windows look out on to the platform. There is a small bar in
the basement. *Seats 40. L Sun 12.30-2.30 D 7-10. Set L £15
Set D from £18 & £30. Closed D Sun & all Mon, 2 weeks Jan &
1 week July.*

Hillsborough   The Hillside Bar
Tel 01846 682765   **P**
21 Main Street Hillsborough Co Down   Map 1 D2

A delightful, well-run bar, The Hillside is easily found in the
centre of this pretty little town – and very well worth finding
it is, too – winner of our Ireland 1995 Pub of the Year award (see
page 89). The atmosphere is warm and cosy in both the main bar
and a smaller one to the side, which has its own fire; throughout,
the atmosphere is gently rustic – dark green paint and soft country
browns and greys in natural materials – and comfortably set
up for eating. At lunchtime there's a self-service arrangement,
giving way to a bar menu served by charming young staff
in uniform T-shirts during the afternoon and evening. Typical
fare from the bar menu might include Hillside paté, a really
excellent rough liver paté served with Cumberland sauce and hot,

toasted wheaten bread, chicken and mushroom pie – crisp home-made pastry over a creamy chicken and mushroom filling – and a ploughman's lunch or tagliatelle carbonara. Home-made beef burgers are flame-grilled and come with hash browns and a choice of sauces; you can finish with a home-baked fruit pie or a daily dessert special. The wine list offers a really good range of wines served by the glass. Outside seating for 30. *Bar Food from 11.30, self-service to 2.30 (Sat to 3); bar menu to 8pm and 12.30-2 Sun (table service). Closed Good Friday & 25 Dec.* AMERICAN EXPRESS® *Access, Diners, Visa.*

Holywood	**Bay Tree**	
Tel 01232 426414		**JaB**
Audley Court 118 High Street Holywood Co Down		**Map 1 D2**

Reached via an archway opposite the police station in the main street (one can also drive through to a small car park at the rear), the Bay Tree is part pottery shop, with the work of over 30 Irish potters on show, and part small coffee shop, where Sue Farmer's delicious cooking is the big attraction. Throughout the day there are various cakes – carrot, chocolate (both 90p), fresh pineapple crunch, chocolate chantilly tart (both £1.50) and tray bakes – while lunchtime brings savoury items like vegetable moussaka (£3.60), ham open sandwich (£4) and vegetable and chicken lasagne (£3.70). Open for dinner on the first and last Friday of each month but booking is essential. There are a couple of tables on a small patio. No smoking. *Seats 34. Open 10-4.30 (D first & last Fri of month only 7.30-11). Closed Sun, 3 days Christmas, 3 days Easter & 2 or 3 days around 12 July. No credit cards.*

Holywood	**Culloden Hotel**	**72%**	£157
Tel 01232 425223 Fax 01232 426777			**HR**
142 Bangor Road Craigavad Holywood Co Down BT18 0EX			**Map 1 D2**

Originally a palace of the Bishops of Down, this splendid 19th-century building in Scottish Baronial style stands in 12 acres of gardens overlooking Belfast Lough. Antiques, stained glass, fine plasterwork and paintings grace the day rooms. Good-sized, well-furnished bedrooms are mostly in an extension. There are two restaurants, an inn in the grounds, various function suites and a well-appointed health and fitness club. No dogs. *Rooms 89. Garden, indoor swimming pool, keep-fit equipment, squash, sauna, spa bath, solarium, tennis, snooker, hairdresser, beauty salon. Closed 24-25 Dec.* AMERICAN EXPRESS® *Access, Diners, Visa.*

The Mitre Restaurant	£65

Comfortable and relaxing, with friendly, efficient service. The menu is quite extensive, ranging from traditional grills and classics such as scampi provençale or garlic snails to more contemporary creations like pan-fried monkfish with vegetable tagliatelle and a tomato/Pernod sauce. Sunday lunch always features a roast on the fixed-price menu. Separate vegetarian menu. There is also a grill bar in the complex, 'The Cultra Inn'. *Seats 140. Private Room 40. L 12.30-2.30 D 7-9.45. Closed L Sat. Set L & D £17.*

Holywood   Sullivans   £55

Tel & Fax 0232 421000   **R**
Sullivan Place Holywood Co Down BT18 9JF   **Map 1 D2**

Bright and cheerful with sunny yellow walls and colourfully
upholstered chairs, Sullivans operates as a coffee shop during the
day (Devon scones, pecan pie and lunchtime savouries like venison
terrine, salmon and leek quiche and soup) before turning into
a fully-fledged restaurant at night. After only a short time the
accomplished cooking of young chef-patron Simon Shaw
(formerly at *Roscoff* in Belfast) has already gained such a loyal
following that booking is advisable at weekends. Dishes like
a crispy duck confit wth roast beetroot and truffle oil, grilled
vegetables on sun-dried tomato bread and pigeon breast with
polenta come in portions substantial enough to satisfy local
appetites. Desserts range from pears poached in Claret with ice
cream to sweet ginger and apricot creme brulée. There's a short
à la carte in addition to the *prix fixe*. Unlicensed, but there are
a couple of wine merchants nearby. *Seats 40. L 10-2.30
D 6.30-10.30. Set D £19. Closed Sun, 1 week July & 25 & 26 Dec.
Access, Visa.*

Holywood   Place of Interest

Ulster Folk and Transport Museum Cultra Tel 01232 428428

Kesh   Lough Erne Hotel   60%   £56

Tel 01365 631275   Fax 01365 631921   **H**
Main Street Kesh Co Fermanagh BT93 1TF   **Map 1 C2**

Located in the town centre but making the most of its position
on the banks of the Glendurragh River, this friendly family hotel
offers homely accommodation in rooms that tend to be on the
small side but have all recently been modernised, with en-suite
bath/shower rooms, TV and tea/coffee facilities. The downstairs
bar and function rooms are particularly attractive, with
direct access to a paved riverside walkway and garden.
Banqueting/conference for 200/250. Children welcome – cots,
baby-listening/sitting, high-chairs and early evening meals
available. *Rooms 12. Garden, fishing. Closed 24 & 25 Dec.*
AMERICAN EXPRESS *Access, Diners, Visa.*

Many hotels offer reduced rates for weekend or out-of-season
bookings. Always ask about special deals.

Larne   Magheramorne House   63%   £66

Tel 01574 279444   Fax 01574 260138   **H**
59 Shore Road Magheramorne Larne Co Antrim BT40 3HW   **Map 1 D1**

53 acres of woodland overlooking Larne Lough provide a fine
setting for a late-Victorian house which offers fresh, bright
bedrooms, banqueting/conference facilities for up to 180 and free
parking for 150 cars. Extensive Victorian gardens. No dogs.
Rooms 22. Garden. AMERICAN EXPRESS *Access, Diners, Visa.*

Larne   Places of Interest

Ballylumford Dolmen Island Magee
Carrickfergus Castle *12 miles*

Londonderry   Beech Hill House Hotel   59%   £85

Tel 01504 49279   Fax 01504 45366   **HR**

32 Ardmore Road Londonderry Co Londonderry BT47 3QP   **Map 1 C1**

Dating from 1726, Beech Hill is a substantial house set in 36 acres
of mature parkland in the rural hinterland south of the city; the
hotel is signposted off the main A6 as you approach Londonderry
from the Belfast direction. Very much centred around its
restaurant and three function/meeting rooms (for up to 100) the
only day room is a comfortable bar/lounge with unusual 'cattle
head' frieze under the ceiling. Attractive, individually decorated
bedrooms vary in shape and size and boast a variety of antique
pieces along with a well-lit desk or work space. Telephones are
standard, as are remote-control TVs (the latter with set-top ariels
so reception is not always perfect). 13 of the bathrooms have
shower and WC only. No dogs. **Rooms** *17. Garden, tennis.
Closed 24 & 25 Dec.* AMERICAN EXPRESS *Access, Visa.*

Ardmore Restaurant   £65

The dining room is a former billiard room where green Regency-
striped wallpaper, brass 'oil lamp' lights and views over the
gardens set the scene for chef Noel McMeel's generously-
portioned, enthusiastic cooking. From the à la carte, start perhaps
with venison sausage on a 'spaghetti' of vegetables surrounded
by juniper berry sauce or some fresh salmon on celeriac chips
with potato rösti, a basil quenelle and tomato cream; follow with
a main dish like best end of lamb roasted with mustard and
Provencal breadcrumbs, a trio of chicken or stuffed roast
tenderloin of pork with a rosemary and garlic crust. A daily-
changing fixed-price menu (you can mix and match) adds to the
choice with dishes like seafood sausage on vegetables with
a tarragon sauce (an excellent sausage but it actually came with
a Meaux mustard sauce at a recent meal), confit of duck with
purée potatoes and pesto dressing, and sirloin of beef with a red
wine and port jus. There is also an interesting vegetarian menu
with a good choice. As an alternative to puds such as white
chocolate and mint gateau with an orange jus or a traditional
plum pudding with brandy sauce try the plated selection of Irish
cheeses that might come with their own home-baked walnut
bread and dried fruit. **Seats** *40. Parties 8. L 12-2.30 D 7-9.30.
Set L £13.95 Set D £18.95.*

Londonderry   Everglades Hotel   59%   £80

Tel 01504 46722   Fax 01504 49200   **H**

Prehen Road Londonderry Co Londonderry BT47 2PA   **Map 1 C1**

South of the town on the banks of the River Foyle, this modern
low-rise hotel is a popular venue for conferences and banqueting
(350/250) besides providing bright, practical accommodation.
Top of the bedroom range are two suites with jacuzzis and turbo
showers. Children up to 12 stay free in parents' room. **Rooms** *52.
Garden. Closed 24 & 25 Dec.* AMERICAN EXPRESS *Access, Diners, Visa.*

Londonderry   Places of Interest

Tourist Information Tel 01504 267284
Derry's Walls
St Columb's Cathedral off London St Tel 01504 262746
O'Doherty's Tower Magazine St Tel 01504 265238
Display Centre Butcher St Tel 01504 362016
Ulster-American Folk Park Omagh Tel 01662 243292
Brachmore Stone Circus nr Cookstown

Newcastle	Slieve Donard Hotel	63%	£99
Tel 013967 23681 Fax 013967 24830			**H**
Downs Road Newcastle Co Down BT33 OAG			Map 1 D2

Imposing red-brick Victorian railway hotel facing the Irish Sea
(next to the Royal County Down Golf Club) with the Mountains
of Mourne in the background. 'The Slieve' caters mainly
to conferences in winter and holidaymakers, tour groups and
weddings in the summer. A grand, galleried entrance hall sets the
tone for public areas which include a large elegant lounge with
conservatory extension (sometimes used for functions), cosy
library sitting room and a bar named after Charlie Chaplin, who
once stayed here. Bedrooms vary in shape and size but, apart from
the third currently being refurbished, share the same blue and
peach colour scheme, polycotton duvets and dark mahogany
furniture. The only advertised room service is breakfast, and that
is not available for conference delegates. Good leisure centre.
Parking for 300 cars. ***Rooms*** *117. Garden, tennis, indoor swimming
pool, gymnasium, solarium, steam room, beauty salon, table tennis,
shop.* AMERICAN EXPRESS *Access, Diners, Visa.*

Newcastle   Places of Interest

Seaforde Gardens Tel 01396 87225 *5 miles*
Castle Ward Strangford Tel 01396 86204 *15 miles*

Portaferry	Portaferry Hotel	63%	£85
Tel 012477 28231 Fax 012477 28999			**H R**
10 The Strand Portaferry Co Down BT22 1PE			Map 1 D2

Formed out of an 18th-century terrace on the seafront, where
the ferry crosses the neck of Strangford Lough, the Portaferry
has been substantially remodelled over recent years to create
a delightful small hotel run with a winning combination of charm
and professionalism by John and Marie Herlihy. Public areas
include a tweedy bar and several tastefully decorated little lounges
sporting pictures of the surrounding area by local artists. Light,
airy bedrooms come with lightwood furniture and matching
floral bedcovers and curtains, neat bathrooms with huge bath
sheets. No dogs. ***Rooms*** *14. Closed 24 & 25 Dec.* AMERICAN EXPRESS
Access, Diners, Visa.

Restaurant   £65

The secret of Anne Truesdale's cooking is the use of the best local
produce in dishes that are essentially simple, although not without
interest. Lamb from the mountains of Mourne and Ulster beef
feature but it's seafood that takes pride of place with amazingly
plump scallops from the Lough (pan-fried with garlic and bacon
perhaps or baked in white wine and cheese), Murlough Bay

mussels, prawns from Portavogie, Ardglass crab (in filo pastry
with tomato and basil sauce), goujons of monkfish (with fresh
lime sauce), salmon (wild Irish in season) and lobsters from their
own tanks. Vegetables, often organically grown, are well handled
too. At lunchtime there is a fairly extensive bar menu that is also
served in the dining room except on Sundays, when there is a
fixed-price menu that always features a traditional roast. *Seats 80.
L 12.30-2.30 D 7-9. Set L (Sun only) £12.95, set D £17.50.
Closed 24 & 25 Dec.*

Portballintrae	Bayview Hotel	58%	£70
Tel 02657 31453 Fax 02657 32360			**H**
2 Bayhead Road Portballintrae nr Bushmills Co Antrim BT57 8RZ			Map 1 C1

Overlooking the tiny harbour and the bay, the long pebbledash
hotel building stands half a mile from the main A2 coastal route.
Functions and conferences (up to 300) are quite big business, but
residents have their own sitting room, and there's also a convivial
bar. Bedrooms include one semi-suite with a small sitting room
area and generally have modern bathrooms. Six cottages are
a short distance from the hotel; these are let as self-catering or as
three-bedroom suites. Dogs by prior arrangement only. *Rooms 16.
Indoor swimming pool, sauna, solarium, snooker. Access, Visa.*

Our inspectors **never** book in the name of Egon Ronay's
Guides. They disclose their identity only if they are
considering an establishment for inclusion in the next
edition of the Guide.

Portrush	Ramore	★	£55
Tel 01265 824313			**R**
The Harbour Portrush Co Antrim BT56 8BN			Map 1 C1

The sheer cosmopolitan buzz of this waterside restaurant, with its
sleek, chic black-and-chrome decor, smoothly operating open
kitchen flanked by huge baskets of freshly baked breads and
serried ranks of highly professional staff, is apt to take the
uninitiated by surprise. It's trendier than one might expect to find
in Portrush town and a tribute to the remarkable style of chef
George McAlpin and the family team that their bright, airy
restaurant continues to attract flocks of enthusiastic diners from
throughout Ireland and beyond. Local seafood still predominates,
but a keen feeling for the mood of the moment imbues the
cooking with unusual immediacy in starters like Dublin Bay
prawns or fresh asparagus with egg-filled ravioli. The wide variety
of modestly priced main dishes (escalopes of peppered fillet steak,
confit of duck, rack of Irish lamb) includes a handful of interesting
'complete dishes' such as a local version of paella or garlic cream
chicken – remarkable value at £7.50. Desserts are a speciality:
there is always a hot soufflé on the list – perhaps hot fresh
fruit and Grand Marnier – and daily blackboard specials like
an excellent tangy lemon tart. Very good coffee, served with petits
fours. *Seats 85. D only 6.30-10.30 (lunchtime wine bar downstairs).
Closed Sun & Mon, 24-26 Dec. Access, Visa.*

Portrush   **Place of Interest**

Dunluce Castle *3 miles*

Templepatrick   **Templeton Hotel**   66%   £100

Tel 0184 94 32984   Fax 0184 94 33406

882 Antrim Road Templepatrick Ballyclare Co Antrim BT39 0AH

H

Map 1 D2

An eye-catching modern hotel a mile from the M2 and handy for Belfast airport. Spacious bedrooms are equipped with the expected up-to-date amenities, and the four Executive rooms have additionally mini-bars and jacuzzis. Day rooms take various decorative themes – sleek black and gold for the cocktail bar, Scandinavian for the banqueting hall (catering for up to 350), echoes of medieval knights in the restaurant. New conference suite for up to 50 in a separate annexe. 24hr room service. Free parking for 165 cars. Weekend reductions. ***Rooms** 20. Garden. Closed 25 & 26 Dec.* *Access, Diners, Visa.*

Tempo   **Tempo Manor**   £100

Tel 01365 541450   Fax 01365 541202

Tempo Co Fermanagh BT94 3FJ

H

Map 1 C2

An impressive Victorian manor house of considerable charm, set in eleven acres of lakes and gardens established in 1869 by the Langham family. Tempo is now in the capable young hands of John and Sarah Langham whose recent restoration, modernisation (including the installation of central heating) and redecoration is in keeping with the style of the house. Many original features and furniture, including three four-poster beds, have been retained and all the spacious bedrooms have lovely views of the surrounding gardens and en-suite bathrooms – an ideal combination of the interesting old and convenient new. Reception rooms are impressive yet welcoming, with crackling log fires, and dinner is served in the beautiful dining room, overlooking the lake and garden. Non-residents may also book for dinner, which is served communally or at separate tables, as preferred. Banqueting for 300 (+ unlimited numbers in marquee, daytime only). Children welcome: under-5s may stay free in their parents room; cot, extra beds, baby-listening/sitting, high-chair, early evening meal available by arrangement. Woodland walks. ***Rooms** 5. Garden, croquet. Closed Christmas week. Access, Visa.*

JAMESON ®

IRISH WHISKEY

Quick Reference Lists

Family-friendly Establishments

listed in county order

Please note that while many establishments claim to be 'family-friendly', many restaurants and pubs may still put time limitations on children in the evenings, and hotels may only provide entertainment during school holiday times or at weekends. We urge readers to confirm the availability of essentials (Z-beds, cots and bedding) and entertainment facilities required when booking and before arrival. Specific requirements for babies and toddlers (high-chairs, changing facilities) may not necessarily be provided in all the following establishments; similarly, amenities for energetic teenagers should also be checked. Nevertheless, we provide this list in the hope that it is a useful starting point for easing the often difficult task of dining and staying away from home *en famille*. If you experience anything that might be described as not 'family-friendly' at any of the establishments listed below, please inform us by using a Readers' Comments form from the back of this Guide.

Republic of Ireland

Co Carlow, Bagenalstown **Lorum Old Rectory** (A)
Co Carlow, Leighlinbridge **Lord Bagenal Inn** (R/P*)
Co Cavan, Ballyconnell **Slieve Russell Hotel** (H)
Co Clare, Ballyvaughan **Monks Pub** (P)
Co Clare, Bunratty **Fitzpatricks Bunratty Shamrock Hotel** (H)
Co Clare, Ennis **The Cloister** (P)
Co Cork, Ahakista **Ahakista Bar** (P)
Co Cork, Ahakista **Hillcrest House** (A)
Co Cork, Baltimore **Bushe's Bar** (P)
Co Cork, Bantry **Anchor Tavern** (P)
Co Cork, Bantry **Westlodge Hotel** (H)
Co Cork, Butlerstown **Dunworley Cottage** (R)
Co Cork, Carrigaline **Gregory's** (R)
Co Cork, Cork **An Spailpín Fánac** (P)
Co Cork, Cork **Fitzpatrick Silver Springs** (H)
Co Cork, Cork **Flemings** (RR)
Co Cork, Crookhaven **O'Sullivan's** (P)
Co Cork, Crosshaven **Cronin's Bar** (P)
Co Cork, Kinsale **Blue Haven Hotel** (HR)
Co Cork, Kinsale **The Dock Bar** (P)
Co Cork, Shanagarry **Ballymaloe House** (AR*)
Co Cork, Timoleague **Dillon's** (P)
Co Donegal, Culdaff **McGuiness's** (P)
Co Donegal, Dunkineely **Castle Murray House** (HR)
Co Donegal, Rossnowlagh **Sand House Hotel** (H)
Co Donegal, Rossnowlagh **Smugglers Creek Inn** (IR/P*)
Dublin 1 **101 Talbot** (R)
Dublin 2 **Chicago Pizza Pie Factory** (JaB)
Dublin 2 **Kilkenny Kitchen** (JaB)
Dublin 5 **The Station House** (P)
Dublin 14 **The Goat** (P)
Co Galway, Clifden **E J King's** (P)
Co Galway, Galway **Brennans Yard** (H)
Co Galway, Galway **Corrib Great Southen Hotel** (H)
Co Galway, Moycullen **Cloonnabinnia House Hotel** (H)
Co Galway, Moycullen **Drimcong House Restaurant** (R*)
Co Galway, Oughterard **Connemara Gateway Hotel** (H)
Co Galway, Renvyle **Renvyle House** (H)
Co Kerry, Beaufort **Dunloe Castle** (H)
Co Kerry, Caherciveen **The Point Bar** (P)
Co Kerry, Caherdaniel **Derrynane Hotel** (HR)
Co Kerry, Caragh Lake **Caragh Lodge** (A)
Co Kerry, Dingle **Dingle Skellig Hotel** (H)
Co Kerry, Killarney **Foley's Town House** (RR)
Co Kerry, Tralee **Brandon Hotel** (H)

Co Kildare, Naas **Manor Inn** (P)
Co Kilkenny, Kilkenny **Kilkenny Kitchen** (R)
Co Kilkenny, Kilkenny **Newpark Hotel** (H)
Co Laois, Mountrath **Roundwood House** (HR)
Co Leitrim, Dromahair **Stanford's Village Inn** (P)
Co Limerick, Limerick **Jurys Hotel** (H)
Co Longford, Moydow **The Vintage** (R)
Co Louth, Carlingford **Carlingford House** (A)
Co Louth, Carlingford **McKevitt's Village Hotel** (H)
Co Mayo, Ballina **Downhill Hotel** (H)
Co Mayo, Westport **The Towers Bar** (P)
Co Offaly, Birr **Tullanisk** (A)
Co Sligo, Drumcliff **Yeats Tavern & Davis's Pub** (P)
Co Sligo, Rosses Point **The Moorings** (R)
Co Sligo, Sligo **McGettigan's** (P)
Co Sligo, Tubbercurry **Killoran's Traditional Restaurant** (P)
Co Tipperary, Cahir **Kilcoran Lodge Hotel** (H)
Co Waterford, Ardmore **Cliff House Hotel** (H)
Co Waterford, Waterford **Jack Meade's Bar** (P)
Co Waterford, Waterford **Jurys Hotel** (H)
Co Westmeath, Mullingar **Crookedwood House** (R)
Co Wexford, Carne **Lobster Pot** (R)
Co Wexford, Rosslare **Great Southern** (H)
Co Wexford, Rosslare **Kelly's Resort Hotel** (HR)

Northern Ireland

Co Antrim, Belfast **Speranza** (R)
Co Antrim, Belfast Int Airport **Aldergrove Airport Hotel** (H)
Co Antrim, Dunadry **Dunadry Inn** (H)
Co Down, Comber **La Mon House** (H)

Accommodation under £70 for two & Restaurants with Rooms

REPUBLIC OF IRELAND

Location	Establishment	Food Price	Cat	Room Price	Grade	No. Rooms	Family
Co Carlow							
Bagenalstown	Lorum Old Rectory		A	£45		5	
Carlow	Barrowville Townhouse		A	£39		7	
Carlow	Royal Hotel		H	£55	60%	34	
Co Clare							
Ballyvaughan	Hyland's Hotel		H	£66	65%	20	
Ennis	West County Inn		H	£55	59%	110	
Kilkee	Halpins Hotel		H	£66	63%	12	
Lisdoonvarna	Sheedy's Spa Hotel		H	£50	66%	11	
Co Cork							
Ahakista	Hillcrest House		A	£33		4	
Baltimore	Bushe's Bar		P	£25		3	Family
Bantry	Westlodge Hotel		H	£68	66%	104	
Butlerstown	Atlantic Sunset		A	£30		4	
Butlerstown	Sea Court House		A	£40		6	
Castletownshend	Bow Hall		A	£56		3	
Cork	Flemings	£55	RR	£55		4	Family
Cork	Forte Travelodge		H	£42		40	
Cork	Jurys Cork Inn		H	£55	60%	133	
Cork	Lotamore House		A	£48	60%	20	
Cork	Seven North Mall		A	£60		5	
Courtmacsherry	Courtmacsherry Hotel		H	£65	60%	14	
Glandore	Marine Hotel		H	£56		16	
Killeagh	Ballymakeigh House		A	£40		5	
Kinsale	The Moorings		A	£70		8	
Kinsale	Old Presbytery		A	£44		6	
Kinsale	The White Lady Inn		H	£50		10	
Midleton	Bailick Cottage		A	£50		6	
Schull	Corthna Lodge		A	£40		6	
Schull	East End Hotel		H	£45	60%	17	
Youghal	Aherne's Seafood Restaurant	£60	RR	£100		10	
Co Donegal							
Ballybofey	Kee's Hotel		H	£65	62%	37	
Bruckless	Bruckless House		A	£40		4	
Donegal	Ardnamona House		A	£60		5	
Dunkineely	Castle Murray House	£55	HR	£48	69%	10	Family
Ramelton	The Manse		A	£40		3	
Rossnowlagh	Smugglers Creek Inn	£40	IR/P*	£40		5	Family

Location	Establishment	Food Price	Category	Room Price	Grade	No. Rooms	Family
Dublin (Central)							
Dublin 2	Grey Door & Pier 32	£50	RR	£99		7	
Dublin 2	No. 31		A	£68		5	
Dublin 4	Aberdeen Lodge		A	£66		16	
Dublin 4	Glenveagh Town House		A	£60		11	
Dublin 4	Merrion Hall		A	£70		15	
Dublin 8	Jurys Christchurch Inn		H	£60	60%	183	
Dun Laoghaire	Chestnut Lodge		A	£50		4	
Co Dublin							
Clondalkin	Kingswood Country House/ Restaurant	£60	RR	£56			
Swords	Forte Travelodge		H	£42		40	
Co Galway							
Clifden	The Quay House	£50	RR	£50		6	
Galway	Jurys Galway Inn		H	£61	60%	128	
Inishbofin Island	Day's Hotel		H	£40	61%	14	
Kingstown	Kille House		A	£50		4	
Leenane	Killary Lodge		A	£56	59%	18	
Leenane	Portfinn Lodge	£55	RR	£35		8	
Moyard	Rose Cottage		A	£30		6	
Moycullen	Cloonnabinnia House Hotel	£45	HR	£55	63%	14	Family
Moycullen	Moycullen House		A	£55		5	
Spiddal	Bridge House Hotel		H	£65	59%	14	
Co Kerry							
Caherdaniel	Derrynane Hotel	£45	HR	£70	62%	75	Family
Dingle	Doyle's Seafood Bar & Townhouse	£65	RR	£62		8	
Dingle	Greenmount House		A	£40		8	
Kenmare	Sallyport House		A	£45		5	
Killarney	Foley's Town House	£80	RR	£70		12	Family
Killarney	Kathleen's Country House		A	£60		17	
Waterville	The Smugglers Inn		A	£33		12	
Co Kildare							
Athy	Tonlegee House	£55	RR	£58		5	
Co Kilkenny							
Kilkenny	Lacken House	£60	RR	£55		8	
Maddoxtown	Blanchville House		A	£50		6	
Co Laois							
Mountrath	Roundwood House	£60	HR	£64	58%	6	Family
Co Leitrim							
Carrick-on-Shannon	Hollywell House		A	£50		3	

Location	Establishment	Food Price	Cat	Room Price	Grade	No. Rooms	Family
Co Limerick							
Adare	Woodlands House Hotel		H	£50	60%	57	
Co Louth							
Ardee	The Gables	£60	RR	£34		5	
Ardee	Red House		A	£60			
Carlingford	Carlingford House		A	£30			
Carlingford	McKevitt's Village Hotel		H	£59	59%		
Co Mayo							
Dugort	Gray's Guest House		A	£36		17	
Mulraney	Rosturk Woods		A	£40		4	
Pontoon	Healy's Hotel	£50	HR	£55	60%	10	
Co Offaly							
Banagher	Brosna Lodge Hotel		H	£44	56%	14	
Banagher	The Old Forge		A	£32		4	
Birr	Dooly's Hotel		H	£50	60%	18	
Co Sligo							
Collooney	Glebe House	£45	RR	£30		4	
Co Tipperary							
Cahir	Kilcoran Lodge		H	£68	62%	23	
Glen of Aherlow	Aherlow House		H	£53	63%	10	
Co Waterford							
Ardmore	Cliff House Hotel		H	£68	59%	20	
Waterford	Foxmount Farm		A	£36		6	
Waterford	Prendiville's	£60	RR	£46		9	
Co Westmeath							
Athlone	Higgins's		P	£28		4	
Ballymurn	Ballinkeele House		A	£60		5	
Newbay	Newbay Country House		A	£60		6	
Co Wexford							
Wexford	Clonard House		A	£32		9	
Co Wicklow							
Blessington	Downshire House		H	£66	59%	25	
Enniskerry	Enniscree Lodge	£60	HR	£55	59%	10	

NORTHERN IRELAND

Location	Establishment	Food Price	Category	Room Price	Grade	No. Rooms	Family
Co Antrim							
Larne	Magheramorne House		H	£66	63%	22	
Portballintrae	Bayview Hotel		H	£65	58%	16	
Co Fermanagh							
Kesh	Lough Erne Hotel		H	£56	60%	12	
Co Londonderry							
Aghadowey	Greenhill House		H	£42		6	
Garvagh	MacDuff's Restnt, Blackheath House	£50	RR	£60		5	

Hotels with Sporting Facilities

REPUBLIC OF IRELAND

Certain facilities may not necessarily be owned by the hotels listed, but they are a major attraction of the establishment; many arrange reduced green fees for golf or have an arrangement, say, with a local angling club. For example, *Halpin's Hotel* in Kilkee, Co Clare is popular with golfers (due to its proximity to a superb golf course), and both *The Davenport* and *Mont Clare* hotels in Dublin offer an arrangement for their guests to have members' rates at the Riverview Racquets and Fitness Club.

Location	Establishment	Category	Indoor Pool	Outdoor Pool	Squash	Tennis	Golf	Fishing	Riding	Croquet
Co Carlow										
Bagenalstown	Lorum Old Rectory	A								▲
Co Cavan										
Ballyconnell	Slieve Russell Hotel	H	▲			▲	▲	▲		
Co Clare										
Ballyvaughan	Gregans Castle	HR	▲							▲
Bunratty	Fitzpatricks Shannon Shamrock	H	▲							
Ennis	Auburn Lodge	H					▲			
Ennis	West County Inn	H					▲			
Kilkee	Halpin's Hotel	H					▲			
Lisdoonvarna	Sheedy's Spa Hotel	H					▲			
Newmarket-on-Fergus	Dromoland Castle	HR					▲	▲	▲	▲
Newmarket-on-Fergus	Clare Inn Hotel	H	▲				▲	▲		▲
Co Cork										
Ballycotton	Bayview Hotel	H					▲			
Ballylickey	Ballylickey Manor House	A		▲				▲		▲
Bantry	Westlodge Hotel	H	▲		▲	▲	▲			
Blarney	Blarney Park Hotel	H	▲			▲				
Butlerstown	Sea Court House	A					▲			
Castlelyons	Ballyvolane House	A						▲		▲
Cork	Arbutus Lodge	HR					▲			
Cork	Fitzpatrick Silver Springs	H	▲	▲	▲		▲			
Cork	Jurys Hotel	H	▲	▲	▲	▲				
Cork	Rochestown Park Hotel	H	▲							
Courtmacsherry	Courtmacsherry Hotel	H					▲	▲	▲	▲
Glandore	Marine Hotel	H						▲		
Innishannon	Innishannon House Hotel	H						▲		
Kanturk	Assolas Country House	AR					▲	▲		
Killeagh	Ballymakeigh House	A					▲			
Kinsale	Actons Hotel	H	▲							
Kinsale	Blue Haven Hotel	HR						▲		

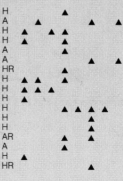

Location	Establishment	Category	Indoor Pool	Outdoor Pool	Squash	Tennis	Golf	Fishing	Riding	Croquet
Mallow	Longueville House	HR						▲		
Midleton	Bailick Cottage	A								▲
Shanagarry	Ballymaloe House	AR	▲			▲	▲			▲
Skibbereen	Liss Ard Lake Lodge	R						▲		

Co Donegal

Location	Establishment	Category	Indoor Pool	Outdoor Pool	Squash	Tennis	Golf	Fishing	Riding	Croquet
Ballybofey	Kee's Hotel	H	▲				▲	▲		
Bruckless	Bruckless House	A						▲		
Donegal	Ardnamona House	A						▲		
Donegal	Harvey's Point Country Hotel	H						▲		
Letterkenny	Castle Grove Country House	A				▲		▲		
Rathmullan	Rathmullan House	HR	▲			▲		▲		▲
Rossnowlagh	Sand House Hotel	H				▲		▲		

Co Dublin

Location	Establishment	Category	Indoor Pool	Outdoor Pool	Squash	Tennis	Golf	Fishing	Riding	Croquet
Dublin 2	The Davenport	H	▲		▲					
Dublin 4	Berkeley Court	H	▲							
Dublin 4	Jurys Hotel and Towers	H	▲	▲						
Dublin 13	Marine Hotel	H	▲			▲				
Dublin 2	Mont Clare Hotel	H	▲		▲					
Howth	Deer Park Hotel	H					▲			
Howth	Howth Lodge Hotel	H	▲							
Killiney	Fitzpatrick's Castle	H	▲		▲	▲				

Co Galway

Location	Establishment	Category	Indoor Pool	Outdoor Pool	Squash	Tennis	Golf	Fishing	Riding	Croquet
Ballynahinch	Ballynahinch Castle	H				▲		▲		▲
Cashel	Cashel House	HR				▲		▲	▲	
Cashel	Zetland House	H				▲		▲		
Clifden	Abbeyglen Castle	H			▲	▲				
Clifden	Rock Glen Manor	HR				▲		▲		▲
Furbo	Connemara Coast Hotel	H	▲			▲				
Galway	Corrib Great Southern Hotel	H	▲							
Galway	Glenlo Abbey	H					▲	▲		
Galway	Great Southern	H	▲							
Leenane	Delphi Lodge	A						▲		
Leenane	Killary Lodge	H				▲				
Letterfrack	Rosleague Manor	HR				▲		▲		
Moycullen	Cloonnabinnia House Hotel	HR						▲		
Oughterard	Connemara Gateway Hotel	H	▲			▲			▲	
Oughterard	Currarevagh House	AR				▲		▲		
Recess	Lough Inagh Lodge	H								
Renvyle	Renvyle House	H		▲		▲	▲	▲	▲	▲

Co Kerry

Location	Establishment	Category	Indoor Pool	Outdoor Pool	Squash	Tennis	Golf	Fishing	Riding	Croquet
Aghadoe	Killeen House Hotel	H				▲				
Beaufort	Dunloe Castle	H	▲			▲		▲	▲	
Caherdaniel	Derrynane Hotel	HR		▲		▲				
Caragh Lake	Caragh Lodge	A				▲		▲		
Caragh Lake	Hotel Ard-na-Sidhe	H				▲				
Dingle	Dingle Skellig Hotel	H	▲			▲				
Kenmare	Dromquinna Manor Hotel	H				▲		▲		
Kenmare	Park Hotel Kenmare	HR				▲	▲	▲		
Kenmare	Sheen Falls Lodge	HR				▲		▲		▲
Killarney	Aghadoe Heights Hotel	HR	▲			▲		▲		

Location	Establishment	Category	Indoor Pool	Outdoor Pool	Squash	Tennis	Golf	Fishing	Riding	Croquet
Killarney	Cahernane Hotel	HR				▲	▲			
Killarney	Great Southern	H	▲			▲				
Killarney	Hotel Europe	H	▲			▲	▲	▲		
Killarney	Kathleen's Country House	A								▲
Killarney	Killarney Park Hotel	H	▲							
Killarney	Randles Court Hotel	H					▲	▲	▲	
Killarney	Torc Great Southern	H	▲			▲				
Parknasilla	Great Southern	H	▲			▲	▲	▲		
Tralee	Brandon Hotel	H	▲							
Waterville	Butler Arms Hotel	H				▲	▲			

Co Kildare

Location	Establishment	Category	Indoor Pool	Outdoor Pool	Squash	Tennis	Golf	Fishing	Riding	Croquet
Castledermot	Kilkea Castle	HR	▲			▲				
Maynooth	Moyglare Manor	HR				▲				
Straffan	Kildare Hotel	HR	▲		▲	▲	▲	▲		

Co Kilkenny

Location	Establishment	Category	Indoor Pool	Outdoor Pool	Squash	Tennis	Golf	Fishing	Riding	Croquet
Kilkenny	Newpark Hotel	H	▲			▲				
Thomastown	Mount Juliet Hotel	HR	▲			▲	▲	▲	▲	▲

Co Laois

Location	Establishment	Category	Indoor Pool	Outdoor Pool	Squash	Tennis	Golf	Fishing	Riding	Croquet
Mountrath	Roundwood House	HR						▲		▲

Co Leitrim

Location	Establishment	Category	Indoor Pool	Outdoor Pool	Squash	Tennis	Golf	Fishing	Riding	Croquet
Carrick-on-Shannon	Hollywell House	A						▲		

Co Limerick

Location	Establishment	Category	Indoor Pool	Outdoor Pool	Squash	Tennis	Golf	Fishing	Riding	Croquet
Adare	Adare Manor	HR	▲					▲	▲	
Adare	Dunraven Arms	HR				▲				
Castleconnell	Castle Oaks House Hotel	H	▲			▲				
Glin	Glin Castle	A				▲				▲
Limerick	Castletroy Park Hotel	HR	▲			▲				
Limerick	Greenhills Hotel	H	▲			▲				
Limerick	Jurys Hotel	H	▲			▲				
Limerick	Limerick Inn Hotel	H	▲			▲				

Co Louth

Location	Establishment	Category	Indoor Pool	Outdoor Pool	Squash	Tennis	Golf	Fishing	Riding	Croquet
Dundalk	Ballymascanlon House	H	▲		▲	▲				

Co Mayo

Location	Establishment	Category	Indoor Pool	Outdoor Pool	Squash	Tennis	Golf	Fishing	Riding	Croquet
Ballina	Downhill Hotel	H	▲		▲	▲				
Ballina	Mount Falcon Castle	AR				▲		▲		
Cong	Ashford Castle	HR				▲	▲	▲	▲	▲
Crossmolina	Enniscoe House	A						▲		
Newport	Newport House	HR						▲		
Pontoon	Healy's Hotel	HR						▲		
Westport	The Olde Railway Hotel	H						▲		
Westport	Westport Woods Hotel	H					▲			

Location	Establishment	Category	Indoor Pool	Outdoor Pool	Squash	Tennis	Golf	Fishing	Riding	Croquet
Co Monaghan										
Carrickmacross	Nuremore Hotel	H	▲			▲	▲			
Scotshouse	Hilton Park	A					▲	▲		
Co Offaly										
Birr	Dooly's Hotel	A						▲		
Birr	Tullanisk	A								▲
Co Sligo										
Ballymote	Temple House	A						▲		▲
Boyle	Cromleach Lodge	HR						▲		
Collooney	Markree Castle	H						▲		
Riverstown	Coopershill House	AR				▲		▲		▲
Sligo	Sligo Park	H	▲			▲				
Co Tipperary										
Cahir	Kilcoran Lodge	H	▲							
Dundrum	Dundrum House	H				▲	▲	▲	▲	
Co Waterford										
Waterford	Foxmount Farm	A				▲				
Waterford	Jurys Hotel	H	▲			▲				
Waterford	Tower Hotel	H	▲							
Waterford	Waterford Castle	HR	▲				▲	▲		
Co Westmeath										
Hodson Bay	Hodson Bay Hotel	H	▲			▲	▲			
Co Wexford										
Ballymurn	Ballinkeele House	A				▲				
Bunclody	Clohamon House	A						▲	▲	
Gorey	Marlfield House	HR				▲				
Rosslare	Great Southern	H	▲		▲	▲				
Rosslare	Kelly's Resort Hotel	HR	▲	▲	▲	▲				▲
Co Wicklow										
Blessington	Downshire House	H					▲			▲
Dunlavin	Rathsallagh House	AR	▲			▲	▲			▲
Rathnew	Tinakilly House	HR					▲			▲

NORTHERN IRELAND

Location	Establishment	Category	Indoor Pool	Outdoor Pool	Squash	Tennis	Golf	Fishing	Riding	Croquet
Co Antrim										
Ballymena	Galgorm Manor	HR						▲	▲	
Bushmills	Bushmills Inn	H						▲		
Dunadry	Dunadry Inn	H	▲					▲		▲
Dunmurry	Forte Posthouse Belfast	H			▲					
Larne	Magheramorne House	H								
Portballintrae	Bayview Hotel	H	▲							
Co Down										
Annalong	Glassdrumman Lodge	HR				▲			▲	
Bangor	Clandeboye Lodge Hotel	H					▲		▲	
Comber	La Mon House	H	▲							
Holywood	Culloden Hotel	HR	▲		▲	▲	▲			
Newcastle	Slieve Donard Hotel	H	▲			▲				
Co Fermanagh										
Kesh	Lough Erne Hotel	H						▲		
Tempo	Tempo Manor	A						▲		▲
Co Londonderry										
Londonderry	Beech Hill House Hotel	HR				▲				
Co Tyrone										
Fivemiletown	Blessingbourne	A	▲			▲	▲			

Establishments
listed in
county order

REPUBLIC OF IRELAND ENTRIES LISTED IN COUNTY ORDER

HR = Hotel with recommended Restaurant open to public **H** = Hotel **RR** = Restaurant with Rooms **R** = Restaurant open to public **P** = Pub
A = Accommodation (classified by Bord Fáilte as a Private House or Irish Home) **AR** = as A but with a recommended Restaurant open to the public
See Starred Restaurants and map on page 13 for **R★** and **R†** restaurant listings. **P★** indicates starred **bar** food (not restaurant) in pubs.
Some hotels are ungraded due to their categorisation as a Private House Hotel or Inns without public rooms;
the former are usually de luxe B&B establishments and their restaurant may not generally be open to non-residents. Restaurants with Rooms are also ungraded.
Restaurants without prices are generally not open to the public and categorised as **JaB = Just a Bite**
Swimming pool refers to an indoor pool (a few places have outdoor pool only – see Sporting Facilities lists pp 374–8)

Location	Establishment	Food Price	Cat	Room Price	%	Rooms	Conf	Banq	Beaut Sit	Family Friendly	Swim Pool	Golf	Address
Co Carlow													
Bagenalstown	Lorum Old Rectory		A	£45		5							Kilgreaney Bagenalstown
Carlow	Barrowville Townhouse		A	£39		7							Kilkenny Road Carlow
Carlow	The Beams Restaurant	£60	R							Family			59 Dublin Street Carlow
Carlow	Buzz's Bar		P										7 Tullow Street Carlow
Carlow	Royal Hotel		H	£55	60%	34	300	200					Dublin Street Carlow
Carlow	Tully's		P										149 Tullow Street Carlow
Fighting Cocks	Fighting Cocks		P										Fighting Cocks
Leighlinbridge	Lord Bagenal Inn	£45	R/P★							Family			Leighlinbridge
Co Cavan													
Ballyconnell	Slieve Russell Hotel		H	£140	78%	150	800	450		Family	yes	yes	Ballyconnell
Blacklion	MacNean Bistro	£40	R										Blacklion
Butlersbridge	Derragarra Inn		P										Butlersbridge

Co Clare

Location	Name									Address	
Ballyvaughan	An Féar Gorta (The Tea Rooms)	JaB								Ballyvaughan	
Ballyvaughan	Gregans Castle	HR	£75	£99	71%	22				Ballyvaughan	
Ballyvaughan	Hyland's Hotel	H		£66	65%	20	150	150	yes	Ballyvaughan	
Ballyvaughan	Monks Pub	P							Family	The Quay Ballyvaughan	
Ballyvaughan	Whitehorn Restaurant	R	£50							Ballyvaughan	
Bunratty	Fitzpatricks Shannon Shamrock	H		£137	60%	115	200	150		Bunratty	
Bunratty	MacCloskey's	R	£70							Bunratty House Mews Bunratty	yes
Clarecastle	Carnelly House	A		£146		5				Clarecastle	
Ennis	Auburn Lodge	H		£70	61%	100	500	400		Galway Road Ennis	
Ennis	The Cloister	P								Abbey Street Ennis	
Ennis	Old Ground Hotel	H		£99	66%	58	250	180	Family	Ennis	
Ennis	West County Inn	H		£55	59%	110	200	500		Clare Road Ennis	
Kilkee	Halpins Hotel	H		£66	63%	12				Erin Street Kilkee	
Lisdoonvarna	Sheedy's Spa Hotel	H		£50	66%	11				Lisdoonvarna	
New Quay	Linnane's Bar	P								New Quay Burrin	
Newmarket-on-Fergus	Clare Inn Hotel	H	£115	£87	64%	121	400	350	yes	Dromoland Newmarket-on-Fergus	yes
Newmarket-on-Fergus	Dromoland Castle	HR†		£262	79%	73	450	450		Newmarket-on-Fergus	yes
Shannon	Oakwood Arms Hotel	H		£96	63%	46	200	250		Shannon	
Shannon Airport	Great Southern	H		£114	64%	115	170	140		Shannon Airport	

Co Cork

Location	Name									Address	
Ahakista	Ahakista Bar	P								Ahakista Bantry	
Ahakista	Hillcrest House	A							Family	Ahakista nr Durrus	
Ahakista	Shiro	R*		£33		4			Family	Ahakista nr Bantry	yes
Ballycotton	Bayview Hotel	H	£80							Ballycotton	
Ballydehob	Annie's Bookshop and Café	JaB		£80	67%	35				Main Street Ballydehob	
Ballydehob	Annie's Restaurant	R	£55							Main Street Ballydehob	
Ballydehob	Levis Bar	P								Corner House Main Street Ballydehob	
Ballylickey	Ballylickey Manor House	A		£99	67%	5				Ballylickey Bantry Bay	yes
Ballylickey	Larchwood House	R	£60							Pearsons Bridge Ballylickey	yes
Ballylickey	Seaview Hotel	HR	£55	£100	70%	17	35			Ballylickey nr Bantry	yes

Location	Establishment	Food Price	Cat	Room Price	%	Rooms	Conf	Banq	Beaut Sit	Family Friendly	Swim Pool	Golf	Address
Baltimore	Bushe's Bar		P	£25		3				Family			Baltimore
Baltimore	Chez Youen	£70	R										The Pier Baltimore
Baltimore	McCarthy's Bar		P										The Square Baltimore
Bantry	Anchor Tavern		P							Family			New Street Bantry
Bantry	Westlodge Hotel		H	£68	66%	104	550	400		Family	yes		Bantry
Blarney	Blarney Park Hotel		H	£110	63%	76	340	350			yes		Blarney
Butlerstown	Atlantic Sunset		A	£30		4							Butlerstown nr Bandon
Butlerstown	Dunworley Cottage	£60	R										Dunworley nr Butlerstown Clonakilty
Butlerstown	O'Neill's		P							Family			Butlerstown Bandon
Butlerstown	Sea Court House		A	£40		6							Bandon nr Butlerstown
Carrigaline	Gregory's	£55	A							Family			Main Street Carrigaline
Castlelyons	Ballyvolane House		A	£80		7							Castlelyons
Castletownbere	MacCarthy's		P										Town Square Castletownbere
Castletownshend	Bow Hall		A	£56		3			yes				Castletownshend
Castletownshend	Mary Ann's Bar & Restaurant	£50	R/P*										Castletownshend nr Skibbereen
Clonakilty	An Sugan	£50	R/P										41 Strand Road Clonakilty
Clonakilty	Fionnula's Restaurant	£35	R										30 Ashe Street Clonakilty
Cobh	Mansworth's		P										Midleton Street Cobh
Cork	An Spailpin Fanac	£80	P										28-29 South Main Street Cork
Cork	Arbutus Lodge		HR*	£80	70%	20	120	180		Family			Montenotte Cork
Cork	Bully's	£25	R										40 Paul Street Cork
Cork	Cliffords	£70	R*										18 Dyke Parade Cork
Cork	Crawford Gallery Café	£45	R										Emmet Place Cork
Cork	Dan Lowrey's Seafood Tavern		P										13 MacCurtain Street Cork
Cork	Fitzpatrick Silver Springs		H	£107	65%	110	1000	750		Family	yes		Tivoli Cork
Cork	Flemings	£55	RR	£55		4				Family			Silver Grange House Tivoli Cork
Cork	Forte Travelodge		H	£42		40							South Ring Rd/Kinsale Rd Cork
Cork													Airport Blackash
Cork	Gingerbread House		JaB										Paul Street Cork
Cork	Harolds Restaurant	£55	R										Douglas Cork
Cork	Imperial Hotel		H	£121	66%	101	600	350					South Mall Cork
Cork	Isaacs	£35	R										48 MacCurtain Street Cork

Cork	Ivory Tower Restaurant	£55	R								35 Princes Street Cork
Cork	Jacques	£55	R								9 Phoenix Street Cork
Cork	Jurys Cork Inn		H		60%	133					Anderson's Quay Cork
Cork	Jurys Hotel		H	£140	66%	185	520	700			Western Road Cork
Cork	Lotamore House		A	£48	60%	20	20				Tivoli Cork
Cork	Lovetts	£72	R						yes		Churchyard Lane off Well Road Douglas Cork
Cork	Metropole Hotel		H	£88	58%	108	500	300			Maccurtain Street Cork
Cork	Michael's Bistro	£45	R								4 Mardyke Street Cork
Cork	Morrisons Island Hotel		H	£119	68%	40	15	15			Morrisons Quay Cork
Cork	Quay Co-Op		JaB								24 Sullivan's Quay Cork
Cork	Reidy's Wine Vaults		P*								Lancaster Quay Western Road Cork
Cork	Rochestown Park Hotel		H	£85	67%	63	150	150			Rochestown Road Douglas Cork
Cork	Seven North Mall		A	£60		5			yes		7 North Mall Cork
Courtmacsherry	Courtmacsherry Hotel		H	£65	60%	14					Courtmacsherry
Crookhaven	O'Sullivan's		P							Family	Crookhaven
Crosshaven	Cronin's Bar		P							Family	Crosshaven
Durrus	Blairs Cove House Restaurant	£60	P*								Blairs Cove Durrus nr Bantry
East Ferry	Marlogue Inn		P						yes		East Ferry Marina East Ferry Cobh
Glandore	Hayes' Bar		P*								Glandore
Glandore	Marine Hotel		H	£56		16					Glandore
Glandore	The Pier House Bistro	£45	R								Glandore
Glengarriff	The Blue Loo	£65	R						yes		Main Street Glengarriff
Innishannon	Innishannon House Hotel		H	£95	63%	14	200	150	yes		Innishannon
Kanturk	Alley Bar		P								Strand Street Kanturk
Kanturk	Assolas Country House	£65	AR*	£104	72%	9	20	20			Kanturk
Kanturk	The Vintage		P	£40					yes		O'Brien Street Kanturk
Killeagh	Ballymakeigh House		A			5					Killeagh
Kinsale	Actons Hotel		H	£100	60%	57	400	300	yes		Pier Road Kinsale
Kinsale	The Bistro	£65	R								Guardwell nr Kinsale
Kinsale	Blue Haven Hotel	£60	HR	£90		18				Family	3 Pearse Street Kinsale
Kinsale	The Bulman Bar										Summer Cove Kinsale
Kinsale	Chez Jean-Marc	£55	R†								Lower O'Connell Street Kinsale
Kinsale	The Dock Bar		P							Family	Castlepark Kinsale

Location	Establishment	Food Price	Cat	Room Price	%	Rooms	Conf	Banq	Beaut Sit	Family Friendly	Swim Pool	Golf	Address
Kinsale	Man Friday	£55	R										Scilly Kinsale
Kinsale	Max's Wine Bar	£40	R										Main Street Kinsale
Kinsale	The Moorings		A	£70		8							Scilly Kinsale
Kinsale	The Old Bank House		A	£80		9							11 Pearse Street Kinsale
Kinsale	Old Presbytery		A	£44		6							Cork Street Kinsale
Kinsale	1601		P										Pearse Street Kinsale
Kinsale	Scilly House		A	£90	65%	7	25						Scilly Kinsale
Kinsale	The Spaniard Inn		P										Scilly Kinsale
Kinsale	The White Lady Inn		H	£50		10							Lower O'Connell Street Kinsale
Mallow	Longueville House	£65	HRt	£110	72%	16	20		yes				Mallow
Midleton	Bailick Cottage		A	£50		6							Midleton
Midleton	Farmgate	£45	R										The Coolbawn Midleton
Midleton	Jameson Heritage Centre		JaB										Midleton
Midleton	Midleton Park Hotel	£75	H	£75	68%	40	300	300					Midleton
Monkstown	The Bosun	£70	P										Monkstown
Oysterhaven	Finders Inn	£70	R										Nohoval Oysterhaven
Oysterhaven	The Oystercatcher	£65	R										Oysterhaven Begooly
Rathpeacon	Country Squire Inn		P										Mallow Road Rathpeacon
Schull	Adele's	£40	R										Main Street Schull
Schull	Bunratty Inn		P										Schull nr Galway
Schull	La Coquille	£55	R										Schull
Schull	Cortkna Lodge		A	£40		6							Schull
Schull	East End Hotel		H	£45	60%	17	120						Schull
Schull	Restaurant in Blue	£50	R										Crookhaven Road Schull
Schull	TJ Newman's		P										Main Street Schull
Shanagarry	Ballymaloe House	£80	AR*	£120	66%	30			yes	Family		yes	Shanagarry
Skibbereen	Liss Ard Lake Lodge	£80	R										Skibbereen
Timoleague	Dillon's		P							Family				Mill Street Timoleague
Timoleague	Lettercolum House	£40	P										Timoleague
Youghal	Aherne's Seafood Restaurant	£60	RR	£100		10							163 North Main Street Youghal

Co Donegal

Town	Name	Rate	Type	Rate	%	No	No	No	Facility		Address
Ballybofey	Kee's Hotel		H	£65	62%	37	300			yes yes	Stranolar Ballybofey
Bruckless	Bruckless House		A	£40		4	250				Bruckless
Bundoran	Le Chateaubrianne	£55	R								Sligo Road Bundoran
Culdaff	McGuinness's		P						Family		Culdaff Inishaven
Donegal	Ardnamona House		A	£60		5					Lough Eske nr Donegal
Donegal	Harvey's Point Country Hotel	£65	H	£99	63%	20	300	200			Lough Eske nr Donegal
Donegal	St Ernan's House Hotel	£55	HR	£130	70%	12					St Ernan's Island Donegal
Dunkineely	Castle Murray House	£55	HR	£48	69%	10	25		Family		Dunkineely
Fahan	Restaurant St John's	£45	R						yes		Fahan Innishowen
Greencastle	Kealy's Seafood Bar	£65	R						yes		The Harbour Greencastle
Letterkenny	Carolina House Restaurant		R						yes		Loughnagin Letterkenny
Letterkenny	Castle Grove House		A	£90		8					Letterkenny
Ramelton	The Manse		A	£40		3					Ramelton
Rathmullan	Rathmullan House	£60	HR	£104	62%	23	20		yes	yes	Rathmullan nr Letterkenny
Rossnowlagh	Sand House Hotel		H	£88	69%	40	75		Family		Rossnowlagh
Rossnowlagh	Smugglers Creek Inn	£40	IR/P*	£40		5			Family		Rossnowlagh

Dublin (Central)

Town	Name	Rate	Type	Rate	%	No	No	No	Facility	Address
Blackrock	Ayumi-Ya	£40	R							Newpark Centre Newtownpark Ave
Blackrock	Clarets	£70	R↑							63 Main Street Blackrock
Dublin 1	Chapter One	£70	R							18/19 Parnell Square
Dublin 1	Gresham Hotel		H	£175	64%	200	325	200		Upper O'Connell Street
Dublin 1	The Harbourmaster		P				200			Custom House Docks
Dublin 1	101 Talbot	£32	R							101 Talbot Street
Dublin 1	Royal Dublin Hotel		H	£108	63%	117	250		Family	40 Upper O'Connell Street
Dublin 2	Ayumi-Ya Japanese Steakhouse	£40	R				230			132 Lower Baggot Street
Dublin 2	Bleeding Horse		P							24 Upper Camden Street
Dublin 2	Blooms Hotel		H	£140	60%	86	30			6 Anglesea Street Temple Bar
Dublin 2	Café en Seine		P							40 Dawson Street
Dublin 2	Central Hotel		H	£139	57%	70	80			1-5 Exchequer Street

Location	Establishment	Food Price	Cat	Room Price	%	Rooms	Conf	Banq	Beaut Sit	Family Friendly	Swim Pool	Golf	Address
Dublin 2	Chicago Pizza Pie Factory	£45	JaB										St Stephen's Green
Dublin 2	The Chili Club	£85	R										1 Anne's Lane South Anne Street
Dublin 2	Commons Restaurant		R							Family			Newman Hse 85-86 St Stephen's Green
Dublin 2	Hotel Conrad	£70	H	£230	75%	191	250	150					Earlsfort Terrace
Dublin 2	Cooke's Café		R										14 South William Street
Dublin 2	Davenport Hotel	£70	H	£182	76%	120	300	400					Merrion Square
Dublin 2	Davy Byrnes		P										21 Duke Street
Dublin 2	Dobbins Wine Bistro	£60	R										15 St Stephen's Lane
Dublin 2	Doheny & Nesbitt		P										5 Lower Baggot Street
Dublin 2	Eamonn Doran		P										3A Crown Alley Temple Bar
Dublin 2	L'Ecrivain	£70	R										112 Lower Baggot Street
Dublin 2	Elephant & Castle	£50	R										18 Temple Bar
Dublin 2	Les Frères Jacques	£80	R										74 Dame Street
Dublin 2	George's Bistro & Piano Bar	£70	R										29 South Frederick Street
Dublin 2	Georgian House	£40	H	£94	56%	33							20 Lower Baggot Street
Dublin 2	Good World		R										18 South Great George's Street
Dublin 2	Gotham Café		JaB										8 South Anne Street
Dublin 2	Grafton Plaza Hotel	£50	H	£90	64%	75	20	36					Johnsons Place
Dublin 2	Grey Door	£40	RR	£99		7							22 Upper Pembroke Street
Dublin 2	Imperial Chinese Restaurant	£65	R										13 Wicklow Street
Dublin 2	Kapriol		R										45 Lower Camden Street
Dublin 2	Kilkenny Kitchen		JaB										Nassau Street
Dublin 2	Little Caesar's Pizza	£65	JaB										5 Chatham House Balfe Street
Dublin 2	Longfield's Hotel	£55	HR	£96	61%					Family			Fitzwilliam Street Lower
Dublin 2	La Mère Zou	£80	R										22 St Stephen's Green
Dublin 2	Le Mistral	£35	R*										16 Harcourt Street
Dublin 2	Mitchell's Cellars		R										21 Kildare Street
Dublin 2	Mont Clare Hotel		H	£157	66%	74	150	120					Merrion Square
Dublin 2	National Museum Café		JaB										Kildare Street
Dublin 2	No. 31		A	£68		5					yes		31 Leeson Close off Lower Leeson St
Dublin 2	O'Dwyer's		P										Mount Street

Location	Name	Price	Type	Price	%					Address
Dublin 2	Oisíns	£95	R							31 Upper Camden Street
Dublin 2	The Old Stand		P							37 Exchequer Street
Dublin 2	Pasta Fresca	£30	R							2-4 Chatham Street
Dublin 2	Patrick Guilbaud	£100	R*†							46 James Place off Lower Baggot St
Dublin 2	The Pembroke		P							31 Lower Pembroke Street
Dublin 2	Periwinkle Seafood Bar		JaB							Powerscourt Thouse Centre South William St
Dublin 2	Pier 32	£30	R							at The Grey Door Upper Pembroke St
Dublin 2	Pierre's	£30	R							2 Crowe Street Temple Bar
Dublin 2	Pigalle	£55	R							14 Temple Bar
Dublin 2	Il Primo	£45	R							16 Montague Street
Dublin 2	Rajdoot	£48	R							26 Clarendon St Westbury Centre
Dublin 2	Shalimar	£50	R							17 South Great George's Street
Dublin 2	Shelbourne Hotel		H	£226	74%	164	500	300		St Stephen's Green
Dublin 2	Stag's Head		R†							1 Dame Court
Dublin 2	La Stampa	£60	P							35 Dawson Street
Dublin 2	Stauntons on the Green		A	£88		33				83 St Stephen's Green South
Dublin 2	Stephen's Hall Hotel	£50	HR	£143	65%	37				14-17 Lower Leeson Street
Dublin 2	Temple Bar Hotel		H	£117	66%					Temple Bar
Dublin 2	Thomas Read		P							Parliament Street
Dublin 2	Toners Pub		P							139 Lower Baggot Street
Dublin 2	Tosca		JaB							20 Suffolk Street
Dublin 2	The Westbury	£85	HR	£189	79%	203	300	170		Off Grafton Street
Dublin 3	Wong's	£60	R							436 Clontarf Road
Dublin 3	The Yacht		P							73 Clontarf Road
Dublin 4	Aberdeen Lodge		A	£66		16				53/55 Park Avenue Ailesbury Road
Dublin 4	Anglesea Town House		A	£90		7				63 Anglesea Road
Dublin 4	Ariel House		A	£100		28				52 Lansdowne Road Ballsbridge
Dublin 4	Berkeley Court		H	£180	76%	207	400	300	yes	Lansdowne Road
Dublin 4	Burlington Hotel		H	£154	70%	450	1000	1000		Upper Leeson Street
Dublin 4	Canaletto's	£35	R							69 Mespil Road
Dublin 4	Le Coq Hardi	£100	R*							35 Pembroke Road Ballsbridge
Dublin 4	Courtyard Restaurant	£45	R							Belmont Court, 1 Belmont Ave Donnybrook
Dublin 4	Doyle Montrose Hotel		H	£114	65%	179	90			Stillorgan Road

Location	Establishment	Food Price	Cat	Room Price	%	Rooms	Conf	Banq	Beaut Sit	Family Friendly	Swim Pool	Golf	Address
Dublin 4	Doyle Tara Hotel	£80	H	£108	61%	114	200	165					Merrion Road
Dublin 4	Ernie's	£65	R										Mulberry Gardens Donnybrook
Dublin 4	Fitzers Café Ballsbridge	£75	R										RDS Merrion Road
Dublin 4	Furama Chinese Restaurant		A										Anglesea House 88 Donnybrook Road
Dublin 4	Glenveagh Town House		A	£60	70%	11							31 Northumberland Road
Dublin 4	Hibernian Hotel	£55	HR	£135	70%	30	40	55					Eastmoreland Place Ballsbridge
Dublin 4	Jurys Hotel and Towers		H	£163	76%	390	850	600			yes		Pembroke Road Ballsbridge
Dublin 4	Kielys		P										22-24 Donnybrook Road Donnybrook
Dublin 4	Kitty O'Shea's Bar		P										23-25 Upper Grand Canal Street
Dublin 4	Langkawi Malaysian Restaurant	£40	R										46 Upper Baggot Street
Dublin 4	Lobster Pot	£70	R										9 Ballsbridge Terrace
Dublin 4	McCormack's Merrion Inn		P										188 Merrion Road
Dublin 4	Merrion Hall		A	£70		15							54-56 Merrion Road
Dublin 4	Raglan Lodge		A	£85		7							10 Raglan Road Ballsbridge
Dublin 4	Roly's Bistro	£50	R†										7 Ballsbridge Terrace
Dublin 4	Sachs Hotel		H	£98	62%	20	170	150					19 Morehampton Road Donnybrook
Dublin 4	Senor Sassi's	£58	P										146 Upper Leeson Street
Dublin 5	The Station House		P							Family			3-5 Station Road Raheny
Dublin 6	Ashtons	£55	R										Clonskeagh
Dublin 6	Ivy Court	£50	R										88 Rathgar Road
Dublin 6	Zen	£45	R†										89 Upper Rathmines Road
Dublin 7	Ta Se Mohogani Gaspipes		R										17 Manor Street Stoneybatter
Dublin 8	Brazen Head		P										20 Lower Bridge Street
Dublin 8	Jurys Christchurch Inn		H	£60	55%	183							Christchurch Place
Dublin 8	Locks Restaurant	£85	R										1 Windsor Terrace Portobello
Dublin 8	The Lord Edward	£60	R										23 Christchurch Place
Dublin 8	Old Dublin Restaurant	£60	R										90-91 Francis Street
Dublin 8	Ryans of Parkgate Street	£55	R										28 Parkgate Street
Dublin 9	Kavanagh's		P										Prospect Square Glasnevin
Dublin 9	P Hedigan: The Brian Boru		P										5 Prospect Road Glasnevin
Dublin 13	Marine Hotel		H	£86	64%	26	150	200		Family	yes		Sutton Cross
Dublin 14	The Goat		P										Goatstown Dublin

Area	Name	Type	Price	Price2	%	No.1	No.2	No.3	Flag	Address
Dublin 14	Yellow House	P								Willbrook Road Rathfarnham
Dun Laoghaire	Chestnut Lodge	A	£75	£50		4				2 Vesey Place Monkstown
Dun Laoghaire	Restaurant Na Mara	R								1 Harbour Road Dun Laoghaire
Dun Laoghaire	Royal Marine Hotel	H		£85	64%	104	700	400		Marine Road Dun Laoghaire
Dun Laoghaire	The South Bank	R	£55							1 Martello Terrace Dun Laoghaire
Howth	Abbey Tavern	P								Howth
Howth	Adrian's	R	£50							3 Abbey Street Howth
Howth	Casa Pasta	JaB								12 Harbour Road Howth
Howth	Deer Park Hotel	H		£80	64%	50	140	100	yes	Howth
Howth	Howth Lodge Hotel	H		£90	65%	46	200	200		Howth
Howth	King Sitric	R	£70							East Pier Harbour Road Howth
Malahide	Bon Appetit	R	£80						yes	9 St James Terrace Malahide
Malahide	Eastern Tandoori	R	£40							1 New Street Malahide
Malahide	Giovanni's	JaB								Townyard Lane Malahide
Malahide	Grand Hotel	H		£90	66%	100	900	600		Malahide
Malahide	Malahide Castle	R	£40							Malahide
Malahide	Roches Bistro	R	£55							12 New Street Malahide
Malahide	Siam Thai Restaurant	R	£45							Gas Lane Malahide
Malahide	Silks Restaurant	R	£45							5 The Mall Malahide
Monkstown	Coopers Restaurant	JaB	£40							8a The Crescent Monkstown
Monkstown	FXB's	P								3 The Crescent Monkstown
Monkstown	Purty Kitchen	R	£55							Old Dunleavy Road Monkstown
Sandycove	Bistro Vino	R	£55							56 Glasthule Road Sandycove
Sandycove	Morels Bistro	R	£55							Glasthule Road Sandycove
Stillorgan	Beaufield Mews	R	£50							Woodlands Avenue Stillorgan
Stillorgan	China-Sichuan Restaurant	R								4 Lower Kilmacud Road Stillorgan
Stillorgan	The Mill House	P								Lower Kilmacud Road Stillorgan
Stillorgan	Stillorgan Orchard	P								Stillorgan

Co Dublin

Area	Name	Type	Price	Address
Clondalkin	Kingswood Country House/Restaurant	RR	£60	Naas Road Clondalkin Dublin
Dalkey	The Queens	P	£56	Castle Street Dalkey

Location	Establishment	Food Price	Cat	Room Price	%	Rooms	Conf	Banq	Beaut Sit	Family Friendly	Swim Pool	Golf	Address
Dublin Airport	Forte Crest		H	£122	57%	188	160	150				yes	Dublin Airport
Glencullen	Fox's Pub & Seafood Kitchen		P										Glencullen
Killiney	Court Hotel		H	£97	68%	86	300	300					Killiney Bay Killiney
Killiney	Fitzpatrick's Castle		H	£160	68%	90	550	400			yes		Killiney
Rathcoole	An Potín Still		P										Rathcoole
Skerries	Red Bank Restaurant	£60	R										7 Church Street Skerries
Swords	Forte Travelodge		H	£42		40							N1 Dublin/Belfast Road Swords bypass
Swords	Old Schoolhouse	£50	R										Coolbanagher Swords

Co Galway

Location	Establishment	Food Price	Cat	Room Price	%	Rooms	Conf	Banq	Beaut Sit	Family Friendly	Swim Pool	Golf	Address
Aughrim	Aughrim Schoolhouse Restaurant	£45	R										Aughrim nr Ballinasloe
Ballyconneely	Erriseask House	£60	HR*	£72	66%	13			yes				Ballyconneely nr Clifden
Ballynahinch	Ballynahinch Castle		H	£114	71%	28	25		yes				Recess Ballynahinch
Barna	Donnelly's of Barna	£60	P										Barna
Barna	Ty Ar Mor	£70	R										The Pier Barna
Cashel	Cashel House		HR	£145	76%	32			yes				Cashel
Cashel	Zetland House		H	£115	65%	20							Cashel
Clarenbridge	Paddy Burke's		P										Clarenbridge Road Galway
Clifden	Abbeyglen Castle		H	£99	60%	40	230	200	yes				Sky Road Clifden
Clifden	Ardagh Hotel	£55	HR	£83	60%	21			yes				Ballyconneely Road Clifden
Clifden	Destry Rides Again												Clifden
Clifden	Doris's Restaurant	£40	jaB										Market Street Clifden
Clifden	E J King's		P							Family			The Square Clifden
Clifden	Foyles Hotel		H	£79	61%	30							The Square Clifden
Clifden	O'Grady's Seafood Restaurant	£50	R										Market Street Clifden
Clifden	The Quay House	£50	RR	£50	61%	6							Beach Road Clifden
Clifden	Rock Glen Manor	£60	HR	£90	71%	29							Ballyconneely Road Clifden
Furbo	Connemara Coast Hotel		H	£120	66%	113			yes		yes		Furbo nr Galway
Galway	Ardilaun House		H	£95		90	400	250					Taylors Hill Galway
Galway	Brennans Yard		H	£90	64%	24				Family			Lower Merchants Road Galway

Location	Establishment		Type									Address
Galway	Bridge Mills Restaurant		JaB									O'Brien's Bridge Galway
Galway	Casey's Westwood Restaurant & Bars	£60	R									Dangan Upper Newcastle Galway
Galway	Corrib Great Southern Hotel		H	£128	68%	180	850	700		Family	yes	Dublin Road Galway
Galway	Glenlo Abbey		H	£115	68%	43	48	75				Bushypark Galway
Galway	Great Southern		H	£113	69%	116	450	350			yes	Eyre Square Galway
Galway	Hooker Jimmy's Seafood Restaurant		JaB									The Fishmarket Spanish Arch Galway
Galway	House of St James		JaB									Castle Street Galway
Galway	Jurys Galway Inn		H	£61	55%	128						Quay Street Galway
Galway	Tigh Neachtain		P									Cross Street Galway
Inishbofin Island	Day's Bar		P									Inishbofin Island
Inishbofin Island	Day's Hotel		H	£40	61%	14						Inishbofin Island
Kilcolgan	Moran's Oyster Cottage		p*									The Weir Kilcolgan
Kingstown	Kille House		A	£50		4						Kingstown Clifden
Kinvara	Sayre's	£38	R									Kinvara
Kinvara	Tully's		p									Kinvara
Kylemore	Kylemore Abbey Restaurant		JaB									Kylemore Connemara
Leenane	Delphi Lodge		A	£70		11			yes			Leenane
Leenane	Killary Lodge		A	£56	59%	18	35		yes			Leenane
Letterfrack	Portfinn Lodge	£55	RR	£35		8			yes			Letterfrack Connemara
Moyard	Rosleague Manor	£65	HR	£90	72%	20			yes			Rockfield Moyard
Moycullen	Rose Cottage		A	£30		6						Ross Lake Moycullen
Moycullen	Cloonnabinnia House Hotel	£45	HR	£55	63%	14				Family		Moycullen
Moycullen	Drimcong House Restaurant	£65	R*							Family		Moycullen
Moycullen	Moycullen House		R	£55	63%	5			yes			Moycullen Village
Oughterard	White Gables Restaurant	£50	H									Oughterard
Oughterard	Connemara Gateway Hotel		AR	£108	66%	62	180	130		Family	yes	Oughterard Connemara
Oughterard	Currarevagh House	£50	P	£91	65%	15			yes			The Square Oughterard
Oughterard	Powers		H									Oughterard
Recess	Sweeney's Oughterard House		H	£98	59%	20						Oughterard
Recess	Lough Inagh Lodge		H	£104	68%	12	24		yes			Inagh Valley Recess
Renvyle	Renvyle House		H	£118	63%	65	120	150		Family	yes	Renvyle
Roundstone	O'Dowd's Seafood Bar & Restaurant		P									Roundstone
Spiddal	Boluisce Seafood Bar		JaB									Spiddal Village Connemara

Location	Establishment	Food Price	Cat	Room Price	%	Rooms	Conf	Banq	Beaut Sit	Family Friendly	Swim Pool	Golf	Address
Spiddal	Bridge House Hotel												Spiddal
Tuam	Cre na Cille	£50	H	£65	59%	14							High Street Tuam
Co Kerry													
Aghadoe	Killeen House Hotel		H	£73	64%	15							Aghadoe Lakes of Killarney
Annascaul	Dan Foley's		P										Annascaul
Ballyferriter	Long's Pub		P										Ballyferriter Village
Ballyferriter	Tigh an Tobuir (The Well House)		R										Ballyferriter
Beaufort	Dunloe Castle	£35	H	£96	71%	120	300	200	yes	Family	yes		Beaufort nr Killarney
Cahersiveen	Brennan's Restaurant	£55	R										13 Main Street Cahirciveen
Cahersiveen	Old Schoolhouse Restaurant	£55	R										Cahirciveen
Cahersiveen	The Point Bar		P							Family			Renard Point Cahirciveen
Caherdaniel	Derrynane Hotel	£45	HR	£70	62%	75							Caherdaniel
Caherdaniel	Loaves & Fishes	£55	R						yes	Family			Caherdaniel nr Derrynane
Caragh Lake	Hotel Ard-na-Sidhe		H	£96	70%	20			yes				Caragh Lake nr Killorglin
Caragh Lake	Caragh Lodge		A	£99	65%	10			yes	Family			Caragh Lake nr Killorglin
Dingle	Beginish Restaurant	£55	R										Green Street Dingle
Dingle	Dick Mack's		P										Green Lane Dingle
Dingle	Dingle Skellig Hotel		H	£86	61%	115	120		yes	Family	yes		Dingle
Dingle	Doyle's Seafood Bar & Townhouse	£65	RR	£62		8							4 John Street Dingle
Dingle	Greenmount House		A	£40		8							Greenmount Dingle
Dingle	Half Door	£55	R										John Street Dingle
Dingle	James Flahive		P										The Quay Dingle
Dingle	Lord Baker's Bar & Restaurant	£60	R/P										Main Street Dingle
Dingle	O'Flaherty's		P										Bridge Street Dingle
Dingle	Tigh Mhaire de Barra		P										The Pier Head Dingle
Kenmare	d'Arcy's		R										Main Street Kenmare
Kenmare	Dromquinna Manor Hotel	£70	H	£85	60%	28							Blackwater Bridge nr Kenmare

Town	Name	Price	Type	%							Address
Kenmare	The Horseshoe	£35	R								3 Main Street Kenmare
Kenmare	Lime Tree	£50	R								Shelbourne Street Kenmare
Kenmare	Packie's	£45	R								Henry Street Kenmare
Kenmare	Park Hotel Kenmare	£90	HR*	87%	50	50	30	yes		yes	Henry Street Kenmare
Kenmare	Purple Heather		P		5						Kenmare
Kenmare	Sallyport House		A							yes	Henry Street Kenmare
Kenmare	Sheen Falls Lodge	£90	HR*	87%	40	120	120	yes			Kenmare
Killarney	Aghadoe Heights Hotel	£100	HR†	70%	60	100	130	yes		yes	Aghadoe Killarney
Killarney	Cahernane Hotel	£65	HR	66%	48			yes			Muckross Road Killarney
Killarney	Dingles Restaurant	£45	R								40 New Street Killarney
Killarney	Hotel Europe	£80	RR	72%	205	500	600	yes		yes	Killorglin Road Fossa Killarney
Killarney	Foley's Town House	£60	R		12	25	95		Family		23 High Street Killarney
Killarney	Gaby's Seafood Restaurant		R								27 High Street Killarney
Killarney	Great Southern	£129	H	69%	180	1000	650			yes	Killarney
Killarney	Kathleen's Country House	£60	A		17						Tralee Road Killarney
Killarney	Killarney Park Hotel	£130	H	73%	66	150	160			yes	Kenmare Place Killarney
Killarney	Killarney Towers Hotel	£120	H	57%	157						College Square Killarney
Killarney	Randles Court Hotel	£120	H		37		130				Muckross Road Killarney
Killarney	Strawberry Tree	£65	R								24 Plunkett Street Killarney
Killarney	Torc Great Southern	£94	H	63%	94					yes	Park Road Killarney
Killarney	West End House	£50	R		3						New Street Killarney
Killarney	Yer Man's Pub		P								24 Plunkett Street Killarney
Killorglin	Nick's Restaurant	£65	R								Lower Bridge Street Killorglin
Parknasilla	Great Southern	£161	H	72%	84	80	70	yes		yes	Parknasilla Sneem
Portmagee	Fishermans Bar		P		4						Portmagee
Tahilla	Long Lake	£350	A		15	180	80				Tahilla nr Sneem
Tralee	Ballyseede Castle Hotel	£85	H	60%	160	1100	550		Family		Tralee
Tralee	Brandon Hotel	£90	H	61%	160	25				yes	Princes Street Tralee
Waterville	Butler Arms Hotel	£100	H	68%	31						Waterville
Waterville	The Huntsman		P								Waterville
Waterville	The Smugglers Inn	£33	A		12						Waterville

Co Kildare

Town	Name	Price	Type	%							Address
Athy	Tonlegee House	£55	RR		5						Athy
Castledermot	Kilkea Castle	£75	HR	70%	45	200	200			yes	Kilkea Castledermot

Location	Establishment	Food Price	Cat	Room Price	%	Rooms	Conf	Banq	Beaut Sit	Family Friendly	Swim Pool	Golf	Address
Maynooth	Moyglare Manor	£75	HR	£136	75%	17	40	70	yes				Moyglare Maynooth
Moone	Moone High Cross Inn		P*										Bolton Hill Moone
Naas	Fletcher's		P										Commercial House Naas
Naas	Manor Inn		P							Family			Main Street Naas
Newbridge	Hotel Keadeen		H	£85	68%	37	800	600					Ballymany Newbridge
Newbridge	The Red House Inn	£55	R										Newbridge
Straffan	Barberstown Castle	£65	HR	£110	70%	10	200	160					Straffan
Straffan	Kildare Hotel	£100	HR	£250	87%	45	70	44	yes		yes	yes	Straffan

Co Kilkenny

Location	Establishment	Food Price	Cat	Room Price	%	Rooms	Conf	Banq	Beaut Sit	Family Friendly	Swim Pool	Golf	Address
Bennetsbridge	Millstone Café		JaB										Bennetsbridge nr Kilkenny
Castlewarren	Langton's		P										Castlewarren
Inistioge	The Motte	£60	R						yes				Inistioge
Kilkenny	Caislean Uí Cuain		P										2 High Street Kilkenny
Kilkenny	Kilkenny Kitchen	£20	R							Family			Kilkenny Design Centre Castle Street
Kilkenny	Lacken House	£60	RR	£55		8	12						Dublin Road Kilkenny
Kilkenny	Langton's		P										69 John Street Kilkenny
Kilkenny	Newpark Hotel		H	£97	58%	84	600	350		Family	yes		Castlecomer Road Kilkenny
Kilkenny	Shem's		P										61 John Street Kilkenny
Kilkenny	Tynan's Bridge House Bar		P										Bridge House 2 Johns Bridge Kilkenny
Maddoxtown	Blanchville House		A	£50		6	30		yes				Dunbell Maddoxtown
Thomastown	Mount Juliet Hotel	£66	HR	£215	84%	56	50	140	yes		yes	yes	Mount Juliet Thomastown

Co Laois

Location	Establishment	Food Price	Cat	Room Price	%	Rooms	Conf	Banq	Beaut Sit	Family Friendly	Swim Pool	Golf	Address
Abbeyleix	Morriseys		P										Main Street Abbeyleix
Mountrath	Roundwood House	£60	HR	£64	58%	6	12			Family			Mountrath

Co Leitrim

Town	Name		Type							Address
Carrick-on-Shannon	Hollywell House		A	£50						Liberty Hill Carrick-on-Shannon
Dromahair	Stanford's Village Inn		P						Family	Dromahair

Co Limerick

Town	Name		Type							Address
Abbeyfeale	The Cellar	£85	P							The Square Abbeyfeale
Adare	Adare Manor	£55	HR†	£220	81%	64	220	yes		Adare
Adare	Dunraven Arms	£45	HR	£133	72%	43	250			Adare
Adare	The Inn Between	£60	R						yes	Adare
Adare	Mustard Seed		R†			300				Main Street Adare
Adare	Woodlands House Hotel	£55	H	£50	60%	57	270			Adare
Ballyneety	Croker's Bistro		R							Limerick County Golf/Country Club
Castleconnell	Bradshaw's Bar		P							Castleconnell
Castleconnell	Castle Oaks House Hotel		H	£72	64%	11	300		yes	Castleconnell
Glin	Glin Castle	£65	A	£256		6	40			Glin
Limerick	Castletroy Park Hotel		HR	£139	74%	107	300		yes	Dublin Road Limerick
Limerick	Greenhills Hotel		H	£119	62%	60	400		yes	Ennis Road Limerick
Limerick	Jurys Hotel		H	£116	68%	96	130		yes	Ennis Road Limerick
Limerick	Restaurant de La Fontaine	£60	R						Family	12 Upper Gerald Griffin Street
Limerick	Limerick Inn Hotel		H	£117	68%	153	800			Ennis Road Limerick
Limerick	Quenelle's Restaurant	£55	R						yes	Upper Henry St (corner of Mallow St)
Limerick	Two Mile Inn		H	£78	63%	125	350			Ennis Road Limerick

Co Longford

Town	Name		Type							Address
Moydow	The Vintage	£45	R						Family	Moydow

Co Louth

Location	Establishment	Food Price	Cat	Room Price	%	Rooms	Conf	Banq	Beaut Sit	Family Friendly	Swim Pool	Golf	Address
Ardee	The Gables	£60	RR	£34		5							Dundalk Road Ardee
Ardee	Red House		A	£60									Ardee
Blackrock	Brake Tavern		P										Main Street Blackrock nr Dundalk
Carlingford	Carlingford House	£55	A	£30									Carlingford
Carlingford	Jordan's Bar & Restaurant	£35	R	£48		7							Carlingford
Carlingford	Magee's Bistro		R										D'Arcy Magee Centre Carlingford
Carlingford	McKevitt's Village Hotel		H	£59	59%					Family			Carlingford
Carlingford	P J O'Hare's Anchor Bar		P										Carlingford
Collon	Forge Gallery Restaurant	£65	R										Collon
Dundalk	Ballymascanlon House		H	£75	61%	35	250	300			yes		Ballymascanlon Dundalk
Dundalk	Quaglino's Restaurant	£55	R										Clanbrassil Street Dundalk
Termonfeckin	Triple House Restaurant	£55	R										Termonfeckin

Co Mayo

Location	Establishment	Food Price	Cat	Room Price	%	Rooms	Conf	Banq	Beaut Sit	Family Friendly	Swim Pool	Golf	Address
Ballina	Downhill Hotel	£50	H	£86	65%	50	500	450		Family	yes		Ballina
Ballina	Mount Falcon Castle	£110	AR	£72	60%	10							Ballina
Cong	Ashford Castle		HR†	£265	88%	83	40	140				yes	Cong
Crossmolina	Enniscoe House	£50	A	£88	63%	6							Castlehill nr Crossmolina Ballina
Dugort	Gray's Guest House		A	£36		17							Dugort Achill Island
Keel	The Beehive		JaB										Keel Achill Island
Lecanvey	Staunton's		P										Lecanvey Westport
Mulraney	Rosturk Woods	£70	A	£40	67%	4							Rosturk Mulraney
Newport	Newport House	£50	HR	£124		20							Newport
Pontoon	Healy's Hotel		HR	£55	60%	10	60	70					Pontoon
Westport	The Asgard		P										The Quay Westport
Westport	Matt Molloy's Bar		P										Bridge Street Westport
Westport	The Olde Railway Hotel		H	£75	63%	24	150	150					The Mall Westport
Westport	Quay Cottage	£50	R										The Harbour Westport

Location	Name	Type	Price	%							Address
Westport	The Towers Bar	P									The Harbour The Quay Westport
Westport	The West Bar	P									Lower Bridge Street Westport
Westport	Westport Woods Hotel	H	£88	62%	57	150	120	Family			Louisburgh Road Westport

Co Meath

Location	Name	Type	Price	%							Address
Bettystown	Coastguard Restaurant	R	£55								Bettystown
Ceanannas Mor (Kells)	O'Shaughnessy's	P									Market Street Ceanannas Mor (Kells)
Kilmoon	Snail Box	P									Kilmoon
Navan	Ardboyne Hotel	HR	£55	60%	27	700	400				Dublin Road Navan
Skryne	O'Connell's Pub	P									Skryne nr Tara

Co Monaghan

Location	Name	Type	Price	%							Address
Carrickmacross	Nuremore Hotel	H	£120	72%	69	300	500		yes	yes	Carrickmacross
Scotshouse	Hilton Park	A	£111		5			yes	yes	yes	Scotshouse nr Clones

Co Offaly

Location	Name	Type	Price	%							Address
Banagher	Brosna Lodge Hotel	H	£44	56%	14						Banagher
Banagher	JJ Hough's	P									Main Street Banagher
Banagher	The Old Forge	A	£32		4						Westend Banagher
Banagher	The Vine House	P									Westend Banagher
Birr	Dooly's Hotel	H	£50	60%	18						Birr
Birr	Tullanisk	A	£76		7						Birr
Dunkerrin	Dunkerrin Arms	P						Family			Dunkerrin Birr

Co Roscommon

Location	Name	Type	Price	%							Address
Athleague	Fitzmaurice's Tavern	P									Athleague

Co Sligo

Location	Establishment	Food Price	Cat	Room Price	%	Rooms	Conf	Banq	Beaut Sit	Family Friendly	Swim Pool	Golf	Address
Ballisodare	The Thatch		P										Ballisodare
Ballymote	Temple House		A	£70		5							Ballymote
Boyle	Cromleach Lodge	£75	HR*	£118	61%	10							Ballindoon Castlebaldwin nr Boyle
Colloony	Glebe House	£45	RR	£30	78%	4							Colloony
Colloony	Markree Castle		H	£97	60%	15	40	100					Colloony
Drumcliff	Yeats Tavern & Davis's Pub		H										Drumcliff
Riverstown	Coopershill House	£50	AR	£88	69%	7			yes	Family			Coopershill Riverstown
Rosses Point	Austie's		P										Rosses Point
Rosses Point	The Moorings	£45	R						yes	Family			Rosses Point
Sligo	Bistro Bianconi	£85	R										The Mall Sligo
Sligo	Hargadon's		P										O'Connell Street Sligo
Sligo	McGettigan's		P							Family			Connolly Street Sligo
Sligo	Sligo Park		P	£95	58%	90					yes		Pearse Road Sligo
Sligo	Truffles Restaurant	£25	R										The Mall Sligo
Tubbercurry	Killoran's Traditional Restaurant		P							Family			Main Street Tubbercurry

Co Tipperary

Location	Establishment	Food Price	Cat	Room Price	%	Rooms	Conf	Banq	Beaut Sit	Family Friendly	Swim Pool	Golf	Address
Birdhill	Matt the Thresher		p										Birdhill
Cahir	Kilcoran Lodge	£70	H	£68	62%	23	300	300		Family	yes		Kilcoran Cahir
Cashel	Chez Hans		R										Rockside Cashel
Cashel	Dowling's		P										Cashel
Cashel	The Spearman	£55	R										Main Street Cashel
Clonmel	Clonmel Arms		H	£83	61%	31	600	400					Sarfield Street Clonmel
Dundrum	Dundrum House		H	£95	66%	55	400	350	yes			yes	Dundrum
Glen of Aherlow	Aherlow House		H	£53	63%	10	280	220	yes				Glen of Aherlow nr Tipperary
Killaloe	Goosers		p*										Killaloe Ballina

Co Waterford

Town	Name	£	Type	£	%						Address
Ardmore	Cliff House Hotel		H	£68	59%	20			Family		Ardmore
Cheekpoint	McAlpin's Suir Inn		P								Cheekpoint
Dunmore East	The Ship		P								Dunmore East
Waterford	Dwyer's Restaurant	£55	R								8 Mary Street Waterford
Waterford	Foxmount Farm		A	£36		6					off Passage East Road Waterford
Waterford	Granville Hotel		H	£83	69%	74	300	200			1 Meagher Quay Waterford
Waterford	Henry Downes		P								10 Thomas Street Waterford
Waterford	Jack Meade's Bar		P								Cheekpoint Road Halfway House
Waterford	Jurys Hotel		H	£106	61%	98	700	600	Family		Ferrybank Waterford
Waterford	Prendiville's	£60	RR	£46		9					Cork Road Waterford
Waterford	Tower Hotel		H	£114	59%	141	500	600	Family	yes	The Mall Waterford
Waterford	Waterford Castle	£80	HR	£220	74%	19		16	yes	yes	The Island Ballinakill Waterford
Waterford	The Wine Vault	£40	R							yes	High Street Waterford

Co Westmeath

Town	Name	£	Type	£	%						Address
Athlone	Le Chateau	£55	R								Abbey Lane Athlone
Athlone	Higgins's		P								2 Pearce Street Athlone
Athlone	Sean's Bar		P	£28		4					13 Main Street Athlone
Glasson	Glasson Village Restaurant	£50	R								Glasson Athlone
Glasson	Grogan's		P								Glasson nr Athlone
Glasson	Wineport Restaurant	£40	R								Glasson nr Athlone
Hodson Bay	Hodson Bay Hotel		H	£90	65%	46	500	400		yes	Hodson Bay nr Athlone
Kinnegad	The Cottage	£25	R								Kinnegad
Mullingar	Crookedwood House	£55	R						Family		Crookedwood Mullingar

Co Wexford

Town	Name	£	Type	£	%						Address
Ballyhack	Neptune Restaurant	£50	R								Ballyhack New Ross
Ballymurn	Ballinkeele House		A	£60	65%	5					Enniscorthy Ballymurn

Location	Establishment	Food Price	Cat	Room Price	%	Rooms	Conf	Banq	Beaut Sit	Family Friendly	Swim Pool	Golf	Address
Bunclody	Clohamon House		A	£80		4			yes				Bunclody
Carne	Lobster Pot	£50	R/P*							Family			Carne
Ferrycarrig Bridge	Ferrycarrig Hotel	£60	HR	£90	61%	40	400	400	yes				Ferrycarrig Bridge nr Wexford
Foulksmills	Horetown House	£50	R										Foulksmills
Gorey	Marlfield House	£90	HR	£154	81%	19	20	30	yes				Gorey
Kilmuckridge	Boggan's		P										Kilmuckridge
Newbay	Cedar Lodge		H	£75	62%	18	100	70					Carrigbyrne Newbawn
Newbay	Newbay Country House		A	£60		6							Newbay nr Wexford
Roslare	Great Southern		H	£91	62%	99	150	200		Family			Rosslare
Roslare	Kelly's Resort Hotel	£55	HR	£99	76%	99	20			Family	yes		Rosslare
Wexford	Archer's		P			9					yes		Redmond Square Wexford
Wexford	Clonard House		A	£32		9					yes		Clonard Great Wexford
Wexford	Granary	£55	R										Westgate Wexford
Wexford	White's Hotel	£55	H	£76	60%	82	600	450					George Street Wexford

Co Wicklow

Location	Establishment	Food Price	Cat	Room Price	%	Rooms	Conf	Banq	Beaut Sit	Family Friendly	Swim Pool	Golf	Address
Blessington	Downshire House		H	£66	59%	25	100	250					Blessington
Bray	Tree of Idleness	£65	R										Seafront Bray
Delgany	Glenview Hotel		H	£90	63%	37	300	200	yes				Glen of the Downs Delgany
Delgany	Wicklow Arms		P										Delgany
Dunlavin	Rathsallagh House	£65	AR	£110	67%	17	50		yes		yes	yes	Dunlavin
Enniskerry	Curlestown House	£50	R										Curlestown Enniskerry
Enniskerry	Enniscree Lodge	£60	HR	£55	59%	10							Glencree Valley nr Enniskerry
Greystones	The Hungry Monk	£55	R										Greystones
Laragh	Mitchell's of Laragh	£45	R						yes				The Old Schoolhouse Laragh
Rathnew	Hunter's Hotel	£55	HR	£80	60%	17	20	30	yes				Newrath Bridge Rathnew
Rathnew	Tinakilly House	£75	HR	£116	76%	29	150	100	yes				Rathnew Wicklow
Roundwood	Roundwood Inn	£60	R/P*										Roundwood
Wicklow	Old Rectory	£60	AR	£90	59%	5			yes				Wicklow

NORTHERN IRELAND ENTRIES LISTED IN COUNTY ORDER

HR = Hotel with recommended Restaurant open to public **H** = Hotel **RR** = Restaurant with Rooms **R** = Restaurant open to public **P** = Pub
A = Accommodation (classified by Bord Fáilte as a Private House or Irish Home) **AR** = as A but with a recommended Restaurant open to the public
See Starred Restaurants and map on page 13 for **R*** and **R†** restaurant listings. **P*** indicates starred **bar** food (not restaurant) in pubs.
Some hotels are ungraded due to their categorisation as a Private House Hotel or Inns without public rooms;
the former are usually de luxe B&B establishments and their restaurant may not generally be open to non-residents. Restaurants with Rooms are also ungraded.
Restaurants without prices are generally of an informal, snackier nature and categorised as **JaB = Just a Bite**

Co Antrim

Location	Establishment	Food Price	Cat	Room Price	%	Rooms	Conf	Banq	Beaut Sit	Family Friendly	Swim Pool	Golf	Address
Ballycastle	House of McDonnell		P										71 Castle Street Ballycastle
Ballymena	Galgorm Manor	£70	HR	£110	71%	23	500	450	yes				136 Fenaghy Road Ballymena
Belfast	Antica Roma	£65	R										67-69 Botanic Avenue
Belfast	Bengal Brasserie	£35	R										339 Ormeau Road
Belfast	Crown Liquor Saloon		P										46 Great Victoria Street
Belfast	Dukes Hotel		H	£98	67%	21	130	140					65 University Street
Belfast	Europa Hotel		H	£130	71%	184	1200	600					Great Victoria Street
Belfast	Kelly's Cellars		P										30/32 Bank Street
Belfast	Manor House Cantonese Cuisine	£40	R										43-47 Donegall Pas
Belfast	Plaza Hotel		H	£82	64%	76	100	100					15 Brunswick Street
Belfast	Roscoff	£75	R*										Lesley House Shaftesbury Square
Belfast	Speranza	£40	R							Family			16 Shaftesbury Square
Belfast	Stormont Hotel	£40	H	£137	69%	110	450	300					587 Upper Newtownards Road Stormont
Belfast	Strand Restaurant	£35	R										12 Stranmillis Road
Belfast	The Warehouse	£45	R										35-39 Hill Street
Belfast	Villa Italia	£45	R										39 University Road
Belfast	Welcome Restaurant	£40	R										22 Stranmillis Road

Location	Establishment	Food Price	Cat	Room Price	%	Rooms	Conf	Banq	Beaut Sit	Family Friendly	Swim Pool	Golf	Address
Belfast	Wellington Park		H	£90	59%	50	160	120					21 Malone Road
Belfast Int Airport	Aldergrove Airport Hotel		H	£80	62%	108	250	180		Family			Belfast International Airport
Bushmills	Bushmills Inn		H	£78	58%	11	85	85					25 Main Street Bushmills
Carnlough	Londonderry Arms		P										20 Harbour Road Carnlough
Carnlough	The Waterfall		P										High Street Carnlough
Carrickfergus	Wind-Rose Bar		JaB										The Marina Carrickfergus
Cushendall	PJ McCollam		P										23 Mill Street Cushendall
Dunadry	Dunadry Inn		H	£105	64%	67	350	300		Family	yes		2 Islandreagh Drive Dunadry
Dunmurry	Forte Posthouse Belfast		H	£85	67%	82	450	350					300 Kingsway Dunmurry
Larne	Magheramorne House		H	£66	63%	22	150	180					59 Shore Road Magheramorne Larne
Portballintrae	Bayview Hotel		H	£70	58%	16	300	220				yes	2 Bayhead Road Portballintrae nr Bushmills
Portrush	Ramore	£55	R*										The Harbour Portrush
Templepatrick	Templeton Hotel		H	£100	66%	20	300	350					882 Antrim Road Templepatrick Ballyclare

Co Down

Location	Establishment	Food Price	Cat	Room Price	%	Rooms	Conf	Banq	Beaut Sit	Family Friendly	Swim Pool	Golf	Address
Annalong	Glasdrumman Lodge	£60	HR	£95	69%	10	16	60					85 Mill Road Annalong
Bangor	Back Street Café	£45	R										14 Queen's Parade Bangor
Bangor	Clandeboye Lodge Hotel		H	£95	61%	43	350	320				yes	10 Estate Road Clandeboye Bangor
Bangor	Shanks	£60	R†										Blackwood Golf Centre 150 Crawfordsburn Rd
Comber	La Mon House		H	£85	59%	38	1100	450		Family			The Mills 41 Gransha Road Comber
Crawfordsburn	Old Inn		I	£90		33	150	90			yes		15 Main Street Crawfordsburn
Dundrum	Buck's Head Inn	£60	P										77 Main Street Dundrum nr Newcastle
Helen's Bay	Deanes on the Square		R										7 Station Square Helen's Bay
Hillsborough	The Hillside Bar		P*										21 Main Street Hillsborough
Hillsborough	Bay Tree		JaB										118 High Street Audley Court Holywood
Holywood	Culloden Hotel	£65	HR	£152	72%	89	500	300				yes	142 Bangor Road Craigavad Holywood

Location	Name	Type	£	£	%				Access	Address
Holywood	Sullivans	R	£55							Sullivan Place Holywood
Newcastle	Slieve Donard Hotel	H		£99	63%	117	1000	500		Downs Road Newcastle
Portaferry	Portaferry Hotel	HR	£65	£80	63%	14	30	80	yes	10 The Strand Portaferry

Co Fermanagh

Location	Name	Type	£	£	%				Access	Address
Enniskillen	Blakes of the Hollow	P								6 Church Street Enniskillen
Kesh	Lough Erne Hotel	H		£56	60%	12	250	200		Main Street Kesh
Tempo	Tempo Manor	A		£100		5	300	300		Tempo

Co Londonderry

Location	Name	Type	£	£	%				Access	Address
Aghadowey	Greenhill House	H		£42	6				yes	24 Greenhill Road Aghadowey Coleraine
Garvagh	MacDuff's Restnt, Blackheath House	RR	£50	£60	5					112 Killeague Road Garvagh nr Coleraine
Londonderry	Beech Hill House Hotel	HR	£50	£75	59%	17	100	80		32 Ardmore Road Londonderry
Londonderry	Everglades Hotel	H		£80	59%	52	350	250		Prehen Road Londonderry

Co Tyrone

Location	Name	Type	£	£	%				Access	Address
Fivemiletown	Blessingbourne	A		£90	4				yes	Fivemiletown

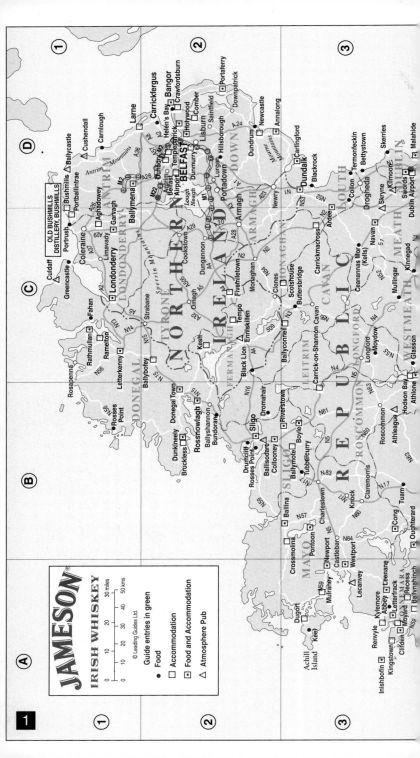

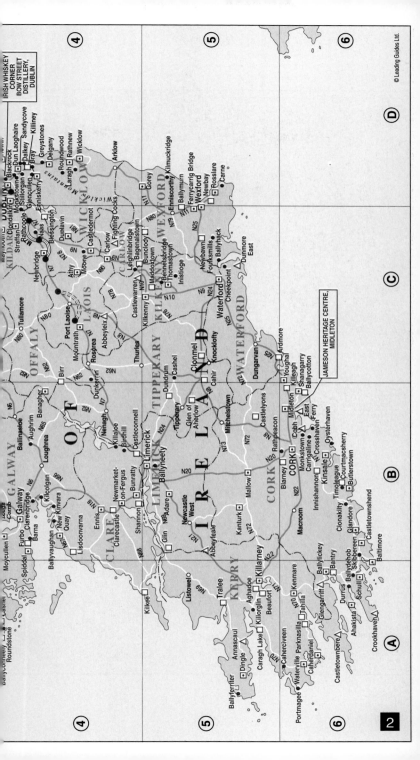

IRISH WHISKEY CORNER BOW STREET DISTILLERY, DUBLIN

JAMESON HERITAGE CENTRE, MIDLETON

© Leading Guides Ltd.

2

N3 to
TRIM 46(28)
KELLS 62(39)
NAVAN 46(29)

N2 to
ASHBOURNE 21(13)
SLANE 46(29)
DERRY 236(147)

Kavanagh's

Forte
Crest,
Dublin
Airport

The
Brian
Boru
Prison

N1 to
AIRPORT 10(6)
BALBRIGGAN 32(20)
DROGHEDA 50(31)
DUNDALK 85(53)
BELFAST 166(104)

Marino

to
MALAHIDE
14(9)

Cabra

PHIBSBOROUGH

CONNOLLY
STATION

Ta Se Mahogani
Gaspipes

Ryans

GUINNESS
BREWERY

CUSTOM HOUSE

Kilmainham

CHRIST CHURCH
CATHEDRAL

CASTLE

MUSEUM

PEARSE STA

ST PATRICK'S
CATHEDRAL

GOVERNMENT
BUILDINGS

Dolphin's
Barn

For central area, see pages 5 & 6

LANDSDOWNE
ROAD STA

San
Merrion
Hall

BALLSBRIDGE

Harold's
Cross

Ranelagh

Sachs

Kielys
Courtyard
Restaurant

SHOWGROUNDS

Ernie's

Fitze
Caf

N7 to
NAAS 34(21)
KILKENNY 117(73)
WATERFORD 157(98)
LIMERICK 197(123)
CORK 258(161)
KILLARNEY 306(191)

Donny
brook

Furama

Anglesea
Town Hous

RATHMINES

Zen

Milltown

Ashtons

RTE
STUDIOS

Ivy Court

Rathgar

Kimmage

Terenure

Windy
Arbour

Universi
Colleg

Club
House

to **N7** for
NAAS 34(21)
KILKENNY 117(73)
WATERFORD 157(98)
LIMERICK 197(123)
CORK 258(161)
KILLARNEY 306(191)
N81 to
BLESSINGTON 30(19)

Milltown
Golf Course

Rathfarnham

Castle
Golf Course

Yellow
House

3

Willbrook

to DUBLIN MTS

Goatsto
The Goa

DUNDRUM

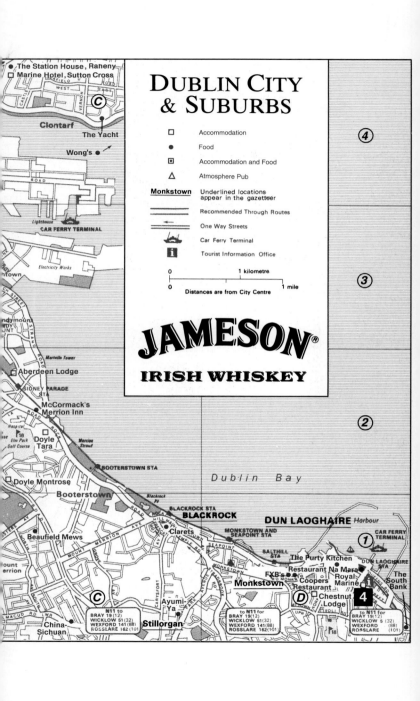

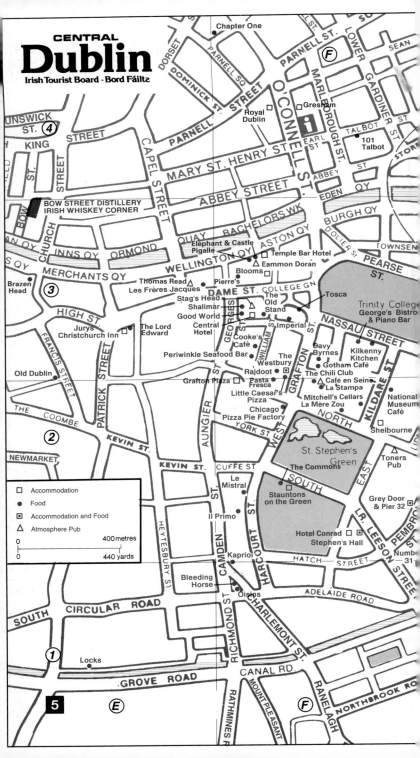

CENTRAL
Dublin
Irish Tourist Board - Bord Fáilte

Chapter One

Royal Dublin

Gresham

101 Talbot

BOW STREET DISTILLERY
IRISH WHISKEY CORNER

Elephant & Castle
Pigalle

Temple Bar Hotel
Eammon Dorán

Blooms

Brazen Head

Thomas Read
Les Frères Jacques

Pierre's

Stag's Head
Shalimar
Good World

The Old Stand

Tosca

Central Hotel

Trinity College
George's Bistro
& Piano Bar

The Lord Edward

Cooke's Café

Imperial

Jurys
Christchurch Inn

Periwinkle Seafood Bar

Davy Byrnes

Kilkenny Kitchen

Old Dublin

The Westbury

Gotham Café

Rajdoot

The Chili Club

Grafton Plaza

Pasta Fresca

Café en Seine
La Stampa

Little Caesar's Pizza

Mitchell's Cellars

La Mère Zou

Chicago

Pizza Pie Factory

National Museum Café

Shelbourne

St. Stephen's Green

Toners Pub

The Commons

Le Mistral

Stauntons on the Green

Grey Door
& Pier 32

Il Primo

Hotel Conrad
Stephen's Hall

Number 31

Kapriol

Bleeding Horse

Oisins

Locks

☐	Accommodation
•	Food
⊡	Accommodation and Food
△	Atmosphere Pub

| 0 | 400 metres |
| 0 | 440 yards |

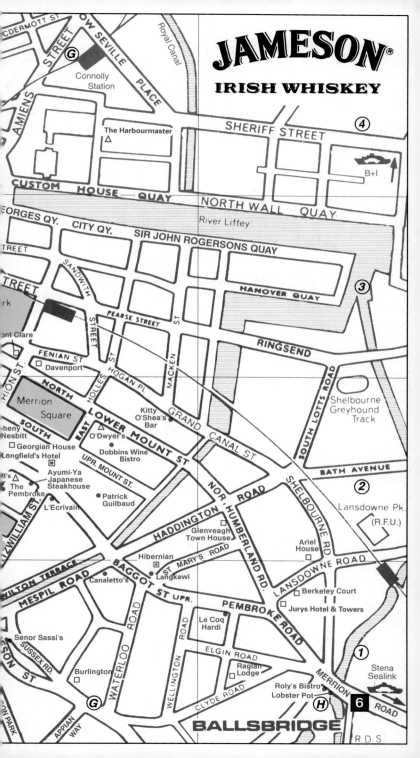

JAMESON

IRISH WHISKEY

Index

Index

Advertisers' Index

Acknowledgements

Egon Ronay's Guides would particularly like to thank Georgina Campbell, our Ireland consultant, for her invaluable assistance in the writing and production of this Guide. We also wish to thank the following for their assistance in supplying photographs:

Page No.	Feature	Credit
61	Cliffords, Cork	John Sheehan
73	Irish Cheeseboard	Bord Fáilte
89	Hillside Bar, Hillsborough, NI	Brian Thompson Photography
93	Shanks, Bangor, NI	Nick Cann
97	Jurys Hotel Group	Frank Fennell Photography

Egon Ronay's Guides would also like to thank all those unnamed persons who kindly supplied photographs to assist in the compilation of this Guide.

Recommended by

EGON RONAY'S GUIDES

1995

YOUR GUARANTEE
OF
QUALITY AND INDEPENDENCE

- Establishment inspections are anonymous

- Inspections are undertaken by qualified
  Egon Ronay's Guides inspectors

- The Guides are completely independent
  in their editorial selection

- The Guides do not accept advertising,
  hospitality or payment from listed
  establishments

Hotels & Restaurants   Pubs & Inns

Europe   Just a Bite

Family Hotels & Restaurants   Paris

Oriental Restaurants   Ireland

New Zealand & South Pacific   Australia

Egon Ronay's Guides are available from all good bookshops or can be
ordered from Leading Guides, 35 Tadema Road, London SW10 0PZ
Tel: 071-352 2485 / 352 0019   Fax: 071-376 5071

READERS' COMMENTS

Please use this sheet, and the continuation overleaf, to recommend hotels, restaurants or pubs of **really outstanding quality** and to comment on existing entries.

Complaints about any of the Guide's entries will be treated seriously and passed on to our inspectorate, but we would like to remind you always to take up your complaint with the management at the time.

We regret that owing to the volume of readers' communications received each year, we will be unable to acknowledge all these forms, but they will certainly be seriously considered. Readers' comments forms are not passed on to the establishments concerned.

Please post to: **Egon Ronay's Guides, 35 Tadema Road, London SW10 0PZ**

Please use an up-to-date Guide. We publish annually. (IRELAND 1995)

Name and address of establishment	Your recommendation or complaint

Readers' Comments continued

Name and address of establishment   **Your recommendation or complaint**

Your Name (BLOCK LETTERS PLEASE)

Address

READERS' COMMENTS

Please use this sheet, and the continuation overleaf, to recommend hotels, restaurants or pubs of **really outstanding quality** and to comment on existing entries.

Complaints about any of the Guide's entries will be treated seriously and passed on to our inspectorate, but we would like to remind you always to take up your complaint with the management at the time.

We regret that owing to the volume of readers' communications received each year, we will be unable to acknowledge all these forms, but they will certainly be seriously considered. Readers' comments forms are not passed on to the establishments' concerned.

Please post to: **Egon Ronay's Guides, 35 Tadema Road, London SW10 0PZ**

Please use an up-to-date Guide. We publish annually. (IRELAND 1995)

Name and address of establishment	Your recommendation or complaint

Readers' Comments continued

Name and address of establishment	Your recommendation or complaint

Your Name (BLOCK LETTERS PLEASE)

Address

READERS' COMMENTS

Please use this sheet, and the continuation overleaf, to recommend hotels, restaurants or pubs of **really outstanding quality** and to comment on existing entries.

Complaints about any of the Guide's entries will be treated seriously and passed on to our inspectorate, but we would like to remind you always to take up your complaint with the management at the time.

We regret that owing to the volume of readers' communications received each year, we will be unable to acknowledge all these forms, but they will certainly be seriously considered. Readers' comments forms are not passed on to the establishments concerned.

Please post to: **Egon Ronay's Guides, 35 Tadema Road, London SW10 0PZ**

Please use an up-to-date Guide. We publish annually. (IRELAND 1995)

Name and address of establishment	Your recommendation or complaint

Readers' Comments continued

Name and address of establishment	Your recommendation or complaint

Your Name (BLOCK LETTERS PLEASE)

Address

READERS' COMMENTS

Please use this sheet, and the continuation overleaf, to recommend hotels, restaurants or pubs of **really outstanding quality** and to comment on existing entries.

Complaints about any of the Guide's entries will be treated seriously and passed on to our inspectorate, but we would like to remind you always to take up your complaint with the management at the time.

We regret that owing to the volume of readers' communications received each year, we will be unable to acknowledge all these forms, but they will certainly be seriously considered. Readers' comments forms are not passed on to the establishments concerned.

Please post to: **Egon Ronay's Guides, 35 Tadema Road, London SW10 0PZ**

Please use an up-to-date Guide. We publish annually. (IRELAND 1995)

Name and address of establishment	Your recommendation or complaint

Readers' Comments continued

Name and address of establishment	Your recommendation or complaint

Your Name (BLOCK LETTERS PLEASE)
_____

Address
_____

_____

_____

_____

READERS' COMMENTS

Please use this sheet, and the continuation overleaf, to recommend hotels, restaurants or pubs of **really outstanding quality** and to comment on existing entries.

Complaints about any of the Guide's entries will be treated seriously and passed on to our inspectorate, but we would like to remind you always to take up your complaint with the management at the time.

We regret that owing to the volume of readers' communications received each year, we will be unable to acknowledge all these forms, but they will certainly be seriously considered. Readers' comments forms are not passed on to the establishments concerned.

Please post to: **Egon Ronay's Guides, 35 Tadema Road, London SW10 0PZ**

Please use an up-to-date Guide. We publish annually. (IRELAND 1995)

Name and address of establishment	Your recommendation or complaint

Readers' Comments continued

Name and address of establishment	Your recommendation or complaint

Your Name (BLOCK LETTERS PLEASE)

Address

READERS' COMMENTS

Please use this sheet, and the continuation overleaf, to recommend hotels, restaurants or pubs of **really outstanding quality** and to comment on existing entries.

Complaints about any of the Guide's entries will be treated seriously and passed on to our inspectorate, but we would like to remind you always to take up your complaint with the management at the time.

We regret that owing to the volume of readers' communications received each year, we will be unable to acknowledge all these forms, but they will certainly be seriously considered. Readers' comments forms are not passed on to the establishments concerned.

Please post to: **Egon Ronay's Guides, 35 Tadema Road, London SW10 0PZ**

Please use an up-to-date Guide. We publish annually. (IRELAND 1995)

Name and address of establishment	Your recommendation or complaint

Readers' Comments continued

Name and address of establishment	Your recommendation or complaint
2 MILES BEFORE BANGOR.	FOLLOW SIGNS FOR N'ANDS
SIGN FOR N'ANDS —	TURN RIGHT AT
LIGHTS	DIXONS GARDEN CENTRE
UNDER BRIDGE	1 at ON LEFT
TUE 8-00 P.M,	

Your Name (BLOCK LETTERS PLEASE)

Address